Professional
Outlook® 2007 Programming

Ken Slovak

D0556306

BICENTENNIAL
1807
WILEY
2007
BICENTENNIAL

Wiley Publishing, Inc.

Professional Outlook® 2007 Programming

Published by
Wiley Publishing, Inc.
10475 Crosspoint Boulevard
Indianapolis, IN 46256
www.wiley.com

Copyright © 2007 by Wiley Publishing, Inc., Indianapolis, Indiana

Published simultaneously in Canada

ISBN-13: 978-0-470-04994-5

Manufactured in the United States of America

10 9 8 7 6 5 4 3 2 1

Library of Congress Cataloging-in-Publication Data:
Slovak, Ken.
  Professional Outlook 2007 programming / Ken Slovak.
      p. cm.
  Published simultaneously in Canada.
  Includes index.
  ISBN 978-0-470-04994-5 (paper/website)
  1. Microsoft Outlook. 2. Personal information management. 3. Business--Computer programs. I. Title.
  HF5548.4.M5255S583 2007
  005.5'7--dc22
                        2007031694

No part of this publication may be reproduced, stored in a retrieval system or transmitted in any form or by any means, electronic, mechanical, photocopying, recording, scanning or otherwise, except as permitted under Sections 107 or 108 of the 1976 United States Copyright Act, without either the prior written permission of the Publisher, or authorization through payment of the appropriate per-copy fee to the Copyright Clearance Center, 222 Rosewood Drive, Danvers, MA 01923, (978) 750-8400, fax (978) 646-8600. Requests to the Publisher for permission should be addressed to the Legal Department, Wiley Publishing, Inc., 10475 Crosspoint Blvd., Indianapolis, IN 46256, (317) 572-3447, fax (317) 572-4355, or online at http://www.wiley.com/go/permissions.

For general information on our other products and services please contact our Customer Care Department within the United States at (800) 762-2974, outside the United States at (317) 572-3993 or fax (317) 572-4002.

Trademarks: Wiley, the Wiley logo, Wrox, the Wrox logo, Wrox Programmer to Programmer, and related trade dress are trademarks or registered trademarks of John Wiley & Sons, Inc. and/or its affiliates, in the United States and other countries, and may not be used without written permission. Outlook and Microsoft are registered trademarks of Microsoft Corporation in the United States and/or other countries. All other trademarks are the property of their respective owners. Wiley Publishing, Inc., is not associated with any product or vendor mentioned in this book.

Wiley also publishes its books in a variety of electronic formats. Some content that appears in print may not be available in electronic books.

This book is dedicated, as always, to my beloved wife, Susie, for her patience in putting up with the long hours of writing and for just being there, and to my dog Casey for keeping me company while I was writing this book and for being my sales manager and the administrator of my Exchange server.

About the Author

Ken Slovak is president of Slovak Technical Services, a company specializing in Outlook, Exchange, and Office custom development and consulting. He has been an Outlook MVP since 1998. He has coauthored *Programming Microsoft Outlook 2000, Professional Programming Outlook 2000, Beginning Visual Basic 6 Application Development;* contributed material to other Outlook books; and written numerous magazine articles about Outlook. He makes his home in central Florida with his wife and dog and enjoys swimming, fishing, cooking, and chasing squirrels for the dog's amusement.

Credits

Acquisitions Director
Jim Minatel

Development Editor
Maureen Spears

Technical Editor
Diane Poremsky

Production Editor
Christine O'Connor

Copy Editor
Foxxe Editorial Services

Editorial Manager
Mary Beth Wakefield

Production Manager
Tim Tate

Project Coordinator
Lynsey Osborne

Compositor
Craig Johnson, Happenstance Type-O-Rama

Proofreader
Christopher Jones

Indexer
Jack Lewis

Anniversary Logo Design
Richard Pacifico

Acknowledgments

A book like this is a team effort, and even though only the author's name is on the cover, everyone on the team makes valuable contributions. I'd like to thank the editors at Wrox for all their work on the book, which I appreciate more than I can ever express, and for their patience during the long waits for new chapters. Maureen Spears has been a patient and painstaking development editor, guiding the book from beginning to end. Jim Minatel, the acquisitions editor is an old friend and also has been a patient and critical part of this book's publication. Everyone else at Wrox has also been great to work with. The technical editor, Diane Poremsky, an Outlook MVP, is an old friend and writing partner, and I was lucky to have her on this book. The editors are responsible for everything that's correct in this book and nothing that's incorrect.

I constantly learn more about Outlook and Outlook development from my fellow Outlook MVPs, especially the ones who also are involved with Outlook development: Sue Mosher, Dmitry Streblechenko, Dave Kane, Jay Harlow, Eric Legault, Michael Bauer, Roberto Restelli, and Ricardo Silva. I'd also like to thank the other Outlook and Exchange MVPs for everything I've learned from them. There is no better group of MVPs and people, and I appreciate being included in their company. I'd also like to thank Patrick Schmid, who although not an Outlook MVP hangs out with us and who has done a lot of pioneering work with Ribbon development for Office 2007.

I'd also like to give special thanks to the people on the Outlook product team responsible for Outlook programmability, Randy Byrne and Ryan Gregg. Randy is an old friend and former Outlook MVP who has helped bring Outlook from the programming Dark Ages by enhancing the Outlook object model to turn it into a complete programming API. Ryan has always been completely helpful and responsive also, and has become a new friend. Finally, Bill Jacob, an Outlook premier support programming specialist in Microsoft PSS, has always been another helpful friend.

Contents

Contents

Contents

Contents

Introduction

Welcome to *Professional Programming Outlook 2007*. This book covers Outlook programming, with the primary emphasis on the many new Outlook 2007 programming features. Existing knowledge of Outlook programming isn't necessary because this book teaches you all you need to know to develop everything from Outlook custom forms and personal productivity macros to advanced COM addins that utilize a range of Microsoft technologies.

When I first was briefed on the programming features of Outlook 2007 early in 2005, I felt like a kid at Christmas. Finally, the Outlook object model had almost all the features Outlook developers had been requesting for many years.

Outlook's object model always has been incomplete. Many properties that are important to Outlook developers were always unavailable in previous versions of the Outlook object model. Some examples of properties that were unavailable are Internet headers in emails, the name of the last person to modify an item, the global object ID for calendar items that was introduced in Outlook 2003 SP2 and calendar labels. Advanced Outlook programming always had to use additional programming APIs such as CDO 1.21 (Collaboration Data Objects), Extended MAPI, and third-party libraries that exposed Extended MAPI properties, such as Redemption, that weren't in the Outlook object model.

Now, with Outlook 2007 you rarely if ever have to leave the Outlook object model to do what you want with your code.

Who Is This Book For

This book is for professional or advanced developers who want to take full advantage of the power of the unified Outlook object model in Outlook 2007, and who want to learn the important new features in the unified object model.

Most of the code samples in this book only require Outlook 2007, and use Outlook VBA code. Code that utilizes COM addins or that uses VSTO requires you to install Visual Studio 2005 plus VSTO 2005 SE.

What Does This Book Cover?

This book covers:

- ❑ The Outlook 2007 object model (OOM).
- ❑ Programming Outlook using VBA, VBScript, VSTO, VB.NET, C#, and VB 6.
- ❑ Outlook macros, custom forms, and COM addins.

- ❑ Importing data into Outlook from other programs such as Word, Excel, and Access.

- ❑ Exporting Outlook data into other programs such as Word, Excel, and Access.

- ❑ Custom user interface elements for Outlook such as menu items, toolbars, and custom Ribbon elements, and the use of custom data input and output forms.

- ❑ Tips and tricks to make your Outlook code run faster and better.

Most short code snippets are presented in VBA (Visual Basic for Applications) code. VBA is useful as a prototyping tool, and code in VBA is easily translated into VB.NET, VBScript, VB 6, and usually even into C#. Longer code segments are presented in either VBA or in both VB.NET and C#. The case study is presented using VB.NET and C#.

Each chapter introduces important Outlook programming concepts, with plenty of sample code to help you make use of the new and old features of the Outlook object model. In more detail, here's what you'll find in each chapter:

- ❑ Chapter 1 introduces you to Outlook 2007 programming and includes how to set up Outlook VBA, how to delve into Outlook and the basics on data storage and data display.

- ❑ Chapter 2 covers what's new in the Outlook object model for Outlook 2007, providing an overview of the important new properties, methods and events in the new unified object model. The chapter also covers new features that can dramatically improve the speed of Outlook code, the essentials of Outlook code security, Outlook syntax, and new features for Outlook forms.

- ❑ Chapter 3 gives you the basics of Outlook development, starting with the decisions about whether to develop using custom Outlook forms, macros or COM addins. It also covers the essential elements of Outlook programming, including the Application, Namespace, Explorer and Inspector objects and collections, Outlook collections and items, and using Outlook's built-in dialogs.

- ❑ Chapter 4 takes a look at Outlook VBA and macros. Outlook VBA isn't only for creating simple macros; it's a great prototyping tool for almost any Outlook project. The VBA Project, macro security, class modules, UserForms, event handling, macro projects and macro distribution are among the topics covered here.

- ❑ Chapter 5 covers Outlook forms, with custom forms both with and without code. The newly exposed form controls such as the calendar controls are discussed, as is prototyping Outlook forms code using VBA, Outlook form publishing and custom form distribution.

- ❑ Chapter 6 shows you Outlook COM addins, both managed and unmanaged, as well as how to use VSTO 2005 SE (Visual Studio Tools for Office) to simplify the development of managed Outlook addins. Creating Outlook property pages, debugging Outlook COM addins and distribution of COM addins are also covered.

- ❑ Chapter 7 covers customizing the Outlook user interface. Working with menus and toolbars as well as the new Office Ribbon interface are covered, as are custom views, custom task panes and form regions.

- ❑ Chapter 8 shows how to interface Outlook with other applications. Interfacing with Word, Excel, Access are all shown.

❑ Chapter 9 discusses real world Outlook programming tips and tricks. Code optimization for speed, support for multiple versions of Outlook, working around Outlook's remaining programming limitations, coping with Outlook security and working with alternate APIs are all covered from the perspective of an Outlook developer.

The rest of the material in the book gives you important learning and reference resources in the form of a chapter devoted to a COM addin case study as well as two appendixes. The study chapter shows how to use Outlook code in solving a real-world programming problem.

❑ Chapter 10 creates a task management system that utilizes the new `PropertyAccessor` and a custom task pane to provide hierarchical task linking.

❑ Appendix A provides a summary of the important features of the Outlook 2007 object model. Important new collections, events, methods, and properties are all covered, as are common property tags used with the new `PropertyAccessor` object.

❑ Appendix B covers Outlook development resources, such as Microsoft and third-party Web sites, resources for Outlook programming code samples, and tools that are useful for Outlook development. It also shows you how to get help and support for Outlook development, covering Microsoft and third-party Web sites, support newsgroups, and support mailing lists.

What You Need to Use This Book

The Outlook VBA code samples in this book require you to have Office 2007 with Outlook 2007 installed. The VB.NET and C# code examples and projects additionally require Visual Studio 2005. The VSTO code examples and projects require VSTO 2005 SE. The sample code and projects will run on any computer with those prerequisites. For readers using Windows Vista, Visual Studio 2005 requires Service Pack 1 to be able to debug code.

Conventions

To help you get the most from the text and keep track of what's happening, we've used a number of conventions throughout the book.

> **Boxes like this one hold important, not-to-be forgotten information that is directly relevant to the surrounding text.**

Tips, hints, tricks, and asides to the current discussion are offset and placed in italics like this.

As for styles in the text:

❑ We *highlight* new terms and important words when we introduce them.

❑ We show keyboard strokes like this: Ctrl+A.

❑ We show file names, URLs, and code within the text like this: `persistence.properties`.

❏   We present code in two different ways:

```
In code examples we highlight new and important code with a gray background.
```

```
The gray highlighting is not used for code that's less important in the
present context, or has been shown before.
```

Source Code

As you work through the examples in this book, you may choose either to type in all the code manually or to use the source code files that accompany the book. All of the source code used in this book is available for downloading at www.wrox.com. The code for the addin templates and the chapters is also available for downloading at www.slovaktech.com. Once at the site, simply locate the book's title (either by using the Search box or by using one of the title lists), and click the Download Code link on the book's detail page to obtain all the source code for the book.

Because many books have similar titles, you may find it easiest to search by ISBN; this book's 097804470049945.

Once you download the code, just decompress it with your favorite compression tool. Alternately, you can go to the main Wrox code download page at www.wrox.com/dynamic/books/download.aspx to see the code available for this book and all other Wrox books.

You can copy the VBA examples in this book into a code module in the Outlook VBA project and run them to display the outputs for the email Internet message header and the Out of Office state. To enter and run the code in VBA by copying it from the book:

1.   Use Alt+F11 to open the VBA project.

2.   Select Insert, Module.

3.   If the Property Window isn't visible, make it show it by selecting View, Properties Window.

4.   Place your cursor in the Name property in the Properties Window, as shown in the following figure, and select the default name text, Module 1.

5.   Change the module name to Chapter 2, and press Enter to save the change.

6.   Place your cursor in the new code module, and type the code into the project.

7.   To run the code, place your cursor in one of the procedures, and use the keyboard shortcut F5 to start code execution.

The VB.NET and C# code examples require Visual Studio 2005 to run, and the VSTO code examples require VSTO 2005 SE.

Errata

We make every effort to ensure that there are no errors in the text or in the code. However, no one is perfect, and mistakes do occur. If you find an error in one of our books, like a spelling mistake or faulty piece of code, we would be very grateful for your feedback. By sending in errata you may save another reader hours of frustration, and at the same time you will be helping us provide even higher-quality information.

To find the errata page for this book, go to www.wrox.com and locate the title using the Search box or one of the title lists. Then, on the book details page, click the Book Errata link. On this page, you can view all errata that has been submitted for this book and posted by Wrox editors. A complete book list, including links to each book's errata, is also available at www.wrox.com/misc-pages/booklist.shtml.

If you don't spot "your" error on the Book Errata page, go to www.wrox.com/contact/techsupport.shtml and complete the form there to send us the error you have found. We'll check the information and, if appropriate, post a message to the book's errata page and fix the problem in subsequent editions of the book.

p2p.wrox.com

For author and peer discussion, join the P2P forums at p2p.wrox.com. The forums are a Web-based system for you to post messages relating to Wrox books and related technologies and interact with other readers and technology users. The forums offer a subscription feature to email you topics of interest of your choosing when new posts are made to the forums. Wrox authors, editors, other industry experts, and your fellow readers are present on these forums.

Introduction

At `http://p2p.wrox.com` you will find a number of different forums that will help you not only as you read this book but also as you develop your own applications. To join the forums, just follow these steps:

1. Go to `p2p.wrox.com` and click the Register link.

2. Read the terms of use and click Agree.

3. Complete the required information to join as well as any optional information you wish to provide and click Submit.

4. You will receive an email with information describing how to verify your account and complete the joining process.

> *You can read messages in the forums without joining P2P, but in order to post your own messages, you must join.*

Once you join, you can post new messages and respond to messages other users post. You can read messages at any time on the Web. If you would like to have new messages from a particular forum emailed to you, click the Subscribe to this Forum icon by the forum name in the forum listing.

For more information about how to use the Wrox P2P, be sure to read the P2P FAQs for answers to questions about how the forum software works as well as many common questions specific to P2P and Wrox books. To read the FAQs, click the FAQ link on any P2P page.

Professional
Outlook® 2007 Programming

An Introduction to Outlook 2007 Programming

Outlook stores items such as mail, appointment, task, and contact items in tables in a hierarchically structured database. This is unlike the underlying document object model that most other Office applications use and requires a change of orientation for programmers experienced in programming applications, such as Word or Excel. For this reason, this chapter explains Outlook's data model and introduces Outlook's data storage and data presentation models.

In this chapter, you first open the Outlook VBA project and set it up for use in creating and running macros and prototype code. Using the Outlook VBA project is often the easiest way to quickly test and prototype your Outlook code. Next, you discover the concept of a `NameSpace` and how to access Outlook data in folders and in individual Outlook items. This is the basis of all Outlook data access and is a building block for all Outlook programming. You next see how Outlook stores its data and how to access that data. In Outlook 2007, you can now access data either with the traditional `Folders` and `Items` collections or with the new `Stores` collection and `Table` object. The new members of the Outlook object model are explained in Chapter 2. Finally, this chapter discusses Inspectors—the windows that display items such as emails or appointments, as well as Explorers—the windows that display folders. Working with these collections is critical for any Outlook program that works with the Outlook display.

Setting Up Outlook VBA

Outlook VBA is a very convenient way of testing and prototyping your code. You can quickly write procedures to test various elements in the Outlook object model, and in VBA code you have an intrinsic Outlook `Application` object that makes it easy to work with Outlook items. Instead of writing your code in a Component Object Model (COM) addin to test something, it's far easier to quickly test in a macro and then place the tested code in your COM addin. In fact, it's even easier to test Outlook forms code, which uses VBScript, in Outlook VBA and then convert the VBA code to VBScript than it is to test the code in an Outlook form.

Setting Up Macro Security

The first thing when using Outlook VBA is to set up your macro security so that your code will run. By default, Outlook's macro security is set to high, which doesn't run code not signed with a code-signing certificate and which warns you when signed code is present. At a minimum, you should set your security to prompt you when macro code is present.

> Never set your security to perform no security checks; that's a very dangerous setting that leaves you with no security at all.

To set security, do the following:

1. Select Tools ⇨ Macro ⇨ Security to open the Security dialog. The Security dialog, shown in Figure 1-1, appears.

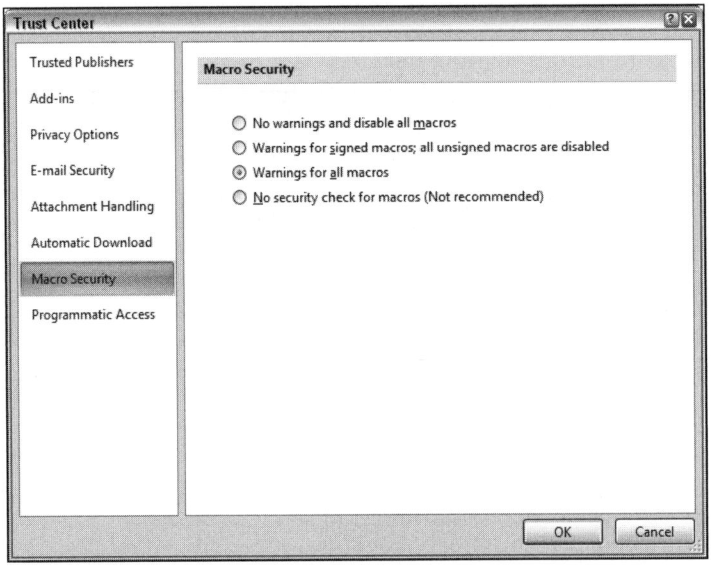

Figure 1-1

2. Set your security:

❑ **Warnings for all macros:** Use this if you don't intend to sign your Outlook VBA project.

❑ **Warnings for signed macros; all unsigned macros are disabled:** If you intend to sign your VBA project, it's recommended that you use this security setting.

3. Click the OK button to save your changes to the macro security and then exit and restart Outlook to apply the new security setting.

After setting up your macro security, you can open the Outlook VBA project by using the keyboard shortcut Alt+F11.

Creating a Code-Signing Certificate

Unlike other Office applications such as Word or Excel, Outlook stores its macros globally and only has one VBA project that you can use. Outlook's VBA project is always named VBAProject.OTM, and signing this code project provides a higher degree of security than just enabling warnings for all macros.

Even if you don't have a standard code-signing certificate from a trusted authority, such as VeriSign or Thawte, you can use the certificate-generating software included with Office 2007, Selfcert.exe, to create a personal signing certificate. You shouldn't use this certificate to distribute code, because it doesn't derive from a trusted authority, but you can use it for your own code on your development computer.

To create a code-signing certificate, follow these steps:

1. Navigate to the folder where your Office 2007 applications are installed, usually C:\Program Files\Microsoft Office\Office12 for Office 2007, and run the Selfcert.exe program. Running this application results in the dialog box shown in Figure 1-2.

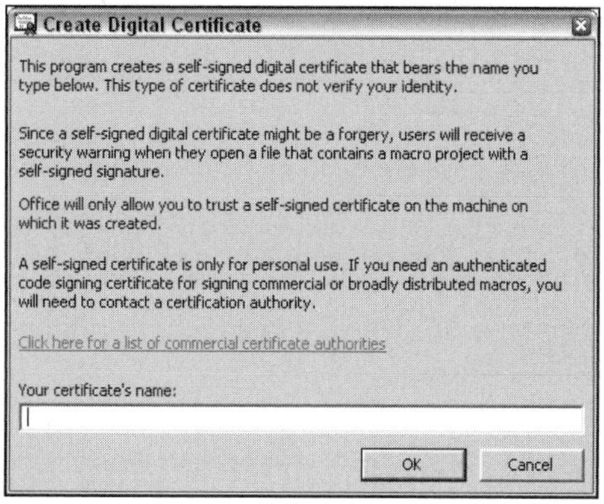

Figure 1.2

2. Enter a name for your certificate—just use your own name—and press Enter to create your personal code-signing certificate.

3. Now open the Outlook VBA project using Alt+F11 in Outlook and select Tools ⇨ Digital Signature to open the dialog shown in Figure 1-3. In this dialog, click the Choose button and select the certificate you created using Selfcert.exe, then click OK twice to choose your certificate and sign your code project with that certificate.

Figure 1-3

4. Now select File ➪ Save VBAProject.OTM to save your VBA project; then exit and restart Outlook. If you are prompted again to save your VBA project when Outlook is closing, save the project again.

5. When you open your VBA project using Alt+F11, you are prompted to enable your macros in the dialog shown in Figure 1-4. You can use this dialog to trust your certificate, which prevents this dialog from appearing again, or you can just enable the macros for that Outlook session. It's recommended to trust your certificate so you don't get prompted to trust your VBA code every time you want to run a macro or go into the Outlook VBA project.

Microsoft Office Outlook Security Notice

- Microsoft Office has identified a potential security concern.

Warning: This publisher has not been authenticated and therefore could be imitated. Do not trust these credentials.

File Path: ThisOutlookSession

Due to your security settings, macros have been disabled. If you choose to enable the macros, your computer may no longer be secure.

More information

Show Signature Details

[Trust all documents from this publisher]   [Enable Macros]   [Disable Macros]

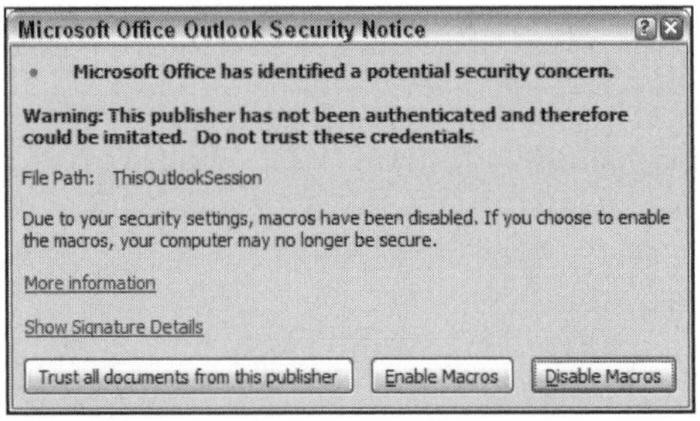

Figure 1-4

6. Click the Trust All Documents from This Publisher button to trust your code-signing certificate and add it to the trusted publishers list. If you open the Trust Center dialog shown in Figure 1-1 again and click the Trusted Publishers area, you will now see your code-signing certificate listed as a trusted publisher. Now you won't get the security prompts, and your VBA code will run without problems.

Reviewing the VBA Editor Interface and Options

Take a few minutes to explore the menus in the Outlook VBA interface and click Tools ➪ Options to set up the VBA editor options so that the settings match what you want:

❑ **The Require Variable Declaration option:** Checking this checkbox is recommended. It inserts an `Option Explicit` statement in every module you add to your project. Declaring your variables before using them is a valuable tool in making sure that you are typing your variables and objects correctly and is good programming practice.

❑ **The Object Browser:** Before leaving the Outlook VBA project use the keyboard shortcut F2 to open the Object Browser, and spend a few minutes reviewing the properties, methods and events in the Outlook object model. The Object Browser is the most useful tool you have when writing Outlook code. It shows what is available in the Outlook object model and provides prototypes of all the Outlook properties, methods, and events that show how they are used. Clicking F1 to call Help when any entry in the Object Browser is selected brings up context-sensitive Help about that Outlook object, usually with some sample code to show how to use and access that object.

Understanding Outlook

When you start Outlook, you are logged into an *Outlook session*. An Outlook session starts when Outlook is started and ends when you close Outlook. The data and properties that you have available to you in this session are set by the *Outlook profile* that logged into that Outlook session. Each Outlook profile consists of a data store, email accounts, and other settings that define the Outlook environment. Most users have only one default Outlook profile, but Outlook allows you to set up as many profiles as you want to define different environments in which to run Outlook.

Outlook can only have one session open at a time and can use the properties from only one Outlook profile at a time. To switch to a different Outlook profile, you must close and reopen Outlook.

Figure 1-5 shows the hierarchical structure used to organize access to Outlook data. The Outlook `Application` opens one session, also known as a `NameSpace`. The session has a `Stores` collection, consisting of all open stores in that session. One or more stores may be opened in a session. Each store has a collection of folders, and each folder has a collection of items that make up the data in that folder.

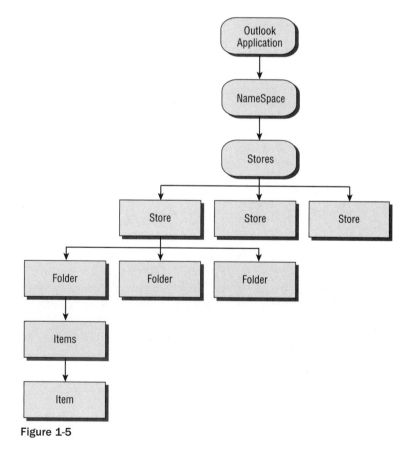

Figure 1-5

Outlook Profiles and Data Store

Each Outlook profile has access to selected data stores, which can be PST files, Exchange mailboxes, Exchange public folders, or special stores known as custom store providers. A profile also has certain email accounts set up, and send/receive groups, which control how certain Outlook features behave, such as sending emails on a deferred basis or sending meeting invitations. Regardless of the profile or profile properties, the Outlook session always opens into a `NameSpace`, which is always "MAPI":

```
Dim oNS As Outlook.NameSpace
Set oNS = Application.GetNameSpace("MAPI")
```

All of the code snippets in this chapter use VBA, Outlook's macro language. VB.NET and C# code samples in the book show similar code in those languages.

MAPI stands for *Messaging Application Programming Interface*, and Outlook uses MAPI protocols for all of its data accesses, and the Outlook data stores are designed around the MAPI storage interface. Outlook wraps most of the MAPI protocols and data storage in the Outlook object model, so most of the time you don't have to deal directly with the complexities of MAPI.

Outlook Sessions and Data Stores

In any Outlook session, the available data stores, such as PST files, are all contained in the `Stores` collection of the `NameSpace` object. Each `Store` object in the `Stores` collection provides access to the top level of that data store. You can also access these stores at a lower level from the `NameSpace` object's `Folders` collection. `Stores` are new to the Outlook object model in Outlook 2007.

Each store has its own `Folders` collection, and each `Folder` object in those collections can contain its own `Folders` collections (subfolders). The user interface represents these collections and folders as Outlook folders and subfolders.

The Evolution of the MAPIFolder object

In previous versions of the Outlook object model, the `Folder` object was called the `MAPIFolder` object. This alias is still accepted in Outlook code, so the forward compatibility of existing code isn't compromised.

The new properties and methods for the `Folder` object, such as the `GetTable()` method used to get a `Table` object for a folder, are also available for the `MAPIFolder` object, although only for Outlook 2007.

The new events for the `Folder` object are not added to the `MAPIFolder` object. If you enhance existing code to use the new `Folder` events, make sure to convert all declarations of `MAPIFolder` objects into `Folder` declarations.

Outlook Folders

Each folder in Outlook is dedicated to containing certain types of items, such as emails, tasks, contacts, or appointments. Folders contain `Items` collections to hold items that are compatible with the type of folder (refer to Figure 1-5). There are also special folders such as Inbox and Deleted Items that can hold items of many different types.

The following VBA code snippet illustrates how to use code to access one item from the Outlook Sent Items folder using Outlook VBA code:

```
Dim oNS As Outlook.NameSpace
Dim oFolder As Outlook.Folder 'note: this is new for Outlook 2007
Dim colItems As Outlook.Items
Dim oMail As Outlook.MailItem

Set oNS = Application.GetNameSpace("MAPI")
Set oFolder = oNS.GetDefaultFolder(olFolderSentMail)
Set colItems = oFolder.Items
Set oMail = colItems.Item(1)
```

> **This code uses the intrinsic** `Application` **object that always represents** `Outlook.Application` **when running in the Outlook VBA project, or in custom form code. In other contexts, such as VBA code running in a Word macro, an** `Outlook.Application` **object needs to be declared and instantiated:**
>
> ```
> Dim oOL As Outlook.Application
>
> Set oOL = CreateObject("Outlook.Application")
> ```

Please note the following regarding this code:

- ❑ The code instantiates a `NameSpace` object and uses the `GetDefaultFolder()` method to retrieve a reference to the Sent Items folder. This folder is declared as a `Folder` object, new for Outlook 2007.

- ❑ The `Folder` object is derived from the `MAPIFolder` object and adds additional methods, properties and events to that object.

- ❑ The code then gets the `Items` collection of the Sent Items folder and returns a reference to one item from the `Items` collection.

This code is typical of how you access an Outlook item from an Outlook data store, navigating the storage and interface hierarchy to access that item. This code assumes that the first item in Sent Items is an email item, which it may not be because email folders can also hold `Post` items.

Many Outlook objects such as `Application`, `Inspector`, *and* `Explorer` *have a* `Session` *property that returns the* `NameSpace` *object and exposes all the properties, methods and events of the* `NameSpace` *object. The* `Session` *object can be used as an alias for the* `NameSpace` *object.*

If you use the `Session` *object make sure you set a* `NameSpace` *object using the* `GetNameSpace(MAPI)` *method once in your code before using the* `Session` *object. The* `Session` *object isn't fully instantiated until you log in to the* `NameSpace` *object at least once, particularly when you start Outlook using automation code.*

Outlook Items

Each Outlook item contains many properties that define the data for that item. Default properties are present in every item and are always defined for an item, such as `Subject` or `Body` (the note text in an item). Users can also add properties to items either from code or the user interface. These `UserProperties` are also called *named properties* and play a prominent role in most advanced Outlook development, often being used to store application-specific data in items.

The following example uses the `oMail` object instantiated in the previous example:

```
Dim colProps As Outlook.UserProperties
Dim oProp As Outlook.UserProperty
Dim sSubject As String

sSubject = oMail.Subject
If InStr(1, sSubject, "support", vbTextCompare) > 0 Then
Set colProps = oMail.UserProperties
Set oProp = colProps.Item("Processed Date")
If oProp Is Nothing Then 'if Nothing add the user property
        Set oProp = colProps.Add("Processed Date", olDateTime)
End If
oProp.Value = #April 21, 2007# 'set a date this item was processed
oMail.Save 'save the change to the MailItem
End If
```

This example tests to see if the `Subject` of a mail item contains the case-insensitive string `"support"`. If so, it tries to get an existing `UserProperty` named `"Processed Date"` from a mail item. If that property doesn't exist, the code adds it to the item. The `Value` property of `"Processed Date"` is set, and then the mail item is saved. You can add data in a `UserProperty` to a view of an Outlook folder, so it's visible to users.

Outlook Data Storage

Programming Outlook is different from programming most other Microsoft Office applications in that it's not centered on documents but rather on individual items stored in databases. Each Outlook item, whether it's an appointment or an email, is really a row in a database with the database columns being individual properties, such as `Subject`. Outlook disguises the underlying data storage with collections of folders and items, but you still access a database when you work with Outlook data.

Outlook data is stored in PST (Personal Storage) files for users not working with Exchange server, and for archive and offloaded data even for Exchange server users. Other Outlook data stores are OST (Offline Storage) files used in offline and cached mode by Exchange server users and Exchange mailboxes. What these data stores have in common are storage organization and the use of a derivative of the JET database used for Access. Using Open DataBase Connectivity (ODBC) database drivers Outlook items can be accessed as recordsets, although only a subset of the properties in an item is available as columns in the recordset.

Outlook data is organized into `Stores`, `Folders`, and `Items`. Each store, such as a PST file, has a one-to-many relationship to folders, including default folders such as Inbox and Calendar, and nondefault folders that the user creates. Each `Folder` object has a `Folders` collection, which can contain many subfolders, with each of those subfolders able to contain subfolders of its own. Folders have one-to-many relationships with items, such as emails and contacts. Each item has many different properties stored in its row in the folder item table, including properties common to all items, such as `Subject`, and special properties related to certain items such as the start date and time of an appointment.

Accessing Data Stores Using NameSpace

When you access an Outlook data store, you do so in one of two ways. The first and familiar way for Outlook programmers is from the `NameSpace.Folders` collection, the other, new way is to use the `NameSpace.Stores` collection. The difference is in the returned object and where you end up in the store hierarchy.

When you use the `NameSpace.Folders` collection, or one of the methods that retrieves a folder from the `NameSpace` object, such *as* `GetDefaultFolder()` or `GetFolderFromID()`, you get a `Folder` (`MAPIFolder`) object. If you use `NameSpace.Folders.Item(1)`, you get a `Folder` that is called the `RootFolder` or Top of Information Store. This is usually shown as something like "Personal Folders" or "Mailbox - Ken Slovak."

The following VBA examples show how to retrieve a `Folder` object using some of the various `NameSpace` methods:

```
Dim oNS As Outlook.NameSpace
Dim oFolder As Outlook.Folder 'note: this is new for Outlook 2007

Set oNS = Application.GetNameSpace("MAPI")

'Get a default Outlook folder
Set oFolder = oNS.GetDefaultFolder(olFolderCalendar) 'get Calendar

'Another way:
Set oFolder = oNS.GetFolderFromID(strFolderID) 'using a string EntryID

'Another way:
Set oFolder = oNS.Folders.Item("Personal Folders") 'get RootFolder
```

The disadvantage of these methods is they can only take you so high in the Outlook folders hierarchy, to the Top of Information Store or `RootFolder`. There are other interesting Outlook folders, however, that aren't visible to the user but are important to programmers, such as the Reminders and Common Views folders, as well as Search Folders and the new To-Do Bar task list folder. Using the new Stores collection, you can access these hidden folders, as well as properties of the store itself, such as the Out of Office state and the support mask that indicates what types of operations the store supports.

Accessing Data with Tables

Some of the new features in the Outlook 2007 object model relate to tables, which provide direct read-only access to an Outlook table, such as an `Items` collection of all items in a folder. These tables provide much faster access to your Outlook data than using other methods, such as a iterating through a folder's `Items` collection or using a filter on an `Items` collection. The disadvantage of table operations is that the data is read-only, so if you need to change your returned data, you must include columns with information that lets you retrieve individual items corresponding to the rows that need to be changed.

To retrieve individual items from the Outlook database, whether from tables or Items collections, you make use of one or both of the GUIDs (Globally Unique Identifiers) that uniquely identify all Outlook items in the Outlook data storage.

The first and most important GUID is named `EntryID`. This GUID uniquely identifies any Outlook item in an Outlook data store, such as a PST file or Exchange mailbox. The other important GUID is `StoreID`, which is unique to any Outlook data store and which you can use in combination with `EntryID` to retrieve any Outlook item stored in any opened Outlook data store:

```
Set oMail = oNS.GetItemFromID(strEntryID, strStoreID)
```

where `strEntryID` and `strStoreID` are string variables that are storing specific GUIDs for an Outlook item and data store.

Outlook Data Display

Now that you know how Outlook stores and accesses data, you need to understand how Outlook displays its data. Outlook has two primary display collections, the `Explorers` and `Inspectors` collections. Outlook also has other user interface objects, such as the familiar menus and toolbars that are composed of the `CommandBars` collection, the new Ribbon displayed in open items such as emails, and various `Panes`, such as the Navigation and Reading (preview) Panes. You learn how to use all those interface elements and to create or modify them in Chapter 7, but for now let's concentrate on the `Explorers` and `Inspectors` collections.

❑ The `Explorers` collection contains all open folder views, such as a view of the Inbox or Calendar. Each open folder view is an `Explorer` object and has a `CurrentFolder` object, which is the folder whose data is currently being displayed in the `Explorer`. The currently active `Explorer` object is also available as the `ActiveExplorer` object. When you open Outlook as a user, one `Explorer` object is opened. You can add additional `Explorers` to the `Explorers` collection by right-clicking a folder in the Navigation Pane and selecting Open in New Window. When you open Outlook using code, there are no open `Explorers` unless you explicitly open an `Explorer` to display the contents of a folder.

❑ The `Inspectors` collection contains all open Outlook items. Each time you open an Outlook item, such as an email, a contact, or an appointment item, you are adding an `Inspector` to the `Inspectors` collection. Logically, the currently active `Inspector` object is available as the `ActiveInspector` object.

The distinction between `Inspectors` and `Explorers` is fundamental to Outlook programming, and they are often confused by new Outlook programmers. If you want to access a folder being displayed in Outlook, use the `Explorers` collection. If you want to access open Outlook items, use the `Inspectors` collection. You cannot access the display of a folder without using an `Explorer`, and you can't access any open Outlook items without using an `Inspector`.

To change the subject of a newly opened email, use the following code to access the `ActiveInspector` and the item being displayed in the `Inspector`:

```
Dim oMail As Outlook.MailItem
Dim oInsp As Outlook.Inspector
```

```
Set oInsp = Application.ActiveInspector
If oInsp.CurrentItem.Class = olMail Then ' check for mail item first
 Set oMail = oInsp.CurrentItem
 oMail.Subject = "Test Message"
 oMail.Save 'save the change
Else
 MsgBox "This is not a mail item"
End If
```

This code first checks the `ActiveInspector` to make sure that the currently displayed item in the `Inspector` is a mail item, and if it is it changes the `Subject` to "Test Message." If the item is not a mail item, it displays a message box describing the problem.

The following code shows how to use the current `ActiveExplorer` object to first display the default Contacts folder and then change the view of that folder to the Business Cards view:

```
Dim oNS As Outlook.NameSpace
Dim oExpl As Outlook.Explorer
Dim oFolder As Outlook.Folder
Dim oView As Outlook.View

Set oNS = Application.GetNamespace("MAPI")

Set oExpl = Application.ActiveExplorer
Set oFolder = oNS.GetDefaultFolder(olFolderContacts)
Set oExpl.CurrentFolder = oFolder
oExpl.CurrentView = "Business Cards"
```

The code gets the default Contacts folder using the `GetDefaultFolder` method, using the `olFolderContacts` constant, and then sets the `CurrentFolder` property object of the `Explorer` to the Contacts folder. The `Explorer`'s `CurrentView` property is then set to "Business Cards."

Summary

In this chapter, you learned how to configure the Outlook VBA project, so you can use it without warning prompts and so your VBA code will run. You also learned:

❑   How to access Outlook items using the Outlook object model.

❑   How Outlook organizes its data storage.

❑   The differences between `Explorers` and `Inspectors` and how they are used to display Outlook objects.

In the next chapter, you learn about some of the most important new features of the Outlook object model and how they are used to display Outlook objects.

What's New in Outlook 2007

This chapter explains the most important new collections, objects, methods, properties, and events in the Outlook object model. So many things were added to the Outlook object model in Outlook 2007 that the object model doubled its size, making it hard to select the most important new features.

At the end of the Outlook 2000 beta, the Outlook MVPs (Microsoft Most Valuable Professionals) involved in Outlook development wrote a whitepaper listing items they wanted added to the Outlook object model so that development could be done using only Outlook code, without dipping into other APIs. Thanks to the splendid work of the Outlook team at Microsoft, spearheaded by Randy Byrne and Ryan Gregg, we finally have almost everything we asked for so many years ago.

The selections for this chapter are the ones I consider the most important, based on many years as an Outlook developer. All new Outlook 2007 features are covered in this book even if they aren't in this chapter:

❑ **The unified object model:** The Outlook object model now has many of the properties and methods of other APIs (Application Programming Interfaces), such as CDO 1.21 (Collaboration Data Objects), making Outlook 2007 a complete development platform. For most programming tasks, Outlook programmers now don't have to master additional APIs to perform basic Outlook programming functions. This chapter explains important new additions to the Outlook object model, such as the `PropertyAccessor`, `Stores`, and `StorageItems`, user interface objects, tables, and accounts. You also learn about the limitations and bugs in some of the new additions to the Outlook object model.

❑ **Improving your performance:** Another part of this chapter explains how to use tables to increase the often slow performance of Outlook in accessing filtered groups and collections of items. Using tables for such accesses instead of filtered or restricted `Items` collections can often yield an order of magnitude performance improvement.

❑ **Increased security:** You learn how the Outlook object model security guard treats trusted and untrusted Outlook code and how to ensure that code in Outlook COM addins is trusted by Outlook.

❑ **DASL:** You discover DASL syntax and why mastering this syntax is so important in Outlook 2007 programming. DASL is the search syntax (DAV Searching and Locating) used in WebDAV (Web Distributed Authoring and Versioning) and also for Exchange and Outlook access based on schemas defined by Microsoft. The more familiar JET syntax for accessing Outlook items is also explained and contrasted with using DASL syntax.

The Unified Object Model

This section and the following sections in this chapter introduce the most important new things in the Outlook object model. Appendix A, which discusses the Outlook object model, contains a complete list of the new collections, objects, properties, methods, and events added to the Outlook 2007 object model.

The Outlook 2007 developer Help file lists the complete Outlook object model reference, with many extensive code samples illustrating the use of the object model components. It also has sections on what was added to the Outlook object model in each major release since Outlook 97 was released. There are sections in Help that list changes since Outlook 97, Outlook 2000, Outlook 2002, and Outlook 2003. There is also a section in Help about the developer issues that can be expected when upgrading code solutions to Outlook 2007. More than ever, the Outlook Help file really is helpful.

The PropertyAccessor

Even with all the added properties in Outlook items, there are still some that aren't exposed in the Outlook object model (OOM). For example, the Internet message headers aren't available as a property in an Outlook `MailItem` object. The headers are available to the new Rules objects, but for some reason aren't exposed in the OOM. There are also properties that are quite useful, but are undocumented or poorly documented and not exposed in the OOM, such as the Out of Office state for Exchange users.

For years Outlook developers used alternate APIs such as CDO 1.21 (CDO) to access `Fields` collections that provided access to properties not exposed in the OOM for items, folders, and stores. The new `PropertyAccessor` object gives Outlook developers parity with developers using other APIs. You now can access any property, if you know the property tag, anywhere in Outlook using the `PropertyAccessor`. As you may have discovered in Chapter 1, Outlook stores data in rows and columns in a database. These columns include not only the properties exposed in the OOM for items, folders, and stores but also all the properties defined in MAPI for those objects. The Outlook defined columns are known to program-mers as properties, or named MAPI properties for properties that are added to an item only when data is stored in the property, such as `BusinessAddressStreet`. User defined properties are known as `UserProperties` or `Named Properties`. `UserProperties` are visible to users, while named proper-ties are not visible to the user. All these types of properties are accessible to the `PropertyAccessor`.

> *Outlook properties and named MAPI properties can't be deleted by using the* `PropertyAccessor`. `UserProperties` *and* `Named Properties` *can be deleted using the* `PropertyAccessor`. *The justification for this is to protect Outlook from essential properties being deleted and causing data loss or crashes, although I can think of many ways to cause either or both with existing methods.*

The `PropertyAccessor` object provides access to properties that aren't exposed to the Outlook object model, so it must use different syntax than the usual `strSubject = oItem.Subject`. The syntax is similar to the syntax for the `AdvancedSearch` method, a DASL schema syntax that resembles an

Internet URL. The arguments passed to the `PropertyAccessor` methods refer to the DASL property identifiers as `SchemaName`.

The following methods are provided to get, set, and delete one or multiple properties at a time:

- ❑   `GetProperty(SchemaName)`, `GetProperties(SchemaNames)`

- ❑   `SetProperty(SchemaName, Value)`, `SetProperties(SchemaNames, Values)`

- ❑   `DeleteProperty(SchemaName)`, `DeleteProperties(SchemaNames)`

   To create a new property using the `PropertyAccessor`, use the `SetProperty` method and make sure to save the Outlook item so that the new property is saved.

The `PropertyAccessor` object also provides helper methods for date/time and binary array conversion:

- ❑   `LocalTimeToUTC`, `UTCToLocalTime`

- ❑   `BinaryToString`, `StringToBinary`

   One thing to be aware of when working with the time conversion methods is that Outlook 2007 rounds the values to convert to the nearest minute; it doesn't use the seconds part of any times. Therefore, any time comparisons between property values need to take this rounding into account. One way to do that is to test for a difference of 1 minute or less as an approximation of time equality.

The `PropertyAccessor` object accepts four types of `SchemaName` syntax to specify the property you want to work with:

- ❑   Property tag syntax uses the string `http://schemas.microsoft.com/mapi/proptag/0x` followed by the property tag of the property. An example is `http://schemas.microsoft.com/mapi/proptag/0x007D001E` for an email's Internet mail headers. This syntax for SchemaName is used for Outlook properties.

- ❑   Property ID syntax uses the string `http://schemas.microsoft.com/mapi/id/` followed by a GUID namespace for the item and property types, followed by a property ID, followed by a string for the data type of the property. An example is `http://schemas.microsoft.com/mapi/id/{00062004-0000-0000-C000-000000000046}/8082001E` for a contact's `EmailAddressType` property. This syntax is used for MAPI `Named Properties` and `UserProperties`.

- ❑   Named Property syntax uses the string `http://schemas.microsoft.com/mapi/string/` followed by a GUID namespace for the item and property types, followed by a property name. An example is `http://schemas.microsoft.com/mapi/string/{00020329-0000-0000-C000-000000000046}/keywords`, which is the `Categories` field in Outlook, containing the category names. This syntax is used for `Named Properties` and some MAPI named properties. This is the syntax you use most often to create named properties in your code.

- ❑   Office document syntax uses the string `urn:schemas-microsoft-com:office:office#` for Office `DocumentItem` support. In this syntax, the name of the property is concatenated to the end of the property tag string. An example is `urn:schemas-microsoft-com:office:office#author` for the author of a document.

The following sections describe all four `PropertyAccessor` syntax types.

PropertyAccessor Syntax 1

The first example of using the `PropertyAccessor` in Listing 2.1 uses the Property Tag syntax, `http://schemas.microsoft.com/mapi/proptag/0x`, concatenated with a property tag string, in this case `007D001E`. The resulting string, `http://schemas.microsoft.com/mapi/proptag/0x007D001E` is the way to retrieve the Internet mail headers from an email item. This example assumes the item selected in the Inbox is an email item that was received using an Internet mail protocol. It doesn't provide any error handling if this is not true.

Listing 2.1

```
Public Sub ShowMailHeaders()
  Dim oNS As Outlook.NameSpace
  Dim oInbox As Outlook.Folder 'using new Folder object
  Dim colItems As Outlook.Items
  Dim oMail As Outlook.MailItem
  Dim oPropAccessor As Outlook.PropertyAccessor
  Dim strHeaders As String

  Const PR_MAIL_HEADER_TAG As String = _
    "http://schemas.microsoft.com/mapi/proptag/0x007D001E"

  Set oNS = Application.GetNameSpace("MAPI")
  Set oInbox = oNS.GetDefaultFolder(olFolderInbox)
  Set colItems = oInbox.Items
  Set oMail = colItems.Item(1)
  Set oPropAccessor = oMail.PropertyAccessor
  'PropertyAccessor property tags are always strings
  strHeaders = oPropAccessor.GetProperty(PR_MAIL_HEADER_TAG)

  MsgBox "Mail Headers: " & vbCRLF & strHeaders
End Sub
```

> You learn more about DASL syntax and the various schemas used for Outlook properties later in this chapter in the section "The Importance of DASL." You also learn about using a different type of DASL filter, the Content Indexer filter in that section of this chapter. The most common DASL property tags for Outlook items are listed in Appendix A and resources for the various schemas used for Outlook and tools to work with Outlook properties are discussed in Appendix B.

For the previous code, notice the following:

- ❑ First, the code gets the `NameSpace` object and uses the `GetDefaultFolder` method to retrieve the Inbox as a `Folder` object. The `Items` collection of the `Folder` contains all visible items in the folder

- ❑ The code assumes that the first item in the `Items` collection is an email and was sent by Internet mail and retrieves it as an Outlook `MailItem`.

❑   The `PropertyAccessor` retrieves the value of the Internet headers, which is a string, and displays the headers in a message box.

Standard Outlook properties use standard property tags, for example `Subject` is always `0x0037001E`. You can always retrieve any standard property value from Outlook, even if the property is available using other, different syntax by using the `http://schemas.microsoft.com/mapi/proptag/0x` syntax and concatenating the property tag value as a string to the schema.

> *An exception to this is the* `Body` *property of an item, which is blocked to the* `PropertyAccessor`. *This limitation is due to the potentially extremely large size of the body of an item.*

All properties have a type, such as Boolean or String8 (ANSI 8-bit string), as well as a property tag. The property tag is a 32.bit integer that is usually expressed as a hexadecimal number (a number in Base16 notation). Property tags have different ranges, with properties in the `0x80000000` range known as named properties. This range contains user-defined as well as Outlook-defined properties that aren't always present on an item, such as `BusinessAddressState` for contact items.

> **The notation** `0x80000000` **is hexadecimal notation for the signed value** `-2147483648`. **There are different ways of expressing hexadecimal numbers, such as the Visual Basic format that precedes the number with** `&H`. **This book uses the** `0x` **notation familiar to C++ and C# programmer. Hexadecimal notation is a convenient way of expressing numbers for programmers and is used extensively in this book. The** `0x` **notation is used because that is the notation used for** `PropertyAccessor` **property tags.**

The biggest limitation of the `PropertyAccessor` is a limitation on how much data you can read from a string or binary property. This limitation applies to user properties, properties whose property tags are above `0x80000000`. In most cases, you can't read any string or binary property that is larger than 4088 bytes. The exceptions to this are online Exchange mailboxes (not in cached mode) and Exchange public folder stores. Those Exchange stores have a limit of 16,372 bytes for read operations. Reading properties larger than that size may return an out of memory error. A `PropertyAcccessor` can write much more data than it can read back, potentially creating a problem. Both CDO and Redemption (a third-party COM wrapper for Extended MAPI functionality) can be used to avoid this problem. CDO and Redemption fall back to retrieving the property data for large properties as streams, working around a MAPI limitation. `PropertyAccessor` does not currently implement this workaround, so it has the 4 KB read limitation on string and binary properties. The value of the property tag for the Internet headers is below `0x80000000`, so headers larger than 4 KB can be retrieved without errors.

The second example of using Property Tag syntax gets the user's Out of Office state. The code to find the Out of Office state first gets the default Outlook store, and if the store is an Exchange mailbox, then retrieves the Boolean value of the Out of Office property. Listing 2.2 defines a constant string for the Out of Office state using the property name used in the MAPI header files, `PR_OOF_STATE`. Outlook programmers often use this type of property name to retain meaning between Outlook and the underlying MAPI.

Listing 2.2

```
Public Sub ShowOutOfOfficeState()
  Dim oNS As Outlook.NameSpace
```

(continued)

Listing 2.2 *(continued)*

```
    Dim colStores As Outlook.Stores
    Dim oStore As Outlook.Store
    Dim oPropAccessor As Outlook.PropertyAccessor
    Dim blnOOF_State As Boolean

    Const PR_OOF_STATE As String = _
      "http://schemas.microsoft.com/mapi/proptag/0x661D000B"

    blnOOF_State = False

    Set oNS = Application.GetNameSpace("MAPI")
    Set colStores = oNS.Stores
    For Each oStore In colStores
      If oStore.ExchangeStoreType = _
        OlExchangeStoreType.olPrimaryExchangeMailbox Then

        Set oPropAccessor = oStore.PropertyAccessor
        'PropertyAccessor property tags are always strings
        blnOOF_State = _
          oPropAccessor.GetProperty(PR_OOF_STATE)

        Exit For
      End If
    Next

    MsgBox "Out of office is " & blnOOF_State

End Sub
```

PropertyAccessor Syntax 2

In Property ID syntax, you create property tags for named properties using a schema, GUID (a globally unique string) defining the property usage, a property ID and the property type. These properties are added to an item either by Outlook or by code when data is added to the property. Examples of properties added to items only when data is added to the properties are `Private` and `Email1AddressType`. You use different GUIDs for different classes of property types with Property ID syntax, for example, properties for tasks or contacts.

❑ The schema for most named properties is `http://schemas.microsoft.com/mapi/id/`.

❑ The GUID for `Email1AddressType` is the contact GUID, `{00062004-0000-0000-C000-000000000046}`.

❑ The property ID for `Email1AddressType` is `8082`.

❑ `Email1AddressType` is a string, so to retrieve the ANSI display name a property type string, use `001E`. To retrieve the Unicode display name string, use `001F` as the property type string.

The complete `SchemaName` for `Email1AddressType` is therefore:

```
http://schemas.microsoft.com/mapi/id/" + "{00062004-0000-0000-C000-000000000046}" +
"/8082" + "001E"
```

The following code blocks for variations of Basic and C# show some common declarations of constants for property types, GUIDs and schemas. Additional schema declarations are shown in the Importance of DASL section of this chapter. The declarations follow MAPI style, where the PT prefix indicates a property type.

VB.NET, VBA, VB 6

```
' Property type constants
Const PT_STRING8 As String = "001E"
Const PT_MV_STRING8 As String = "101E"
Const PT_UNICODE As String = "001F"
Const PT_MV_UNICODE As String = "101F"
Const PT_BINARY As String = "0102"
Const PT_MV_BINARY As String = "1102"
Const PT_BOOLEAN As String = "000B"
Const PT_SYSTIME As String = "0040"
Const PT_LONG As String = "0003" ' 32 bits
Const PT_DOUBLE As String = "0005"

'8 byte integer (64 bits) - this is not a usable type for VB 6 or VBA
'only use with VB.NET
Const PT_I8 As String = "0014"

' GUIDs for various named property types
Const MAPI_NAMED_PROP As String = _
"{00020329-0000-0000-C000-000000000046}"
Const MAPI_NAMED_TASK_PROP As String = _
"{00062003-0000-0000-C000-000000000046}"
Const MAPI_NAMED_APPT_PROP As String = _
"{00062002-0000-0000-C000-000000000046}"
Const MAPI_NAMED_CONTACT_PROP As String = _
"{00062004-0000-0000-C000-000000000046}"
Const MAPI_NAMED_MAIL_PROP As String = _
"{00062008-0000-0000-C000-000000000046}"

' Property Schemas
Const PROPERTY_TAG_SCHEMA As String = _
"http://schemas.microsoft.com/mapi/proptag/0x"
Const PROPERTY_ID_SCHEMA As String = _
"http://schemas.microsoft.com/mapi/id/"
```

C#

```
// Property type constants
const string PT_STRING8 = "001E";
const string PT_MV_STRING8 = "101E";
const string PT_UNICODE = "001F";
const string PT_MV_UNICODE = "101F";
const string PT_BINARY = "0102";
const string PT_MV_BINARY = "1102";
const string PT_BOOLEAN = "000B";
const string PT_SYSTIME = "0040";
const string PT_LONG = "0003"; // 32 bits
const string PT_DOUBLE = "0005";
const string PT_I8 = "0014"; // 64 bits
```

(continued)

C# (continued)

```
// GUIDs for various named property types
const string MAPI_NAMED_PROP = "{00020329-0000-0000-C000-000000000046}";
const string MAPI_NAMED_TASK_PROP = "{00062003-0000-0000-C000-000000000046}";
const string MAPI_NAMED_APPT_PROP = "{00062002-0000-0000-C000-000000000046}";
const string MAPI_NAMED_CONTACT_PROP = "{00062004-0000-0000-C000-000000000046}";
const string MAPI_NAMED_MAIL_PROP = "{00062008-0000-0000-C000-000000000046}";

// Property Schemas
const string PROPERTY_TAG_SCHEMA =
"http://schemas.microsoft.com/mapi/proptag/0x";
const string PROPERTY_ID_SCHEMA =
"http://schemas.microsoft.com/mapi/id/";
```

An easy way to find the DASL definition of most Outlook properties is to use the filter definition window for Outlook views. To do so:

1. Select View ⇨ Current View ⇨ Define Views to open the Custom View Organizer.

2. Click the New button to open the Create a New View dialog, and click OK to accept the defaults.

3. In the Customize View: New View dialog, click the Filter button.

4. Select the Advanced tab, and use the Field button to select the property in which you are interested.

5. For a string value, such as `Email1AddressType`, select "is empty" in the Condition drop-down.

6. Click the Add to List button to accept the query.

7. Select the SQL tab, and check the Edit These Criteria Directly checkbox to enable you to view and copy the generated `SchemaName` for use with the `PropertyAccessor`.

8. Cancel the custom view dialogs after copying the `SchemaName` to avoid actually creating the custom view.

Figure 2.1 shows the SQL shown for the query `Email1AddressType is empty`, with the information needed to access the `Email1AddressType` property.

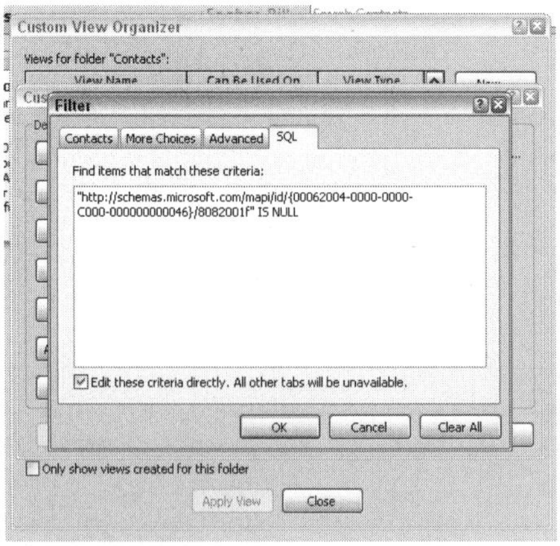

Figure 2.1

Using the SQL tab in the custom view designer is also a handy way to learn the SQL syntax used with AdvancedSearch, *and in other places in Outlook.*

The code to retrieve the string value of the Email1AddressType from an already instantiated PropertyAccessor object for a contact item is:

```
' To retrieve the Unicode string use "001F" instead of "001E"
strAddyType = _
"http://schemas.microsoft.com/mapi/id/" & _
"{00062004-0000-0000-C000-000000000046}" & "/8082" & "001E"

strAddrType = oPropertyAccessor.GetProperty(strAddyType)
```

You add task properties to flagged items so that you can view the items in the To-Do Bar. When the item is marked complete, it's removed from the To-Do Bar. The code to set the Complete status for a contact, where Complete is used to control viewing a flagged contact in the To-Do Bar, is:

```
strTaskComplete = _
"http://schemas.microsoft.com/mapi/id/" & _
"{00062003-0000-0000-C000-000000000046}" & "/811C" & "000B"

oPropertyAccessor.SetProperty(strTaskComplete, True)
```

In this code, the task GUID {00062003-0000-0000-C000-000000000046} is concatenated with the property ID /811C and the property type value for a Boolean property, 000B. The property is set to True, which marks the associated task in the To-Do Bar complete. Make sure to save the Outlook item so that your changes are preserved.

PropertyAccessor Syntax 3

The third PropertyAccessor syntax is also for named properties, but you use it for named properties that have names instead of property IDs. Named properties you create in code use this syntax, as do some Outlook properties. For example the Categories property is a multi-valued string property that uses the name Keywords instead of a property ID. The schema for these properties is http://schemas .microsoft.com/mapi/string/, followed by a GUID and then the property name. This name may not be the name used in the Outlook object model for the property, just as the Categories property is represented in the schema as Keywords.

After a named property is created, you cannot change its data type and name. You must delete the property and create a new one with the changed data type or name.

The SchemaName for Categories uses the GUID {00020329-0000-0000-C000-000000000046}, so the complete SchemaName for Categories is:

```
http://schemas.microsoft.com/mapi/string/{00020329-0000-0000-C000-000000000046}/
keywords.
```

This is a different SchemaName from that shown in the SQL tab of the custom view filter dialog, urn:schemas-microsoft-com:office:office#Keywords. Both of these work to retrieve the categories from an Outlook item, demonstrating that you can retrieve many properties in Outlook using different SchemaName values.

`Categories` is an array of strings, so the Outlook property is a multi-valued string property. Listing 2.3 shows code to retrieve the property value from the Outlook item as a string array, then display the list of all categories in the item displays in a message box. The code shows both `SchemaName` variations for the `Categories` property, with the `urn:schemas-microsoft-com:office:office#Keywords` variation commented out. Uncomment this variation and comment out the earlier `strSchemaName` lines to verify that both return the same results from any item selected in Outlook:

Listing 2.3

```
Public Sub ShowCategories()
    Dim colSelection As Outlook.Selection
    Dim oExpl As Outlook.Explorer
    Dim oPropAccessor As Outlook.PropertyAccessor
    Dim aryCats() As String
    Dim strDisplay As String
    Dim i As Long
    Dim strSchemaName As String

    strSchemaName = "http://schemas.microsoft.com/mapi/string/"
    strSchemaName = strSchemaName & _
"{00020329-0000-0000-C000-000000000046}"
    strSchemaName = strSchemaName & "/keywords"

    'strSchemaName = "urn:schemas-microsoft-com:office:office#Keywords"

    Set oExpl = Application.ActiveExplorer
    Set colSelection = oExpl.Selection
    Set oPropAccessor = colSelection.Item(1).PropertyAccessor
    aryCats() = oPropAccessor.GetProperty(strSchemaName)
    For i = LBound(aryCats) To UBound(aryCats)
        strDisplay = strDisplay & aryCats(i) & vbCrLf
    Next i

    MsgBox "Categories are " & strDisplay
End Sub
```

PropertyAccessor Syntax 4

The final syntax for accessing Outlook properties is used primarily for `DocumentItem` support. You access properties such as `Comments`, `Title`, `Author`, and other document properties using the schema `urn:schemas-microsoft-com:office:office#`, followed by the name of the property.

This schema is the same shown as an alternate schema for Categories. Just substitute the name of the document property you want to access for `Keywords`. For example, to access `Comments`, the `SchemaName` would be `urn:schemas-microsoft-com:office:office#Comments`.

Accessing Multiple Properties

The multiple property methods of the `PropertyAccessor`: `GetProperties`, `SetProperties`, and `DeleteProperties` take variant array arguments for the `SchemaNames` and `Values` arguments. If you are creating new named properties, the property types are determined from the types of the values passed to the `SetProperties` method.

VB.NET and C# do not support a `Variant` *array variable type, so for development using those languages, use an* `Object` *array. For VB.NET use* `Dim colArgs As Object()`, *and for C# use* `object[] colArgs;`.

The code in Listing 2.4 shows how to set two properties at the same time on a currently opened email item, a category and text for a follow-up flag. If any errors occur, they are returned to a variant array, which is tested to see if the array contains any errors.

Listing 2.4

```
Public Sub Set2Properties()
    Dim astrProps() As Variant
    Dim astrValues() As Variant
    Dim avarErrors() As Variant
    Dim sProp1 As String
    Dim sProp2 As String
    Dim sVal1 As String
    Dim sVal2 As String
    Dim oInsp As Outlook.Inspector
    Dim oMail As Outlook.MailItem
    Dim oPropAccessor As Outlook.PropertyAccessor
    Dim i As Long

    Set oInsp = Application.ActiveInspector
    Set oMail = oInsp.CurrentItem
    Set oPropAccessor = oMail.PropertyAccessor

    sProp1 = "urn:schemas:httpmail:messageflag"
    sProp2 = "urn:schemas-microsoft-com:office:office#Keywords"
    astrProps = Array(sProp1, sProp2)

    sVal1 = "Please follow up"
    sVal2 = "Red Category"
    astrValues = Array(sVal1, sVal2)

    avarErrors = oPropAccessor.SetProperties(astrProps, astrValues)
    If Not (IsEmpty(avarErrors)) Then
        For i = LBound(avarErrors) To UBound(avarErrors)
            If IsError(avarErrors(i)) Then
                MsgBox CVErr(avarErrors(i))
            End If
        Next i
    End If

    oMail.Save
End Sub
```

The `DeleteProperties` and `GetProperties` methods also return a variant error array, which you should test to see if any errors occurred during the method calls. You should always test each element in the returned array as shown. Even if no errors occurred, the return error array may not be empty, so each array element should be tested to see whether it's an error.

The Date/Time and Binary/String Methods

You use the remaining methods of the `PropertyAccessor` object to convert from Outlook and MAPI formats to formats that Outlook programmers use. Outlook stores all dates internally in UTC values, where dates and times are normalized to the setting for Greenwich Mean Time with offsets for the local time zone and daylight savings time. When dates and times are returned as properties in the Outlook object model, such as `CreationTime`, they are converted into local time, which is shown as the property value.

The `PropertyAccessor` object sets and returns all date and time properties using UTC values, so methods to convert to and from UTC and local time are provided. These methods are `LocalTimeToUTC` and `UTCToLocalTime`, both of which take `Date` values and return converted `Date` values. For example, to convert the local date and time January 1, 2007 4:00 PM to UTC time, the code would use:

```
datConvertedDate = oPropAccessor.LocalTimeToUTC(#1/1/2007 4:00 PM#)
```

These time conversion methods round the time to be converted to the nearest minute, so the converted results are only accurate to plus 1 minute of the time that was converted.

Some properties returned from the Outlook object model, such as `EntryID` and `StoreID`, are retrieved and used as strings, but are actually stored internally as binary data. Technically, these properties aren't strings, but are really `PT_BINARY` properties (Property Type Binary), and they are retrieved as binary arrays. Of course, you can use the Outlook object model to retrieve an `EntryID` or a `StoreID` from a `Folder` object, but using a `PropertyAccessor` is useful even for a property such as `StoreID`. `StoreID` can be retrieved from an Outlook item. However, when using the Outlook object model you must retrieve the parent `Folder` object where the item exists before you can retrieve the `StoreID`.

To convert a binary property to a string, use the `BinaryToString` method. To convert a string to a binary property, use the `StringToBinary` method. The following short code snippet shows how to retrieve the `StoreID` from an instantiated `MailItem` object as a usable string value, using the `BinaryToString` method:

```
Set oPropAccessor = oMail.PropertyAccessor
' Schema for StoreID
strSchema = "http://schemas.microsoft.com/mapi/proptag/0x0FFB0102"
strStoreID = oPropAccessor.BinaryToString(oPropAccessor.GetProperty(strSchema))
```

Stores and Storage Items

Outlook stores are the top level of Outlook storage. Examples of stores are PST files and Exchange mailboxes. Storage items are invisible items stored in Outlook folders used to contain configuration information that should remain invisible to the user. In this section, you learn about working with stores and `StorageItems`.

Working with Stores

Although stores are new to the Outlook object model, programmers have used them for many years from alternate APIs, such as CDO 1.21. A `Store` object is the highest level of storage in Outlook and corresponds to a PST file or Exchange mailbox or the Exchange public folders. Not only do `Store` objects provide access to properties such as Out of Office, explored earlier in this chapter, but they also provide other unique properties that are only available on the `Store` object. The store's support mask property enables you to learn what operations, such as Unicode storage, are available. The access level property exposes the permissions that the current user has on objects in the store, and the offline state shows the current online status of that store, as examples of various store properties.

In addition to store properties, the `Store` object provides access to special folders, such as the Reminders folder and the To-Do Search folder that the new To-Do Bar uses and all user-created search folders, as well as storage for views and other things that are only retrieved from a `Store` object or its derivatives. All loaded stores are contained in the `Stores` collection, where you can add and remove stores as well as enumerate individual loaded stores. Among other properties and methods for `Store` objects in this book, you learn to work with the new `GetRules` method@@mda new feature that Outlook developers have requested for years, which retrieves the rules defined for that store and uses code to create and modify rules.

The following code gets the `Rules` collection of all rules from the default `Store`:

```
Dim oNS As Outlook.NameSpace
Dim oStore As Outlook.Store
Dim colRules As Outlook.Rules

Set oNS = Application.GetNameSpace("MAP")
Set oStore = oNS.DefaultStore
Set colRules = oStore.GetRules
```

You learn much more about working with stores and rules from code later in this chapter, and in other chapters in this book.

Working with StorageItems

`StorageItems` are standard Outlook items that are invisible to the user. This makes them valuable as repositories for storing user configurations, special program settings, and other uses where you don't want a user to view the item and change settings in an unstructured way. For years, Outlook programmers have used APIs, such as CDO 1.21, to add messages to the `HiddenMessages` collection or `Associated Contents` collections to create hidden Outlook items. Now programmers using only the Outlook object model have this option.

The following code creates a `StorageItem` in the Inbox to store special properties related to an application:

```
Dim oFolder As Outlook.Folder
Dim oNS As Outlook.NameSpace
Dim oStorage As Outlook.StorageItem

Set oNS = Application.GetNameSpace("MAPI")
Set oFolder = oNS.GetDefaultFolder(olFolderInbox)
Set oStorage = oFolder.GetStorage("STS_MyInboxStorage", _
    OlStorageIdentifierType.olIdentifyBySubject)
```

You can call the `GetStorage` method in one of three ways depending on the value of the `StorageIdentifierType` argument. This argument uses a member of the `OlStorageIdentifier` enumeration:

❑ Use `OlStorageIdentifier.olIdentifyByEntryID` to retrieve a `StorageItem` by its `EntryID`, the unique GUID that identifies items in each data store. If no `StorageItem` exists with that `EntryID`, an error is raised.

❑ Use `OlStorageIdentifier.olIdentifyByMessageClass` to retrieve or create a `StorageItem` by its `MessageClass`. If no `StorageItems` exist in the folder with the specified `MessageClass`, one is created. If more than one `StorageItem` exists with the same `MessageClass`, the item with the latest modification time is retrieved when `GetStorage` is called.

❑ Use `OlStorageIdentifier.olIdentifyBySubject` to retrieve or create a `StorageItem` by its `Subject`. `GetStorage` creates a new item with the requested `Subject` if an item with that `Subject` does not already exist. If more than one `StorageItem` exists with the same `Subject`, the item with the latest modification time is retrieved when `GetStorage` is called. When a `StorageItem` is created this way the `MessageClass` is always `IPM.Storage`.

After you have a `StorageItem`, you can set its `Body` property to store your settings, set individual properties on the item, and add attachments to the item, just as with any other Outlook item. Always remember to save the `StorageItem` to persist any change you make in the item.

The following code retrieves a storage item with the message class of `IPM.Note.MyStorage` and sets a Boolean `UserProperty` named `ItemSynched`:

```
Dim oProp As Outlook.UserProperty

Set oStorage = oFolder.GetStorage("IPM.Note.MyStorage ", _
    OlStorageIdentifierType.olIdentifyByMessageClass)

Set oProp = oStorage.UserProperties.Add("ItemSynched, olYesNo)
oProp = True
oStorage.Save
```

`StorageItems` as implemented by Outlook 2007 have two limitations and one major bug:

❑ You cannot create or read `StorageItems` in Exchange public folders.

❑ To retrieve `StorageItems` where multiple items exist in the same folder with identical `Subject` or `MessageClass` properties, you must use a `Table` object. You can't use the `GetStorage` method.

❑ If you create a `StorageItem` in a non-mail folder, the item is created as a visible item in the Inbox. Although this is likely to be among the first bugs fixed in Outlook 2007, I recommend not using `StorageItems` in folders other than mail folders unless you can ensure that your users will have the required bug fix. A workaround is to store `StorageItems` for non-mail folders in the Inbox, using the `MessageClass` or `Subject` to make the `StorageItems` unique.

User Interface Objects

In the past, Outlook has always been weak in letting you access and work with various aspects of the user interface, such as views and the `NavigationPane`. Outlook 2007 finally provides access to these user interface objects in a structured object model.

Views

Views have been programmable in Outlook since Outlook 2002, but the method of creating a custom view in code was awkward and not fully documented. About the only way to define a custom view was to create that view in the user interface and then read the XML that defined the view. This method was prone to mistakes and did not provide full access to all the formatting you could apply to a view in the user interface. For example, you could not apply autoformatting colors or turn in-cell editing on or off.

The new view specific objects, such as `TableView`, `TimelineView`, and `CardView`, have properties that allow you to set in-cell editing, apply autoformatting rules, set fonts, set properties to view, and more.

You can read more about creating custom views using the new view objects in Chapter 6.

NavigationPane, NavigationFolders, and NavigationGroups, and Modules

Before Outlook 2007, you could not program the Navigation Pane in Outlook. You could find and hack the XML file that defines the Navigation Pane, but even adding a shortcut was never a sure thing. Sometimes it worked, sometimes it didn't, and Microsoft never supported hacking the XML file. Another shortcoming of hacking the XML file was that Outlook only read it at startup and always overwrote whatever was there when it shut down.

Outlook 2007 provides an object interface to the Navigation Pane using the `Explorer.NavigationPane` object. You can now retrieve modules from the Navigation Pane, such as the Email and Contacts modules, retrieve or set the current module, see how many modules are displayed, and discover if the Navigation Pane is collapsed. New Navigation Pane modules cannot be created using the `NavigationPane` object. Each module, such as the `MailModule`, has methods to retrieve the `NavigationGroups` for that module, and you can add and remove folders from a `NavigationGroup`. You can also get the Navigation Pane's Shortcuts module and add or remove folders from the shortcuts.

You learn to more about working with the Navigation Pane in Chapter 6.

SelectNamesDialog

The `SelectNamesDialog` is familiar to all Outlook users as the dialog you see when you click the To button in an email. This dialog, known as the `AddressBook` method in CDO 1.21, has previously never been exposed to Outlook programmers. This enables you to show the dialog on demand in your code in Outlook 2007 without using the CDO `AddressBook` dialog. The CDO `AddressBook` dialog returns a CDO `Recipient`, which can't be used in OOM code. To get the equivalent Outlook `Recipient`, you must get the `ID` property of the CDO `Recipient` and use that as the `EntryID` argument for the Outlook `NameSpace.GetRecipientFromID` method.

When you display a `SelectNamesDialog`, it appears as a modal dialog, and on return from the dialog, you can access the selected names from the `SelectNamesDialog` class's `Recipients` collection. The following code (Listing 2.5) returns one recipient for a select names dialog that is set up as an email selection dialog. You can also set up this dialog to resemble the ones that display for assigning a task, selecting attendees for a meeting, assigning delegates, selecting members of a distribution list, and other types of name selection dialogs.

Listing 2.5

```
Public Sub AddRecipient()
   Dim oSelect As Outlook.SelectNamesDialog
   Dim colRecipients As Outlook.Recipients
   Dim oRecip As Outlook.Recipient
   Dim oMail As Outlook.MailItem

   Set oMail = Application.CreateItem(olMailItem)
   Set oSelect = Application.Session.GetSelectNamesDialog
```

(continued)

Listing 2.5 *(continued)*

```
With oSelect
  .AllowMultipleSelection = False
  SetDefaultDisplayMode _
    OlDefaultSelectNamesDisplayMode.olDefaultMail

  .ForceResolution = True
  .Caption = "My Mail Selector Dialog"
  .ToLabel = "My To Selector"

  .NumberOfRecipientSelectors = _
    OlRecipientSelectors.olShowTo

  .Display

  If .Recipients.Count = 1 Then
    Set oRecip = _
      oMail.Recipients.Add(.Recipients.Item(1).Name)
  End If
End With

  oMail.Display
End Sub
```

Accounts

In past versions, the installed email accounts in an Outlook profile have never been accessible from Outlook object model code, and there was never a way to control what account was used to send out an Outlook item. However, Outlook 2007 now provides a `NameSpace.Accounts` collection that includes all the accounts set up in that Outlook profile. In addition, you can send mail, appointment, task, and sharing items using a specific account from code.

Listing 2.6 creates a new mail item and iterates the `Accounts` collection to find the first POP3 account; then the code uses that account to send the email.

Listing 2.6

```
Public Sub SendUsingPOP3()
  Dim oMail As Outlook.MailItem
  Dim colAccounts As Outlook.Accounts
  Dim oNS As Outlook.NameSpace
  Dim oAccount As Outlook.Account
  Dim strUser As String
  Dim strAddress As String
  Dim strAccountName As String
  Dim blnFound As Boolean

  blnFound = False

  Set oNS = Application.GetNameSpace("MAPI")
```

Listing 2.6 *(continued)*

```
      Set colAccounts = oNS.Accounts
      For Each oAccount In colAccounts
         If oAccount.AccountType = OlAccountType.olPOP3 Then
            strAddress = oAccount.SmtpAddress
            strUser = oAccount.UserName
            strAccountName = oAccount.DisplayName

            blnFound = True

            Exit For
         End If
      Next

      If blnFound Then
         Set oMail = Application.CreateItem(olMailItem)
         oMail.Subject = "Sent using: " & strAccountName

         oMail.Body = "Sent by " & strUser & vbCRLF & _
         "Sent using the " & strAddress & " SMTP address."

         oMail.Recipients.Add("test@test.com")
         oMail.Recipients.ResolveAll

         oMail.SendUsingAccount = oAccount

         oMail.Send
      End If
End Sub
```

The `Account` object enables you to test the `AccountType` property for the type of user email account. The supported types in the `OlAccountType` enumeration are:

- ❑ `olExchange`
- ❑ `olHttp`
- ❑ `olIMAP`
- ❑ `olOtherAccount`, used to mark accounts using alternate account providers
- ❑ `olPOP3`

Although you cannot add new email accounts or configure email accounts using the new accounts properties, the ability to send using a specified account and examine the installed email accounts in an Outlook profile adds features that Outlook developers have long been requesting.

> *The line* `oMail.SendUsingAccount = oAccount` *in listing 2.6 does not use the* `Set` *keyword to assign the value of the object property* `SendUsingAccount`. *When a new instance of an object is created, the* `Set` *keyword is used.* `Set` *is not used when setting object properties. This syntax is used for all object properties added since Outlook 2003. It was not used before that, which can be confusing when you're using VBA or VB 6 for Outlook programming.* `SendUsingAccount` *does not use* `Set`, *but* `Explorer.CurrentFolder` *uses* `Set` *even though both are object properties because* `Explorer` `.CurrrentFolder` *was added to the OOM prior to Outlook 2003.*

Performance Improvements

Using the Outlook object model to work with large collections of items has always been rather slow. Processing a collection of 15,000 Outlook items and reading a property on each item could literally take hours. However, there are ways of speeding up Outlook object model accesses, such as filtering, restricting a large collection so only items of interest are retrieved, or using the SetColumns method to force Outlook to only load properties of interest. But even with the best optimizations, the code can be slow. Alternatives have included using CDO 1.21 Messages collections instead of Outlook Items collections, but all the alternatives suffered from not being standard or requiring optional components.

Working with Tables Instead of Items

The new Table objects in Outlook 2007 are a huge performance boost, offering order of magnitude improvements in reading collections of Outlook objects. Tables use rows and columns, where each row is one Outlook item and the columns in the row are the properties that have been retrieved from the item. Tables are read-only, so you have to return the EntryID and StoreID of the item with the row data if you need to retrieve an Outlook item and write to it. Even with this extra step, working with a Table object is still much faster than conventional Outlook methods.

Tables are read-only dynamic recordsets that are forward only. Any changes you make to items included in the table are shown in the table. You can only move forward in the table; however, you can reset the table pointer at any time to the start of the table using the Table.MoveToStart method. If there are no rows in the table, or you if have navigated to the end of the table, the Table.EndOfTable Boolean property becomes True, so this property is valuable as a termination condition when looping through a table's rows.

The code in Listing 2.7 retrieves a Table object from the Sent Items folder, removes all the columns in the table, and adds EntryID and Importance columns. It then adds a user property to each item that is marked as High importance.

Listing 2.7

```
Public Sub PlayWithTable()
  Dim oTable As Outlook.Table
  Dim colColumns As Outlook.Columns
  Dim oColumn As Outlook.Column
  Dim oFolder As Outlook.Folder
  Dim oMail As Outlook.MailItem
  Dim oRow As Outlook.Row
  Dim oProp As Outlook.UserProperty
  Dim aryValues() As Variant
  Dim strEntryID As String

  Set oFolder = _
    Application.Session.GetDefaultFolder(olFolderSentMail)

  Set oTable = oFolder.GetTable 'returns all items in folder
  Set colColumns = oTable.Columns
  colColumns.RemoveAll
  Set oColumn = colColumns.Add("EntryID")
  Set oColumn = colColumns.Add("Importance")
```

Listing 2.7 *(continued)*

```
      Do While oTable.EndOfTable = False
        Set oRow = oTable.GetNextRow
        aryValues = oRow.GetValues
        If aryValues(1) = OlImportance.olImportanceHigh Then
          strEntryID = aryValues(0)

          Set oMail = _
            Application.Session.GetItemFromID(strEntryID)

          Set oProp = _
            oMail.UserProperties.Add("VeryImportant", olYesNo)

          oProp.Value = True
          oMail.Save
        End If
      Loop
    End Sub
```

Note the following about the code in Listing 2.7:

- ❑ You can specify columns you add and remove from a `Table` object using the Outlook object model name (English only) or any of the appropriate schema names for that column (property).

- ❑ The `FolderGetTable` method takes two optional arguments. The first argument is a filter, which uses JET or DASL syntax and returns a filtered subset of the items in the folder. The second argument, which defaults to `OlTableContents.olUserItems`, returns visible items from the `Folder`. If this argument is set to `OlTableContents.olHiddenItems`, the table returns the `StorageItems` in the folder, the collection of hidden folder items.

- ❑ The `GetValues` method of the `Row` object returns a 1-dimensional `Variant` array containing all the requested columns in the table for that row in the table. Users of VB.NET and C# should use `Object` arrays to retrieve the values from the `GetValues` method.

- ❑ To retrieve a 2-dimensional array containing all the columns from a specified number of rows, use the `Table.GetArray` method and specify the number of rows to retrieve with a 32-bit integer value as the argument for `GetArray`.

Filtering Tables

The code in Listing 2.7 looped through the collection of `Rows` returned in the `Table` object and checked each one for a High Importance. You can simplify this code and make it even faster by filtering the `Table` for only items with High Importance. The code in Listing 2.8 implements a filter for the table based on the Importance level of the items in the folder:

Listing 2.8

```
    Public Sub PlayWithFilteredTable()
      Dim oTable As Outlook.Table
      Dim colColumns As Outlook.Columns
      Dim oColumn As Outlook.Column
```

(continued)

Listing 2.8 (continued)

```
    Dim oFolder As Outlook.Folder
    Dim oMail As Outlook.MailItem
    Dim oRow As Outlook.Row
    Dim oProp As Outlook.UserProperty
    Dim aryValues() As Variant
    Dim strEntryID As String
    Dim strFilter As String

    Set oFolder = _
      Application.Session.GetDefaultFolder(olFolderSentMail)

    strFilter = "[Importance] = 2"

    Set oTable = oFolder.GetTable(strFilter)
    Set colColumns = oTable.Columns
    colColumns.RemoveAll
    Set oColumn = colColumns.Add("EntryID")
    Set oColumn = colColumns.Add("Importance")

    Do While oTable.EndOfTable = False
      Set oRow = oTable.GetNextRow
      aryValues = oRow.GetValues
      If aryValues(1) = OlImportance.olImportanceHigh Then
        strEntryID = aryValues(0)

        Set oMail = _
          Application.Session.GetItemFromID(strEntryID)

        Set oProp = _
          oMail.UserProperties.Add("VeryImportant", olYesNo)

        oProp.Value = True
        oMail.Save
      End If
    Loop
End Sub
```

Please note the following about the code in Listing 2.8:

❑ The filter you use can be a standard Outlook filter string or a DASL syntax filter string. If you use a DASL filter, you must precede it with @SQL=. For example, you could have expressed the filter in the previous example as @SQL=http://schemas.microsoft.com/mapi/proptag/ 0x00170003 = 2. Another type of DASL filter uses the new Content Indexer in Outlook, Filters of that type are discussed in the section "The Importance of DASL."

❑ The Table object allows you to retrieve a filtered table, or to retrieve an unfiltered table and filter the table on the fly using the FindRow(strfilter) and FindNextRow methods. You can also restrict the table, using the Table.Restrict method. You can also sort a table in either ascending or descending order.

Filtering and restricting a table have performance and store load implications. Filtering a table is faster if there are a small number of items in the table. If only a small subset of items in a large table is required, restricting is faster than filtering. These performance issues are the same as those you face when you decide to use a filter or a restriction on an Outlook Items collection.

Table Default Columns

By default, tables return certain default columns. All tables return, in this order:

1. EntryID
2. Subject
3. CreationTime
4. LastModificationTime
5. MessageClass

Each type of item also returns additional default columns, as shown in the following table.

Item Type	Column #	Default Columns
Calendar Item	6.	Start
	7.	End
	8.	IsRecurring
Contact Item	6	FirstName
	7.	LastName
	8.	CompanyName
Task Item	6.	DueDate
	7.	PercentComplete
	8.	IsRecurring

If you need to retrieve other properties, you can add additional columns or you can remove all existing columns and just add the ones you need.

Table Limitations

Tables have certain limitations, depending on the store provider and property types. There are four limitations of which you need to be aware when using tables:

❑ Depending on the store provider, you may only be able to retrieve 255 characters from string properties. Exchange is an example of a store provider that can only return 255 characters in a table. You can either check to see if the store is an Exchange store or use the NameSpace .GetItemFromID method to retrieve the Outlook item and read the property value from the item.

❑ If a `Date` value property is defined as part of the Outlook object model and is retrieved using the Outlook property name, for example, `CreationTime`, the date value is returned in local time. If the column is retrieved using a schema name the value is returned in UTC, and you must use the `Row.UTCToLocalTime` method to convert the value to local time. To convert a local time retrieved from a row, use the `Row.LocalTimeToUTC` method. These methods round any times to the nearest minute.

❑ Properties that are defined in Outlook as strings but stored internally as binary properties are returned as strings if accessed using the Outlook property name, for example `EntryID` or `StoreID`. If the property is not defined in the Outlook object model or is retrieved using a schema name, the column is returned as a binary array. You can use the `Row.BinaryToString` method to convert the binary array into a string value.

❑ You cannot add computed property values such as `Sent` or `AutoResolvedWinner` to the `Columns` collection.

Security

Since its introduction in Outlook 2000 SP2, the Outlook object model guard has been a source of frustration for Outlook developers. It displays various security dialogs when any restricted property or method is accessed using the Outlook object model or CDO 1.21. The object model guard restricts such accesses as reading the `Body` property of an item because it can be used to harvest email addresses. Many other properties and methods are also restricted in the object model guard, the complete list is at MSDN, in an article "Code Security Changes in Outlook 2007," which also lists changes in how the object model guard is applied. This article is located at `http://msdn2.microsoft.com/en-us/library/ms778202.aspx`.

This section lists the changes that make it far easier to live with the Outlook object model guard than ever before in Outlook 2007. The Web page `www.outlookcode.com/d/sec.htm` contains additional information on the object model guard for developers working with untrusted code and code that must run on earlier versions of Outlook. Outlook code falls into one of two categories:

❑ Trusted code has access to all the properties and methods in the object model, and never causes a security prompt from the object model guard.

❑ Untrusted code causes a security prompt or failure of a method or property access with an error when accessing a restricted property or method.

In previous secure versions of Outlook, all out-of-process code running in other applications was always untrusted. In-process code running in Com addins was untrusted in Outlook 2002 and earlier, as was VBA macro code. In Outlook 2003, COM addins and VBA code were trusted if they derived all Outlook objects from the `Application` object passed in the COM addin's startup code or from the intrinsic `Application` object in VBA code.

Untrusted code or code that had to run on multiple versions of Outlook had to use Extended MAPI code or third-party libraries to avoid the Outlook object model guard. However, Extended MAPI is very difficult to learn and work with and can only be programmed using C++ or Delphi. Extended MAPI is not supported in any .NET language. The use of third-party libraries is the standard for most Outlook code that must run across multiple Outlook versions, but some organizations don't want to use third-party libraries or require the source code for any third-party libraries used.

Trusted Code

By default, all Outlook 2007 code, both in process and out of process, is trusted if the user is running up-to-date antivirus software that is indicated as in good health status in the Windows Security Center. This is a huge change in security, because now code running in a Word or Excel macro, or an `.exe` or `.dll` program can be treated as trusted code.

If group policies have been implemented for programmability, or the Exchange public folder security form is in use, the settings applied in the policy or form are honored. However, under normal circumstances, most Outlook code can now run as trusted code on secure computers.

If "healthy" antivirus software isn't running on an Outlook 2007, computer code is trusted if it's running in process with Outlook. That means if you derive your Outlook objects from the available intrinsic `Application` object, your COM addin and VBA code is trusted.

You can check to see if your application is trusted by checking the new `Application.IsTrusted` Boolean property.

Untrusted Code

Untrusted code will cause the security prompts to appear when the code accesses any restricted property or method. The new `PropertyAccessor` and `Table` objects are not available in untrusted code and will return errors if used in untrusted code.

In general, restricted properties and methods can be used to harvest address or private information, return `AddressEntry` objects, save to external storage, access properties with schema names, and send Outlook items. Your only alternative if you need to access any restricted properties or methods is to use Extended MAPI or a third-party library, such as Redemption or MAPI33.

You can learn more about these alternate libraries in Appendix B.

The Importance of Using DASL

This section uses a number of terms that may not be familiar to all Outlook developers such as DAV, DASL, JET, and CI. Some DASL syntax was used earlier in this chapter to set up filters and property schemas for the `PropertyAccessor` and `Table` objects, so at least the look of DASL should be becoming somewhat familiar.

DAV is an abbreviation for WEBDav, which stands for Web Distributed Authoring and Versioning. This is an Internet standard, which is discussed at `www.ietf.org/html.charters/webdav-charter.html`, if you are interested in learning more about this term. For this book, the use of DAV is mostly about the search features implemented in DASL.

DASL is an abbreviation for DAV Searching and Locating query syntax. Outlook has its own implementation of DASL, which is what is used in this book. DASL is used for creating queries for search folders, restrictions for `Table` and `Items` collections, and the schemas used in DASL form the basis of the property schemas used for the `PropertyAccessor`.

JET query syntax is based on the Access Expression Service. JET searches have been the standard used for most Restriction and Filter clauses for `Items` collections, such as `"[Subject] = 'Test'"`. This syntax is still supported in Outlook 2007, but DASL and CI searches can be more flexible and in the case of CI searches far faster than using JET syntax.

CI search syntax uses Content Indexer instant search syntax that queries the indexes created by the new Outlook full-text indexing engine. This instant search engine may not be installed or running, so before using any CI searches always test for `Store.IsInstantSearchEnabled`, a Boolean property.

DASL Namespaces

Outlook supports various DASL schemas and namespaces, as you've learned in this chapter. These namespaces are oriented to specific MAPI, Office, or DAV schemas. The following namespaces are specifically supported in Outlook:

`"DAV:"`	`"urn:schemas:calendar:"`	`"http://schemas`
		`.microsoft.com/mapi/`
		`proptag/0x"`

`"urn:schemas:httpmail:"`	`"urn:`
	`schemas-microsoft-com:`
	`office:office#"`
		`"http://schemas.microsoft`
		`.com/mapi/id/"`

`"urn:schemas:`
`mailheader:"`
	`"urn:`
	`schemas-microsoft-com:`
	`office:outlook#"`
		`"http://schemas.microsoft`
		`.com/mapi/string/"`

`"urn:schemas:contacts:"`	`"http://schemas.microsoft` `.com/exchange/"`	

You can find more information about these various namespaces at the following Web URLs:

❑ MAPI format and namespace: `http://msdn.microsoft.com/library/`
`default.asp?url=/library/en-us/e2k3/e2k3/_cdo_schema_mapi.asp`

❑ Office format and namespace: `http://msdn.microsoft.com/library/`
`default.asp?url=/library/en-us/e2k3/e2k3/_cdo_schema_office.asp`

❑ DAV formats and namespaces such as: `http://msdn.microsoft.com/library/`
`default.asp?url=/library/en-us/e2k3/e2k3/_cdo_schema_calendar.asp`

Using DASL and JET Syntax

Searching in Outlook can be confusing because two types of search syntax can be used. The older and more familiar JET syntax references properties by using their names, which is more readable, but only searches on properties exposed in the Outlook object model. The newer DASL syntax is more flexible and allows more comparison operators but is less readable. DASL references properties using property schemas and can search on properties not exposed in the Outlook object model. Understanding both types of searching is important to get maximum performance in your Outlook applications.

JET Syntax

JET syntax uses only standard property names, such as *"[Subject]"* or *"[Location]"*. You can also reference user defined properties in JET syntax, but only if the specific `UserProperty` is exposed as a property in the folder. User properties added only to specific items cannot be used in a JET syntax search or query. Note the following about JET syntax:

❑   JET allows a limited set of comparison operators: =, <>, <, >, >=, and <=. You cannot use substring searches or qualifiers such as "begins with" or "includes".

❑   JET syntax is supported for `Items.Find` and `Items.Restrict`, for `Table.FindRow` and `Table.Restrict`, and for `Folder.GetTable`. JET syntax is not supported for View filters or the `AdvancedSearch` method.

You will find many examples of JET search syntax in this book, but it isn't discussed further in this chapter, because it's not a new technology for Outlook.

DASL Syntax

DASL syntax is a newer technology for Outlook and in addition to the comparison operators used by JET, DASL syntax also can use other SQL query type operators such as `LIKE` and `IS`.

Although DASL search syntax is newly supported for Outlook 2007 in areas such as `Items.Find` *and* `Items.Restrict`*, you can also use the syntax with Outlook 2002 and 2003. Microsoft doesn't document or support that, but a DASL search string preceded by "@SQL=" will work for filters and restrictions in Outlook 2002 and 2003.*

DASL syntax is supported for `Items.Find` and `Items.Restrict`, for `Table.FindRow` and `Table.Restrict`, and for `Folder.GetTable`. For all those areas, the search string must be preceded by `@SQL=`, with no spaces between that string and the DASL search string. For use in `AdvancedSearch` and view filters, you must not use the `@SQL=` string at the beginning of the search string. Some examples of using DASL search syntax for an `Items.Restrict` clause are:

❑   `@SQL=urn:schemas:httpmail:subject LIKE '%store%'`: Searches for items with a `Subject` including the substring `store`.

❑   `@SQL=urn:schemas:httpmail:importance = 2`: Searches for items with a High `Importance`.

❑   `@SQL=http://schemas.microsoft.com/mapi/id/{00062003-0000-0000-C000-000000000046}/81050040 <= 'today'`: Searches for tasks that are overdue or due today.

❑   `@SQL=urn:schemas:httpmail:subject IS NULL`: Searches for items with a blank `Subject`.

❑   `@SQL=NOT(urn:schemas:httpmail:subject IS NULL)`: Searches for items with a `Subject` that isn't blank.

CI Syntax

The new CI syntax is a subset of DASL syntax, but you can expect it to be much faster for searches in large datasets. Of course, that's only if the instant search feature is installed, which is optional. Even if instant search is installed, it may be disabled, so always check the `IsInstantSearchEnabled` Boolean property of the `Store` object before attempting to use a CI syntax search for any particular store. Because this property is set on a store-by-store basis, make sure to check it for any store you are searching. Note the following about CI syntax:

❑ CI searches provide two operators you can use, `CI_STARTSWITH` and `CI_PHRASEMATCH`. One important thing to remember is that mixing JET and DASL syntax is not permitted in a search and will cause an error.

❑ CI search keywords are only permitted in an `Items.Restrict` or `Table.Restrict` filter clause. They are not permitted for `Table.FindRow` or `Items.Find` filter clauses.

❑ `CI_STARTSWITH` searches for a match on the beginning of a word, using a case insensitive search. For properties that can contain more than one word the match can be on any word in the property. For properties such as `Subject`, the initial RE: or FWD: (if any) is ignored.

❑ `CI_PHRASEMATCH` searches for a word or words in a property that exactly match the search phrase. This search is also case-insensitive, and the word or words do not have to be the first word or words in the property.

❑ Operators such as `LIKE` or = can only be used in non-CI searches that use DASL syntax.

Here are some examples of CI searches:

❑ `urn:schemas:httpmail:subject CI_STARTSWITH 'stor'`: Searches for items with a `Subject` including words that start with "stor". This search returns "store" and "storage" but does not return "restore".

❑ `urn:schemas:httpmail:subject CI_PHRASEMATCH 'install'`: Searches for items with a `Subject` including words or phrases that start with "install". This search does not return "installation".

❑ `urn:schemas:httpmail:subject CI_PHRASEMATCH 'install from disk'`: Searches for items with a `Subject` including words or phrases that start with "install from disk". This search returns "Install from disk" and "install from disk drive" but not "installed from disk".

CI searches may seem limited due to only offering two keywords, but their speed makes them the first choice if you are working with an object that supports CI searching and your search can conform to using only the `CI_STARTSWITH` or `CI_PHRASEMATCH` keywords.

Summary

In this chapter, you learned about some of the new features in the Outlook object model. Important new bjects such as the `PropertyAccessor` and `Table` objects were introduced and discussed in some depth, while other new features such as stores, accounts, and interface objects were briefly introduced.

A discussion about Outlook security introduced the new, more relaxed security restrictions for Outlook 2007 code development. New performance enhancements were discussed in relation to the `Table` object, and various search and schema syntaxes such as DASL, JET, and CI were introduced. With this foundation, you are now ready to start exploring the many new ways to work with Outlook code.

In the next chapter, you will start exploring in depth the top-level Outlook development objects such as `NameSpace` and the `Explorers` and `Inspectors` collections, as well as some of the new forms and user interface elements in Outlook 2007.

3

Outlook Development

This chapter focuses on the `Application` and `NameSpace` objects. As you've already learned in Chapter 1, these objects are your entry point into Outlook programming and are used throughout your Outlook applications. To help you understand the `Application` object, this chapter introduces methods for instantiating globally available and trusted `Application` and `NameSpace` objects for COM addins programmed using languages such as VB.NET and C#, with Visual Studio 2005 and VSTO 2005 SE development platforms. You then learn about some of the new methods, properties, and events of the `Application` object. You discover how to program context menus, and you get to work with context menus in many of the examples in this book. To better understand the `NameSpace` object, this chapter introduces you to the new `Categories` collection and `Category` objects, Exchange information, and user interface dialogs.

> *The version of VSTO used for Outlook 2007 development is VSTO 2005 SE. It is referred to as VSTO in this book.*

The Application Object

The Outlook object model guard is much less intrusive in Outlook 2007 than in any previous secure version of Outlook, as you learned in Chapter 2. There are times, however, when tighter security is in effect, so it's important to handle the `Application` object correctly, and to verify if your code is trusted. Even if your code is running on Outlook 2003, security policies are more relaxed for trusted code so it's important to handle `Application` correctly.

Form and VBA code have intrinsic `Application` objects, and COM addins are passed an `Application` object in their `OnConnection` events. This `Application` object is what's trusted, and all Outlook objects must be derived from this object, or they won't inherit this trust. Code can verify trusted status by checking the new `IsTrusted` property. Generally, the `Application` object is stored in a global variable or as a public property of a class that has scope during the life of the application.

Chapter 3: Outlook Development

Outlook form code also has an intrinsic Item *object that refers to the item in which the code is running. The* Item *object in form code is also a trusted object, much like* Application. *You will learn about form coding in Chapter 5.*

The code in Listing 3.1 shows how to initialize globally trusted Outlook Application and NameSpace objects that you can use throughout an application. Both objects are exposed as public properties of a class that is available throughout the application. The class is only initialized if the Application object is trusted.

Code for a COM addin is shown in both VB.NET and C# using Visual Studio 2005. Only VSTO startup and shutdown code is shown; the class code is unchanged when used with VSTO.

Listing 3.1: VB.NET

```
Private applicationObject As Outlook.Application

Public gClass As Class1

Public Sub OnConnection(ByVal application As Object, ByVal connectMode As
    Extensibility.ext_ConnectMode, ByVal addInInst As Object, ByRef custom As
    System.Array) Implements Extensibility.IDTExtensibility2.OnConnection

    applicationObject = TryCast(application, _
      Outlook.Application)

    If applicationObject.IsTrusted Then
      gClass = New Class1(applicationObject)
    End If
End Sub

Public Sub OnDisconnection(ByVal RemoveMode As Extensibility.ext_DisconnectMode,
    ByRef custom As System.Array) Implements
    Extensibility.IDTExtensibility2.OnDisconnection

    ' call to release all other objects
    Call Shutdown

    applicationObject = Nothing
    gClass = Nothing

End Sub

' Beginning of the Class1 definition
Imports Outlook = Microsoft.Office.Interop.Outlook

Friend Class Class1
    ' The WithEvents declarations allow handling
    '  events for the Application and NameSpace objects
    Private WithEvents _app As Outlook.Application
    Private WithEvents _ns as Outlook.NameSpace

    Public Sub New(ByVal app As Outlook.Application)
      _app = app
      _ns = _app.GetNameSpace("MAPI")
    End Sub
```

40

Listing 3.1: VB.NET *(continued)*

```
    Public ReadOnly Property Application() As Outlook.Application
      Get
        Return _app
      End Get
    End Property

    Public ReadOnly Property NameSpace() As Outlook.NameSpace
      Get
        Return _ns
      End Get
    End Property
End Class
```

VB.NET with VSTO

```
public class ThisAddIn
  Friend gClass As Class1

  Private Sub ThisApplication_Startup(ByVal sender As Object, ByVal e As
    System.EventArgs) Handles Me.Startup

    If Me.IsTrusted Then
      gClass = New Class1(Me.Application)
    End If
  End Sub

  Private Sub ThisApplication_Shutdown(ByVal sender As Object, ByVal e As
    System.EventArgs) Handles Me.Shutdown

    ' call to release all other objects
    Call Shutdown

    gClass = Nothing
  End Sub

End class
```

C#

```
namespace CS_Addin
{
  using Outlook = Microsoft.Office.Interop.Outlook;

  public partial class Connect : Object, Extensibility.IDTExtensibility2
  {
    private Outlook.Application m_Application;
    public Class1 gClass;

    public void OnConnection(object application, Extensibility.ext_ConnectMode
      connectMode, object addInInst, ref System.Array custom)
    {
```

(continued)

C# *(continued)*

```csharp
      m_Application = application as Outlook.Application;

      if(m_Application.IsTrusted)
      {
        gClass = new Class1(m_Application);
      }
    }

    public void OnDisconnection(Extensibility.ext_DisconnectMode disconnectMode,
      ref System.Array custom)
    {
      // call to release all other objects
      ShutdownAddin();

      m_Application = null;
      gClass = null;
    }
    // Other code before the closing brace of the Connect class and namespace
  }
}

// Beginning of the Class1 class
using Outlook = Microsoft.Office.Interop.Outlook;

namespace CS_Addin
{
  class Class1
  {
    private Outlook.Application _app;
    private Outlook.NameSpace _ns;

    // Class Constructor
    public Class1(Outlook.Application app)
    {
      _app = app;
      _ns = _app.GetNamespace("MAPI");

    }

    public Outlook.Application Application
    {
      get
      {
        return _app as Outlook.Application;
      }
    }

    public Outlook.NameSpace NameSpace
    {
      get
      {
        return _ns as Outlook.NameSpace;
      }
    }
  }
}
```

C# with VSTO

```csharp
namespace CS_Addin
{
  public partial class ThisAddIn
  {
    private Outlook.Application m_Application;
    public Class1 gClass

    private void ThisApplication_Startup(object sender, System.EventArgs e)
    {
      m_Application = this.Application as Outlook.Application;
      if(m_Application.IsTrusted)
      {
        gClass = new Class1(m_Application);
      }

    }

    private void ThisApplication_Shutdown(object sender, System.EventArgs e)
    {
      // call to release all other objects
      ShutdownAddin();

      m_Application = null;
      gClass = null;
    }
}
```

It's very important that you release all of your Outlook objects in the appropriate shutdown procedure. Outlook 2007 takes extra measures to ensure that Outlook can close even if global objects (and event handlers if necessary) aren't released, but it doesn't always succeed. Earlier versions of Outlook will hang in memory if your global objects aren't released.

The code releases global Outlook and class objects and calls a ShutdownAddin procedure that isn't shown to release any other global objects. In general, Outlook 2007 is less sensitive to shutdown problems than earlier versions of Outlook. VSTO addins are less sensitive to shutdown problems than addins created using only Visual Studio 2005. If you are programming Outlook on the .NET platform, you might have to take additional steps to ensure that Outlook can close properly, especially if you are supporting earlier versions of Outlook. Explicitly calling the garbage collector and waiting for it to complete may be necessary. If you program in C#, you have to unsubscribe from any event handlers to which you are subscribed.

VSTO Outlook addins use a special Startup method in their ThisAddIn class in place of the OnConnection event. The details of handling the IDTExtensibility2 interface that provides the connection between the addin and Outlook are handled behind the scenes by VSTO. The objects and properties provided in OnConnection are available in the System.EventArgs variable in the Startup method.

- ❑ **VB.NET**: OnConnection(ByVal application As Object, ByVal connectMode As Extensibility.ext_ConnectMode, ByVal addInInst As Object, ByRef custom As System.Array) Implements Extensibility.IDTExtensibility2.OnConnection

- ❑ **VB.NET with VSTO:** Private Sub ThisAddIn_Startup(ByVal sender As Object, ByVal e As System.EventArgs) Handles Me.Startup

The call to initialize the instance of `Class1` is made using the `Me.Application` object in VSTO VB.NET addins, which represents the `Application` object. VSTO C# addins use the `this.Application` object instead of `Me.Application`.

When using the `Application` object in Outlook VBA or forms code, the object is already global, so you don't have to instantiate a global object. A global `NameSpace` object would still have to be instantiated.

If you've used VSTO 2005 with Outlook 2003, there are some differences in VSTO 2005 SE, the VSTO version used for Outlook 2007 development. VSTO 2005 SE uses `ThisAddIn` instead of `ThisApplication` and exposes the `Outlook.Application` object differently. The following table shows how to reference the `Application` object in both versions of VSTO.

	VSTO 2005 SE	VSTO 2005
VB	Me.Application	Me
C#	this.Application	this

New Methods, Properties, and Events

The following new methods, properties, and events have been added to the `Application` object for Outlook 2007.

GetObjectReference

`GetObjectReference(Item As Object, ReferenceType)` is a method you use to get either a strong or weak reference to an object. A *strong reference* is a reference that won't get garbage collected until the reference is explicitly released. A *weak reference* is a reference that can be released by the garbage collector at any time, so the reference essentially must be used immediately while you know it's still valid. Weak references are mostly for objects that have a large memory impact that you can re-reference, if needed, but that you don't want to persist if you don't need to. The call to `GetObjectReference(Item As Object, ReferenceType)` returns an `Object` reference and is passed either `OlReferenceType.olStrong` or `OlReferenceType.olWeak` as the `ReferenceType` argument.

DefaultProfileName

`DefaultProfileName` is a read-only property that returns a string specifying the default profile name of the Outlook setup. The default profile name is not necessarily the current profile name in the current Outlook session. The currently active Outlook profile can be retrieved using the `NameSpace.CurrentProfileName` property.

IsTrusted

`IsTrusted` is a new, Boolean read-only property that lets you know if your code is running under a trusted context. Outlook 2007 trusts more code than previous secure versions of Outlook, including in many cases out of process code such as code running in `.exe` applications and as macros in other Office applications such as Excel, but there are times when your code won't be running in a trusted context and certain parts of the Outlook object model won't be available to you, such as the `PropertyAccessor` object. In those cases, you must use workarounds or handle the untrusted condition in other ways.

Context Menus

The new events presented in the following table are fired when a context menu is about to display in Outlook, the result of right-clicking in an area of the Outlook UI. Outlook developers have requested this feature for years. Before Outlook 2007, you could only use a hack of trapping the `Office.CommandBars.OnUpdate` event, which did not return the context that was clicked and was prone to various problems such as crashing Outlook.

> An example of using the `OnUpdate` event is shown at www.outlookcode.com/codedetail .aspx?id=314, along with comments that indicate the problems to which this method is prone.

The `CommandBar` argument, passed to all the event handlers shown in the following table, is used as the target for any new menu items you are adding, removing, or repurposing in the context menu that is about to be displayed. These events all fire before the context menu is displayed.

Event	Purpose
`AttachmentContextMenuDisplay(CommandBar As CommandBar, Attachments As AttachmentSelection)`	Fires when you right-click the attachment well that shows the attachments in an Outlook item, either in a folder view in the reading pane (`Explorer`) or in an open Outlook item (`Inspector`). The `AttachmentSelection` collection passed as an input to this event handler contains all the attachments selected in the attachment well, allowing you to process all selected attachments.
`FolderContextMenuDisplay(CommandBar As CommandBar, Folder As Folder)`	Fires when you right-click a folder in the Navigation Pane, passing the `Folder` object that was clicked. This event fires when you right-click a folder anywhere in the Navigation Pane, including in the lists of folders such as My Calendars.
`ItemContextMenuDisplay(CommandBar As CommandBar, Selection As Selection)`	Fires when you right-click one item or a selection of items in a folder view.
`ShortcutContextMenuDisplay(CommandBar As CommandBar, Shortcut As OutlookBarShortcut)`	Fires when you right-click an item listed in the Shortcuts section of the Navigation Pane. The new `OutlookBarShortcut` object has a `Target` property that returns a `Folder` object for selected folder shortcuts, including shortcuts to the new To-Do List folder, or a string URL for shortcuts to Web URLs such as Microsoft Office Online.

Continued

45

Event	Purpose
`StoreContextMenuDisplay(CommandBar As CommandBar, Store As Store)`	Fires when you right-click a `Store` object in the Navigation Pane, such as Personal Folders, Mailbox - Casey Slovak or Exchange Public Folders.
`ViewContextMenuDisplay(CommandBar As CommandBar, View As View)`	Fires when you right-click a view in a folder view or in the To-Do Bar
`ContextMenuClose(ContextMenu As OlContextMenu)`	Fires when a context menu is about to close. The `OlContextMenu` enumeration contains members for each type of context menu for which there is a display event, such as Item or Store. This event is used to clean up any changes you've made to the context menu or anything you've instantiated during the use of your display event handler.

You can place the following code in the `ThisOutlookSession` class module in the Outlook VBA project. It demonstrates adding a menu control to the context menu that's displayed when you right-click an item in an Outlook folder, in this case the Inbox or other email folder. The menu item is added as a temporary `CommandBarButton` control that fires the `oButton_Click` event when the menu item is clicked. The menu item displays the subject of the selected email item and the click event displays a message box. The cleanup for this menu item is performed in the `ContextMenuClose` event handler, where the menu item is deleted and the referenced `CommandBar` and `CommandBarButton` objects are set to `Nothing` (`null` in C#). These object references are declared as module level class objects, so they retain scope after the procedure instantiating them is finished.

```
Private WithEvents oButton As Office.CommandBarButton
Private oBar As Office.CommandBar

Private Sub Application_ContextMenuClose(ByVal ContextMenu _
  As OlContextMenu)

  Dim oControl As Office.CommandBarControl

  If ContextMenu = OlContextMenu.olItemContextMenu Then
    Set oControl = oBar.FindControl(msoControlButton, , "MyTag")
    If Not (oControl Is Nothing) Then
      oControl.Delete
      Set oButton = Nothing
      Set oBar = Nothing
    End If
  End If
End Sub

Private Sub Application_ItemContextMenuDisplay(ByVal CommandBar _
  As Office.CommandBar, ByVal Selection As Selection) _

  Dim strCaption As String
  Dim strTag As String
```

```
    If (Selection.Count = 1) And (Selection.Item(1).Class = _
       OlObjectClass.olMail) Then

       strCaption = Selection.Item(1).Subject & " Context Menu"
       strTag = "MyTag"

       Set oButton = _
         CommandBar.Controls.Add(msoControlButton, , , , True)

       oButton.Caption = strCaption
       oButton.Tag = strTag

       Set oBar = CommandBar
    End If

 End Sub

 Private Sub oButton_Click(ByVal Ctrl As Office.CommandBarButton, _
    CancelDefault As Boolean)

   MsgBox "My button clicked"
 End Sub
```

The module level `CommandBar` object is declared so that it's easy to work with the context menu `CommandBar`; otherwise, it would be very hard to locate it among the overall `CommandBars` collection. A unique `Tag` property is assigned to the button when it's created so that the button can be found and deleted when the context menu is closed. Unique `Tag` properties are also important when handing multiple `Inspectors` and `Explorers`, so each button you create in an `Explorer` or `Inspector` can later be located and so the button's `Click` event only fires in the desired event handler and not in event handlers in every open `Inspector` or `Explorer`.

Various variations of Visual Basic allow passing a missing parameter in a function call as a missing argument with just the comma as a placeholder. If you are using C# you have to supply each specified argument in the parameter list, you cannot just use comma placeholders. This can be done by declaring a reference to private object `System.Reflection.Missing.Value` *and using that reference wherever there's a missing argument.*

C# use of missing parameter values:

```
 private object missing = System.Reflection.Missing.Value;

 oButton = CommandBar.Controls.Add(MsoControlType.msoControlButton, missing,
 missing, missing, true);
```

BeforeFolderSharingDialog

The `BeforeFolderSharingDialog(FolderToShare As Folder, Cancel As Boolean)` event fires just before the dialog for sharing a folder is displayed. For example, when using Exchange server, you can select to share your calendar folder with someone. If you right-click the Calendar folder in the Navigation Pane and select Share Calendar, the sharing dialog is displayed and the event fires. This applies to any folder that can be shared. If you set the `Cancel` property equal to `True` in your event handler code, the dialog display is canceled. This provides a way of repurposing the existing menu item to perform your own function either in addition to or instead of the original function. You can also perform pre-processing work that you might want, for example, setting up some properties in the shared folder before the dialog is displayed.

If you create a sharing item using the NameSpace.CreateSharingItem *method to create a sharing item the* BeforeFolderSharingDialog *event handler will not fire.*

ItemLoad

The ItemLoad event provides an Object representing the item about to be loaded into memory. Outlook loads an item into memory when the item is accessed in any way, for example when you view it in the Reading Pane or right-click an item and select it to add a follow-up flag. Previous versions of Outlook had no way to detect those actions using the Outlook object model. Prior to Outlook 2007, Extended MAPI code was the only way to detect when Outlook loaded an item into memory.

The Object is a weak reference that only provides Class and MessageClass as valid properties. All other item properties are unavailable and return an error if referenced in this event. As a weak reference, you cannot control when Outlook unloads this reference, so if you want to preserve this reference you must assign it to another, strong reference. When the reference is about to be destroyed, the Unload event fires, as shown in the following code.

```
Dim WithEvents oMail As Outlook.MailItem

Private Sub Application_ItemLoad(ByVal Item As Object)
  If Item.Class = olMail Then
    Set oMail = Item
  End If
End Sub

Private Sub oMail_Unload()
  ' Use this event to unload any wrapper class
  '  instantiated to work with loaded items.
End Sub
```

One way of using the ItemLoad event is to detect changes made to items during in-cell editing. A wrapper class that handles the Unload event as well as any other item events in which you're interested is created to handle each item that's loaded. These wrapper classes are stored or referenced in a global collection or a hashtable to prevent them from going out of scope or being garbage collected. For changes made during in-cell editing, events for PropertyChange and UserPropertyChange are handled.

There is no way to determine when Outlook will unload items from memory.

Other Important Collections, Methods, Properties, and Events

The Explorers collection and Explorer object are one of the ways you interact with the Outlook user interface, with an Explorer object used to display an Outlook folder. The Explorers collection contains all currently open Explorer objects, with ActiveExplorer the currently active Explorer object.

The following code retrieves the `ActiveExplorer` as well as the currently displayed folder in the Explorer. If the folder is a mail folder, the code turns on the To-Do Bar.

```
Dim oExpl As Outlook.Explorer
Dim oFolder As Outlook.Folder

If Not (Application.ActiveExplorer Is Nothing) Then
  Set oExpl = Application.ActiveExplorer
  Set oFolder = oExpl.CurrentFolder

  If oFolder.DefaultItemType = OlItemType.olMailItem Then
    Call oExpl.ShowPane(OlPane.olToDoBar, True)
  End If
End If
```

`Inspectors` are used to display Outlook items, and the `ActiveInspector` object is the currently active displayed item. If no Outlook items are displayed, `ActiveInspector` is `Nothing`. The item being displayed in the `Inspector` is retrieved using the `CurrentItem` property, as the following code illustrates.

```
Dim oInsp As Outlook.Inspector
Dim oMail As Outlook.MailItem

If Not (Application.ActiveInspector Is Nothing) Then
  Set oInsp = Application.ActiveInspector
  If oInsp.CurrentItem.Class = OlObjectClass.olMail Then
    Set oMail = oInsp.CurrentItem
  End If
End If
```

`ActiveWindow` returns an Object that represents the currently active Outlook window, either an `Explorer` or `Inspector`. If Outlook isn't displaying a UI, `ActiveWindow` returns `Nothing`. You use this procedure to work with the active Outlook window, as well as to find out where the user is working at any point in time. The following code checks the active window type and instantiates an Outlook object based on the window type.

```
Dim oInsp As Outlook.Inspector
Dim oExpl As Outlook.Inspector
Dim oWindow as Object

Set oWindow = Application.ActiveWindow
If Not (oWindow Is Nothing) Then
  If TypeName(oWindow) = "Inspector" Then
    Set oInsp = Application.ActiveInspector
  ElseIf strType = "Explorer" Then
    Set oExpl = Application.ActiveExplorer
  End If
End If
```

CreateItem and CreateItemFromTemplate

CreateItem and CreateItemFromTemplate are some of the ways to create new Outlook items. CreateItemFromTemplate creates new items from published Outlook forms that are saved as .OFT files. CreateItem takes a member of the OlItemType enumeration as its argument and creates a new item of that type, as shown in the following code:

```
Set oContact = Application.CreateItem(OlItemType.olContactItem)

Set oAppointment = Application.CreateItemFromTemplate("C:\Forms\Appt.oft", _
  oMyCalendar)
```

CreateItem creates the new item in the default folder for that item type. For mail items, the default folder is Drafts. To create an item in a folder other than the default folder, use the Add method of the folder's Items collection. Another option is to use CreateItem and move the item to the correct destination folder after the item is created.

You use the optional InFolder Folder argument for CreateItemFromTemplate to create the item in the specified folder.

NewMail and NewMailEx

NewMail is one of the most useless events in the Outlook object model. It fires only at intervals of every few minutes and misses any incoming item that arrives too soon after the previous NewMail event has fired. It also doesn't tell you which item just arrived in the Inbox.

NewMailEx is a much better event to use to monitor incoming items. It passes a string that contains a list of the EntryID properties, separated by commas, of the items that have arrived since the last NewMailEx event. You use the text processing to collect an array of EntryID properties. The items are retrieved using the NameSpace.GetItemFromID(EntryID) method.

The NewMail event has a major limitation, in that if more than 16 items arrive at once the event won't fire at all. The underlying MAPI, which only fires a change event if more than 16 items arrive at one time, causes this limitation. This limitation is shared with the events that monitor Add, Change and Remove for a folder's Items collection. A limitation of the NewMailEx event is that when over 1000 items are received at once, NewMailEx misses some of the items. This limitation can usually be ignored because it happens so infrequently.

Reminder and Reminders

The Reminder(Item As Object) event fires when a reminder is about to be displayed. The Item object can be any Outlook item that supports a reminder. Reminders are supported for Mail, Contact, Appointment, Meeting, Task, and Post items. Journal and Note items don't support reminders.

The Reminders collection is the complete collection of items in the Reminders search folder. This collection provides events for when reminders are added, removed and changed. Other events are provided for when a reminder snoozes or fires and before the Reminders window is displayed. These events are useful when you process reminders, for example, to cancel showing the Reminders window and sending an email instead when a reminder fires. The Reminders collection also provides access to individual Reminder items.

The following code sample initializes a `Reminders` collection object and shows an event handler for sending an email when a reminder fires. The Reminders window is canceled and the reminder snoozes for 1 hour. The initialization code can be in any class or code module in the VBA project. The event handler must be in a class module or `UserForm`. For this code, the intrinsic `ThisOutlookSession` can be used.

```vba
'Initialization code in ThisOutlookSession
Private WithEvents colReminders As Outlook.Reminders

Private Sub Application_Startup()
   Set colReminders = Application.Reminders
End Sub


'Event handlers
Private Sub colReminders_BeforeReminderShow(Cancel As Boolean)
   Cancel = True 'cancel showing reminders window
End Sub


Private Sub colReminders_ReminderFire(ByVal ReminderObject _
   As Reminder)

   Dim oMail As Outlook.MailItem

   Set oMail = Application.CreateItem(olMailItem)
   With oMail
      .Subject = ReminderObject.Caption
      .Body = "Reminder: " & CStr(ReminderObject.NextReminderDate)
      .To = "tester@test.org" 'substitute real email address
      .Recipients.ResolveAll
      .Send
   End With

   ReminderObject.Snooze 60 '60 minutes
End Sub
```

Startup, MAPILogonComplete, and Quit

The `Startup` and `MAPILogonComplete` events fire in that order. The `Startup` event handler is used to initialize any application-wide events in which you are interested and initialize any global variables. `MAPILogonComplete` fires after Outlook finishes logging in to the MAPI store provider, usually a PST file or an Exchange mailbox. COM addins mostly use the `Startup` or `OnConnection` events instead of `Application_Startup` for initializations. `Application_Startup` is used mostly in Outlook VBA code and out-of-process applications that have started Outlook.

By the time the `Quit` event fires in Outlook VBA, all Outlook objects are already out of scope and will cause an exception if referenced.

ItemSend

The `ItemSend(Item As Object, Cancel As Boolean)` event is an application-wide event that fires every time any Outlook item is sent out through the email transport. The item being sent is passed to the event-handling procedure as a general `Object` because the item may also be a task request, a meeting request, or other type of item. To check what type of item is passed to the event handler, use `Item.Class` and test for values representing members of the `OlObjectClass` enumeration.

You can use `ItemSend` for purposes such as attaching corporate disclaimers to emails and adding required recipients for meetings, as the following code shows.

VB.NET

```
Private Const Disclaimer = "This message is private"

Private Sub Application_ItemSend(ByVal Item As Object, _
  Cancel As Boolean)

  If Item.Class = olMail Then ' If a MailItem

     ' If this is HTML use HTMLBody for
     '  formatting the text.
     Item.Body = Item.Body & vbCRLF & Disclaimer
  End If
End Sub
```

C#

```
// Hook up the event handler
Application.ItemSend += new Microsoft.Office.Interop.Outlook.ApplicationEvents_11_
ItemSendEventHandler(Application_ItemSend);

// This can be any disclaimer message
const String Disclaimer = "This message is private";

private void Application_ItemSend(object Item, ref bool Cancel)
{
  try
  {
    // Try casting the Item to an Outlook.MailItem
    Outlook.MailItem oMail = (Outlook.MailItem)Item;

    // Add a newline and the disclaimer.
    // If this is HTML use HTMLBody for
    // formatting the text.
    Item.Body = Item.Body + "\n" + Disclaimer;
  }
  catch
  {
    // Any error in the type casting comes here
  }
}
```

Version

The `Version` property returns a string that tells you what version of Outlook is running. This is important if you plan to support multiple versions of Outlook, if you only want your code to run on certain Outlook versions, or if you support certain features only with specific versions of Outlook. The following table lists the leftmost part of the `Version` property for each version of Outlook. The `Version` property string for Outlook 2007 would be something like "12.0.0.4518", identifying the leftmost two digits of the string as "12" would identify the running Outlook version as 2007.

Outlook Version	Value
97	"8.0"
98	"8.5"
2000	"9.0"
2002	"10.0"
2003	"11.0"
2007	"12.0"

The NameSpace Object

The `NameSpace` object is the current Outlook session. Only one Outlook session can run at a time, and to switch sessions you must exit and restart Outlook. The `Session`, an alias for `NameSpace`, logs in to a specific Outlook profile, which provides the settings for which data store to use and which email accounts are configured, among other things. The `NameSpace` object in Outlook 2007 provides new methods and properties you learn about in this section.

`CompareEntryIDs` is a new method that determines if two objects are the same based on a comparison of their `EntryID` properties. You can use this method not only for Outlook items, such as mail items, but also for `Folder` and `Store` objects, as well as for any other objects that have an `EntryID` property. This not only allows comparisons between a stored `EntryID` and the `EntryID` of a new object but also between different `EntryID` formats. When using Outlook with Exchange, you can retrieve two variations of the `EntryID` property. The short-term `EntryID` is only valid for that Outlook session and may change when Outlook is run again. The long-term `EntryID` is a permanent GUID that never changes as long as that item retains its `EntryID`. `CompareEntryIDs` enables you to compare IDs with both of those formats without concerning yourself with whether an ID is short-term or long-term.

The `CurrentProfileName` property returns the current Outlook profile, which may be different from the default profile name that the `Application.DefaultProfileName` property returns. If the user has more than one Outlook profile, the current profile is the one that Outlook is logged in to.

The `SendAndReceive` method is the equivalent of the Send/Receive All menu command in the user interface. This synchronous method sends and receives for all accounts defined in the current profile. For more granular sending and receiving, use the `SyncObjects` collection. Setting the optional `ShowProgressDialog` argument displays the send and receive progress dialog for the send and receive operation.

Exchange

Outlook 2003 introduced the `ExchangeConnectionMode` property for determining how Outlook connects to Exchange, which is necessary because of the cached connection modes introduced in

Outlook 2003. Outlook 2007 adds three new properties for retrieving information about an Exchange server:

❑ ExchangeMailboxServerName returns the name of the Exchange server that hosts the default mailbox. If no Exchange server is used, a null string is returned. If Exchange is used, but Outlook is offline, an error is returned.

❑ ExchangeMailboxServerVersion returns the version of the Exchange server that hosts the default mailbox. If no Exchange server is used a null string is returned. If Exchange is used but Outlook is offline an error is returned, for example:

```
If oNS.ExchangeConnectionMode <> OlExchangeConnectionMode.olOffline Then
    strServerName = oNS.ExchangeMailboxServerName
    strServerVersion = oNS.ExchangeMailboxServerVersion
End If
```

❑ The AutoDiscoverXML property returns the XML string, which is used to discover an Exchange connection for Exchange 12. For connections to earlier versions of Exchange or where Exchange isn't used, the property returns a null string.

Categories

Outlook categories have always been strings defined in specific items, stored as default categories hard-coded into Outlook or stored as a Master Category List in the registry. Outlook 2007 retains that definition for the Item.Categories property and adds a new Categories collection to the NameSpace object. Each Category object has properties to identify or set the category color, name, and shortcut key, as shown in the following code:

```
Set colCategories = oNS.Categories

Set oCategory = colCategories.Add("Professional Programming Outlook 2007", _
    OlCategoryColor.olCategoryColorLightTeal, _
    OlCategoryShortcutKey.olCategoryShortcutKeyNone)
```

This code snippet adds a light teal book category to the Categories collection and makes it available to the user.

Picking Folders

The PickFolder dialog isn't new to Outlook 2007, but the PickFolder dialog is useful anywhere your code needs the user to select a folder, for example as the target for moving an item. The function returns a Folder object if the user selected a folder, and Nothing (null in C#) if the user canceled the dialog.

```
Dim oFolder As Outlook.Folder
Dim oNS As Outlook.NameSpace

Set oNS = Application.GetNameSpace("MAPI")
Set oFolder = Nothing
Set oFolder = oNS.PickFolder()
If oFolder Is Nothing Then
   'user canceled the dialog
```

```
Else
   'code to use the selected folder
End If
```

Picking Names

The `GetSelectNamesDialog` function is the equivalent for the Outlook object model of the old CDO `AddressBook` dialog, which was never available in the Outlook object model. You have complete control over this dialog, unlike the `PickFolder` dialog, which you cannot customize. With the `GetSelectNamesDialog` dialog, you can control the dialog caption, the number of and labels for the recipient wells, the initial address list shown, and whether the user can select other address lists, whether only one or multiple recipients can be selected, the display mode, and whether to force resolution of recipients.

The `SetDefaultDisplayMode` method enables you to tailor the dialog to modes such as selecting email, or meeting or task request recipients. The `OlDefaultSelectNamesDisplayMode` enumeration lists the default display modes that are available. In the following table, the column labeled as Wells refers to the recipient wells available in the dialog, such as To, Cc and Bcc. The column labeled Group refers to the ability to select more than one recipient in the dialog.

Member	Caption	Wells	Labels	Edit box	Group
olDefaultDelegates	Add Users	To	Add	To	Y
olDefaultMail	Select Names	To, Cc, Bcc	To, Cc, Bcc	To, Cc, Bcc	Y
olDefaultMeeting	Select Attendees and Resources	To, Cc, Bcc	Required, Optional, Resources	Required, Optional, Resources	Y
olDefaultMembers	Select Members	To	To	To	Y
olDefaultPickRooms	Select Rooms	To	Rooms	Resource recipient	Y
olDefaultSharingRequest	Select Names	To	To	To	Y
olDefaultSingleName	Select Name				
olDefaultTask	Select Task Recipient	To	To	To	Y

If you don't set a display mode, the default `olDefaultMail` mode is used when the dialog is displayed. The `SetDefaultDisplayMode` method sets many of the `GetSelectNamesDialog` class's properties, so if you plan to customize the dialog properties, do so after you call the `SetDefaultDisplayMode` method.

```
Function SelectSignee() As Outlook.Recipient
  Dim oDialog As Outlook.SelectNamesDialog
  Dim colRecips As Outlook.Recipients
  Dim oRecip As Outlook.Recipient

  Set oRecip = Nothing

  Set oDialog = Application.Session.GetSelectNamesDialog
  With oDialog
    .SetDefaultDisplayMode olDefaultDelegates
    .AllowMultipleSelection = False
    .Caption = "Wrox"
    .ToLabel = "Sign Up:"
    .Display

    If .Recipients.Count > 0 Then
      Set oRecip = .Recipients.Item(1)
    End If
  End With

  If (oRecip Is Nothing) Then
    MsgBox "No recipient selected"
  Else
    MsgBox oRecip.Name
  End If

  Set SelectSignee = oRecip
End Function
```

Figure 3.1 shows the resulting GetSelectNamesDialog with the custom Sign Up button and Wrox dialog caption. The Sign Up button label is used in place of the default To label.

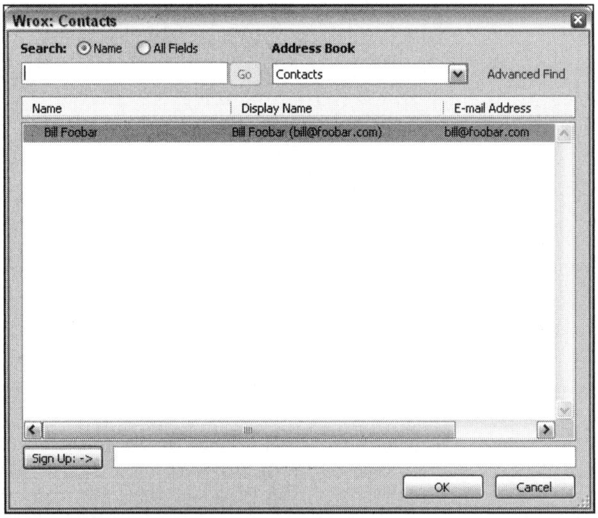

Figure 3.1

Summary

In this chapter, you learned more about the `Application` and `NameSpace` objects and some of their properties, methods, and events. You learned how to initialize global `Application` and `NameSpace` objects and make them available throughout your code, especially in COM addins. You also learned about additions to the Outlook object model such as `Categories`, context menus, user interface dialogs, and the `ItemLoad` event.

The many new properties, methods and events added to the `Application` and `NameSpace` objects are key to developing in Outlook without having to use other APIs, but possibly the most important change for developers is the new more relaxed security model. If your Outlook objects are directly or indirectly derived from the trusted `Application` or `Item` objects passed to Outlook VBA, form code, or COM addins, the code you write is trusted by Outlook and won't fire the security warnings that have been a problem since the Outlook Object Model Guard was introduced in Outlook 2000 SP2. This, along with the trust extended to external programs that run on computers with up-to-date antivirus protection, may be the biggest new features in Outlook 2007 development.

In the next chapter, you start learning to put these pieces together in the Outlook VBA project to work with `SyncObjects` and `Accounts`, `AddressBooks`, `Stores`, `Folders`, and `Items` collections.

Outlook VBA

In this chapter, you learn more about working with the Outlook VBA project, and how to use it to create macros and to prototype code destined for use in COM addins and standalone projects.

The code in this chapter uses the intrinsic ThisOutlookSession class module, custom classes, and VBA UserForms for user input and data display to create macros that you can run on demand as well as code that runs automatically when Outlook starts or in response to specific Outlook events. These types of uses are common not only for VBA macro code but also in almost every Outlook application you write, including COM addins and standalone projects.

The Outlook VBA Project

Unlike Office applications such as Word, where the VBA project is document oriented, Outlook code is oriented towards the application. This orientation is similar to the orientation of COM addins and standalone projects, and makes Outlook VBA especially useful as a prototyping tool. The VBA project is also used for creating two classes of macros, macros that run automatically and those that are run on demand by the user, which you learn about in this chapter.

The Project File

Outlook has one global VBA project file, stored in the file system as VBAProject.OTM. This file is usually located in the C:\Documents and Settings\<windows logon>\Application Data\Microsoft\Outlook folder, where <windows logon> is the current user logon name for Windows. All Outlook VBA code is contained in this project file. This is unlike Word or Excel VBA projects, which are tied to the document or workbook and where you can have many different VBA projects.

ThisOutlookSession

You learned in Chapter 1 about the ThisOutlookSession class module, which has special backing for Outlook's application-wide events. This class is always present in all Outlook VBA projects and can be used for all of your macros and prototyping code. However, it's usually better to group code into related functions contained in separate code and class modules.

The ThisOutlookSession class is used in this chapter primarily to contain code that references the built-in Application events, and for startup code that initializes event-handling objects. Most other event-handling code in this chapter is grouped into custom class modules, with examples shown of handling application-wide events in custom class modules.

Macros and VBA Procedures

Outlook VBA code uses three types of procedures:

- ❑ Functions, procedures that may take zero or more input arguments and return a value
- ❑ Subs, procedures that may take zero or more input arguments and do not return a value
- ❑ Macro Subs, procedures that take zero input arguments that are declared global in scope, either explicitly or implicit

Macro Subs are special cases of standard Sub procedures. Only Subs with no input arguments that are declared globally can be macros. A Sub may be declared globally by using the Public keyword in the Sub declaration, or it may be declared as implicitly global by omitting any scope keyword in the Sub declaration. The following examples show the difference between macro and non-macro Sub declarations:

Subs That Are Not Macros

```
Private Sub Test()
Sub Test(strValue As String)
Public Sub Test(strValue As String)
```

Subs That Are Macros

```
Sub Test()
Public Sub Test()
```

Only macro Subs can be run from the Tools ➪ Macros menu list or from a custom toolbar button. Figure 4.1 shows the macro list opened from the Macros menu list. Running a macro from a custom toolbar button immediately executes the macro without opening a list for macro selection.

Macro Security

As you learned in Chapter 1, Outlook defaults to disabling all VBA code that isn't signed. You learned how to create a code signing certificate and to sign code using the certificate with the Selfcert utility in Chapter 1. If you have not signed your code and do not want to set a lower security level you should go back to Chapter 1 now and create your code signing certificate and sign your VBA project.

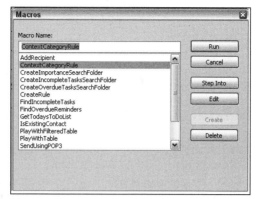

Figure 4.1

Security Levels

Select Tools ⇨ Trust Center to open the new Trust Center dialog and select the Macro Security section to view the available security levels for Outlook VBA code. The security settings apply to all VBA code, whether or not it is macro code by strict definition.

The following security levels are available for VBA code:

- ❑   No warnings and disable all macros
- ❑   Warnings for signed macros; all unsigned macros are disabled
- ❑   Warnings for all macros
- ❑   No security checks for macros (not recommended)

If you don't sign your code with a certificate created using Selfcert or with a code signing certificate issued by a recognized certificate authority such as VeriSign or Thawte, you can only run VBA code if you enable one of the last two security levels, which are not as secure as the first two security levels. The first, most secure, macro security level prevents all VBA code from running, so it's not a setting you want to use if you are developing Outlook VBA code.

Signed Macro Code

Even with the recommended second security level set and signed code, you will still get warnings every time Outlook is opened. This quickly gets annoying, so to disable the startup macro warnings add your signature to the Trusted Publishers list. You learned how to do this in Chapter 1.

Class Modules

The code for this chapter uses both the `ThisOutlookSession` class and user classes you add to the VBA project. `ThisOutlookSession` is intrinsic to the Outlook VBA project and appears in all Outlook project files.

In general the best way to utilize `ThisOutlookSession` is to handle application-wide events in this class module and to instantiate objects and classes that will be used by other code in the project. If you add all your event-handling code and class-level code to `ThisOutlookSession`, it will quickly become packed with code and it will be hard to segregate the code into logically grouped sets of procedures and event handlers.

ThisOutlookSession

The code for this chapter that's placed in `ThisOutlookSession` falls into three categories: initialization code, application-wide event handlers and initializations for event handlers that are in user classes. This shows a common mix of uses for code in `ThisOutlookSession`.

The initialization code consists of module-level declarations and code in the `Application_Startup` event handler. This is the equivalent of code for a COM addin that's in the `OnConnection` event handler, or for VSTO applications, code that's in the `ThisAddIn` class in the `Startup` event handler.

Module-level declarations are placed before any procedures or event handlers in `ThisOutlookSession`:

```
Private WithEvents oInbox As Outlook.Folder 'Inbox folder events
Private WithEvents colInspectors As Outlook.Inspectors 'Inspectors events

Private oDeletedItems As Outlook.Folder 'Deleted Items folder
```

The `WithEvents` modifier for the declarations allows those objects to handle any events exposed for that type of object. Declaring variables at module level enables those variables to retain scope throughout the life of the module, unlike variables declared within procedures, which go out of scope when the procedure ends. `ThisOutlookSession` has scope for the lifetime of the Outlook session, so variables declared in this class at module level also have scope for the life of the Outlook session.

User Classes

The code for this chapter uses four user classes:

- ❑ `clsCategorizeRule`
- ❑ `clsContactWrap`
- ❑ `clsMailWrap`
- ❑ `clsSearch`

To add a class module to the VBA project:

1. Select Insert ➪ Class Module.

2. Add four user classes now, and name them as indicated in the list above. You will use these classes and populate them with code later in this chapter.

Classes that are inserted by the user can be used for any code that can be inserted in the `ThisOutlookSession` class. The main difference is that for user classes you must instantiate an `Outlook.Application` object declared `WithEvents` to be able to handle application-wide events. User classes have access to the same intrinsic `Application` object that is available elsewhere in the Outlook VBA project. Another difference is that a user class must be instantiated, whereas `ThisOutlookSession` is automatically instantiated when Outlook and the VBA project start up.

Code Modules

The code in this chapter uses one code module for macros and for global object and variable declarations. Select Insert ➪ Module to insert a new code module in the VBA project. Name the code module `Chapter_4`.

Add the code declarations shown in Listing 4.1 to the `Chapter_4` code module.

Listing 4.1

```
Public g_oNS As Outlook.NameSpace 'global NameSpace object

'to keep contact wrapper classes alive
Public colContactWrapper As New Collection

'to keep mail item wrapper classes alive
Public colMailWrapper As New Collection

Public cSearch As clsSearch 'AdvancedSearch class
Public cRule As clsCategorizeRule 'Categorize Rule class

Public g_lngID As Long
```

These lines declare a global `NameSpace` object used throughout the code in this chapter, two collections, two classes, and a global `Long`.

> `Long` *data types in VBA and VB 6 are 32-bit integers, equivalent to the* `Integer (int)` *data type in VB.NET and C#.*

The two collections, `colContactWrapper` and `colMailWrapper`, are used to maintain references to the `clsEmailWrap` and `clsContactWrap` classes and keep them alive and in scope. Using collections for this allows you to handle multiple contacts and emails that are open or accessed at the same time, and to separately handle the properties, methods, and events of those items without any interference from other open or accessed items of the same type.

The code for `clsEmailWrap` is shown in Listing 4.13. The code for `clsContactWrap` is shown in Listing 4.14.

> *In C#, you would add a reference to a wrapper class to a* `hashtable` *or* `List` *to keep the reference alive, just as collections are used for that purpose in VBA, VB 6, and VB.NET.*

Add one macro `Sub` now to the code in the code module. The code in Listing 4.2 is used to initialize a class that adds a custom menu item to the item context menu. This menu is displayed when you right-click an item in a folder view in Outlook.

Listing 4.2

```
'Initialize the Categorize Rule class
Public Sub ContextCategoryRule()
  Set cRule = New clsCategorizeRule
End Sub
```

This macro instantiates an instance of the `clsCategorizeRule` class as the global `cRule` object. Making this class object global to the VBA project gives it scope throughout the life of an Outlook session, from the time the macro is run until Outlook is closed. The code for the `clsCategorizeRule` class is shown in Listing 4.16.

To add the context menu entry automatically when Outlook starts, add this line to in the `Application_Startup` code in Listing 4.4:

```
Set cRule = New clsCategorizeRule
```

Office UserForms

VBA `UserForms` are the VBA equivalent of Windows Forms in .NET code or standard Forms in VB 6 code. `UserForms` can be used to get user input and also to display information or data gathered by procedural code elsewhere in the VBA project. `UserForms` are classes with a user interface component, so any code that can be used in a class module, such as event handling code, can also be used in a `UserForm`.

All controls used in VBA `UserForms` are ActiveX controls; .NET form controls cannot be used in `UserForms`. The standard controls used in `UserForms` (labels, textboxes, command buttons, etc.) all come from the MS Forms 2.0 library, the same library that provides the controls for Outlook forms.

Creating the Macro User Interface

The code in this chapter uses two VBA `UserForms`, one for the automatic macro that checks for a `Subject` in all outgoing emails, and the other form for the macro to check today's To-Do list. This section shows you how to add the two `UserForms` to the project.

To add the two `UserForms` to the project, select Insert ➪ UserForm in the VBA project menu twice.

The NoSubjectForm

The first form, `NoSubjectForm`, shown in Figure 4.2, will be used by the procedure that runs every time an outgoing email is sent. This code, shown in Listing 4.13, checks for no `Subject` in the email, and displays the `NoSubjectForm` if the email is sent with no `Subject`. This macro is an example of an automatic macro that runs with no user intervention when circumstances are appropriate, in this case when an email is sent.

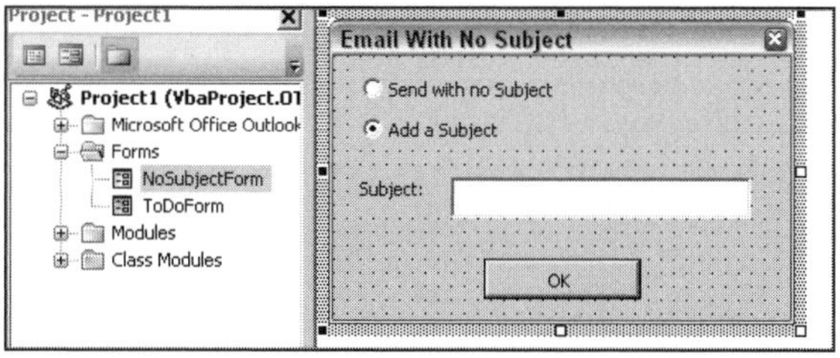

Figure 4.2

1. Set the properties of the form as shown in the following table.

Form Property	Value
Name	NoSubjectForm
Caption	Email With No Subject
Height	141
Width	72

2. Add an OptionButton control to the form. To add any control to a form, select the control on the Control Toolbox, and draw the selected control on the form. If the Control Toolbox isn't displayed when the form is selected, display it by clicking the Toolbox icon on the toolbar or by selecting View ⇨ Toolbox.

3. Select the OptionButton control you just added by clicking it, and set its properties to those in the following table.

OptionButton Property	Value
Name	optNoSubject
Caption	Send with no Subject
Height	18
Left	12
Top	6
Value	False
Width	174

4. Add another `OptionButton`, and set its properties as shown in the following table.

OptionButton Property	Value
Name	optSubject
Caption	Add a Subject
Height	18
Left	12
Top	24
Value	True
Width	174

5. Add a `Label` control, and set its propertes as shown in the following table.

Label Property	Value
Name	lblSubject
Caption	Subject
Height	18
Left	12
Top	54
Width	42

6. Add a `TextBox` control, and set its properties to those in the following table.

TextBox Property	Value
Name	txtSubject
Height	18
Left	54
Top	54
Width	138

7. Finally, add a `CommandButton` control, and set its properties as shown in the following table.

CommandButton Property	Value
Name	cmdOK
Caption	OK
Height	18
Left	69
Top	90
Width	72

The code in Listing 4.13 displays the `NoSubjectForm` when an email is sent with a blank `Subject`.

The ToDoForm

The second `UserForm` in this chapter, shown in Figure 4.3, is used to display a list of all tasks due for today that are listed in the To-Do Bar. This form is used in the Today's ToDo List macro, shown in Listing 4.18, which is run on demand by the user.

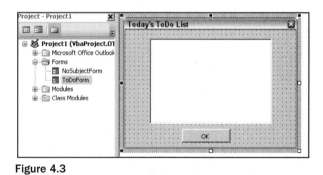

Figure 4.3

1. Set the form properties for the Today's ToDo List form as shown in the following table.

Form Property	Value
Name	ToDoForm
Caption	Today's ToDo List
Height	180
Width	240

2. Add a `Listbox` control to the form and set its properties as shown in the following table.

ListBox Property	Value
Name	lstToDo
ColumnCount	3
Height	113
Left	34
Top	12
Width	168

3. Add a `CommandButton` control to the form and set its properties as shown in the following table.

CommandButton Property	Value
Name	cmdOK
Caption	OK
Default	True
Height	18
Left	78
Top	132
Width	66

4. Save your work to make sure that the forms are available for use later in this chapter with the code for the macros.

Working with Outlook Events

Events in VBA can only be handled in classes or forms. Code modules cannot handle any events. Forms can handle events but are rarely used in VBA because forms are usually shown only for a brief time and then unloaded. A form could be hidden and still handle events, but in general most event handlers are located in class modules.

Place the code in Listing 4.3 in the `ThisOutlookSession` class module, at the module level before any procedures in the class.

Listing 4.3

```
Private WithEvents oInbox As Outlook.Folder 'Inbox folder events

'Inspectors events
Private WithEvents colInspectors As Outlook.Inspectors

Private oDeletedItems As Outlook.Folder 'Deleted Items folder
```

The `oInbox Folder` object declared at the module level in `ThisOutlookSession` is declared `WithEvents`, meaning that it can handle events exposed for the `Folder` object. Two events are exposed for `Folder` objects in Outlook 2007, `BeforeFolderMove` and `BeforeItemMove`. These events are new to Outlook 2007. Code that uses the `BeforeItemMove` event is shown in Listing 4.10.

The `colInspectors Inspectors` collection object also is declared `WithEvents`, and is used to handle the one exposed event for the `Inspectors` collection, `NewInspector`. This event fires when a new `Inspector` is opened, whenever a user opens a new or existing item. Code that uses the `NewInspector` event is shown in Listing 4.12.

The `oDeletedItems Folder` object is also used in the `BeforeItemMove` event handler code.

Application Events

The `Application` events you'll be working with in this chapter are:

- ❑ `Application_Startup`
- ❑ `Application_ItemSend`
- ❑ `Application_ItemLoad`
- ❑ `Application_NewMailEx`
- ❑ `Application_ContextMenuClose`
- ❑ `Application_ItemContextMenuDisplay`
- ❑ `Application_AdvancedSearch`

User classes are used to handle the `Application_ContextMenuClose`, `Application_ ItemContextMenuDisplay` and `Application_AdvancedSearch` events. The other event handlers are coded in the `ThisOutlookSession` class module.

Startup

The `Application_Startup` event handler is automatically available to you in the `ThisOutlookSession` class module. To expose the event, select `Application` in the Object drop-down at the top left of the code window. Click the drop-down, which starts out showing (General) and select `Application`. In the right-hand drop-down, select the `Startup` event to add a prototype of the `Application_Startup` event handler to the code.

Add the code in Listing 4.4 to the `Application_Startup` event handler procedure in `ThisOutlookSession`.

Listing 4.4

```
Private Sub Application_Startup()
  'global NameSpace object
  Set g_oNS = Application.GetNamespace("MAPI")

  'Inbox (handles events)
  Set oInbox = g_oNS.GetDefaultFolder(olFolderInbox)

  'Deleted Items folder
  Set oDeletedItems = g_oNS.GetDefaultFolder(olFolderDeletedItems)

  'Inspectors collection (handles events)
  Set colInspectors = Application.Inspectors
End Sub
```

This code first instantiates the global `NameSpace` object declared in the `Chapter_4` code module, making a `NameSpace` object available throughout the VBA project code.

The `oInbox Folder` object declared at the module level is instantiated as the Inbox folder, using the `NameSpace.GetDefaultFolder()` method. This method accepts any of the `OlDefaultFolders` enumeration members, or the equivalent numeric values. The enumeration member for the Inbox is `olFolderInbox`.

The `GetDefaultFolder` method is used with the `olFolderDeletedItems` enumeration member to instantiate the `oDeletedItems Folder` object as the Deleted Items folder. This object is instantiated once on startup to save time in the event handler code.

Most Outlook events are not reentrant. If your code takes too long to execute in an event handler, you may miss the next instance of that event. When it comes time to optimize your code for production use, you should always make an effort to minimize the time you spend in your event handlers.

Finally, the `colInspectors Inspectors` collection object is instantiated using the intrinsic `Application.Inspectors` collection.

Every time Outlook starts up with macros enabled, the code in `Application_Startup` is executed, providing you with a way to run selected code on startup.

ItemSend

With `Application` selected in the Object drop-down, select the `ItemSend` event in the right-hand drop-down. You learned about `Application_ItemSend` in Chapter 3, with code that added a disclaimer to outgoing emails.

The `Application_ItemSend` code in Listing 4.5 might be used in a corporate environment, where there's a policy that no emails can be sent using private email addresses. This code uses the new `Account` object to see if the sending account is an Exchange server account.

After making sure the outgoing item has a `Class` of `olMail`, an `Account` object is instantiated in the line `Set oAccount = oMail.SendUsingAccount`.

The `AccountType` property is checked to see if the sending account is an Exchange email account. Production code would check for and handle other outgoing item types such as meeting and task requests, and handle any possible errors.

Listing 4.5

```
Private Sub Application_ItemSend(ByVal Item As Object, Cancel As Boolean)
  Dim oMail As Outlook.MailItem
  Dim oAccount As Outlook.Account
  Dim strMessage As String

  strMessage = "You must send emails using your Exchange email account"

  'if this is a mail item
  If Item.Class = olMail Then
    Set oMail = Item

    'get the account used to send the email
    Set oAccount = oMail.SendUsingAccount

    'check for not sending using an Exchange account
    If oAccount.AccountType <> olExchange Then
      'if not Exchange cancel the send
      Cancel = True

      MsgBox MsgBox strMessage, vbOKOnly + vbExclamation
    End If
  End If

  Set oMail = Nothing
  Set oAccount = Nothing
End Sub
```

Some properties related to sending aren't populated when the `ItemSend` *event fires; they are populated later when the transport, an email service such as POP3, Exchange, or IMAP populates them. Accessing properties such as* `MailItem.SenderEmailAddress` *or* `MailItem.SenderEmailType` *in* `ItemSend` *causes automation errors or returns blank values. The new* `SendUsingAccount` *object is populated and works very well in* `ItemSend`; *in fact, the default sending account is only populated in the* `Application` `.ItemSend` *and* `Item.Send` *events. At all other times,* `SendUsingAccount` *returns* `Nothing` *(null) if the default sending account is used.*

Other common uses for the `ItemSend` event are to add recipients to outgoing email such as new `To`, `Cc`, or `Bcc` recipients and to add or remove attachments from emails.

ItemLoad

You learned in Chapter 3 that the `ItemLoad` event fires when Outlook is loading an item into memory. This event fires whenever an item is accessed in any way, unless the item is already cached in memory. The code in Listing 4.6 checks to see if the loaded item is a contact item, and if so, it instantiates an instance of the contact wrapper class, `clsContactWrap`.

```
Set clsContact = New clsContactWrap
```

The wrapper class's internal ContactItem object is instantiated as the contact which is being loaded, and a Key value is set for that instance of the wrapper class. The global g_lngID is then incremented for the next use as a Key value.

```
With clsContact
   .Contact = oContact
   .Key = CStr(g_lngID)
End With
```

The new contact wrapper is then added to the colContactWrapper collection, so its reference stays alive and in scope.

Listing 4.6

```
Private Sub Application_ItemLoad(ByVal Item As Object)
  Dim clsContact As clsContactWrap
  Dim oContact As Outlook.ContactItem
  Dim sKey As String

  'if a contact is opened or read in a folder view
  If Item.Class = olContact Then
    'create an instance of the contact wrapper class
    Set oContact = Item
    sKey = CStr(g_lngID)

    Set clsContact = New clsContactWrap

    With clsContact
       .Contact = oContact
       .Key = CStr(g_lngID)
    End With

    'add the class to a collection to keep it alive
    colContactWrapper.Add clsContact, sKey

    g_lngID = g_lngID + 1
  End If

  Set clsContact = Nothing
  Set oContact = Nothing
End Sub
```

The clsContactWrap code marks the contact as a task that is due next week if the loaded contact is marked as Private. This action automatically displays the contact task in the new To-Do Bar. The code for clsContactWrap is shown in Listing 4.14.

NewMailEx

The NewMailEx event is an excellent event to use when you need to process incoming items for purposes such as processing that you don't want to do using the Rules Wizard, or that cannot be done using the Rules Wizard. This NewMailEx event handler scans incoming emails for those with a flag marked for follow-up. Any items with follow-up flags are marked as completed.

The code in this `NewMailEx` event handler in Listing 4.7 splits the comma-separated list of incoming `EntryID`s into a string array. The array is iterated in a `For` loop, and each item is instantiated as an `Object`. This is done because an incoming Outlook item can also be a meeting request, a non-delivery report, a task request, or a number of other types of items.

If the `Object` is a mail item, a `MailItem` object is instantiated from the `Object`, and the `MailItem's` `PropertyAccessor` is instantiated. The `FlagStatus` property is not directly available in the Outlook object model for mail items, so you need to access that property using the `PropertyAccessor` object.

To access `FlagStatus`, you use the DASL property tag `"http://schemas.microsoft.com/mapi/proptag/0x10900003"`. The status is evaluated to see if the flag property is set by checking for the `olFlagMarked` value. If that value is found, the setting is changed to `olFlagComplete` and the item is saved to persist the change.

Listing 4.7

```vba
Private Sub Application_NewMailEx(ByVal EntryIDCollection As String)
    Dim oItem As Object
    Dim oMail As Outlook.MailItem
    Dim oPropAccessor As Outlook.PropertyAccessor
    Dim oNs As Outlook.NameSpace
    Dim aryItems() As String
    Dim FlagStatus As Long
    Dim i As Long

    'property tag for FlagStatus, used for follow up flags
    Const PR_FLAG_STATUS As String = _
      "http://schemas.microsoft.com/mapi/proptag/0x10900003"

    'EntryIDCollection is a comma separated list of EntryID's
    aryItems = Split(EntryIDCollection, ",")

    Set oNS = Application.GetNameSpace("MAPI")

    For i = LBound(aryItems) To UBound(aryItems) 'iterate the array
      Set oItem = oNS.GetItemFromID(aryItems(i)) 'Object
      If oItem.Class = olMail Then 'look for mail items
        Set oMail = oItem 'set MailItem from Object
        Set oPropAccessor = oMail.PropertyAccessor

        'read flag status property
        FlagStatus = oPropAccessor.GetProperty(PR_FLAG_STATUS)

        'if marked for follow up
        If FlagStatus = olFlagMarked Then
          'mark the flag completed
          oPropAccessor.SetProperty PR_FLAG_STATUS, olFlagComplete
          'save change
          oMail.Save
        End If
      End If
    Next i
```

(continued)

Listing 4.7 *(continued)*

```
  Set oNS = Nothing
    Set oItem = Nothing
    Set oMail = Nothing
    Set oPropAccessor = Nothing
  End Sub
```

AdvancedSearch

The `AdvancedSearch` method is used to perform filtered searches of one or more folders in a `Store`, returning the results of the search in a `Results` collection. This is the same search that is performed in the user interface with the Advanced Find method.

`AdvancedSearch` works by creating a temporary search folder that contains the `Results` collection from the search. This search folder is not visible to the user, and is discarded by Outlook when the search results go out of scope. Searching using `AdvancedSearch` has the same limitation as any search folder, the results can span only one `Store` object. Searching across multiple `Stores` is not supported.

Each `AdvancedSearch` has filter, search scope and tag properties that are used to qualify the search. The `SearchSubfolders`' Boolean property is used to modify the scope of the search to include or exclude subfolders of the scoped folders.

The following table contains some examples of scoping the search. All scope arguments are strings, enclosed in single quotation marks.

Scope	SearchSubfolders	Folders searched
`'//Personal Folders'`	True	The top of store of a PST file and all subfolders
`'//Mailbox - Casey Slovak'`	True	The top of store of an Exchange mailbox and all subfolders
`'Inbox', 'Sent Items', 'Drafts'`	True	The Inbox, Sent Items, and Drafts and all of their subfolders
`'Inbox', 'Sent Items', 'Drafts'`	False	The Inbox, Sent Items, and Drafts folders only
`'Contacts', 'Inbox'`	False	The Contacts and Inbox folders only

Searches can work in different types of folders, as in the example above that searches in the Contacts and Inbox folders. However, a successful search across folder types will search only for properties that are common to the types of items that are in all the searched folders, such as `Subject` *or* `Body`.

The filter used for the search must be a DASL syntax filter, as shown in Listing 4.8 for this example of finding incomplete tasks. The `Completed` property is represented in DASL syntax as `"http://schemas.microsoft.com/mapi/id/{00062003-0000-0000-C000-000000000046}/811C000B"`. Searching for tasks that aren't complete would look for that property with a value of `False` in all scoped items.

Any item flagged as a task for the To-Do Bar uses the new task-related properties and will be returned by the search.

Listing 4.8

```
Public Sub FindIncompleteTasks()
  Dim objSch As Outlook.Search
  Dim strFilter As String
  Dim strScope As String
  Dim strTag As String
  Dim Completed As String

  'Task completed
  Completed = "http://schemas.microsoft.com/mapi/id/"

  Completed = Completed & _
    "{00062003-0000-0000-C000-000000000046}/811C000B"

  strFilter = Completed & " = 'False'"

  'Scope is entire store, either Personal Folders or Exchange mailbox.

  'Uncomment the following lines as appropriate for the store type

  strScope = "'//Personal Folders'"
  'strScope = "'//Mailbox - Casey Slovak'"

  strTag = "xxxyyy" 'unique tag property

  Set cSearch = New clsSearch 'new instance of search class
  cSearch.Tag = strTag 'this allows the class to handle completion of this search

  Set objSch = Application.AdvancedSearch(Scope:=strScope, _
    Filter:=strFilter, SearchSubFolders:=True, Tag:=strTag)

  Set objSch = Nothing
End Sub
```

For the code in Listing 4.8, remember to change the mailbox name to the name of your mailbox if you are testing the code with an Exchange profile or to uncomment the line strScope = "//Personal Folders'" *if you are testing it with a PST file profile. Change "Personal Folders" if your PST file has a different name.*

The Tag argument is used to identify which search was completed, which is useful when performing multiple searches at the same time, and to make sure the correct AdvancedSearchComplete event handles the results of the related search.

The filter for a search can include multiple logical clauses, separated by the OR and AND operators. The NOT operator may also be used to construct a search filter. All filter clauses must use DASL syntax. For example, the following filter would add a clause to the previous filter that limits the search to only items that contain the MessageClass IPM.NOTE:

```
strFilter = strFilter & _
  " AND http://schemas.microsoft.com/mapi/proptag/0x001A001E LIKE 'IPM.Note'"
```

This search returns standard and custom email items that have the `IPM.Note` base `MessageClass` and are marked as completed tasks. It will not return task items that aren't complete. Using DASL syntax ,the `MessageClass` property is referenced as `"http://schemas.microsoft.com/mapi/proptag/0x001A001E"`.

> *A good way to derive the DASL syntax for a filter is to use the view customization dialog. Select View ⇨ Current View ⇨ Customize to open the customization dialog, and click the Filter button. Use the Advanced tab to set up the filter using the available properties and logical operators, and then click the SQL tab to view the DASL syntax for the filter.*

The `FindIncompleteTasks` macro shown in Listing 4.8 can be run from the Macros dialog. The `AdvancedSearchComplete` event handling is done by the code in `clsSearch`. The line in `FindIncompleteTasks, Set cSearch = New clsSearch` instantiates an instance of the `clsSearch`, created in Listing 4.9. To ensure that the correct instance of the class handles the correct `AdvancedSearchComplete` event, the `Tag` property for the search is used to set the `Tag` property of `clsSearch`.

Place the following code in the `clsSearch` class module you created earlier.

Listing 4.9

```
Private WithEvents oOL As Outlook.Application 'handles events

Private m_sTag As String

Public Property Let Tag(sTag As String)
  'the Tag lets us know we're handling the correct
  ' AdvancedSearchComplete event
  m_sTag = sTag
End Property

Private Sub Class_Initialize()
  Set oOL = Application
End Sub

Private Sub Class_Terminate()
  Set oOL = Nothing
End Sub

Private Sub oOL_AdvancedSearchComplete(ByVal SearchObject As Search)
  Dim colResults As Outlook.Results
  Dim oItem As Object
  Dim strMessage As String
  Dim lngReply As Long
  Dim i As Long

  If SearchObject.Tag = m_sTag Then 'check to see it's the correct Tag
    Set colResults = SearchObject.Results 'get the Results collection

    If colResults.Count > 0 Then
      strMessage = CStr(colResults.Count) & " items were found." _
        & vbCrLf
```

Listing 4.9 *(continued)*

```
        strMessage = strMessage & "Do you want to open them?"

        lngReply = MsgBox(strMessage, vbInformation + vbOKCancel)
        If lngReply = vbOK Then
          'open the items if the user wants them opened
          For i = 1 To colResults.Count
            Set oItem = colResults.Item(i)
            oItem.Display
            Set oItem = Nothing
          Next
        End If
      Else
        strMessage = "No items were found."

        MsgBox strMessage, vbInformation + vbOKOnly
      End If
    End If

    Set colResults = Nothing
    Set oItem = Nothing
End Sub
```

The `Public Property Let Tag(sTag As String)` line in the code establishes a public property that is set to the value of the `Tag` for the `AdvancedSearch`. This is compared to the `SearchObject.Tag` property passed in the `AdvancedSearchComplete` event handler, and if the tags match, the event handler code is executed.

```
If SearchObject.Tag = m_sTag Then 'check to see it's the correct Tag
```

A `Results` collection is instantiated from the `SearchObject.Results` collection and is checked to make sure that the collection isn't empty.

```
    Set colResults = SearchObject.Results 'get the Results collection
    If colResults.Count > 0 Then
```

The user is then asked if he or she wants to open the items returned by the search, and if the answer is yes, the `Results` collection is iterated through in a loop, with each item in the collection being opened for viewing.

The `AdvancedSearch` object was added to the Outlook object model in Outlook 2002, so it can be used in any Outlook code that needs to support Outlook 2002 or later.

Folder Events

Outlook 2007 added two new events for the `Folder` object. Previous versions of Outlook have no events exposed for the `MAPIFolder` object. The two new events are `BeforeItemMove` and `BeforeFolderMove`. Both work in similar fashion, firing if an item or folder is being moved or deleted. The fact that the event fires before the item or folder is moved or deleted and has a `Cancel` argument means that you now can finally trap all deletions and cancel them or take action based on which items are deleted. This is something that Outlook developers have been requesting for years, and finally have in Outlook 2007.

BeforeItemMove

In previous versions of Outlook, there was no event for knowing that an item was deleted unless the item was opened and the File ⇨ Delete menu selection was used. Only under those circumstances does the `BeforeDelete` event fire. If an item was deleted from a folder view, the only way to identify the item was to handle the `ItemAdd` event of the `Items` collection of the Deleted Items folder. If an item was hard deleted (using Shift+Delete to delete the item and bypass the Deleted Items folder) or if more than 16 items were deleted at once, you wouldn't know about it. The `ItemRemove` event of the Items collection doesn't pass a reference to what was deleted, so all it's good for is telling you that something was deleted from a folder, not what was deleted.

There are workarounds, such as maintaining a table of items located in the current folder and seeing if any are missing at timed intervals. But those workarounds are ugly hacks, are very inefficient, and only let you know that something was deleted. There's no way to cancel the deletion, as there is with the limited `BeforeDelete` event.

Place the following code for Listing 4.10 in the `ThisOutlookSession` module to handle deletions or items being moved in the Inbox folder. The `oInbox` object was declared `WithEvents` at the module level in `ThisOutlookSession` and was instantiated in the `Application_Startup` event in Listing 4.4.

Listing 4.10

```
Private Sub oInbox_BeforeItemMove(ByVal Item As Object, _
    ByVal MoveTo As MAPIFolder, Cancel As Boolean)

    Dim lngReply As Long
    Dim strMessage As String
    Dim blnDeleted As Boolean

    strMessage = _
      "Are you sure you want to delete this item without reading it?"

    blnDeleted = False

    If Item.Class = olMail Then 'mail items only
      If (MoveTo Is Nothing) Then
         'if hard deleted the target folder is Nothing
        blnDeleted = True
      ElseIf g_oNS.CompareEntryIDs(MoveTo.EntryID, _
        oDeletedItems.EntryID) Then

         'moved to Deleted Items folder
        blnDeleted = True
      End If

      If blnDeleted Then
        If Item.UnRead Then 'check UnRead status
           lngReply = MsgBox(strMessage, vbExclamation + vbYesNo)

           If lngReply = vbNo Then
             'cancel the deletion if user says to.
             'works for hard deletes too.
             Cancel = True
```

Listing 4.10 *(continued)*

```
            End If
          End If
        End If
      End If
    End Sub
```

Three arguments are passed in the `BeforeItemMove` event handler: `Item`, `MoveTo`, and `Cancel`. The first two arguments are `ByVal`, meaning the objects passed are local copies of the original objects. The `Cancel` argument is passed `ByRef`, meaning that any changes to that Boolean value affect the original item and can be used to cancel the move operation.

> *The `BeforeItemMove` and `BeforeFolderMove` events do not fire as a result of actions taken in auto-archiving or synchronizing operations; they do fire in response to code or the user moving or deleting objects.*

When any item is moved or deleted in the Inbox folder, the target folder is passed as the `MoveTo` argument to the `BeforeItemMove` event handler. If the item is being hard deleted (Shift+Delete), an action that bypasses the Deleted Items folder, the value of `MoveTo` is `Nothing` or `null`. The code tests for deletions only, using the following two lines:

```
If (MoveTo Is Nothing) Then
ElseIf g_oNS.CompareEntryIDs(MoveTo.EntryID, oDeletedItems.EntryID) Then
```

The first line checks to see if `MoveTo` is `Nothing`, which indicates that the item was hard deleted. The second line compares the `EntryID` properties for the `MoveTo` folder and the Deleted Items folder, and if the values are the same the item is moved to the Deleted Items folder. The new `CompareEntryIDs` method is used to compare the `EntryIDs`.

Comparing `EntryID` values using equality operators can produce unexpected errors. An `EntryID` for an object can be short or long term. Short-term `EntryIDs` are valid only for that session; long-term `EntryIDs` are permanent. Some `Store` providers, such as the provider for PST files, only use long-term `EntryID` values. Some, such as the Exchange transport, use both types of `EntryIDs`. The two properties are usually different lengths and will return not equal in comparison operations. The `CompareEntryIDs` method takes account of the differences and will return equal as the result of a comparison between short and long-term `EntryIDs` representing the same object.

The code then checks the `UnRead` property of the mail item to see if the item is unread and prompts the user to see if he or she really wants to delete an unread item.

> *Although the event fires when an item is hard deleted and can be canceled even in that case, the prompt from Outlook about permanently deleting the item will be displayed before the `BeforeItemMove` code is called.*

BeforeFolderMove

The `BeforeFolderMove` event fires when a folder is moved or deleted. It works the same as the `BeforeItemMove` event but only passes two arguments, `MoveTo` and `Cancel`:

```
BeforeFolderMove(MoveTo As Folder, Cancel As Boolean)
```

The `BeforeFolderMove` event does not fire if a subfolder of the folder that's being monitored is moved or deleted. Only moving or deleting the monitored folder will fire this event.

User Events

Code in the Outlook VBA project can not only handle Outlook events but also can be used to create or handle user-defined events. User events are created in classes or forms and can be handled by event handlers in classes or forms.

The code for `NoSubjectForm` in Listing 4.11 demonstrates creating a user event; the event is handled in the code for the `clsMailWrap` class, shown in Listing 4.13.

Code for the NoSubjectForm

Place the following code in the `NoSubjectForm`. To place code in a form, right-click the form in the Project Explorer and select View Code. The code in Listing 4.11 works in conjunction with the code in the `clsMailWrap` class module to handle cases where emails are sent out with no subjects. The `clsMailWrap` class module code is shown in Listing 4.13.

The form event is declared in the line `Public Event DataReady(ByVal sSubject As String)`, which declares a `DataReady` event that passes a subject string when it fires. Firing the event is the job of the line `RaiseEvent DataReady(txtSubject.Text)`, which notifies any code that has subscribed to the event that data is ready for reading. The `RaiseEvent` keyword is used to cause the firing of the event.

Listing 4.11

```
Public Event DataReady(ByVal sSubject As String)

Private Sub cmdOK_Click()
  RaiseDataReadyEvent 'fire DataReady event
  Unload Me
End Sub

Private Sub optNoSubject_Click()
  txtSubject.Enabled = False
  txtSubject.Text = ""
End Sub

Private Sub optSubject_Click()
  txtSubject.Enabled = True
  txtSubject.SetFocus
End Sub

Private Sub RaiseDataReadyEvent()
  'this event is handled externally to the form
  'it passes the new subject text
  RaiseEvent DataReady(txtSubject.Text)
End Sub
```

The `NoSubjectForm` uses option buttons to let the user select whether to send the email with no subject or to add a subject to the outgoing email. The text box on the form is used to enter the subject, which is then passed to the `DataReady` event handler when the user clicks the OK button on the form.

Wrapper Classes and Collections

Wrapper classes and collections are widely used in Outlook programming to handle the events for various Outlook objects and collections. The collections are used to store instances of the wrapper classes, keeping them alive until they are no longer needed, when the wrapper classes are removed from the collection and released.

The question of the life of an object is something that is a concern to all programmers but especially so for .NET programmers. COM code automatically keeps class references alive until the classes are released or go out of scope. In .NET code, you have to pay special attention to keeping references alive so that they aren't released by the running of the garbage collector. Adding a class reference to a collection, or in the case of C# code to a List or hashtable, ensures that the references are kept alive until they are no longer needed.

Using the NewInspector Event to Instantiate a Wrapper Class

The Inspectors collection has one event, NewInspector. This event fires when any item is opened and provides a handle to the new Inspector object. As you learned in Chapter 3, Inspectors are the windows used to view Outlook items, while Explorers are the windows used to view Outlook folders.

You previously declared an Inspectors collection object WithEvents in the ThisOutlookSession class module, in Listing 4.3.

```
Private WithEvents colInspectors As Outlook.Inspectors 'Inspectors events
```

Place the code in Listing 4.12 in ThisOutlookSession to handle any new Inspector objects that are opened.

Listing 4.12

```
Private Sub colInspectors_NewInspector(ByVal Inspector As Inspector)
  Dim clsMail As clsMailWrap
  Dim oMail As Outlook.MailItem
  Dim sKey As String

  'if a mail item is opened in a new Inspector
  If Inspector.CurrentItem.Class = olMail Then
    'create an instance of the email wrapper class
    Set oMail = Inspector.CurrentItem
    sKey = CStr(g_lngID)

    Set clsMail = New clsMailWrap

    With clsMail
      .Email = oMail
      .Key = CStr(g_lngID)
    End With

    'add the class to a collection to keep it alive
    colMailWrapper.Add clsMail, sKey

    g_lngID = g_lngID + 1
```

(continued)

Listing 4.12 *(continued)*

```
    End If

    Set clsMail = Nothing
    Set oMail = Nothing
End Sub
```

When the `NewInspector` event fires, the `Inspector.CurrentItem.Class` property is checked to see if the item is a `MailItem`. If so, an instance of `clsMailWrap` is instantiated and the `Email` and `Key` properties of the wrapper class are set:

```
    Set oMail = Inspector.CurrentItem
    sKey = CStr(g_lngID)

    Set clsMail = New clsMailWrap

    With clsMail
      .Email = oMail
      .Key = CStr(g_lngID)
    End With
```

The wrapper class is then added to the global `colMailWrapper` collection, using the same key property set in the wrapper class as the `Key` for the collection item. This makes it very easy later for the class to dereference itself and remove itself from the collection when it's time for the class to be released.

Email Wrapper

The code in Listing 4.13 for the email wrapper class should be placed in the `clsMailWrap` class module.

Listing 4.13

```
Private WithEvents m_oMail As Outlook.MailItem 'handles mail item events

'we are handling DataReady event from the form
Private WithEvents m_UserForm As NoSubjectForm

'the key lets us access this class in the collection
Private m_Key As String

Public Property Let Email(oMail As Outlook.MailItem)
  Set m_oMail = oMail 'instantiate the mail item
End Property

Public Property Get Email() As Outlook.MailItem
  Set Email = m_oMail
End Property

Public Property Let Key(sKey As String)
  m_Key = sKey 'set the key
End Property

Public Property Get Key() As String
  Key = m_Key
```

Listing 4.13 *(continued)*

```
    End Property

    Public Sub Dispose()
      'release module level objects and remove from the wrapper collection
      Set m_UserForm = Nothing
      Set m_oMail = Nothing

      colMailWrapper.Remove m_Key
    End Sub

    'handle the Send event for the mail item
    Private Sub m_oMail_Send(Cancel As Boolean)
      If m_oMail.Subject = "" Then 'if Subject is blank
        Set m_UserForm = New NoSubjectForm
        m_UserForm.Show vbModal 'see if the user wants to add a Subject
      End If
    End Sub

    Private Sub m_oMail_Unload()
      Call Dispose
    End Sub

    Private Sub m_UserForm_DataReady(ByVal sSubject As String)
      'we get the Subject from the form, passed by the raised form event.
      'we get this event before m_oMail_Send finishes so any Subject we add
      ' gets added to the mail item before it goes out.
      m_oMail.Subject = sSubject
    End Sub
```

The code in this class declares two objects `WithEvents` so that they can be used to handle events fired by those types of objects:

```
    Private WithEvents m_oMail As Outlook.MailItem 'handles mail item events
    Private WithEvents m_UserForm As NoSubjectForm
```

Declaring a `MailItem` for event handling allows you to handle all `MailItem`-generated events. The `WithEvents` declaration for an instance of the `NoSubjectForm` allows you to handle the `DataReady` event that the form generates.

The `MailItem` events being handled in this mail wrapper are the `Send` and `Unload` events. Other events exposed by a `MailItem` can also be handled by adding event handler code for those events. The nice thing about these wrappers is they enable you to separately handle events for many different items that are open at the same time. Only the events related to that item are fired in the wrapper class, so each wrapper can work with only its own item and not be concerned about any other open items.

```
    Public Property Let Email(oMail As Outlook.MailItem)
      Set m_oMail = oMail 'instantiate the mail item
    End Property
```

After `m_oMail` is set in the `Email` property procedure, the code in the wrapper class can handle any exposed events that fire, and only the events for that specific item will fire in the wrapper class.

The `Unload` event is used to know when to release the wrapper class and remove it from the wrapper collection. The `Close` event can also be used for this purpose. When `Unload` fires, the `Dispose` procedure is called:

```
Public Sub Dispose()
    'release module level objects and remove from the wrapper collection
    Set m_UserForm = Nothing
    Set m_oMail = Nothing

    colMailWrapper.Remove m_Key
End Sub
```

The `Dispose` procedure releases the class's module-level objects, `m_UserForm` and `m_oMail`, by setting them to `Nothing`, then the code removes the wrapper class from the wrapper collection by using the `Key` property as the index for the collection's `Remove` method. This provides a very neat way for the class to clean up after itself.

When the `Send` event is fired, the following code is executed:

```
Private Sub m_oMail_Send(Cancel As Boolean)
    If m_oMail.Subject = "" Then 'if Subject is blank
        Set m_UserForm = New NoSubjectForm
        m_UserForm.Show vbModal 'see if the user wants to add a Subject
    End If
End Sub
```

The code tests the email `Subject` to see if it's blank — a null string. If so, it opens a modal instance of the `NoSubjectForm` to let the user decide whether to send the email with no `Subject` or to add a `Subject`. The form must be opened modally, which suspends execution of the `Send` event code until the `NoSubject` form is closed. This is very important; otherwise, the `Send` event would continue execution and the email would be sent by the time the user decided what to do about the blank `Subject`.

Finally, the code in the wrapper class handles the `NoSubjectForm`'s `DataReady` event, which is fired when the user clicks the OK button in the form. This event handler fires before the form is closed, and before the `Send` event code returns to finish up the `Send` procedure. The `Subject` property of the email is set to the subject string passed by the `DataReady` event. Then the event handler code is executed and the form closes. Finally, the `Send` event finishes and the email is sent.

```
Private Sub m_UserForm_DataReady(ByVal sSubject As String)
    'we get the Subject from the form, passed by the raised form event.
    'we get this event before m_oMail_Send finishes so any Subject we add
    ' gets added to the mail item before it goes out.
    m_oMail.Subject = sSubject
End Sub
```

You can use these wrapper classes and collections for any cases where multiple instances of Outlook objects can be opened at any one time. All such classes follow a similar pattern:

1. Create a class that wraps the object of interest and that handles all events of interest fired by that object.

2. Create properties in the class for setting the object and a key property, plus any other properties that need to be set from outside the class or that need to be available to other code outside the class.

3. When an object of interest is opened, create a new instance of the class and populate its object and key properties, as well as any other properties that need to be set on class startup.

4. Add the new class instance to a collection that was declared with scope that keeps the collection alive for the duration of the application. This keeps the class alive as long as it's needed.

5. When the object is closed or no longer needed, release all internal class objects and use the Key property to remove the class from the collection, allowing the class to be released as it goes out of scope.

Contacts Wrapper Class for Mark as Task

Place the code for the contacts wrapper class shown in Listing 4.14 in the clsContactWrap class module created earlier in this chapter. An instance of this class is created whenever a contact is loaded by Outlook, in the Application_ItemLoad event handler. The Application_ItemLoad code is shown in Listing 4.6.

Listing 4.14

```
Private WithEvents m_oContact As Outlook.ContactItem
'handles contact events

Private m_Key As String
'the key lets us access this class in the collection

Public Property Let Contact(oContact As Outlook.ContactItem)
  Set m_oContact = oContact 'instantiate the contact
End Property

Public Property Get Contact() As Outlook.ContactItem
  Set Contact = m_oContact
End Property

Public Property Let Key(sKey As String)
  m_Key = sKey 'set the key
End Property

Public Property Get Key() As String
  Key = m_Key
End Property

'release module level objects and remove from wrapper collection
Public Sub Dispose()
  Set m_oContact = Nothing

  colContactWrapper.Remove m_Key
End Sub

Private Sub m_oContact_PropertyChange(ByVal Name As String)
  On Error Resume Next

  'if the Sensitivity property value is changing...
  If Name = "Sensitivity" Then
    With m_oContact
```

(continued)

Listing 4.14 *(continued)*

```
        If .Sensitivity = olPrivate Then
            'mark private items for follow up in the ToDo Bar
            'set as a ToDo for this week
            If Not .IsMarkedAsTask Then
                .MarkAsTask olMarkThisWeek
                .TaskSubject = "Follow up with this contact: " & .FullName
                .TaskStartDate = Date
                'due 7 days from now
                .TaskDueDate = DateAdd("d", 7, Date)
            End If
        Else
            'if no longer private mark as completed
            If .IsMarkedAsTask Then
                .TaskCompletedDate = Date
            End If
        End If
    End With
  End If
End Sub


'when the contact is unloaded from Outlook cache
Private Sub m_oContact_Unload()
    Call Dispose
End Sub
```

When a contact is loaded the following code is executed to create a new instance of the `clsContactWrap` class. The code then sets the `Contact` and `Key` properties of the class to the newly loaded contact and the current key value. The new class is then added to the `colContactWrapper` collection to keep the class alive while the contact remains loaded.

```
    Set clsContact = New clsContactWrap

    With clsContact
        .Contact = oContact
        .Key = CStr(g_lngID)
    End With

    'add the class to a collection to keep it alive
    colContactWrapper.Add clsContact, sKey
```

The class code in Listing 4.14 handles two contact events, `PropertyChange` and `Unload`. The `Unload` event handler is used the same way that the `Unload` handler is used in the email wrapper class code, to release the module-level `ContactItem` object and to remove that instance of the class from the `colContactWrapper` collection.

The `PropertyChange` event fires for any Outlook item when any built-in property is changed, such as changes to the `Subject` or `Body` of an item. User-defined properties fire the `CustomPropertyChange` event when any user-defined property value is changed.

The `PropertyChange` event passes the name of the property being changed to the event handler; in this case, the `Sensitivity` property is being monitored for changes. `Sensitivity` is the property that sets an item as Normal, Private, Personal, or Confidential to restrict access to the item in contexts where Outlook data is shared, such as Exchange server.

The code checks the `Name` property, which is passed as an argument to the event handler and which contains the name of the property being changed. If `Name = "Sensitivity"` the code checks to see if `Sensitivity` is being set as `Private`. If so, the new task properties that allow an item to be shown in the To-Do Bar are set.

```
    If Name = "Sensitivity" Then
       With m_oContact
          If .Sensitivity = olPrivate Then
             'mark private items for follow up in the ToDo Bar
             'set as a ToDo for this week
             If Not .IsMarkedAsTask Then
                .MarkAsTask olMarkThisWeek
                .TaskSubject = "Follow up with this contact: " & .FullName
                .TaskStartDate = Date
                'due 7 days from now
                .TaskDueDate = DateAdd("d", 7, Date)
             End If
```

The `IsMarkedAsTask` property is read to see if the item is already marked as a task. If not, the `MarkAsTask` property is set to `olMarkThisWeek`, which sets the flag used to display the item in the Next Week section of the To-Do Bar. A subject is set for the task, using the `ContactItem.FullName` property with an indication to follow up with this contact. The `TaskStartDate` property is set to 7 days from the current date, using the VBA `DateAdd` function to add 7 days to the current date.

The follow-up flagging is indicated in the InfoBar of the open contact, as shown in Figure 4.4.

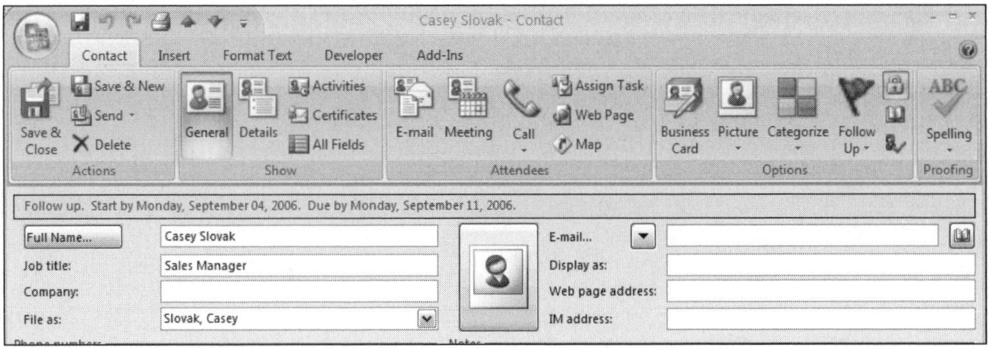

Figure 4.4

The new task properties set on the contact ensure that the follow-up is also shown in the To-Do Bar, as a follow-up to do in the next week, with a due date 1 week from the current date, as shown in Figure 4.5.

Figure 4.5

If `Sensitivity` is set to something other than `Private` (`olPrivate`) the contact is checked to see if it's marked as a task using the `IsMarkedAsTask` property, and if it is, the task is marked as complete with a completed date of the current date.

```
If .Sensitivity = olPrivate Then
Else
    'if no longer private mark as completed
    If .IsMarkedAsTask Then
        .TaskCompletedDate = Date
    End If
End If
```

When the task is marked as completed, the InfoBar in the open contact is changed to show the follow-up as completed, as shown in Figure 4.6. The completed task is automatically removed from the To-Do Bar list.

Figure 4.6

Macro Projects

The code in the next two sections of this chapter show how to work with the new `Rules` collection added to the Outlook 2007 object model. The code in Listing 4.15 shows how to use a macro to create a new rule, and the code in Listing 4.16 shows how to use a macro that runs automatically to create a context menu entry that creates a new rule.

Custom Rules

Creating custom rules looks very complex when you first look at the Rules object model. Custom rules aren't really that hard to understand, however; they follow the model used in the Rules Wizard:

1. Setting the rule as either a send or receive rule. Send rules run after an item is sent; receive rules run after an item is received. This is the same as using a blank template in the Rules Wizard and selecting the option to use a send or receive template.

2. One or more conditions used to test items to see if the rule should be run on them.

3. One or more actions to take if the item meets the rule condition or conditions, such as moving an item or playing a sound.

4. Zero or more exceptions that prevent the rule from running on a specific item based on the exception condition or conditions.

Each rule also has a name and can be enabled or disabled, and can be run on demand when needed.

Family Rule

The Family rule is a receive rule that looks at the sender of an email. If the email was sent by one of a group of specific people, the email is moved to a Family folder that's a subfolder of the Inbox. This rule has two exceptions: If the name "Irene" is used in the subject or text of the email or if the email if Low importance, the email isn't moved to the Family folder. If the Family folder doesn't exist, it's created as a subfolder of the Inbox.

Place the code in Listing 4.15 in the `Chapter_4` code module you created earlier in this chapter.

Listing 4.15

```
Public Sub CreateRule()
  Dim colRules As Outlook.Rules
  Dim oRule As Outlook.Rule
  Dim colActions As Outlook.RuleActions
  Dim oMoveAction As Outlook.MoveOrCopyRuleAction
  Dim oToCondition As Outlook.ToOrFromRuleCondition
  Dim oExceptImportance As Outlook.ImportanceRuleCondition
  Dim oExceptText As Outlook.TextRuleCondition
  Dim oInbox As Outlook.Folder
  Dim oTarget As Outlook.Folder
  Dim blnFound As Boolean

  On Error Resume Next

  Set oInbox = g_oNS.GetDefaultFolder(olFolderInbox)

  'See if target folder exists, create it if not
  Set oTarget = oInbox.Folders.Item("Family")
  If oTarget Is Nothing Then
    Set oTarget = oInbox.Folders.Add("Family", olFolderInbox)
  End If
```

(continued)

Listing 4.15 *(continued)*

```
'Get Rules collection from DefaultStore object
Set colRules = g_oNS.DefaultStore.GetRules()
blnFound = False
For Each oRule In colRules
  'check for the Family rule
  If oRule.Name = "Family" Then
    blnFound = True

    'if the rule already exists just make sure it's enabled.
    If Not oRule.Enabled Then
      oRule.Enabled = True
    End If
  End If
Next

If Not blnFound Then
  'Add a receive rule to Rules collection.
  'Rules are either send or receive rules.
  Set oRule = colRules.Create("Family", olRuleReceive)

  'Every rule has one or more conditions and one or more actions

  'Using a ToOrFromRuleCondition object
  Set oToCondition = oRule.Conditions.From
  With oToCondition
    .Enabled = True

    'sent to one of the following recipients
    .Recipients.Add "Ken Slovak"
    .Recipients.Add "Casey Slovak"

    .Recipients.ResolveAll
  End With

  'Using a MoveOrCopyRuleAction object
  Set oMoveAction = oRule.Actions.MoveToFolder
  With oMoveAction
    .Enabled = True
    .Folder = oTarget
  End With

  'A rule may have one or more exceptions.
  'Exception conditions are standard rule conditions.

  'Add rule exceptions:
  '1. Don't move if low importance.
  'or
  '2. body/subject contains specified text.

  'Using an ImportanceRuleCondition object
  Set oExceptImportance = oRule.Exceptions.Importance
  With oExceptImportance
    .Enabled = True
```

Listing 4.15 *(continued)*

```
        .Importance = olImportanceLow
    End With

    'Using a TextRuleCondition object
    Set oExceptText = oRule.Exceptions.BodyOrSubject
    With oExceptText
      .Enabled = True
      'condition words or phrases are in a comma separated array
      .Text = Array("Irene")
    End With
  End If

  'Save the new rule.
  colRules.Save

  'Uncomment this line to execute the rule after saving it.
  'oRule.Execute
End Sub
```

The first thing the code does is get a reference to the Inbox folder and check to see if the Family folder exists. If the folder doesn't exist, it's created.

```
Set oInbox = g_oNS.GetDefaultFolder(olFolderInbox)

'See if target folder exists, create it if not
Set oTarget = oInbox.Folders.Item("Family")
If oTarget Is Nothing Then
  Set oTarget = oInbox.Folders.Add("Family", olFolderInbox)
End If
```

Setting the target folder, `oTarget`, is done by using the `Folders` collection of the Inbox folder. Every folder has a `Folders` collection, holding all subfolders of that folder. If the Family folder doesn't exist, `oTarget` is `Nothing`, and an error is thrown. The `On Error Resume Next` statement at the beginning of the executable code in the macro allows code execution to continue, which enables you to test to see if the folder exists and to create the folder if not. If that error handler statement wasn't in the code, an error message would be displayed if Family doesn't already exist.

When you create a new folder you can only create folders of certain existing types. Those types are indicated with enumeration values named for the folder type. Using the value `olFolderInbox` doesn't create a new Inbox folder; that type is used for any email folder you create in code.

Every `Store` has a `Rules` collection. In this case you're working with incoming emails, so you're using the `Rules` collection of the `DefaultStore` object of the global `NameSpace` object.

```
Set colRules = g_oNS.DefaultStore.GetRules()
```

After you have a `Rules` collection, the code iterates through the collection to see if a `Rule` with the `Name` "Family" exists. If that `Rule` exists, the `Rule` is enabled; if the `Rule` doesn't exist, a flag is set so that the Rule is created.

```
   blnFound = False
For Each oRule In colRules
  'check for the Family rule
  If oRule.Name = "Family" Then
    blnFound = True

    'if the rule already exists just make sure it's enabled.
    If Not oRule.Enabled Then
      oRule.Enabled = True
    End If
  End If
Next
```

The `Create` method of the `Rules` collection is used to create a new `Rule` object. `Create` is called with the name of the new `Rule` and a value indicating if the `Rule` is a send or receive `Rule`.

```
If Not blnFound Then
  'Add a receive rule to Rules collection.
  'Rules are either send or receive rules.
  Set oRule = colRules.Create("Family", olRuleReceive)
```

The Family rule uses a `From RuleCondition` that's assigned to a `ToOrFromRuleCondition` `RuleCondition`. Not all conditions that are supported in the Rules Wizard are exposed in the `RuleConditions` object. Those conditions that are supported have defined `RuleCondition` properties available in the `RuleConditions` object.

Two recipients are added to the `ToOrFromRuleCondition` and then resolved. When multiple condition tests are added to a `RuleCondition` the tests are `OR`'d together. In this case, the condition is true if the sender of the email was Ken Slovak `OR` Casey Slovak.

```
    'Using a ToOrFromRuleCondition object
    Set oToCondition = oRule.Conditions.From
    With oToCondition
      .Enabled = True

      'sent to one of the following recipients
      .Recipients.Add "Ken Slovak"
      .Recipients.Add "Casey Slovak"

      .Recipients.ResolveAll
    End With
```

A `Rule` can have more than one `RuleCondition`. To add additional conditions to a `Rule`, declare one or more additional types and set their properties and enable the conditions. Multiple conditions are AND'd together, so all conditions must be true for the rule to be executed. If the rule exception for importance was added to the existing rule condition, the logic of the rule would be:

```
If the email ((was sent by (Ken Slovak OR Casey Slovak)) AND (the Importance is
Low)) then move the email to the Family folder.
'adding an additional condition
Set oExceptImportance = oRule.Conditions.Importance
```

The action for the Family rule is to move the email to a folder, the Family folder. A `MoveToFolder` action is added to the rule, and the target folder is set to `oTarget`. Multiple actions can be added to a rule, in which case the actions are all performed.

```
'Using a MoveOrCopyRuleAction object
Set oMoveAction = oRule.Actions.MoveToFolder
With oMoveAction
    .Enabled = True
    .Folder = oTarget
End With
```

The line `.Folder = oTarget` *illustrates a subtle distinction in Outlook syntax. No* `Set` *keyword is used to set the* `Folder` *object property to* `oTarget` *because you aren't instantiating an object reference; you are setting a property that's an object. In earlier versions of Outlook, this distinction wasn't always followed, so setting* `Explorer.CurrentFolder` *uses the* `Set` *keyword.*

Two exceptions are added to the rule:

1.   An Importance condition with its Importance property set to Low

2.   A `TextRuleCondition` that tests the contents of the `Subject` and `Body` of the email for the name "Irene"

```
'Add rule exceptions:
'1. Don't move if low importance.
'or
'2. body/subject contains specified text.

'Using an ImportanceRuleCondition object
Set oExceptImportance = oRule.Exceptions.Importance
With oExceptImportance
    .Enabled = True
    .Importance = olImportanceLow
End With

'Using a TextRuleCondition object
Set oExceptText = oRule.Exceptions.BodyOrSubject
With oExceptText
    .Enabled = True
    'condition words or phrases are in a comma separated array
    .Text = Array("Irene")
End With
End If
```

Every condition, action and exception for a rule must be enabled for that test to be applied by the rule. The rule itself can be enabled or disabled to determine whether or not the rule is run. Rules can be executed on demand by calling the `Execute` *method of the rule.*

Figure 4.7 shows the Rules Wizard dialog with the Family rule that was just created, with the Family subfolder of the Inbox shown in the Mail Folders section of the Navigation Pane.

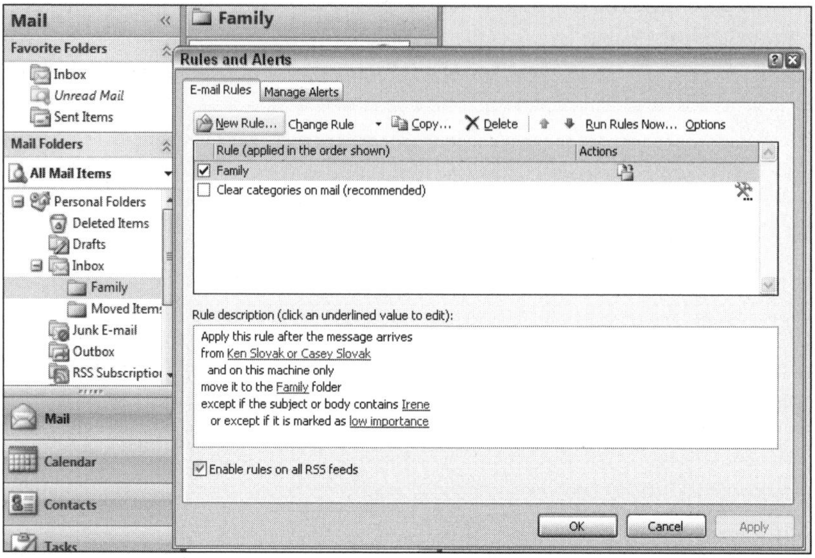

Figure 4.7

Context Menu Rule

The context menu rule is an example of creating a rule on the fly, using information received when a context menu is opened. The code for this rule also demonstrates how to add your own menu item to a context menu, in this case the `ItemContextMenu`, where a new context menu entry to categorize all emails from the sender as Business is created. The code is initiated by running the `ContextCategoryRule` macro created in Listing 4.2. If you added the line `Set cRule = New clsCategorizeRule` to the `Application_Startup` code in Listing 4.4, running the macro is unnecessary; the context menu item will display automatically when the `ItemContextMenu` displays.

```
'Initialize the Categorize Rule class
Public Sub ContextCategoryRule()
  Set cRule = New clsCategorizeRule
End Sub
```

Place the code in Listing 4.16 in the `clsCategorizeRule` class module you created earlier in this chapter.

Listing 4.16

```
'handles Click event
Private WithEvents oButton As Office.CommandBarButton

Private oBar As Office.CommandBar 'context menus are CommandBar objects

'handles context menu events
Private WithEvents oOL As Outlook.Application

Private m_sTag As String
Private m_EntryID As String
```

Listing 4.16 *(continued)*

```
Public Property Let Tag(sTag As String)
  m_sTag = sTag
End Property

Private Sub Class_Initialize()
  Set oOL = Application
End Sub

Private Sub Class_Terminate()
  'release module level objects
  Set oButton = Nothing
  Set oBar = Nothing
  Set oOL = Nothing
End Sub

'this is the meat, this event fires
'when our context menu item is clicked
Private Sub oButton_Click(ByVal Ctrl As Office.CommandBarButton, _
  CancelDefault As Boolean)

  Dim oMail As Outlook.MailItem
  Dim colRules As Outlook.Rules
  Dim oRule As Outlook.Rule
  Dim oRuleCondition As Outlook.AddressRuleCondition
  Dim oRuleAction As Outlook.AssignToCategoryRuleAction
  Dim colCategories As Outlook.Categories
  Dim oCategory As Outlook.Category
  Dim sName As String
  Dim sEmail As String
  Dim sCategories As String
  Dim aryEmail(0) As String
  Dim aryCategories(0) As String

  Set oMail = g_oNS.GetItemFromID(m_EntryID) 'get the context item
  If Not (oMail Is Nothing) Then
    sEmail = oMail.SenderEmailAddress 'get the sender address

    'name for the new rule we're creating
    sName = "Categorize " & sEmail & " as Business"

    'get the Categories collection
    Set colCategories = g_oNS.Categories
    'see if there's a "Business" category
    Set oCategory = colCategories.Item("Business")
    If (oCategory Is Nothing) Then 'if not, create it
      Set oCategory = colCategories.Item("Business")
      oCategory.Color = olCategoryColorLightTeal 'light teal color
    End If

    'get the Rules collection
    Set colRules = g_oNS.DefaultStore.GetRules
    'assume here the rule doesn't already exist.
    'we could iterate the Rules collection to verify that.
```

(continued)

Listing 4.16 *(continued)*

```vba
      'create new receive rule
      Set oRule = colRules.Create(sName, olRuleReceive)

      'rule condition: sender email address
      aryEmail(0) = sEmail
      Set oRuleCondition = oRule.Conditions.SenderAddress
      With oRuleCondition
        .Enabled = True 'enable the condition
        .Address = aryEmail 'this takes an array of email addresses
      End With

      'rule action: assign to one or more categories
      aryCategories(0) = "Business"
      Set oRuleAction = oRule.Actions.AssignToCategory
      With oRuleAction
        .Enabled = True 'enable the action
        .Categories = aryCategories 'takes an array of categories
      End With

      colRules.Save 'save the rule

      'to run the rule immediately
      'oRule.Execute
    End If

    Set oMail = Nothing
    Set colRules = Nothing
    Set oRule = Nothing
    Set oRuleCondition = Nothing
    Set oRuleAction = Nothing
    Set colCategories = Nothing
    Set oCategory = Nothing
End Sub

'fires when any context menu is closed
Private Sub oOL_ContextMenuClose(ByVal ContextMenu As OlContextMenu)
  Dim oControl As Office.CommandBarControl

  'look for the Item context menu
  If ContextMenu = olItemContextMenu Then
    If Not (oBar Is Nothing) Then
      'find our control (menu item) and delete it if it exists
      Set oControl = oBar.FindControl(msoControlButton, , _
        "BusinessCategoryRule")

      If Not (oControl Is Nothing) Then
        oControl.Delete
        Set oButton = Nothing
        Set oBar = Nothing
      End If
    End If
  End If

  Set oControl = Nothing
End Sub
```

Listing 4.16 *(continued)*

```
'fires when the Item context menu is opened
Private Sub oOL_ItemContextMenuDisplay(ByVal _
  CommandBar As Office.CommandBar, ByVal Selection As Selection)

  Dim strCaption As String
  Dim strTag As String

  'only if 1 mail item is selected
  If (Selection.Count = 1) And _
    (Selection.Item(1).Class = olMail) Then

    'get the GUID for the selected item,
    'store it for the Click event handler
    m_EntryID = Selection.Item(1).EntryID

    strCaption = "Categorize all emails from this sender as Business"
    strTag = "BusinessCategoryRule" 'tags should be unique

    'create the button (menu item)
    Set oButton = CommandBar.Controls.Add(msoControlButton, , , , True)
    With oButton
      .Caption = strCaption
      .Tag = strTag
      .BeginGroup = True 'add a menu separator
    End With

    Set oBar = CommandBar
  End If
End Sub
```

A menu item on any Outlook folder menu is a CommandBarControl. Menus are CommandBar objects and are members of the CommandBars collection. In previous versions of Outlook, the menus for Explorers and Inspectors both follow this model, where the CommandBars collection is exposed as a part of the Office library and CommandBar objects are accessed as properties of the Explorer or Inspector objects.

This still applies with Outlook 2007, but in Outlook 2007 Inspector CommandBar objects and controls are relegated to the Add-Ins tab in the new Ribbon interface. The Ribbon can't be programmed using Outlook VBA; programming the Ribbon requires using a COM addin. Ribbon programming is covered in the chapters on COM addins.

The following code lines in Listing 4.16 declare WithEvents a CommandBarButton object that will be your context menu item. This enables the oButton object to handle the Click event that fires when the menu item is clicked. The code also declares a CommandBar object, which is used to hold a reference to the ItemContextMenu.

```
'handles Click event
Private WithEvents oButton As Office.CommandBarButton

Private oBar As Office.CommandBar 'context menus are CommandBar objects
```

When the context menu is displayed, which happens for the ItemContextMenu when any item is right-clicked in an Outlook folder view (Explorer), the ItemContextMenuDisplay event handler is executed.

The `Selection` collection passed in the `ItemContextMenuDisplay` procedure is checked to see if only one item is selected. If so, the code adds a new menu item, a `CommandBarButton`, to the context menu:

```
Set oButton = CommandBar.Controls.Add(msoControlButton, , , , True)
```

The code also sets a module-level variable, `m_EntryID`, to save the `GUID` of the selected item. The selection is not available in the button click event handler, so it's saved for future use when the context menu is opened. The custom menu item is shown in Figure 4.8.

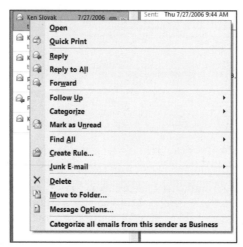

Figure 4.8

When the menu item is clicked, the `oButton_Click` event handler procedure is called, which creates a new rule based on the email address of the sender of the selected email.

```
sEmail = oMail.SenderEmailAddress 'get the sender address

'name for the new rule we're creating
sName = "Categorize " & sEmail & " as Business"
```

The `Categories` collection of the `NameSpace` object is checked to see if there's already a "Business" category, and if not, the `Category` is created. The `Category.Color` property is set to light teal.

```
'get the Categories collection
Set colCategories = g_oNS.Categories
'see if there's a "Business" category
Set oCategory = colCategories.Item("Business")
If (oCategory Is Nothing) Then 'if not, create it
  Set oCategory = colCategories.Item("Business")
  oCategory.Color = olCategoryColorLightTeal light teal color
End If
```

The code then creates a new receive `Rule` (no checking is done to see if the `Rule` already exists) with a `SenderAddress Condition` that the sender email address is the same as the email address of the selected email. The `Rule Action` is to assign the new Business `Category` to the email.

```
'get the Rules collection
Set colRules = g_oNS.DefaultStore.GetRules
'assume here the rule doesn't already exist.
'we could iterate the Rules collection to verify that.
'create new receive rule
Set oRule = colRules.Create(sName, olRuleReceive)

'rule condition: sender email address
aryEmail(0) = sEmail
Set oRuleCondition = oRule.Conditions.SenderAddress
With oRuleCondition
  .Enabled = True 'enable the condition
  .Address = aryEmail 'this takes an array of email addresses
End With

'rule action: assign to one or more categories
aryCategories(0) = "Business"
Set oRuleAction = oRule.Actions.AssignToCategory
With oRuleAction
  .Enabled = True 'enable the action
  .Categories = aryCategories 'takes an array of categories
End With
```

The SenderAddress property takes an array of email addresses. In this case, only one email address is being tested; a larger array would be used if more than one address were being tested. The AssignToCategory Action also takes an array as its Categories property that allows the rule to assign more than one category to the item if desired.

An enhancement to this rule could check to see if the sender is in the user's contacts, and if so, add all the sender's email addresses to the SenderAddress property by setting up a larger array for the aryEmail variable.

The results of creating this Rule are shown in Figure 4.9, which shows the Categorized Mail search folder with the new Business category in its teal color.

Figure 4.9

Additional Macros

The macros in this section of the chapter show additional uses for the Accounts collection, an example of working with the Table object and the hidden All Tasks folder, and how to create search folders from AdvancedSearch objects.

Check for Existing Contact

The code in Listing 4.17 demonstrates using the Accounts collection and Account objects to determine if an email was sent to someone who is in a contacts list or Exchange Global Address List. Place this code in the Chapter_4 code module, and select an email and run the macro to test this code.

Listing 4.17

```
Public Sub IsExistingContact()
  Dim oMail As Outlook.MailItem
  Dim oAE As Outlook.AddressEntry
  Dim oContact As Outlook.ContactItem
  Dim oRecip As Outlook.Recipient
  Dim colAccounts As Outlook.Accounts
  Dim oAccount As Outlook.Account
  Dim oEXUser As Outlook.ExchangeUser
  Dim blnExchange As Boolean

  'get a selected mail item, no error checking for item type
  Set oMail = Application.ActiveExplorer.Selection.Item(1)
  'get first recipient
  Set oRecip = oMail.Recipients.Item(1)
  'get AddressEntry object from Recipient
  Set oAE = oRecip.AddressEntry
  'get contact from AddressEntry
  'this will not return an entry in the GAL or a DL
  Set oContact = oAE.GetContact

  If oContact Is Nothing Then
    'see if it's an entry in the GAL
    Set colAccounts = g_oNS.Accounts
    For Each oAccount In colAccounts
      If oAccount.AccountType = olExchange Then
        'see if Exchange is being used
        blnExchange = True
        Exit For
      End If
    Next

    If blnExchange Then 'if Exchange used
      Set oEXUser = oAE.GetExchangeUser 'get the GAL entry
      If Not (oEXUser Is Nothing) Then
        'if the GAL entry exists show it
        oEXUser.Details
      Else
        'not a contact or GAL entry
        MsgBox "Not a contact or GAL entry", vbOKOnly + vbInformation
      End If
```

Listing 4.17 *(continued)*

```
    Else
        'not a contact or GAL entry
        MsgBox "Not a contact or GAL entry", vbOKOnly + vbInformation
    End If
Else
    oContact.Display 'show the contact item
End If

Set oMail = Nothing
Set oAE = Nothing
Set oContact = Nothing
Set oRecip = Nothing
End Sub
```

The code first sets a `MailItem` object from the first item in the `Selection` collection of the `ActiveExplorer`. This is the `Explorer` that is currently displaying an Outlook folder. If more than one item is selected, only the first item in the `Selection` collection is used for this code. No error checking is performed to make sure the item is an email item.

```
Set oMail = Application.ActiveExplorer.Selection.Item(1)
'get first recipient
Set oRecip = oMail.Recipients.Item(1)
```

The code then gets the first `Recipient` of the email from the `Recipients` collection. Each `Recipient` object has an `AddressEntry` property that represents an entry in an Outlook `AddressList`. Outlook `AddressLists` can be Contacts folders, the Exchange Global Address List if you are using Exchange server, and `AddressLists` returned using LDAP queries.

The new `AddressEntry.GetContact` method is used to return a `ContactItem` object from the `AddressEntry`:

```
'get first recipient
Set oRecip = oMail.Recipients.Item(1)
'get AddressEntry object from Recipient
Set oAE = oRecip.AddressEntry
'get contact from AddressEntry
'this will not return an entry in the GAL or a DL
Set oContact = oAE.GetContact
```

If the `AddressEntry` isn't in a Contacts list, the `oContact` object is `Nothing` and the code then checks to see if the user is using Exchange server. The `Accounts` collection is iterated and each `Account` is examined to see if the `AccountType` is `olExchange`, indicating that an Exchange account is present.

```
Set colAccounts = g_oNS.Accounts
For Each oAccount In colAccounts
    If oAccount.AccountType = olExchange Then
        'see if Exchange is being used
        blnExchange = True
        Exit For
    End If
Next
```

If Exchange was found as an `AccountType`, an `ExchangeUser` object is instantiated from the `AddressEntry` `.ExchangeUser` property. The `Details` method of the `ExchangeUser` property is called to display the Global Address List properties of the `ExchangeUser` represented by the recipient of the email.

```
Set oEXUser = oAE.GetExchangeUser 'get the GAL entry
If Not (oEXUser Is Nothing) Then
  'if the GAL entry exists show it
  oEXUser.Details
```

If a `ContactItem` was found as the recipient of the email, the contact is displayed.

Check Today's To-Do List

The `GetTodaysToDoList` code scans the hidden All Tasks folder that's used to populate the To-Do Bar and lists all tasks due today in the `ToDoForm`, you created earlier in this chapter. This macro uses the new `Table` object exposed by the hidden All Tasks folder to quickly scan the folder and return only tasks due today.

Place the code for Listing 4.18 in the `Chapter_4` code module and run it to display today's to-do list.

Listing 4.18

```
Public Sub GetTodaysToDoList()
  Dim oStore As Outlook.Store
  Dim oFolder As Outlook.Folder
  Dim oTable As Outlook.Table
  Dim FilteredTable As Outlook.Table
  Dim colColumns As Outlook.Columns
  Dim oColumn As Outlook.Column
  Dim oRow As Outlook.Row
  Dim strFilter As String
  Dim aryValues() As Variant
  Dim i As Long

  'DueDate
  strFilter = "http://schemas.microsoft.com/mapi/id/"

  strFilter = strFilter & _
    "{00062003-0000-0000-C000-000000000046}/81050040"

  'using the "@SQL=" syntax for the table filter
  strFilter = "@SQL=" & Chr(34) & strFilter & Chr(34) _
    & " = '" & Format(Date, "General Date") & "'"

  Set oStore = g_oNS.DefaultStore

  'get the hidden folder used for the ToDo Bar
  Set oFolder = oStore.GetSpecialFolder(olSpecialFolderAllTasks)

  Set oTable = oFolder.GetTable 'Table for the ToDo Bar folder
  Set FilteredTable = oTable.Restrict(strFilter) 'filter for due today
```

Listing 4.18 (continued)

```vba
    If FilteredTable.EndOfTable Then
      MsgBox "Nothing to do today, a good day for fishing!", _
        vbInformation + vbOKOnly
    Else
      i = 0

      Set colColumns = FilteredTable.Columns
      With colColumns
        'remove default columns and add our own.
        'EntryID and Subject would be there as default columns
        .RemoveAll
        Set oColumn = .Add("Subject")
        Set oColumn = .Add("EntryID")

        'if this was not a named property we would have to convert
        ' from UTC to local time using the Row.UTCToLocalTime method
        Set oColumn = .Add("DueDate")
      End With

      ToDoForm.lstToDo.Clear 'clear the ToDo list ListBox control

      Do While Not (FilteredTable.EndOfTable)
        Set oRow = FilteredTable.GetNextRow 'get a row
        aryValues = oRow.GetValues 'get the 3 values we asked for

        With ToDoForm.lstToDo
          'add a new row to the list and add 3 columns of data
          .AddItem
          .Column(0, i) = aryValues(0) 'Subject
          .Column(1, i) = aryValues(2) 'DueDate
          .Column(2, i) = aryValues(1) 'EntryID
        End With

        i = i + 1
      Loop

      ToDoForm.Show vbModal
    End If

    Set oStore = Nothing
    Set oFolder = Nothing
    Set oTable = Nothing
    Set FilteredTable = Nothing
    Set colColumns = Nothing
    Set oColumn = Nothing
    Set oRow = Nothing
  End Sub
```

The filter used to return only tasks due today is constructed using the property tag `"http://schemas .microsoft.com/mapi/id/{00062003-0000-0000-C000-000000000046}/81050040"`, which is the

`DueDate` of a task. The filter uses the `"@SQL="` syntax to compare the `DueDate` property for each item in the `Table` for the folder with the date today.

```
strFilter = "@SQL=" & Chr(34) & strFilter & Chr(34) _
    & " = '" & Format(Date, "General Date") & "'"
```

A `Store` object is instantiated from the `NameSpace.DefaultStore` and the hidden All Tasks folder is instantiated as a `Folder` object using the `GetSpecialFolder` method of the `Store` object. This method enables you to get references to the All Tasks folder and the Reminders folder. Both folders are special search folders that are hidden in the Outlook user interface. The `Folder`'s `Table` is returned by the `GetTable` method used to get the `Table` for any folder.

```
Set oStore = g_oNS.DefaultStore

'get the hidden folder used for the ToDo Bar
Set oFolder = oStore.GetSpecialFolder(olSpecialFolderAllTasks)

Set oTable = oFolder.GetTable 'Table for the ToDo Bar folder
Set FilteredTable = oTable.Restrict(strFilter) 'filter for due today
```

After the filter is applied as a `Table.Restrict` clause, the only available rows in the `Table` will be rows that match the filter condition.

The `Table.Columns` collection normally contains default columns representing commonly used properties such as `EntryID`. In this case, the default columns are cleared using the `RemoveAll` method and three new columns are added to the `Table` for `Subject`, `EntryID`, and `DueDate`. If `DueDate` were not a named property the date would have to be converted from UTC time into local time using the `Row.UTCToLocalTime` method. A corresponding `Row.LocalTimeToUTC` method is available to convert UTC time to local time for properties that don't get automatically converted by Outlook into local time. Under the hood, all times are stored by Outlook and MAPI as UTC time values.

```
Set colColumns = FilteredTable.Columns
With colColumns
   'remove default columns and add our own.
   'EntryID and Subject would be there as default columns
   .RemoveAll
   Set oColumn = .Add("Subject")
   Set oColumn = .Add("EntryID")

   'if this was not a named property we would have to convert
   ' from UTC to local time using the Row.UTCToLocalTime method
   Set oColumn = .Add("DueDate")
End With
```

After the table filter and columns are set up, the code checks to make sure that something was returned by evaluating the `Table.EndOfTable` property. If that property is false the code reads each row in turn using the `GetNextRow` method into a `Row` variable. The columns in the row are put into a multi-column `listbox` control that displays the `Subject` and `DueDate` and hides the `EntryID` property. If a `Row` is double-clicked, the code opens that item for review.

```
Do While Not (FilteredTable.EndOfTable)
   Set oRow = FilteredTable.GetNextRow 'get a row
```

```
    aryValues = oRow.GetValues 'get the 3 values we asked for

    With ToDoForm.lstToDo
      'add a new row to the list and add 3 columns of data
      .AddItem
      .Column(0, i) = aryValues(0) 'Subject
      .Column(1, i) = aryValues(2) 'DueDate
      .Column(2, i) = aryValues(1) 'EntryID
```

Incomplete Tasks Search Folder

Place the code in Listing 4.19 in the Chapter_4 code module and run it as a macro to create a search folder that aggregates all items marked as tasks that aren't marked as complete. This code is very similar to the code in Listing 4.8; the difference is this code saves the completed search as a search folder, visible and usable in the user interface.

Listing 4.19

```vba
Sub CreateIncompleteTasksSearchFolder()
    Dim objSch As Outlook.Search
    Dim strFilter As String
    Dim strScope As String
    Dim strTag As String
    Dim Completed As String

    'task complete
    Completed = "http://schemas.microsoft.com/mapi/id/"

    Completed = Completed & _
        "{00062003-0000-0000-C000-000000000046}/811C000B"

    strFilter = Completed & " = 'False'"

  'Scope is entire store, either Personal Folders or Exchange mailbox.

  'Uncomment the following lines as appropriate for the store type

    strScope = "'//Personal Folders'"
    'strScope = "'//Mailbox - Casey Slovak'"

    strTag = "notcompleted"

    Set objSch = Application.AdvancedSearch(Scope:=strScope, _
      Filter:=strFilter, SearchSubFolders:=True, Tag:=strTag)

    If objSch Is Nothing Then
      MsgBox "Sorry, the search folder could not be created."
    End If

  'Saving this search creates a new search folder
    objSch.Save "Uncompleted Tasks"

    Set objSch = Nothing
End Sub
```

The property tag `"http://schemas.microsoft.com/mapi/id/{00062003-0000-0000-C000-000000000046}/811C000B"` is used for the `Complete` property. This is done because the `Complete` property isn't exposed in the Outlook object model for items that aren't `TaskItems`.

Make sure to change the scope string in Listing 4.19 to the name of your Exchange mailbox or PST file as shown in the Outlook user interface for this code to work.

To create a search folder from a completed `AdvancedSearch`, save the search with the name to use for the search folder:

```
objSch.Save "Uncompleted Tasks"
```

Overdue Tasks Search Folder

Place the code in Listing 4.20 in the `Chapter_4` code module, and run it as a macro to create a search folder that aggregates all overdue tasks in the default Tasks folder and its subfolders into a search folder named Overdue Tasks.

Listing 4.20

```
Sub CreateOverdueTasksSearchFolder()
  Dim objSch As Outlook.Search
  Dim strFilter As String
  Dim strScope As String
  Dim strTag As String

  'task due date
  Const DueDate As String = _
    "http://schemas.microsoft.com/mapi/id/{00062003-0000-0000-C000-000000000046}/81050040"

  'Create a folder that shows all tasks due and overdue
  strFilter = DueDate & " <= 'today'"

  'Scope is Tasks folder and any subfolders
  strScope = "Tasks"

  strTag = "RecurSearch"

  Set objSch = Application.AdvancedSearch(Scope:=strScope, Filter:=strFilter, _
    SearchSubFolders:=True, Tag:=strTag)

  If objSch Is Nothing Then
    MsgBox "Sorry, the search folder could not be created."
  End If

  'Saving this search creates a new search folder
  objSch.Save "Overdue Tasks"

  Set objsearch = Nothing
End Sub
```

The property tag `"http://schemas.microsoft.com/mapi/id/{00062003-0000-0000-C000-000000000046}/81050040"` is used for the `DueDate` property.

The TaskItem.DueDate *property doesn't have a time component. Any search filter or restriction using* DueDate *should always strip out the time component of the filter data to ensure that the filter works as intended.*

Importance Search Folder

Place the code in Listing 4.21 in the Chapter_4 code module, and run it as a macro to create a search folder named High that finds all items marked as High Importance in the Inbox and Sent Items folders and their subfolders.

Listing 4.21

```
Sub CreateImportanceSearchFolder()
    Dim objSch As Outlook.Search
    Dim strFilter As String
    Dim strScope As String
    Dim strTag As String

    'item Importance
    strFilter = "urn:schemas:httpmail:importance"

    strFilter = strFilter & " = '2'" ' OlImportanceHigh

    'Scope is Inbox and Sent Items folders and subfolders of those folders
    strScope = "'Inbox', 'Sent Items'"

    strTag = "High"

    Set objSch = Application.AdvancedSearch(Scope:=strScope, Filter:=strFilter, _
        SearchSubFolders:=True, Tag:=strTag)

    If objSch Is Nothing Then
        MsgBox "Sorry, the search folder could not be created."
    End If

    'Saving this search creates a new search folder
    objSch.Save "High" 'Change search folder name to what you want

    Set objSch = Nothing
End Sub
```

The property tag "urn:schemas:httpmail:importance" is used for the Importance property.

Most Outlook items have an Importance *property. Changing the search scope to the name of your Exchange mailbox or PST file populates the search folder with Outlook items of every type that have* Importance *set to* OlImportanceHigh.

Overdue Reminders Search Folder

Place the code in Listing 4.22 in the Chapter_4 code module, and run it as a macro to create a search folder named Overdue that finds all items with overdue reminders.

Listing 4.22

```
Sub CreateOverdueRemindersSearchFolder()
  Dim objSch As Outlook.Search
  Dim strFilter As String
  Dim strScope As String
  Dim strTag As String

  'reminder time
  Const ReminderTime As String = "urn:schemas:calendar:remindernexttime"

  strFilter = ReminderTime & " < 'today'"

  'Scope is entire store, either Personal Folders or Exchange mailbox.

  'Uncomment the following lines as appropriate for the store type

  strScope = "'//Personal Folders'"
  'strScope = "'//Mailbox - Casey Slovak'"

  strTag = "overduereminders"

  Set cSearch = New clsSearch
  cSearch.Tag = strTag

  Set objSch = Application.AdvancedSearch(Scope:=strScope, Filter:=strFilter, _
    SearchSubFolders:=True, Tag:=strTag)

  'Saving this search creates a new search folder
  objSch.Save "Overdue" 'Change search folder name to what you want

  Set objSch = Nothing
End Sub
```

The property tag `"urn:schemas:calendar:remindernexttime"` is used for the `ReminderSet` property. The code finds items of every Outlook type that supports reminders.

> *Make sure to change the scope string in Listing 4.22 to the name of your Exchange mailbox or PST file as shown in the Outlook user interface for this code to work.*

Running and Distributing Macros

In this section, you learn the various ways that Outlook macros can be run, and how to distribute Outlook macros and the VBA project.

Running Macros

There are three ways to manually run a macro in the Outlook VBA project:

1. Select the macro in the Macros dialog, as shown in Figure 4.1, and click the Run button in the Macros dialog.

2. Open the Outlook VBA project, find the macro in your VBA code, place your cursor in the macro procedure, and click the Run icon or press F5.

3. Put the macro on an Outlook toolbar or menu line and use the button to run the macro.

To put the macro on a button in a toolbar or menu line, right-click a toolbar or menu line and select Customize. In the Customize dialog, select the Commands tab and select Macros in the left-hand list. Scroll the right-hand list down to find your macro, and use the mouse to drag it to the toolbar or menu line where you want the button to appear.

Figure 4.10 shows a macro placed on the Menu Bar line, to the right of the Help menu. While in Customize mode you can right-click the new macro button, select Name, and rename the button to something meaningful.

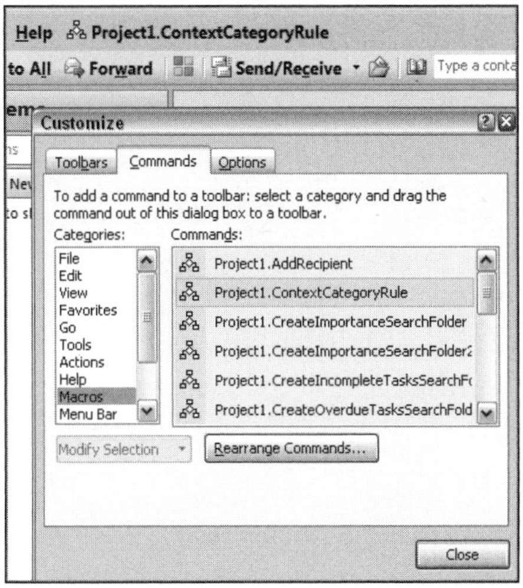

Figure 4.10

In general, it's a good rule to only add macros you run frequently to the existing toolbars or menu line.

Distributing the VBA Project

Distributing a VBA project to other people is an exercise in overwriting any existing macros the people may have. You have to send the other people your VBAProject.OTM file, and they have to replace any existing VBA file they have with the distributed VBAProject.OTM file while Outlook isn't running. This automatically wipes out any existing macros the people have in their old VBA project.

The usual path to the OTM file is hidden by default in Windows and may not be available even if hidden files and folders are set to be visible in Windows Explorer because of user permissions.

VBA projects are intended to be personal code, used for macros or prototyping, not for distribution. A far better solution is to prototype your code in VBA, then write a COM addin that encapsulates your functionality and distribute the COM addin to other people. This also has the advantage of avoiding problems with macro security settings and signing macro code. The certificate generated by the Selfcert utility is not traceable back to a verified signing authority, so usually that certificate cannot be trusted on a different computer than the one you used to generate the certificate.

Distributing Individual Macros

You can distribute individual macros by putting the macro code in a code module and exporting the code module, using the File menu's Export function. The resulting exported code module is a file with an extension of .BAS, which can be opened in Outlook VBA using the File, Import menu function. The code module file can also be opened directly in VB 6.

This is certainly not an automated process; the sender has to export the macro code and transfer it to the recipient, and the recipient has to import the .BAS file into his or her VBA project, but at least the process can be done and it doesn't overwrite any existing macros the user might have.

Summary

In this chapter, you learned more about Outlook VBA code and creating and running macros in Outlook. Macros in this chapter work with:

- ❑ The `Rules` collection
- ❑ Application-wide events
- ❑ `UserForms`
- ❑ Classes and user-created events
- ❑ Wrapper classes
- ❑ Context menus

In the next chapter, you will learn about customizing Outlook forms and how to add form regions to forms.

Outlook Forms

The forms Outlook uses to show open items can be customized by adding controls and code. You often use custom form applications for things such as Help Desk tickets, routing of approval or review forms, and human resources forms. These custom forms and form applications were the only way of providing a custom user interface for Outlook items until Outlook 2007. Form regions are a new way to customize an item's user interface and provide opportunities for customization that aren't available with standard custom forms.

No investment was made in new features for custom forms in Outlook 2007, and none has been made for many versions of Outlook. Microsoft is encouraging forms development for Outlook 2007 to concentrate on using form regions. Of course, this approach works only if every user is running Outlook 2007 and won't work if the forms are used with earlier versions of Outlook.

In this chapter, you learn how to customize Outlook forms, and the advantages and disadvantages of using custom forms. You also learn about form regions and how to design and use them.

> *A complete discussion of Outlook custom forms is a big topic that can take up an entire book, so only the basics of custom forms are covered in this chapter. For more information about designing and working with custom forms and lots of information about various problems and solutions for custom forms, I recommend looking at the material at* www.outlookcode.com/d/forms.htm.

Working with Standard Forms

All Outlook items have a `MessageClass` property that determines what type of object the item is: contact, appointment, task, email, post, journal entry, or variations of those basic types. Note items aren't included. They can't be customized and, more often than not, attempting to work with them in code causes the item or Outlook to crash.

All Outlook forms have a `MessageClass` that starts with "IPM," which stands for Inter-Personal Message. The standard Outlook form types are all derived from that basic building block, such as `IPM.Appointment` for appointment forms and `IPM.Activity` for journal entry forms. When you customize an Outlook form it's published as a derived `MessageClass`, such as `IPM.Contact.MyContactForm`.

The only way to create a completely new `MessageClass` derived from the "IPM" base class is to use Extended MAPI and C++ or Delphi. You cannot create a new `MessageClass` with the Outlook object model.

Forms Libraries

Standard forms are stored in the Standard Forms Library. To choose a form for customization, select Tools ➪ Forms ➪ Design a Form and choose a form from the Standard Forms Library in the Look In drop-down, as shown in Figure 5-1.

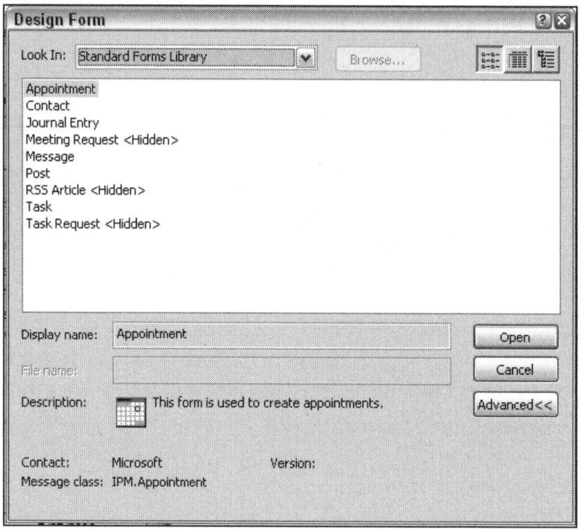

Figure 5-1

To open an Outlook template stored in the file system as an OFT (Outlook form template) file, select User Templates in the File System in the Look In drop-down; then click the Browse button to navigate to where the OFT file is stored.

> *The previous alternate method of opening OFT files by double-clicking them in Windows Explorer does not work with Outlook 2007 in most cases. This change was made by Microsoft for security reasons. Form code won't run in OFT files, also for security reason. Form code only runs in published forms. The only OFT files that can be opened from the file system are those with no custom controls and no code, a very small subset of all custom forms.*

OFT files are a good way to distribute forms that will be published using code. OFT files are also a good way to transfer custom forms so they can be designed on different computers.

Published Forms

Publishing a form saves the form in one of the Outlook forms repositories with the custom `MessageClass` you supply. It also enables the form to run code and makes the form available to anyone who has access to the location where the form is published. The following forms repositories are available by default:

- ❑ Standard Forms Library
- ❑ Organizational Forms Library
- ❑ Personal Forms Library
- ❑ Outlook Folders
- ❑ Standard Templates
- ❑ User Templates in File System
- ❑ List of Outlook Folders

The Organizational Forms Library is only available if you are using Exchange server.

To open previously published forms for design, select the Personal Forms Library (or other location where the form was published) in the Look In drop-down of the Design Form dialog shown in Figure 5-1.

Form Customization

The following table lists the standard forms that are available for customization in the Standard Forms Library, their `MessageClass` and whether you can customize their default pages.

Form	MessageClass	Customize Default Pages
Appointment	IPM.Appointment	No
Contact	IPM.Contact	General tab only
Journal Entry	IPM.Activity	No
Meeting Request (Hidden)	IPM.Schedule.Meeting.Request	No
Message	IPM.Note	Yes
Post	IPM.Post	Yes
RSS Article (Hidden)	IPM.Post.Rss	No
Task	IPM.Task	No
Task Request (Hidden)	IPM.TaskRequest	No

Forms have five pages available for customization, named P.2 to P.6. Some form types also allow you to customize one or more of the default pages, as indicated by the previous table. A form page that is available for customization is a design surface, a place to put controls for data input or display. The standard controls used on a form belong to the MS Forms 2.0 library, listed as MSForms in the Outlook VBA project references. You can also place Active X controls on a form page, although many Active X controls do not run correctly when placed on a form. The only way to tell if a specific Active X control will work on a form is to try it. .NET Windows Forms controls can't be used as controls on a form page.

All customization for a form is stored in the `FormDesign` property for that `MessageClass`, a binary property that contains any controls, customization instructions and settings, and form code. Form code is only written using VBScript, no other language can be used, including any of the other scripting languages such as JavaScript.

> *In previous versions of Outlook, you could place an open form into design mode by selecting Tools ⇨ Forms ⇨ Design This Form. To display this option in the Outlook 2007 Ribbon, the Developer tab must be enabled. To enable the Developer tab select the Office menu in an open item and click the Editor Options button. Check the Show Developer tab in the Ribbon to enable the tab in all Office applications.*

Custom forms don't show the new controls added to Outlook forms, such as the new time zone controls in appointments or the picture control that was added to Outlook contact forms in Outlook 2003. Custom forms also do not use any Windows theming, making custom form pages look different from standard forms or form pages. What you see on a form page that can be customized is what that form type looked like in Outlook 2002, with none of the later form features added to the form.

Advantages and Disadvantages of Custom Forms

Custom forms are the only way to customize the form user interface other than form regions with Outlook 2007. However, they are old technology that hasn't been updated very much since the early days of Outlook, and custom forms aren't the most robust solution possible, being prone to various forms of corruption.

Advantages of Custom Forms

The following list shows some of the advantages of using custom forms for Outlook solutions:

❑ Custom forms are the only way to customize the user interface for Outlook items that's compatible with all versions of Outlook. Form regions are only usable for Outlook 2007, and InfoPath forms are only usable for Outlook 2003 and 2007.

❑ Custom forms can use Active X controls to display data from other applications, such as data retrieved from a database and displayed in a grid control in the Outlook form.

❑ Form customizations integrate with standard forms. Other technologies, such as forms displayed from menu or Ribbon commands are separate forms and are not integrated into the item user interface.

❑ Individual custom forms are very small in size, the bulk of the form design is stored in the forms cache and the published form, so complex forms can take up very little space in an Outlook store.

❑ Custom forms can be made the default forms for folders, automatically opening or being used in those folders for all items.

❑ Custom forms can be set to open as the standard form for a default `MessageClass` using a registry setting, allowing you to substitute a custom form for all standard forms of the replaced `MessageClass`. An example is a custom contact form that is set to be the default contact form used by an organization in Outlook.

Disadvantages of Custom Forms

The following list shows some of the disadvantages of using custom forms for Outlook solutions:

❑ When you first open a custom form, the form design is stored in the forms cache. Whenever you open a new form of that `MessageClass`, the form design is subsequently retrieved from the forms cache. This saves bandwidth and time for forms published on a server, such as forms published in the Organizational Forms Library. However, the forms cache is prone to corruption when a previous version of a form is used instead of the latest version, or the default form for the base class of the custom `MessageClass` is used instead of the custom `MessagClass`.

❑ Custom forms can become one-offed, with the form design embedded in the form instead of coming from the forms cache or forms library. One-offed forms cannot run code, and because the form design is embedded in the item, are much larger than forms where the form design is not embedded in the item. One-offed forms don't use any revisions to the form; they always use the embedded form design.

❑ You can only view custom forms in Outlook, and sending them over the Internet can be problematical. The forms description for the custom form is sent using Rich Text, encapsulated in what Microsoft calls Transport Neutral Encapsulation Format (TNEF). If a custom form is sent using plain text or HTML, the form description is not transmitted and the form arrives as a standard item of that base type. Sending using Rich Text is dependent on Outlook global settings, settings on the Exchange server if one is used, and individual settings for sending to that contact. Many things can go wrong to prevent a form from being transmitted correctly over the Internet. When the form isn't transmitted correctly, the recipient receives a standard form, which may or may not be accompanied by an attached `Winmail.dat` file that holds the TNEF component of the form. The `Winmail.dat` attachment is usually hidden and used to reconstruct the custom form.

❑ Custom forms sent to others won't display correctly, and any code they contain won't run, unless the form is published and the published form is accessible to the recipient.

❑ Care must be taken when publishing custom forms to always mark changes using the `Version` property; otherwise, the forms cache will become corrupted, and old versions of the form will be used. Care must also be taken to ensure that a form is published to only one forms repository. Publishing a form to multiple places is another recipe for forms cache corruption.

❑ Forms can become unstable if you add too many controls to a custom form. How many controls is too many depends on what version of Outlook you use to open a form, and whether or not you're using Exchange. A good rule of thumb is to use fewer than 100 controls on a custom form. Custom forms created in one version of Outlook may disappear from memory or even crash Outlook when opened in a different version of Outlook.

Back to the Past: the Forms Development Environment

If you're used to developing code and forms in VBA, VB 6, or any of the .NET platforms, you are likely to be dismayed by the primitive development environment for custom forms development:

❑ The code editor is a slightly modified version of Notepad.

❑ There is no Intellisense or other code helpers in the forms development environment.

❑ Limited subsets of the events available for an Outlook item are available as templates in the event handler.

❑ The forms script debugger is the Microsoft Script Debugger, which has limited functionality when used with forms code.

❑ Form code uses VBScript, so all variables are untyped Variants.

Because of these limitations, it often makes sense to prototype form code using the VBA environment, which has a much better code development environment.

When you open a custom form for design, it opens to the default page, the same page displayed when a standard form is opened. This page may or may not be customizable, see the table in the "Form Customization" section for a list of forms that permit you to customize the default pages. You can easily recognize a customizable page by the grid displayed in the form background and controls that don't use Windows theming.

Figure 5-2 shows the P.2 customizable page for a task form, with the forms design Ribbon displayed in the Developer tab of the form.

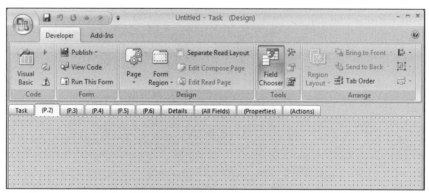

Figure 5-2

The following table shows the functions performed by the menu items in the Developer tab of the Ribbon.

Ribbon Group	Ribbon Menu Item	Menu Function
Code	Visual Basic	Opens the Outlook VBA project
	View Macros	Display the Macros selection dialog
	Script Debugger	Opens the script debugger window in a running form that has code
	Macro Security	Opens the Macro Security page of the Trust Center
Form	Publish	Form publication choices
	View Code	Opens the form code window
	Run This Form	Runs the form being designed
Design	Page	Selections to display and rename the form page
	Form Region	Selections to create, open, save, and close form regions
	Separate Read Layout	Checkbox to enable or disable separate read and compose layouts for the form
	Edit Compose Page	Edits the compose page when separate layouts are enabled
	Edit Read Page	Edit the read page when separate layouts are enabled
Tools	Field Chooser	Opens the Field Chooser window
	Control Toolbox	Opens the Control Toolbox window
	Property Sheet	Opens the Properties window for the selected page or control
	Advanced Properties	Opens the Advanced Properties window for the selected page or control

Continued

117

Ribbon Group	Ribbon Menu Item	Menu Function
Arrange	Region Layout	Layout and sizing for form region controls
	Bring to Front	Brings the selected controls to the front of the Z-order
	Send to Back	Sends the selected controls to the back of the Z-order
	Tab Order	Opens the Tab Order dialog for setting the tab order of the controls on a form
	Align	Selections for aligning the selected controls in various formats
	Group	Groups the selected controls into a control group
	Size	Selections for sizing selected controls

The About This Form Help menu command is not available in the Ribbon. This command displays information that can be useful when debugging custom forms such as version, file number, contact, and description text. You can add this command to the QAT to make it available when running a custom form, but because each Ribbon is different, the command must be added to each form where you want it to be available.

The following sections show how to use the controls in the Developer tab of the Ribbon to design a custom form.

Using the Field Chooser

Form pages are only design surfaces. The controls on a page don't retain values unless the controls are bound to an Outlook property. One of the most common mistakes that a new Outlook forms programmer makes is to expect controls on Outlook custom forms to retain data when the controls aren't bound to Outlook properties. Outlook properties store the data for a form and the controls on the form display that data when the form is loaded, if the controls are bound to Outlook properties. If the controls are not bound to Outlook properties, the only way to populate the controls with stored data is to use code.

Controls can be bound to built-in or custom Outlook properties. The Field Chooser provides an easy way to bind controls to properties, both built in and custom. The Field Chooser is also used to create new properties.

Figure 5-3 shows an Appointment form in design mode, with the P.2 page selected. Open the Field Chooser by clicking the Field Chooser item in the Tools section of the Developer Ribbon tab. Make sure Frequently used fields is selected in the drop-down control at the top of the Field Chooser, and drag the All Day Event item from the Field Chooser to the form. This automatically creates a CheckBox control on the form page and binds that CheckBox control to the AllDayEvent Outlook property.

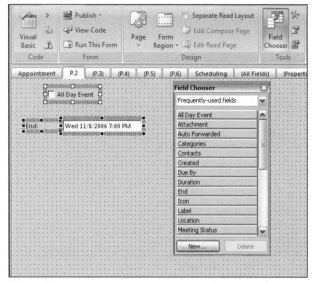

Figure 5-3

Many properties in the Field Chooser use the same controls used by Outlook for the properties, however some Outlook controls aren't exposed through the Field Chooser. Dragging the End property to the form creates a label control and a textbox with the End date and time, not the standard Outlook End time and date picker controls.

Clicking the New button at the bottom of the Field Chooser enables you to create a new Outlook property that can be bound to a suitable control added to a form. The new property is shown in the Field Chooser when the user-defined fields in the folder selection are made in the drop-down control at the top of the Field Chooser. Other selections in the drop-down control enable you to select all controls exposed for a type of item, such as appointment or contact, and to select fields previously created in the folder or in custom Outlook forms.

Using the Control Toolbox

You open the Control Toolbox by clicking the tools icon in the Ribbon, which by default displays only some of the controls from the MS Forms 2.0 controls library. If a control you want to use is not shown in the Control Toolbox, right-click on the Control Toolbox and select Custom Controls to open a list of all Active X controls registered on that development computer. All Microsoft Forms 2.0 controls can be added to the Toolbox and used in forms. Many other registered Active X controls can also be used, with limitations on the properties and events that are usable in a form. Figure 5-4 shows the Control Toolbox with the Forms 2.0 controls and the Outlook View Control, Body control, and the Recipient control. These controls are the only controls guaranteed to be compatible with custom forms.

> *It's tempting to use the new themed Outlook controls such as the date and time pickers in your forms, but only do so after testing the control in your form application to make sure that it works correctly. The controls may work most of the time but aren't tested or guaranteed for use in custom forms, so if you use any of these controls, test them each time you use them.*

119

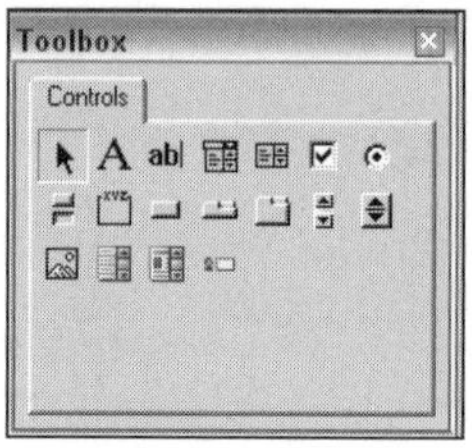

Figure 5-4

Active X controls used on an Outlook form usually expose only a `Click` or `Change` event. Most other control events won't fire when used on a custom form. Many properties exposed by Active X controls aren't available in custom forms. If they are used they will return errors or crash the form. There's no general rule as to which control properties will be available in a form; that's unique to a control and must be determined empirically by testing.

If you use an Active X control that requires licensing on a custom form, you must also distribute the license for the control with your custom form. This usually requires registering the control and providing a license key for it to be installed on the user's computer, although details of distributing licensed controls vary with the control vendor.

Using the Code Window

The code window is where VBScript code for the form is stored. The code editor is a simple Notepad-like editor that's very limited and doesn't provide a modern code development environment. To open the code window, click the View Code item in the Form group of the Developer tab. To add a prototype of an event handler to the form's code window, select Script ⇨ Event Handler in the code window, as shown in Figure 5-5.

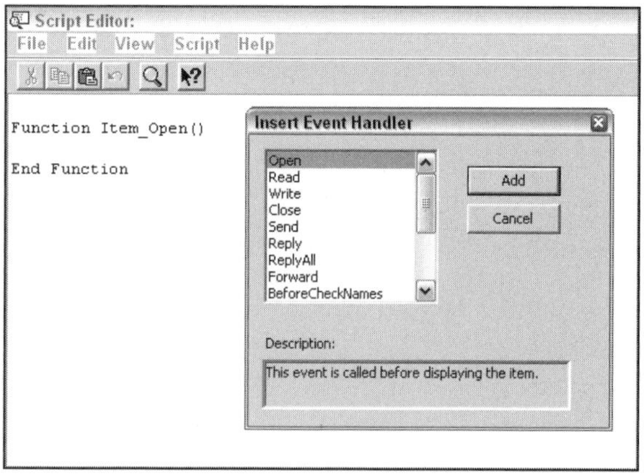

Figure 5-5

The list of prototype event handlers in the code window doesn't include any events added after Outlook 2002. To handle any newer events, you must manually enter the event handler function prototype in the code window. The following table shows the available Outlook item events and the prototypes for those events in VBA and form code.

VBA	Form Code	In Event Handler
`Sub Item_AttachmentAdd(ByVal Attachment As Attachment)`	`Sub Item_AttachmentAdd(ByVal NewAttachment)`	Yes
`Sub Item_AttachmentRead(ByVal Attachment As Attachment)`	`Sub Item_AttachmentRead(ByVal ReadAttachent)`	Yes
`Sub Item_AttachmentRemove(ByVal Attachment As Attachment)`	`Sub Item_AttachmentRemove(ByVal RemoveAttachment)`	No
`Sub Item_BeforeAttachmentAdd(ByVal Attachment As Attachment, Cancel As Boolean)`	`Function Item_BeforeAttachmentAdd(ByVal AddAttachment)`	No
`Sub Item_BeforeAttachmentPreview(ByVal Attachment As Attachment, Cancel As Boolean)`	`Function Item_BeforeAttachmentPreview(ByVal PreviewAttachment)`	No
`Sub Item_BeforeAttachmentRead(ByVal Attachment As Attachment, Cancel As Boolean)`	`Function Item_BeforeAttachmentRead(ByVal ReadAttachment)`	No
`Sub Item_BeforeAttachmentSave(ByVal Attachment As Attachment, Cancel As Boolean)`	`Function Item_BeforeAttachmentSave(ByVal SaveAttachment)`	Yes
`Sub Item_BeforeAttachmentWriteToTempFile(ByVal Attachment As Attachment, Cancel As Boolean)`	`Function Item_BeforeAttachmentWriteToTempFile(ByVal WriteAttachment)`	No
`Sub Item_BeforeAutoSave(Cancel As Boolean)`	`Function Item_BeforeAutoSave()`	No
`Sub Item_BeforeCheckNames(Cancel As Boolean)`	`Function Item_BeforeCheckNames()`	Yes
`Sub Item_BeforeDelete(ByVal Item As Object, Cancel As Boolean)`	`Function Item_BeforeDelete(ByVal Item)`	Yes

Continued

121

VBA	Form Code	In Event Handler
`Sub Item_Close(Cancel As Boolean)`	`Function Item_Close()`	Yes
`Sub Item_CustomAction(ByVal Action As Object, ByVal Response As Object, Cancel As Boolean)`	`Function Item_CustomAction(ByVal Action, ByVal NewItem)`	Yes
`Sub Item_CustomPropertyChange(ByVal Name As String)`	`Sub Item_CustomPropertyChange(ByVal Name)`	Yes
`Sub Item_Forward(ByVal Forward As Object, Cancel As Boolean)`	`Function Item_Forward(ByVal ForwardItem)`	Yes
`Sub Item_Open(Cancel As Boolean)`	`Function Item_Open()`	Yes
`Sub Item_PropertyChange(ByVal Name As String)`	`Sub Item_PropertyChange(ByVal Name)`	Yes
`Sub Item_Read()`	`Function Item_Read()`	Yes
`Sub Item_Reply(ByVal Response As Object, Cancel As Boolean)`	`Function Item_Reply(ByVal Response)`	Yes
`Sub Item_ReplyAll(ByVal Response As Object, Cancel As Boolean)`	`Function Item_ReplyAll(ByVal Response)`	Yes
`Sub Item_Send(Cancel As Boolean)`	`Function Item_Send()`	Yes
`Sub Item_Unload()`	`Sub Item_Unload()`	No
`Sub Item_Write(Cancel As Boolean)`	`Function Item_Write()`	Yes

Most of the form code events are declared as `Functions`, only the `AttachmentAdd`, `AttachmentRead`, `AttachmentRemove`, `CustomPropertyChange`, `PropertyChange` and `Unload` events are declared as `Subs`. Events that provide a `Cancel` argument used to cancel the event don't provide that argument in form code event handlers. To cancel the event, set the event `Function` to `False` in the event handler code.

Prototyping Forms Code in VBA

I strongly recommend using the VBA environment as a prototyping environment for all but the most trivial form code. This makes code development and debugging much easier than developing from scratch in the forms design environment and makes available the enhanced editor, Intellisense, code formatting, Object Browser, Help, and other facilities of the VBA design environment.

Simulating the Form Environment in VBA

The following steps are used to simulate the code environment for a form in the VBA environment:

1. Create the form, and add the desired controls to the form.

2. Run the form so that it's available to the VBA environment. Use the Run This Form item in the Form group of the Developer tab to run the form.

3. Set focus to the main Outlook Explorer window, and use the Alt+F11 keyboard shortcut to open the Outlook VBA window.

4. Add a class module to the VBA project to contain the code and event handlers for the form. Select Insert ⇨ Class Module to insert the class and give it a descriptive name associated with the form so that you know later what the class is used for. Code modules cannot handle events, so the event handler code must be placed in a class module. In this case, for a custom appointment form, use the name `AppointmentCode` for the class module.

You can use the `ThisOutlookSession` class module to contain your event-handling code, but that class will quickly become packed with code that is specific to certain forms, so it's better to use a different class for each form to which you want to add code.

5. Add a class level declaration for `Item` that's set to the form item when the code class is initialized. This `Item` declaration should be declared `WithEvents` so that the code in the class can handle various `AppointmentItem` events.

6. Select Class in the Object drop-down control at the top left of the class and in the right-hand Procedure drop-down control select Initialize to add a class initialization procedure to the code.

The code in the class should look like this when the initial setup is complete:

```
' Change this item type based on the custom form type
Private WithEvents Item As Outlook.AppointmentItem

Private Sub Class_Initialize()
  Set Item = Application.ActiveInspector.CurrentItem
End Sub
```

To create an instance of the class and instantiate it, create the following object declaration and macro in a code module or `ThisOutlookSession` class module:

```
Public AppointmentTestCode As AppointmentCode

Sub RunAppointmentCode()
  Set AppointmentTestCode = New AppointmentCode
End Sub
```

When the macro is executed, and a new instance of the class is instantiated the `Class_Initialize` procedure in the class module runs automatically. This sets the `Item` object in the class to the item displayed in the `ActiveInspector` object. The `ActiveInspector` object should be the custom form that was placed into run mode. This provides the class with access to the equivalent of the `Item` object intrinsic to form code, as well as the `Application` object intrinsic to both form and VBA code. The `AppointmentCode` object variable declared at module level is used to keep the reference to the class alive so that it doesn't close and go out of scope after the initialization code finishes running.

The `StopAppointmentCode` macro is placed in the same module as the `RunAppointmentCode` macro and is used to release the `AppointmentCode` class when you are finished using it.

```
Sub StopAppointmentCode()
   Set AppointmentTestCode = Nothing
End Sub
```

Developing and Debugging Using VBA

Most VBA code you develop for use as form code can be copied unchanged to the form code window and used as VBScript code. The exceptions to this rule are:

❑ **Item event handlers:** Use the standard `Item` event handlers listed in the VBA column of the table in the section "Using the Code Window" in your VBA code and translate the event handler declarations to the declarations listed in the Form Code column when porting the code to VBScript.

❑ **Object declarations:** All variables in VBScript are `Variant` types. VBScript does not have the typed variables available in VBA or other higher-level languages. Comment out any `As` clauses in variable declarations in the VBA code to translate the declarations into VBScript code. The use of `Variants` instead of typed declarations implies that all objects in VBScript code are late-bound and the object references are resolved at runtime.

❑ **Constants:** VBScript doesn't recognize any Outlook constants or enumerations. Declare any Outlook constants you plan to use with `Const` declarations in the code, or use the numeric equivalent of the constant in your code. VBScript does recognize many of the VB-related constants such as `vbYes` and `vbNo`, which are used in the `MsgBox` function.

❑ **Error handling:** VBScript only supports the `On Error Resume Next` error-handling construct, so only use that error-handling construct when developing in VBA for eventual use as form code.

Custom Form Walkthrough

In this section, you create a custom appointment form and develop code for it in the Outlook VBA project. The walkthrough takes you from start to finish with the process of creating and deploying a custom form, including opening a new form in design mode, adding controls to the form and binding the controls to Outlook properties, to publishing and running the form. You also learn about the choices of where to publish a form, how to publish a form using code, and how to test the code for a form.

Creating, Publishing, and Running a Form

In this section, you follow the steps required to create a custom form, add controls to the form and bind the controls to Outlook `UserProperties`, and then publish and run the form.

1. Open an appointment form by selecting Tools ➪ Forms@@Design a Form. Then, select Appointment from the Standard Forms Library in the Design Form dialog.

2. Select the P.2 page of the form. The default Appointment and Scheduling pages can't be customized in an appointment form, as shown in the table in the section "Form Customization."

3. Display the Control Toolbox by clicking the Control Toolbox icon in the Tools section of the Ribbon's Developer tab.

4. Drag a `CheckBox` control to the form.

5. Right-click the `CheckBox` control you just added and select Properties. Set its properties to the following settings:

CheckBox Property	Properties Tab	Value
Name	Display	chkTravelTime
Caption	Display	Travel Time
Top	Layout	40
Left	Layout	48
Height	Layout	24
Width	Layout	144

6. Select the Value tab in the Properties dialog for the `CheckBox` control and click New. Set the Name of the field to TravelTime, set the Type to Yes/No, set the format to True/False, and click OK. This saves the new property as an Outlook `UserProperty`.

7. Click OK to close the Properties dialog and accept the settings.

8. Open the Field Chooser and click New. In the New Field dialog, set the Name to TravelTo, set the type to Duration, and leave the default format as 12h. Click OK to save the new property.

9. Click New again, and in the New Field dialog set the Name to TravelFrom, set the type to Duration, and leave the default format as 12h. Click OK to save the new property.

10. Drag TravelTo from the Field Chooser to the form, and then drag TravelFrom from the Field Chooser to the form. Each field dragged to the form adds both a `Label` control and a `TextBox` control.

11. Click in the form to deselect the controls, and set the properties of the controls to the following settings:

Label1 Property	Properties Tab	Value
Name	Display	lblTravelTo
Caption	Display	Travel To:
Top	Layout	72
Left	Layout	48
Height	Layout	13
Width	Layout	50
TextBox1 Property	**Properties Tab**	**Value**
Name	Display	txtTravelTo
Top	Layout	70
Left	Layout	120
Height	Layout	21
Width	Layout	144
Label2 Property	**Properties Tab**	**Value**
Name	Display	lblTravelFrom
Caption	Display	Travel From:
Top	Layout	108
Left	Layout	48
Height	Layout	13
Width	Layout	72
TextBox2 Property	**Properties Tab**	**Value**
Name	Display	txtTravelFrom
Top	Layout	104

Label1 Property	Properties Tab	Value
Left	Layout	120
Height	Layout	21
Width	Layout	144

12. Click the Page drop-down, and select Rename Page. Name the custom page Travel Time.

13. Select the Properties page, and enter **1.00** in the Version field as shown in Figure 5-6. Set a version, and increment it for every change to the design of a published form. This helps prevent forms cache corruption and ensures that the latest version of a form is loaded. The Properties page is also used to set text-only category and subcategory fields, to assign a form number, and to set other properties that help in classifying forms for archiving and identification. The form category and subcategory properties are unique to custom forms and do not use Outlook Categories.

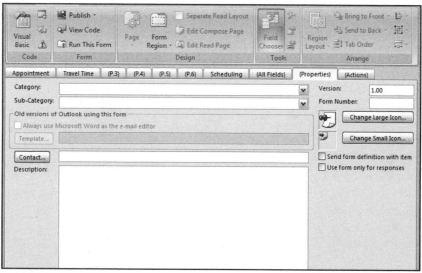

Figure 5-6

You no longer can protect your forms with passwords in Outlook 2007. Passwords were never a strong protection for forms because the Password *property was exposed in the* FormDesign *object. The* Password *property is now hidden to deprecate it, and if a password exists in a form it's ignored by Outlook 2007. Although setting a password on a form only kept the casual user away from a custom form's design, it worked with most users and the loss of this setting makes custom forms less secure than in earlier versions of Outlook.*

14. By default, all custom forms display using Post form icons, as shown in Figure 5-6. To change the icon to an appropriate Outlook or custom form icon, use the Change Large Icon and Change Small Icon buttons. The Outlook supplied icons are usually located in the `C:\Program Files\ Microsoft Office\Office12\FORMS\1033 folder`. If you are using Outlook 2003, change "Office12" to "Office11". The "1033" is the language ID for Office; change the path if you are not using an American English installation of Outlook.

Separate large and small icons are used for different displays. Large icons are 16x16 pixels at 96 dpi with a 32-bit color depth. Small icons are 32x32 pixels at 96 dpi with a 32-bit color depth. Both file types are saved with an `.ICO` *file extension. Any icons you create for use with Outlook forms must follow these specifications.*

15. To publish the form to the Personal Forms Library, click the Publish drop-down, and select Publish Form As. In the Look-In drop-down select Personal Forms Library, and in the Display name field name the form TravelTime. Click Publish to publish the form as `IPM.Appointment .TravelTime`.

16. Close the form, but don't save any changes to it. Saving changes to a custom form in design mode will one-off the form by embedding the form design in the form, and is not the same as publishing a form.

To run a form published in the Personal Forms Library, select Tools ➪ Forms ➪ Choose Form and select Personal Forms Library in the Look In drop-down. Highlight TravelTime and click Open. The custom TravelTime page is selected in Figure 5-7 to show the travel time controls and illustrate that custom form pages and controls aren't themed, causing those pages to have a different look than standard pages.

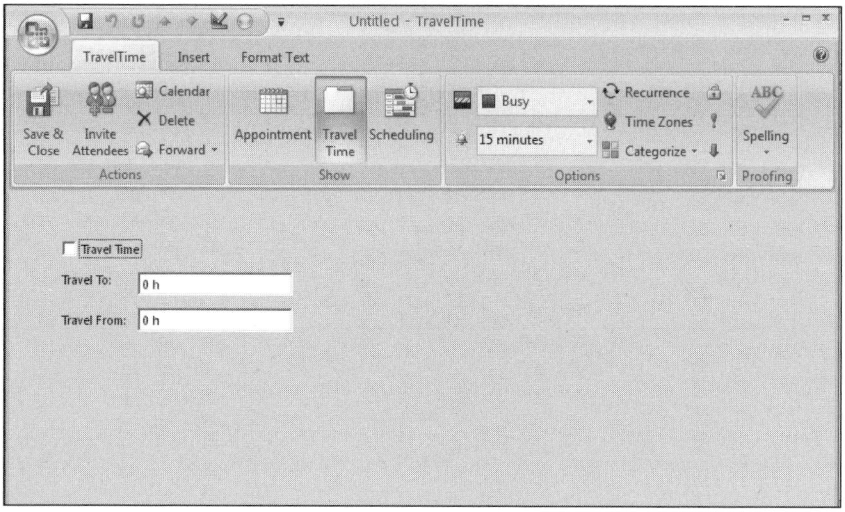

Figure 5-7

Where to Publish Forms

In this section, you learn about the choices of where to publish forms and what determines the best location for publishing a form under various conditions.

Forms are usually published to the Personal or Organizational Forms Libraries, or to an Outlook folder. The following guidelines often determine where a form is published:

❑ Forms used only in one folder can be published to that folder. This allows the opening of a new instance of the form by selecting the form's display name from the folder's Actions menu. Never publish a form to more than one folder; this is a cause of forms cache corruption.

❑ Forms used in more than one folder should be published to the Personal Forms Library.

❑ Forms that should be available in an Exchange organization should be published to the Organizational Forms Library, if Exchange Public Folders are enabled and an Organizational Forms Library has been created. Publishing forms to the Organizational Forms Library requires Owner permissions on the Library folder in the Exchange data store.

❑ Forms for distribution to users or other developers can be saved to the file system as .OFT files. Forms saved as OFT files aren't considered to be published but do contain the custom form design in an easy-to-distribute format.

Publishing Forms Using Code

When custom forms are part of a project, you often need to distribute and publish the form as part of your application. To do so, save the finished form as an OFT file that will be distributed as part of your application. The OFT file is usually installed with the program components in the installation folder. The VBA code in Listing 5-1 publishes an OFT file and makes the custom fields in the form fields in the folder and the item.

Listing 5-1

```
Public Sub PublishForm(FormPath As String)
   Dim oFolder As Outlook.Folder
   Dim oFormItem As Outlook.AppointmentItem
   Dim oFormDesc As Outlook.FormDescription
   Dim oItem As Outlook. AppointmentItem
   Dim oUserProperties As Outlook.UserProperties
   Dim oUserProperty As Outlook.UserProperty
   Dim iUserPropCount As Integer
   Dim iCount As Integer
   Dim strVersion As String
   Dim blnNew As Boolean
   Dim blnPublished As Boolean
   Dim strID As String
   Dim strStoreID As String

   Const CUSTOM_MESSAGECLASS = "IPM.Appointment.TravelTime"
   Const CUSTOM_FORM_DISPLAY_NAME = "Travel Time"

   On Error Resume Next
```

(continued)

```
' FormPath is passed as the path to the OFT file to be published

blnNew = False
blnPublished = False

Set oFolder = Application.Session.GetDefaultFolder(olFolderCalendar)
```

The constants CUSTOM_MESSAGECLASS and CUSTOM_FORM_DISPLAY_NAME are used for the MessageClass and display name for the form to publish. The code then gets the target folder, where the custom form will be used, in this case the default Calendar folder. A new item is then created from the custom form using the CreateItemFromTemplate method. If the Version property of the FormDescription property of the template is empty, the version is set to "1.00". The FormPublish function is then called to check to see if the form is already published to the target destination.

```
' Create Outlook form from template
Set oFormItem = Application.CreateItemFromTemplate(FormPath, oFolder)

If Not (oFormItem Is Nothing) Then
  ' Get Outlook form description
  Set oFormDesc = oFormItem.FormDescription
  If oFormDesc.Version = "" Then
    oFormDesc.Version = "1.00"
  End If
  strVersion = oFormDesc.Version

  ' see if need to publish form to folder
  Err.Clear

  strStoreID = oFolder.StoreID
  blnNew = FormPublish(oFolder.EntryID, _
    strStoreID, strVersion, CUSTOM_MESSAGECLASS, oFolder)
```

If the form has not already been published, it's published to the Personal Forms Library using the FormDescription.PublishForm method. This method takes an argument from the OlFormRegistry enumeration:

❑   olDefaultRegistry

❑   olFolderRegistry

❑   olOrganizationRegistry

❑   olPersonalRegistry

A dummy item is then created in the folder and set to the custom MessageClass of the newly published form. Each UserProperty in the custom form is then added to the dummy item's UserProperties collection with the AddToFolderFields argument set to True, which makes the user properties available for use in filters and restrictions.

```
If blnNew Then
  If Not blnPublished Then
```

```
            oFormDesc.DisplayName = CUSTOM_FORM_DISPLAY_NAME
            oFormDesc.PublishForm olPersonalRegistry

            blnPublished = True
        End If

        ' Add dummy item to folder
        Set oItem = oFolder.Items.Add(CUSTOM_MESSAGECLASS)
        oItem.MessageClass = CUSTOM_MESSAGECLASS

        ' Get Outlook user properties of Outlook form,
        Set oUserProperties = oFormItem.UserProperties

        ' Loop through existing Outlook user properties
        iCount = oUserProperties.Count
        For iUserPropCount = 1 To iCount
            ' Add Outlook user property to dummy item
            Set oUserProperty = Nothing
            Set oUserProperty = oItem.UserProperties.Add _
              (oUserProperties.Item(iUserPropCount).Name, _
               oUserProperties.Item(iUserPropCount).Type, True)

            Err.Clear
        Next
      End If

      Set oFormItem = Nothing
      Set oItem = Nothing
    Else
      ' Error
    End If

    Set oFormItem = Nothing
    Set oFormDesc = Nothing
    Set oItem = Nothing
    Set oUserProperties = Nothing
    Set oUserProperty = Nothing
    Set oFolder = Nothing
End Sub
```

The FormPublish function checks to see if a new item of the specified MessageClass can be created in the target folder, and if the item can be created, what Version the item has. If the Version is less than the version passed to the function or the form cannot be created, the code returns a Boolean value indicating that the custom form should be published.

```
'*****************************************************************************
Private Function FormPublish(strEntryID As String, _
  strStoreID As String, strVersion As String, _
  strMessageClass As String, oFolder As Outlook.Folder) As Boolean

  Dim oItem As Outlook.ContactItem
  Dim oDesc As Outlook.FormDescription
```

```
        Dim strPublishedVersion As String
        Dim strID As String

        On Error Resume Next

        FormPublish = False

        Set oItem = oFolder.Items.Add(strMessageClass)

        Set oDesc = oItem.FormDescription
        strPublishedVersion = oDesc.Version

        If strPublishedVersion = "" Then
          FormPublish = True
        ElseIf CSng(strPublishedVersion) < CSng(strVersion) Then
          FormPublish = True
        ElseIf oItem.MessageClass <> strMessageClass Then
          FormPublish = True
        Else
          FormPublish = False
        End If

        Set oItem = Nothing
        Set oDesc = Nothing
    End Function
```

Testing Code for the Form

Code isn't required in Outlook custom forms, and code in a form does have the disadvantage that it causes the form to not be displayable in the preview pane. However, to add business logic to a form, code is usually required. In this section, you learn about testing your code in VBA before placing it in a form and how to transfer that code to the form after the code is tested.

The TravelTime form currently has fields for enabling travel time and time spent traveling to and from the appointment to be tracked. In this exercise, you add two additional fields to the Travel Time page for total travel time and for total appointment time, including travel time. The fields are populated using code that fires for the `CustomPropertyChange` and `PropertyChange` events to populate the calculated fields.

The duration fields `TravelTo` and `TravelFrom` are 32-bit `Long` properties that store the time in minutes. The total of To and From travel time is, therefore, the sum of the `TravelTo` and `TravelFrom` fields. The calculation for the total travel time could be created using a calculated field formula, but in this case code is used to perform the calculation.

1. Open the `TravelTime` form by selecting Tools ➪ Forms ➪ Design a Form and choosing the Personal Forms Library in the Look In drop-down, then selecting TravelTime and clicking Open.

2. Add two new duration fields to the Travel Time page by clicking New in the Field Chooser and creating duration fields named `TotalTravel` and `TotalTime`. Follow steps 8, 9, and 10 in the

Custom Form Walkthrough in this chapter to create these fields and add them to the form. Set the control properties as follows:

Label1 Property	Properties Tab	Value
Name	Display	lblTotalTravel
Caption	Display	Total Travel:
Top	Layout	148
Left	Layout	48
Height	Layout	13
Width	Layout	72
TextBox1 Property	**Properties Tab**	**Value**
Name	Display	txtTotalTravel
Top	Layout	144
Left	Layout	120
Height	Layout	21
Width	Layout	144
Label2 Property	**Properties Tab**	**Value**
Name	Display	lblTotalTime
Caption	Display	Total Time:
Top	Layout	196
Left	Layout	56
Height	Layout	13
Width	Layout	60
TextBox2 Property	**Properties Tab**	**Value**
Name	Display	txtTotalTime
Top	Layout	192
Left	Layout	120
Height	Layout	21
Width	Layout	144

3. On the Properties page of the form, change the Version to 1.01.

4. Select Publish ⇨ Publish Form to publish the new version of the form.

5. Close the form, and choose not to save changes to the form.

6. Open the VBA project by using Alt+F11, and add event handlers for PropertyChange and CustomPropertyChange to the AppointmentCode class module you created earlier in this chapter. To add the event handlers, select Item in the Object drop-down at the top of the code editor for the AppointmentCode class, select PropertyChange, and then select CustomPropertyChange.

7. Add the code in Listing 5-2 to the CustomPropertyChange event handler.

Listing 5-2

```
Private Sub Item_CustomPropertyChange(ByVal Name As String)
   Dim TotalTime As Long
   Dim TravelTime As Long

   If Name = "TravelTo" Or Name = "TravelFrom" Then
     TravelTime = Item.UserProperties.Item("TravelTo") + _
       Item.UserProperties.Item("TravelFrom")

     TotalTime = Item.Duration +TravelTime

     Item.UserProperties.Item("TotalTravel") = TravelTime
     Item.UserProperties.Item("TotalTime") = TotalTime

     Item.Save
   End If
End Sub
```

8. Add the code in Listing 5-3 to the PropertyChange event handler.

Listing 5-3

```
Private Sub Item_PropertyChange(ByVal Name As String)
   Dim TotalTime As Long
   Dim TravelTime As Long

   If Name = "Duration" Then
     TravelTime = Item.UserProperties.Item("TravelTo") + _
       Item.UserProperties.Item("TravelFrom")

     TotalTime = Item.Duration + TravelTime

     Item.UserProperties.Item("TotalTravel") = TravelTime
     Item.UserProperties.Item("TotalTime") = TotalTime

     Item.Save
   End If
End Sub
```

9. Open a new instance of the `TravelTime` form in the Personal Forms Library, and give the form start and end times for the appointment and a location.

10. Open the VBA editor, place your cursor in the `RunAppointmentCode` macro you created earlier in this chapter, and press F5 to run the macro.

11. Make changes to the duration of the appointment by changing the end time and add travel times to the `TravelTo` and `TravelFrom` fields on the Travel Time page of the form. As you change those settings, the new Total Travel and Total Time fields are automatically updated by the `PropertyChange` and `CustomPropertyChange` event handlers.

12. Add breakpoints to both the `PropertyChange` and `CustomPropertyChange` event handlers, and step the code through those procedures to see how the code works. The `Name` property passed to both event handlers is used to test for changes to the properties you're interested in, if one of those properties is changed, the code calculates total travel time and total time for the appointment, including travel time, and stores those values in `UserProperties`. Because the `UserProperties` are bound to the controls on the form, the form is updated as soon as the `UserProperties` change to display the changes.

13. Run the `StopAppointmentCode` macro you created earlier in this chapter to stop the event-handling code from running, and close the test appointment form.

14. To modify the code in Listing 5-2 for use as form code, delete the `As` clauses in the procedure declaration and variable declarations, as shown in Listing 5-4. Also delete the `Private` scope declaration for the procedure. Make the same changes to the code in Listing 5-3 for the `PropertyChange` event handler.

Listing 5-4

```
Sub Item_CustomPropertyChange(ByVal Name)
   Dim TotalTime
   Dim TravelTime

   If Name = "TravelTo" Or Name = "TravelFrom" Then
     TravelTime = Item.UserProperties.Item("TravelTo") + _
       Item.UserProperties.Item("TravelFrom")

     TotalTime = Item.Duration + TravelTime

     Item.UserProperties.Item("TotalTravel") = TravelTime
     Item.UserProperties.Item("TotalTime") = TotalTime

     Item.Save
   End If
End Sub
```

15. Open the `TravelTime` form in design mode, and change the Version to 1.02; then click View Code in the Form section of the Ribbon to open the form's code window. Paste the code into the form from the Listing 5-4 code and the code modified for the `PropertyChange` event handler in Listing 5-3. Publish the 1.02 version of the form, and the code in the form will now run whenever a property or `UserProperty` is changed in the form.

Forms Management

Forms management involves a number of issues:

❏ Maintaining forms cache integrity by changing the form's `Version` property each time you modify the form.

❏ Managing the forms cache to clear the cache and remove items from the cache.

❏ Setting custom forms to be loaded automatically when a new form is opened in a folder.

❏ Setting existing items in a folder to use a specific custom form.

❏ Making a custom form the default form for all items of that type.

To manage the cache, select Tools ➪ Options ➪ Other tab ➪ Advanced Options button ➪ Custom Forms button. This opens the Custom Forms Options dialog, where you can set the size for the forms cache, allow some forms to bypass Outlook, and set a password on the forms cache manager. Click the Manage Forms button to open the Forms Manager. In the Forms Manager, you can select any forms repository and copy forms to a different repository, update cached forms with the latest versions from a forms repository, delete forms from the cache, and clear the entire forms cache. You can also install forms into the cache from a repository, save a published form as an OFT file, and review information about forms in a repository or the forms cache.

The default form for a folder is set in the user interface, or with code. To set a custom form to be the default form, opened when creating new items in a folder, right-click the folder in the Navigation Pane and select Properties. In the General tab, select the form from the When posting to this folder, use: drop-down.

To make a custom form the default for a folder with code, you set two properties, the custom form `MessageClass` and the custom from name. The code in Listing 5-5 is called with the folder, custom `MessageClass`, and custom form name to set the default form for the folder.

Listing 5-5

```
Private Sub SetFolderForCustomForm(oFolder As Outlook.Folder, _
    CUSTOM_MESSAGECLASS As String, CUSTOM_FORM_DISPLAY_NAME As String)

    Dim oPropAccessor As Outlook.PropertyAccessor

    Dim defFormName As String
    Dim defMsgClass As String

    Const PR_DEF_FORM_NAME = "0x36E6001E"
    Const PR_DEF_MSG_CLASS = "0x36E5001E"
    Const PROPTAG = "http://schemas.microsoft.com/mapi/propag/"

    defFormName = PR_DEF_FORM_NAME & PROPTAG
    defMsgClass = PR_DEF_ MSG_CLASS & PROPTAG

    Set oPropAccessor = oFolder.PropertyAccessor
```

Listing 5-5 *(continued)*

```
    'Set the default form MessageClass for the folder
    If oPropAccessor.GetProperty(defMsgClass) <> CUSTOM_MESSAGECLASS Then
      oPropAccessor.SetProperty(defMsgClass, CUSTOM_MESSAGECLASS)
    End If

    'Set the name for the default form for the folder
    If oPropAccessor.GetProperty(defFormName) <> CUSTOM_FORM_DISPLAY_NAME Then
      oPropAccessor.SetProperty(defFormName, CUSTOM_FORM_DISPLAY_NAME)
    End If

    Set oPropAccessor = Nothing
End Sub
```

For Outlook versions earlier than Outlook 2007, which don't have a `PropertyAccessor` *object, you must use CDO, Extended MAPI, Redemption, or another MAPI wrapper to set the folder properties for the default form for the folder.*

If you change the default form in the Contacts, Calendar, Journal, or Tasks folder, the new form will be used whenever you click the New button for that type of item, even if you're not currently in that default folder.

Making a custom form the default for a folder doesn't change existing items in the folder, it only affects new forms created in that folder. To make all existing items in a folder use the custom form, you must iterate through each item in the folder and change its `MessageClass` to the `MessageClass` of the custom form. The following VBA code sets each item in the current folder to use a custom form, which must be a published form. The code does not check to see whether all the items in the folder are the correct types:

```
    Dim oFolder As Outlook.Folder
    Dim oItems As Outlook.Items
    Dim oAppt As Outlook.AppointmentItem
    Set oFolder = Application.ActiveExplorer.CurrentFolder
    Set oItems = oFolder.Items
    For Each oAppt In oItems
      oAppt.MessageClass = "IPM.Appointment.TravelTime"
      oAppt.Save
    Next
```

Setting the `MessageClass` of the item to the custom form's `MessageClass` sets the item to use the custom form when it's opened. This does not populate custom fields in the form with data unless the data comes from existing Outlook properties. To add data to custom fields in the form, you must enter data in those fields using code or manually enter the data.

Making a custom form the default form for all items of that type is done by modifying the Windows registry. Microsoft has a tool that can be downloaded for that, but unfortunately the tool hasn't been updated since Outlook 2000. The tool can be downloaded from `http://office.microsoft.com/en-us/ork2000/HA011384301033.aspx`. After running the tool export the registry key at `HKCU\Software\Microsoft\Office\9.0\Outlook\Custom Forms` and change the version value "9.0" for Outlook 2000 to "12.0" for Outlook 2007, then import the registry key back into the registry to enable the custom form substitution for Outlook 2007.

Form Behavior

In this section, you learn about some changes made to form behavior in Outlook 2007 and Outlook 2003. These changes were all made in the name of security by Microsoft. The changes limit what unpublished forms can do, where form script will run, and what controls work in unpublished forms. In all cases, the changes were made to prevent forms that aren't trusted from causing damage to data or to Outlook.

Trusted Forms

In Outlook 2003 and Outlook 2007, code in published Outlook forms that aren't one-offed is trusted. Normally, blocked properties and methods will not trigger security prompts, as long as all objects are derived from the intrinsic `Application` and `Item` objects available to form code.

Code will not run in items created from unpublished or one-off forms, and in Outlook 2002 SP3, Outlook 2003, and Outlook 2007 some Active X controls are blocked from running on unpublished or one-off forms.

This affects:

- ❑ Items created from .OFT files
- ❑ Items created from forms that were published with the Send Form Definition with Item checkbox checked
- ❑ Items created from published forms that later became one-offed due to the addition of code in the form or a new custom property

To ensure that a form does not become one-offed, don't check the Send Form Definition with Item checkbox on the Properties page of the form. Outlook suggests checking this setting whenever you publish a form to ensure that the recipient will have the custom form. Only use this setting when sending custom forms over the Internet, and make sure that the form has no code in it when using this setting. A better approach is to have the recipient publish a copy of the form on his or her computer, so the form is trusted and not one-offed when it's received.

Active X Controls

Outlook 2002 SP3, Outlook 2003, and Outlook 2007 all added restrictions on which Active X controls will run on one-off forms. In Outlook 2003 and Outlook 2007, only the MS Forms 2.0 controls and intrinsic Outlook controls load on a one-off form. In Outlook 2002 SP3, Active X controls not marked safe for scripting won't load on one-offed forms.

When a form page in a one-off form with a blocked control is displayed, an error message is shown. The best solution for this problem is to avoid one-off forms. If a one-off form must be used, and you are using Outlook 2003 or Outlook 2007, a registry entry or group policy can be used to control the blocking of Active X controls.

To control Active X control behavior from the registry, a DWORD value named `AllowActiveXOneOffForms` is added to the `HKCU\Software\Microsoft\Office\12.0\Outlook\Security\` registry key ("11.0" for Outlook 2003) set to one of these values:

AllowActiveXOneOffForms Registry Value	Active X Control Behavior
0	Only load Forms 2.0 controls, the Outlook View Control, Outlook Recipient Control, and the Outlook message body control.
1	Only load controls marked as "safe for initialization."
2	All Active X controls can load.

Script in Forms

Script won't run at all in unpublished forms, and by default won't run in shared folders or Exchange Public Folders. Shared folders are folders in Exchange delegate mailboxes and in nondefault PST files. To allow script to run in shared or Public Folders, select Tools ⇨ Trust Center. In the Trust Center, select the e-mail Security tab. The Script in Folders section has checkboxes to allow script in shared and Public Folders. The setting for shared folders also affects whether folder Home Page code will run.

> *To change the settings for script in shared folders and Public Folders in Outlook 2003, select Tools ⇨ Options. Select the Other tab, and click the Advanced Options button to open the Advanced Options dialog.*

Form Regions

Form Regions are the new way to customize Outlook forms. Form regions have the advantage of using themed controls that match the look of standard Outlook forms in Outlook 2007, as well as access to new controls for date and time picking, categories, contact photos, and time zones.

> *Don't use any of the new controls exposed in the object model as Olk* type controls, where "*" is used to indicate any control whose name starts with "Olk" in a custom form page. These controls are not designed for use in custom form pages, and while they may work in certain circumstances, they may crash the form or cause data loss.*

Form regions are used as replacements for all pages of a standard form, to add new pages at the bottom of an Outlook form, to display as custom form pages, and to display in the reading pane. Controls on form regions can be bound to Outlook properties or left as unbound controls.

Most form regions will be designed to work in conjunction with a COM addin, but that's only necessary if the form region requires business logic to be implemented or if unbound controls are used and the data in the controls must be stored in the Outlook item. In the next two sections, you learn about form region basics and how to create new form regions.

Form Region Locations, Properties, and Registry Settings

Form regions store the form design in OFS files created using the Outlook forms designer. The form region location and properties are supplied using an XML file referenced in the registry. When Outlook 2007 opens an item, it checks the item's `MessageClass` and looks in the registry for an entry for a form region that's designed for that `MessageClass`.

❑ Use a standard `MessageClass` in the registry entry, such as `IPM.Appointment`, to use the form region with all items based on that `MessageClass`. Custom forms derived from that `MessageClass` will also use that form region.

❑ Use a custom `MessageClass` in the registry entry, such as `IPM.Appointment.TravelTime2`, to use the form region only with custom forms of that `MessageClass`.

❑ Use the `<exactMessageClass>` tag in your XML file to limit the form region to the exact `MessageClass in the registry entry`.

The registry location for the form region setting is `HKCU\Software\Microsoft\Office\Outlook\FormRegions\`. If the registry key doesn't exist, add the `MessageClass` key to use the form region with that `MessageClass`:

❑ `HKCU\Software\Microsoft\Office\Outlook\FormRegions\IPM.Appointment` uses the form region with all standard and custom appointment items.

❑ `HKCU\Software\Microsoft\Office\Outlook\FormRegions\IPM.Appointment.TravelTime2` uses the form region only with `IPM.Appointment.TravelTime2` custom forms.

In the registry key, add a string value for the form region, using the form region name. The registry entry has the following format:

Registry Value	Type	Data
TravelTime	REG_SZ	File path and file name for TravelTime.XML

The code in Listing 5-6 shows the XML for a `TravelTime` form region. The XML file must be saved with the location and name referenced by the registry entry. The `<layoutFile>` tag in the XML file provides the path to the OFS file.

Listing 5-6

```xml
<?xml version="1.0" encoding="utf-8"?>
<FormRegion xmlns="http://schemas.microsoft.com/office/outlook/12/formregion.xsd">
    <!-- Internal name for the form region OFS file -->
    <name>TravelTime</name>

    <!-- Title for the form region -->
    <title>Travel Time</title>

    <!-- Separate region has an icon in the Pages section of the Ribbon -->
    <!-- Adjoining is region placed at the bottom of the form -->
    <formRegionType>adjoining</formRegionType>
```

Listing 5-6 *(continued)*

```
        <!-- The OFS file that defines the Form Region -->
        <!-- No UNC file paths -->
        <!-- Relative paths can be used -->
        <layoutFile>TravelTime.OFS</layoutFile>

        <!-- Show in preview pane -->
        <showPreview>true</showPreview>

        <!-- Show for Inspector read mode for -->
        <showInspectorRead>true</showInspectorRead>

        <!-- Show for Inspector compose mode -->
        <showInspectorCompose>true</showInspectorCompose>
    </FormRegion>
```

Form Region Walkthrough

To create a form region, follow these steps:

1. Open an appointment form by selecting Tools ⇨ Forms ⇨ Design a Form, then select Appointment from the Standard Forms Library in the Design Form dialog.

2. Click the Form Region drop-down in the Ribbon, and select New Form Region. A form region design surface opens, with the Field Chooser open.

3. Display the Control Toolbox by clicking the Control Toolbox icon in the Tools section of the Ribbon's Developer tab.

4. Drag a CheckBox control to the form.

   Outlook proxies controls from the MS Forms 2.0 collection automatically with themed controls. Add only the Microsoft Office Outlook controls that aren't in Forms 2.0 to the Control Toolbox.

5. Right-click the CheckBox control you just added, and select Properties. Set its properties to the following settings:

CheckBox Property	Properties Tab	Value
Name	Display	chkTravelTime
Caption	Display	Travel Time
Top	Layout	8
Left	Layout	24
Height	Layout	24
Width	Layout	144

6. Select the Value tab in the Properties dialog for the `CheckBox` control, and click Choose Field. In the User-defined fields in folder flyout, select TravelTime and click OK. If the TravelTime property doesn't exist, use the New button to create it, following the steps in the custom form walkthrough earlier in this chapter.

Steps 6 and 7 demonstrate two ways to bind a property to a control on a form.

7. In the Field Chooser drag the `TravelFrom` and `TravelTo` fields to the form region design surface, and set the properties as follows:

OlkLabel1 Property	Properties Tab	Value
Name	Display	lblTravelTo
Caption	Display	Travel To:
Top	Layout	40
Left	Layout	24
Height	Layout	13
Width	Layout	50
OlkTextBox1 Property	**Properties Tab**	**Value**
Name	Display	txtTravelTo
Top	Layout	38
Left	Layout	96
Height	Layout	21
Width	Layout	144
OlkLabel2 Property	**Properties Tab**	**Value**
Name	Display	lblTravelFrom
Caption	Display	Travel From:
Top	Layout	76
Left	Layout	24
Height	Layout	13
Width	Layout	72

OlkTextBox2 Property	Properties Tab	Value
Name	Display	txtTravelFrom
Top	Layout	72
Left	Layout	96
Height	Layout	21
Width	Layout	144

8. Click the Page drop-down, and select Rename Page. Name the custom page Travel Time. The form should look like the form shown in Figure 5-8.

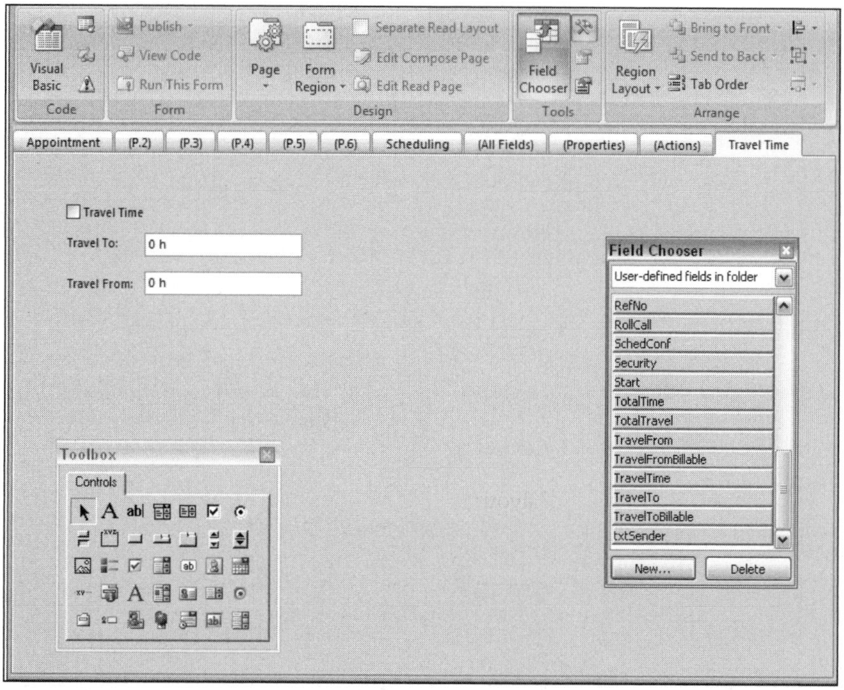

Figure 5-8

9. Click the Form Region drop-down, and select Save Form Region. Save the file to the file system as TravelTime.OFS.

10. Set the form Version and icons on the Properties tab of the form.

11. Publish the form to the Personal Forms Library as "IPM.Appointment.TravelTime2."

12. Close the form, but don't save any changes to it.

13. Use the code in Listing 5-5 to create a new XML file named `TravelTime.XML` in the same folder where you saved the `TravelTime.OFS` file in step 9.

14. Create a registry entry `HKCU\\Software\Microsoft\Office\Outlook\FormRegions\ IPM.Appointment.TravelTime2`, with a string value in that registry key named `TimeTravel`. Set the value of `TimeTravel` to the file path and name where you saved the XML file in step 13.

15. Exit and restart Outlook to use the form region when `IPM.Appointment.TravelTime2` forms are opened.

Figure 5-9 shows the adjoining Travel Time form region in an open Travel Time 2 form. The form region is also visible in the preview pane. The look of the form region and the controls on the form region match the look of the appointment form, in contrast to the custom Outlook form in Figure 5-7.

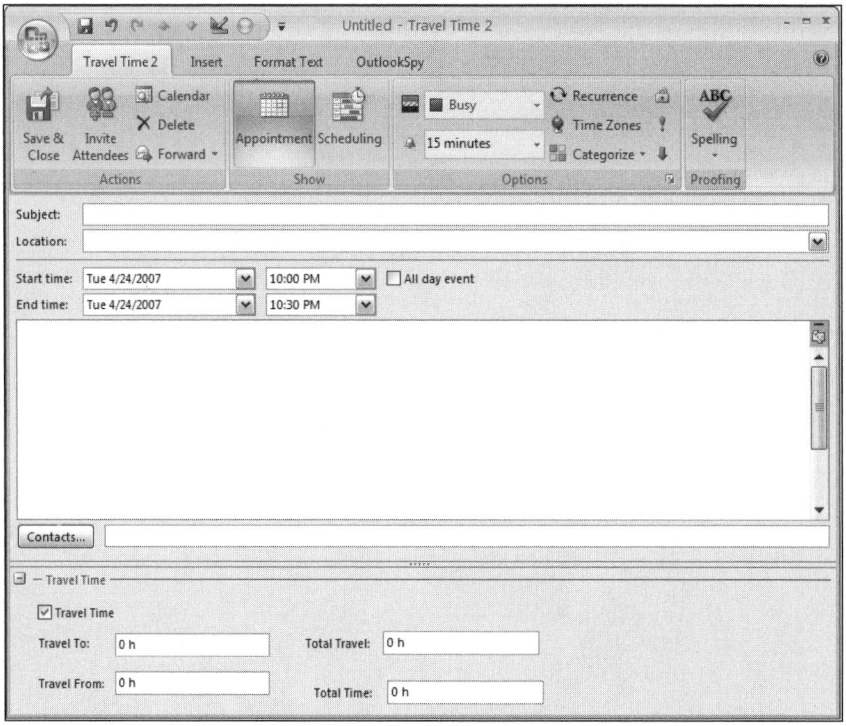

Figure 5-9

The adjoining form region is displayed in the preview pane even if code is in the form when the `<showPreview>` tag value in the form region XML is true. Using a form region in the preview pane can cause problems, however. `TextBox` controls and any compound controls, such as `ComboBoxes` that contain `TextBox` controls, pass the Delete keypress to the parent Explorer window. The Backspace key isn't handled in the control at all. If the form region is displayed in the preview pane, set the `Enabled` property of such controls to false when designing the form, or when responding to the `Read` event when the form isn't open.

Summary

In this chapter, you learned how to create, use, and manage Outlook custom forms. You also learned about the new Form Regions introduced in Outlook 2007.

A complete discussion of Outlook custom forms is a big topic that can take up an entire book, so only the basics of custom forms were covered in this chapter. For more information about designing and working with custom forms and lots of information about various problems and solutions for custom forms, I recommend looking at the material at `www.outlookcode.com/d/forms.htm`.

Form regions can be used without a COM addin, as standalone form regions, as you learned in this chapter. However, to add business logic to form regions, you must use a COM addin. You will learn about COM addins in the next chapter, and you will learn to use COM addins with Form Regions in Chapter 7.

COM Addins

In this chapter, you learn how to create Outlook COM addins, including property pages that are shown when the Tools ⇨ Options and folder Properties dialogs are displayed. COM addins are the preferred way to create and deploy Outlook customization code. A COM addin is the only way to work with such features as the Ribbon interface for Outlook Inspectors, code behind form regions and custom task panes. COM addin code is more robust than Outlook VBA or forms code, and problems with COM addin code can usually be isolated strictly to that addin. You will also learn how to communicate with a COM addin by using external code.

The VB.NET and C# projects associated with this book are available for download in shared addin and VSTO 2005 SE formats for Outlook 2007–only code. Other templates are also available for download. The templates are available for download on the Wrox Web site (www.wrox.com) as well as on my Web site at www.slovaktech.com.

Managed or Unmanaged Code?

COM addins can be written using many different languages and development platforms. Any language that can work with COM interfaces, either directly or indirectly using the COM Interop provided by the Microsoft Framework, can be used to write an Outlook COM addin. The language and development platform you use to develop COM addins depends on your familiarity with the language and development platform, and the versions of Outlook you plan to target with your addin.

The COM addin examples in this book use VB.NET and C#, with Visual Studio 2005 as the development platform. Examples for VB 6 development are also shown, as are examples for VSTO 2005 SE using VB.NET and C#.

Managed code is what's being promoted by Microsoft, in line with their move away from the use of unmanaged code. Managed code can use the new features of the .NET Framework, a richer development platform than the unmanaged Visual Studio 6 platform, and has the advantage of being potentially more isolated in its own development space than unmanaged code. Managed code is slower than unmanaged code due to working with essentially late-bound objects provided by the Outlook PIAs and the overhead of the Framework.

Unmanaged code in VB 6 can do everything managed code can do and does it faster, due to early object binding and the lack of Framework overhead. Even now, some 5 years after the release of the first development platform for managed code, the majority of released COM addins still use unmanaged code. The main disadvantage of unmanaged code using VB 6 is that the language is dead with no further development of it being performed, and in the future, its compatibility with new operating systems and versions of Office is not guaranteed

VSTO provides a framework around managed code that wraps the complexity of working with COM addins, but it is only usable if you are planning to support only Outlook 2003 Professional or above version and Outlook 2007. If you plan to support earlier versions of Outlook than Outlook 2003, or need to support other versions of Outlook 2003, such as the Standard or Learning versions, you cannot use VSTO.

IDTExtensibility2 and Trusted COM Addins

All Outlook addins, whether managed or unmanaged, require an implementation of the IDTExtensibility2 interface of the Extensibility library. This interface supplies five methods that must be handled in your addin for Outlook to run it as a COM addin:

- ❑   OnConnection: Fires when the addin is started by Outlook.
- ❑   OnDisconnection: Fires when Outlook is shutting down the addin.
- ❑   OnStartupComplete: Fires when Outlook startup is completed.
- ❑   OnAddInsUpdate: Any change in the status of any addin causes this event to fire.
- ❑   OnBeginShutdown: Fires when Outlook begins its shutdown procedures.

If the user manually connects or disconnects your addin using the COM Add-Ins dialog, your addin will not receive the OnStartupComplete and OnBeginShutdown events. These events refer to Outlook startup and shutdown, not your addin's startup and shutdown.

The OnConnection event supplies an application object in its input arguments; this is a trusted instance of the Outlook.Application object. It's important that all Outlook objects are derived from this Application object, so your addin code is trusted and does not cause the Outlook security prompts to display or to deny your code access to restricted Outlook properties.

VSTO addins don't supply an Application *object in their startup events. Instead they supply a* Me *(VB) or* this *(C#) object that passes a trusted* Application *object. VSTO 2005 SE changes prior VSTO code to pass this* Application *object as a member of* Me (Me.Application) *or* this (this.Application).

In many cases no code is used in the OnAddinsUpdate or OnBeginShutdown events, and often OnStartupComplete isn't used either. Even if you don't have any code for these events, it's important that they be in your code so that you correctly implement the IDTExtensibility2 interface.

The VSTO 2005 SE Startup *event fires when the Outlook* OnStartupComplete *event fires, not when* OnConnection *fires, as was the case in earlier versions of VSTO. This change was made to allow Outlook to fully initialize itself before the startup code is executed.*

Version Differences

An addin implemented for Outlook 2003 will run in Outlook 2007 as a COM addin, but doing so prevents you from using any properties, methods or events that were added in Outlook 2007. Additionally, changes were made to VSTO 2005 SE implementations for Outlook 2003 and 2007, so code can't be directly transported from VSTO 2003 or VSTO 2005 addins for Outlook 2003 to Outlook 2007 VSTO 2005 SE code. The Application object isn't directly exposed in VSTO 2005 SE as Me or this, and the name of the primary addin class was changed from ThisApplication to ThisAddin.

*The code shown in this chapter is for Outlook 2007 shared addins and VSTO 2005 SE addins. This code is used in this and the next chapter to develop functional Outlook addin templates for VB.NET, VB.NET with VSTO, C#, and C# with VSTO. These and other templates are available for download on the Wrox Web site (*www.wrox.com*) as well as at my Web site at* www.slovaktech.com.

The following sections show typical implementations of the IDTExtensibility2 interface events for VB.NET and C#, with typical implementations for VSTO 2005 SE also shown. All references to VSTO in this chapter are references to VSTO 2005 SE.

VB.NET Addin Implementations

The code in Listing 6.1 shows how to implement the IDTExtensibility2 interface in VB.NET.

Listing 6.1

```
Private m_objOutlook As Outlook.Application

    Public Sub OnConnection(ByVal application As Object, _
      ByVal connectMode As Extensibility.ext_ConnectMode, _
      ByVal addInInst As Object, _
      ByRef custom As System.Array) _
      Implements Extensibility.IDTExtensibility2.OnConnection

      ' Addin initialization code called here
      m_objOutlook = CType(application, Outlook.Application)
    End Sub

    Public Sub OnDisconnection(ByVal RemoveMode As _
      Extensibility.ext_DisconnectMode, ByRef custom As _
      System.Array) Implements _
      Extensibility.IDTExtensibility2.OnDisconnection

        If m_blnTeardown = False Then
            TearDown()
        End If
    End Sub
```

(continued)

Listing 6.1 *(continued)*

```
    Public Sub OnBeginShutdown(ByRef custom _
      As System.Array) Implements _
      Extensibility.IDTExtensibility2.OnBeginShutdown

    End Sub

    Public Sub OnAddInsUpdate(ByRef custom As _
      System.Array) Implements _
      Extensibility.IDTExtensibility2.OnAddInsUpdate

    End Sub

    Public Sub OnStartupComplete(ByRef custom As _
      System.Array) Implements _
      Extensibility.IDTExtensibility2.OnStartupComplete

    End Sub
```

VB.NET with VSTO

VSTO hides the internal implementation of the IDTExtensibility2 interface events and provides Startup and Shutdown events, as shown in Listing 6.2.

Listing 6.2

```
  Private m_objOutlook As Outlook.Application

    Private Sub ThisAddIn_Startup(ByVal sender As Object, _
      ByVal e As System.EventArgs) Handles Me.Startup

        ' Store a reference to the Outlook.Application object.
      m_objOutlook = Me.Application
    End Sub

    Private Sub ThisAddIn_Shutdown(ByVal sender As Object, _
      ByVal e As System.EventArgs) Handles Me.Shutdown

        ' clean up the Outlook objects and other public objects.
      TearDown()
    End Sub
```

C# Addin Implementations

Listing 6.3 shows how the IDTExtensibility2 interface is implemented in C#.

Listing 6.3

```
  private Outlook.Application applicationObect;

      public void OnConnection(object application,
          Extensibility.ext_ConnectMode connectMode,
          object addInInst, ref System.Array custom)
```

Listing 6.3 *(continued)*

```
        {
            applicationObject = application;
        }

        public void OnDisconnection(Extensibility.ext_DisconnectMode
            disconnectMode, ref System.Array custom)
        {
            if (m_Teardown == false) TearDown();
        }

        public void OnAddInsUpdate(ref System.Array custom)
        {
        }

        public void OnStartupComplete(ref System.Array custom)
        {
        }

        public void OnBeginShutdown(ref System.Array custom)
        {
        }
```

C# with VSTO

VSTO hides the internal implementation of the `IDTExtensibility2` interface events and instead provides `Startup` and `Shutdown` events, as shown in Listing 6.4.

Listing 6.4

```
private Outlook.Application m_Outlook;

    private void ThisAddin_Startup(object sender, System.EventArgs e)
    {
        m_Outlook = this.Application;
    }

    private void ThisAddin_Shutdown(object sender, System.EventArgs e)
    {
        // This cleans up the Outlook objects and other public objects.
        TearDown();
    }
```

Addin Templates

An addin template that doesn't add any additional functionality is pretty useless. There is no handling for new `Inspectors` or `Explorers` as the user opens them, and other functionality such as handling changes to Outlook items or folders doesn't exist. The addin templates presented in this chapter add handling for collections of `Inspectors` and `Explorers`, show property pages for the Options and folder Properties dialogs and provide for communication with the addin from outside code. Additional functionality for handling changes to collections of items, adding user interface elements, such as toolbars and menus, handling of the new `Inspector` Ribbon interface and other things are added to the templates in the next chapter.

Explorer and Inspector Event Handlers

When a user opens an item, an `Inspector` is opened and the `NewInspector` event of the `Inspectors` collection is fired. When a user opens a view of a folder in a new window, a new `Explorer` is opened and the `NewExplorer` event of the `Explorers` collection is fired. This section shows how to set up to handle those events and shows how to manage open `Inspectors` and `Explorers` in collections used to separately reference each open object and work with it, without impacting any other open object of the same class. The collections used for this also serve to keep these object references alive, so the .NET garbage collector doesn't remove the references while you still need them.

> *One exception to the rule that the `NewInspector` event fires each time an Outlook item is opened is when Send To ⇨ Mail Recipient is used to send a file. This uses Simple MAPI to create an Outlook email item and does not fire the `NewInspector` event. In Outlook 2002 and later, the email item is added to the `Inspectors` collection, but the `NewInspector` event will not fire.*

If Outlook is opened with no `Explorers`, such as when Send To ⇨ Mail Recipient is used to open a new email or when software that syncs Outlook with a PDA device is started, you should not initialize your addin in most cases. The addin templates monitor for cases such as this and wait for an `Explorer` to be opened before calling initialization procedures.

The `Inspector.Close` and `Explorer.Close` events should be handled in only one of two places:

❑ If wrapper classes are being used to handle `Inspectors` and `Explorers` the `Close` events should be handled in the wrapper class.

❑ If wrapper classes aren't being used, the `Close` events should be handled in the class where the `NewInspector` and `NewExplorer` events are handled.

The code in this chapter uses wrapper classes for `Inspectors` and `Explorers`. If you don't use wrapper classes, use `Close` event handlers in the connection class.

Setting Up Explorer and Inspector Event Handlers

The following sections complete the module-level declarations for the VB.NET and C# templates and add initialization for the `NewExplorer` and `NewInspector` event handlers.

VB.NET

Declaring an object variable `WithEvents` notifies the compiler that the variable will be handling events for that object, as the declarations for the `Outlook.Application`, `NameSpace`, `Explorers`, `Inspectors`, `Explorer`, and `Inspector` objects show in Listing 6.5.

The values of the `GuidAttribute` and `ProgIdAttribute` directives should be different for each addin you create, to make sure each addin is uniquely identified to the Framework and to Outlook.

Listing 6.5

```
Imports Extensibility
Imports System.Runtime.InteropServices
Imports Outlook = Microsoft.Office.Interop.Outlook
```

Listing 6.5 (continued

```
Imports Office = Microsoft.Office.Core
Imports System.Windows.Forms
Imports System.Text

<GuidAttribute("E79C3DDB-C8B2-4920-AF07-20B7D9D670E8"), _
ProgIdAttribute("VBAddinTemplate.Connect")> _
Public Class Connect

#Region "Interface implementations"
    Implements Extensibility.IDTExtensibility2
#End Region

#Region "Module level declarations"
    Private addInInstance As Office.COMAddIn

    Private WithEvents m_objOutlook As Outlook.Application
    Private WithEvents m_objNS As Outlook.NameSpace

    'Event-aware references to Explorers collection & Explorer object
    Private WithEvents m_colExplorers As Outlook.Explorers
    Private WithEvents m_olExplorer As Outlook.Explorer

    'Event-aware references to Inspectors collection & Inspector object
    Private WithEvents m_colInspectors As Outlook.Inspectors
    Private WithEvents m_olInspector As Outlook.Inspector

    ' State flags
    Private m_blnTeardown As Boolean
    Private m_blnInit As Boolean

#End Region
```

The `OnConnection` handler in this section adds code to determine if Outlook was opened with a user interface, with an `Explorer` being displayed. If no `Explorer` is shown, the code continues to run to monitor the `Explorers` collection and starts the addin initialization when an `Explorer` is displayed. If no `Explorer` is displayed before Outlook shuts down, the call to the `Teardown()` procedure ensures that all Outlook objects have been released so that Outlook can close correctly. This code will run correctly for both Outlook 2007 and Outlook 2003.

First, the module-level `Outlook.Application` object `m_objOutlook` is instantiated by casting it from the `application` object passed in `OnConnection`. A `NameSpace` object is instantiated; then an `Explorers` collection object, `m_colExplorers`, is instantiated from `m_objOutlook.Explorers`. The count of open `Explorers` is checked to see if there is at least one `Explorer`, if there is, Outlook has been started with a user interface. If this is the case an `Explorer` object, `m_olExplorer`, is instantiated that represents the open `Explorer`, and the `Explorer` is added to an `Explorer` wrapper collection. `Explorer` and `Inspector` objects should be instantiated to handle `Close` events if you aren't using wrapper classes. Listing 6.6 shows the code for the `OnConnection` event handler, which follows the code in Listing 6.5 in the `Connect` class of the addin.

Listing 6.6

```
#Region "IDTExtensibility events"
    Public Sub OnConnection(ByVal application As Object,_
    ByVal connectMode As Extensibility.ext_ConnectMode,_
    ByVal addInInst As Object, ByRef custom As System.Array)_
    Implements Extensibility.IDTExtensibility2.OnConnection

        m_blnTeardown = False

            'set module level reference to COMAddIn object
            Try
                m_objOutlook = CType(application, Outlook.Application)
                m_objNS = m_objOutlook.GetNamespace("MAPI")

                'event-aware reference to Explorers collection
                'use NewExplorer event to watch for UI creation
                m_colExplorers = m_objOutlook.Explorers

                Try
                    'Are we starting with UI?
                    If m_colExplorers.Count > 0 Then
                        'For Explorer.Close if not using wrappers
                        m_olExplorer = m_objOutlook.Explorers.Item(1)

                        'we have UI
                        InitHandler()

                        If m_blnInit = True Then
                            AddExpl(m_olExplorer)
                        End If
                    Else
                        'do nothing
                        'monitor Explorers collection (in this module)
                        'if NewExplorer event is raised then we have UI
                    End If
                Catch ex As Exception
                    TearDown()
                End Try

            Catch ex As Exception
                TearDown()
            End Try
    End Sub
#End Region
```

The NewExplorer event is handled in the m_colExplorers_NewExplorer event handler, which assigns the ActiveExplorer object to the module level Explorer object variable that handles various Explorer events. NewExplorer won't fire for the Explorer displayed when Outlook starts, so that Explorer is added to the Explorer wrapper collection in the OnConnection event handler. Any other new Explorers that are opened are handled and added to the Explorer wrapper collection in the NewExplorer event handler, shown in Listing 6.7.

Listing 6.7

```
#Region "Explorer (folder window) related events"
    ' NewExplorer event will be raised if there is UI
    Private Sub m_colExplorers_NewExplorer(ByVal Explorer As _
        Outlook.Explorer) Handles m_colExplorers.NewExplorer

        'assign ActiveExplorer
        m_olExplorer = Explorer

        If m_blnInit = False Then
            'we didn't have UI before - initialize addin objects
            InitHandler()
        End If

        If m_blnInit = True Then
            AddExpl(Explorer)
        End If
    End Sub
```

The OnDisconnection Catch-22 Bug

In most cases Outlook 2007 correctly handles Outlook shutting down by firing the OnDisconnection event. However, Outlook 2003 and earlier versions suffer from what's known as the OnDisconnection Catch-22 bug. This bug prevents Outlook from firing OnDisconnection, and keeps Outlook hung in memory unless all Outlook objects are released. Once all the Outlook objects have been released OnDisconnection will fire, but the bug is that OnDisconnection is used to know when to release your Outlook objects. The code in Listing 6.8 should be used to determine when the last Explorer is closing. The code does no harm in Outlook 2007 and will work around the Catch-22 bug in earlier versions of Outlook. In fact, there are cases even in Outlook 2007 where this code is needed, for example when out-of-process Outlook code closes Outlook. In cases like that, this code will let Outlook 2007 close gracefully, so I recommend that you use this code in all cases, even with Outlook 2007.

If an Explorer wrapper isn't used, declare an event-handling Explorer object variable. Assign the Explorer passed in NewExplorer or the initial Explorer in OnConnection to this event-handling Explorer variable. Use the Explorer_Close event to determine if any Explorers and Inspectors are still open, and, if not, call your release code. If any Explorers are open, assign the ActiveExplorer object to the Explorer variable so that the Explorer variable is still instantiated and can handle the closing of the final Explorer. Similar code is used instead in Explorer.Close event handlers in the wrapper classes if wrappers are used.

Listing 6.8

```
    ' Monitor Explorer_Close to see when UI "disappears"
    Private Sub m_olExplorer_Close() Handles m_olExplorer.Close
        'release current reference
        m_olExplorer = Nothing

        Try
            m_olExplorer = m_objOutlook.ActiveExplorer
```

(continued)

Listing 6.8 (continued)

```
        Catch ex As Exception
            Err.Clear()
            If m_objOutlook.Inspectors.Count = 0 Then
                'release addin objects
                If m_blnTeardown = False Then
                    TearDown()
                End If
            End If
        End Try
    End Sub
#End Region
```

When the current `Explorer` closes, an attempt is made to assign the `ActiveExplorer` object to the module-level `Explorer` object, as shown in Listing 6.8. If that fails, then no other `Explorers` are present. If no `Inspectors` are present either, that indicates that Outlook wants to close down, so the code calls the `Teardown` method to release all the Outlook objects so that Outlook can close correctly. The code in Listing 6.8 is not used if wrapper classes are used.

The code in Listing 6.9 handles the `NewInspector` event to detect when Outlook opens a new `Inspector` window. This `Inspector` is added to the `Inspector` wrapper collection, unless the `Inspector` is for a Note item. Note items do not correctly implement an interface, so they are brain dead and do not get handled by the `NewInspector` code.

Listing 6.9

```
#Region "Inspector (item window) related events"
    Private Sub m_colInspectors_NewInspector(ByVal Inspector As _
        Outlook.Inspector) Handles m_colInspectors.NewInspector

        'No handling of Inspectors for Notes, they are brain dead
        If Not (TypeOf (Inspector.CurrentItem) Is Outlook.NoteItem) Then
            m_olInspector = Inspector
            AddInsp(Inspector)
        End If
    End Sub
```

Similarly to the `Explorer.Close` code, the `Inspector.Close` code in Listing 6.10 attempts to assign the `ActiveInspector` object to the module-level `Inspector` object. If this fails and there are no open `Explorers`, then Outlook wants to close down, so a call to `Teardown` is made to release all the Outlook objects. The code in Listing 6.10 is not needed if you use `Inspector` wrappers or if you are using VSTO 2005 SE. Similar code is used in the `Inspector` wrapper to handle the `Close` event.

Listing 6.10

```
    Private Sub m_olInspector_Close() Handles m_olInspector.Close
        m_olInspector = Nothing

        Try
            m_olInspector = m_objOutlook.ActiveInspector
```

Listing 6.10 *(continued)*

```
            Catch ex As Exception
                MessageBox.Show(ex.Message)

                If m_olInspector Is Nothing Then
                    If m_objOutlook.Explorers.Count = 0 Then
                        If m_blnTeardown = False Then
                            TearDown()
                        End If
                    End If
                End If
            End Try
        End Sub
    #End Region
```

VB.NET With VSTO

The module-level declarations and `Startup` event handler code for VSTO in Listing 6.11 are almost identical to the plain VB.NET code shown in Listings 6.5 and 6.6 and perform the same functions. The code for the `NewExplorer`, `Explorer.Close`, `NewInspector`, and `Inspector.Close` event handlers is identical to the code for the plain VB.NET template in Listings 6.7 to 6.10.

Listing 6.11

```
Imports Office = Microsoft.Office.Core
Imports System.Windows.Forms
Imports System.Runtime.InteropServices
Imports System.Reflection

Partial Public Class ThisAddIn

#Region "Class level declarations"
    Private m_objOutlook As Outlook.Application

    Private WithEvents m_objNS As Outlook.NameSpace

    'Event-aware references to Explorers collection & Explorer object
    Private WithEvents m_colExplorers As Outlook.Explorers
    Private WithEvents m_olExplorer As Outlook.Explorer

    'Event-aware references to Inspectors collection & Inspector object
    Private WithEvents m_colInspectors As Outlook.Inspectors
    Private WithEvents m_olInspector As Outlook.Inspector

    ' State flags
    Private m_blnTeardown As Boolean
    Private m_blnInit As Boolean
    Private _disposed As Boolean

    Private m_strProgID As String
#End Region
```

(continued)

Listing 6.11 *(continued)*

```
#Region "Startup and Shutdown"
    Private Sub ThisAddIn_Startup(ByVal sender As Object,_
    ByVal e As System.EventArgs) Handles Me.Startup

        ' Store a reference to the Outlook.Application object.
        m_objOutlook = Me.Application
        m_objNS = m_objOutlook.GetNamespace("MAPI")

        m_blnTeardown = False

        Try
            'event-aware reference to Explorers collection
            'use NewExplorer event to watch for UI creation
            m_colExplorers = m_objOutlook.Explorers

            Try
                'Are we starting with UI?
                If m_colExplorers.Count > 0 Then
                    m_olExplorer = m_objOutlook.Explorers.Item(1)

                    'we have UI
                    InitHandler()

                    If m_blnInit = True Then
                        AddExpl(m_olExplorer)
                    End If
                Else
                    'do nothing
                    'monitor Explorers collection (in this module)
                    'if NewExplorer event is raised then we have UI
                End If
            Catch ex As Exception
                TearDown()
            End Try

        Catch ex As Exception
            TearDown()
        End Try

    End Sub
```

C#

C# doesn't have a `WithEvents` statement like VB.NET, so all event handlers are added using the `+= new EventHandler` construct, such as:

```
m_Explorers.NewExplorer += new
Outlook.ExplorersEvents_NewExplorerEventHandler(m_Explorers_NewExplorer);
```

C# also doesn't have a `Collection` object, so in this case the open `Explorers` and `Inspectors` are wrapped in `System.Collections.SortedList` objects, which makes them available for later use and prevents the garbage collector from prematurely releasing the `Inspector` and `Explorer` references.

The code in Listings 6.12 and 6.13 show the C# equivalent of VB.NET code in Listings 6.5 to 6.10. If wrapper classes are used, the Close event handling for Inspectors and Explorers is handled in the wrapper classes and not in the main code class.

Listing 6.12

```csharp
using System;
using Extensibility;
using System.Runtime.InteropServices;
using System.Reflection;
using System.Windows.Forms;
using Outlook = Microsoft.Office.Interop.Outlook;
using Office = Microsoft.Office.Core;

public class Connect : Object, Extensibility.IDTExtensibility2
{
    #region Module_level_declarations

    // start of COM objects
    private object applicationObject = null;

    private Outlook.Application m_Outlook = null;
    private Outlook.NameSpace m_NameSpace = null;

    private Office.COMAddIn addInInstance = null;

    // Event-aware references to Explorers collection & Explorer object
    private Outlook.Explorers m_Explorers = null;
    private Outlook.ExplorersClass m_ExplorersClass = null;

    private Outlook.Explorer m_Explorer = null;
    private Outlook.ExplorerClass m_ExplorerClass = null;

    // Event-aware references to Inspectors collection & Inspector object
    private Outlook.Inspectors m_Inspectors = null;
    private Outlook.InspectorsClass m_InspectorClass = null;

    private Outlook.Inspector m_Inspector = null;
    private Outlook.InspectorClass m_InspectorClass = null;

    // end of COM objects
```

SortedList *objects are used for the collections of open* Explorers *and* Inspectors.

```csharp
    // Explorer Wrapper Collection
    private System.Collections.SortedList m_ExplWrap = null;

    // Inspector Wrapper Collection
    private System.Collections.SortedList m_InspWrap = null;

    private string m_ProgID = "";

    private int m_WrapperID = 0;
```

```
            private int m_OutlookVersion = 0;

            //Initialization flags
            private bool m_Teardown = false;

            private bool m_Init = false;
        #endregion
```

The OnConnection code in Listing 6.13 adds the current Explorer to a sorted list, used to maintain the Explorer wrapper class collection. The sorted list is initialized to hold 10 simultaneously open Explorer wrapper classes.

Listing 6.13

```
        public void OnConnection(object application, Extensibility.ext_ConnectMode
connectMode, object addInInst, ref System.Array custom)
        {
            applicationObject = application;

                try
                {
                    m_Outlook = (Outlook.Application)application;
                    m_NameSpace = m_Outlook.GetNamespace("MAPI");

                    //event-aware reference to Explorers collection
                    //use NewExplorer event to watch for UI creation
                    m_Explorers = m_Outlook.Explorers;

                    try
                    {
                        m_Teardown = false;

                        //Are we starting with UI?
                        if (m_Explorers.Count > 0)
                        {
                            m_Explorer = m_Outlook.Explorers[1];

                            //we have UI - initialize base class
                            InitHandler();

                            if (m_Init == true)
                            {
                                // allot space initially for 10 open Explorers at a time
                                m_ExplWrap = new System.Collections.SortedList(10);

                                OutExpl adder = new OutExpl();

                                m_WrapperID = adder.AddExpl(m_Explorer,
m_WrapperID, ref m_ExplWrap);

                                adder = null;
                            }

                            m_Inspectors = m_Outlook.Inspectors;
```

After the initializations are finished for the open Explorer to put it in a sorted list and the Inspectors collection is initialized, the event handlers are added for the NewExplorer, ExplorerClose, and NewInspector events.

```
                    m_Explorers.NewExplorer += new
    Outlook.ExplorersEvents_NewExplorerEventHandler(m_Explorers_NewExplorer);

                    m_ExplorerClass = (Outlook.ExplorerClass)m_Explorer;

                    m_ExplorerClass.ExplorerEvents_Event_Close += new
    Outlook.ExplorerEvents_CloseEventHandler(m_Explorer_Close);

                    m_InspectorsClass = (Outlook.InspectorsClass)m_Inspectors

                    m_InspectorsClass.NewInspector += new
    Outlook.InspectorsEvents_NewInspectorEventHandler(m_InspectorsClass_NewInspector);
                }
                else
                {
                    //do nothing
                    //monitor Explorers collection (in this module)
                    //if NewExplorer event is raised then we have UI
                }
            }
            catch (Exception ex)
            {
                MessageBox.Show(ex.Message);
                TearDown();
            }
        }
        catch (Exception ex)
        {
            MessageBox.Show(ex.Message);
            TearDown();
        }
    }
```

The code in Listing 6.14 shows the NewExplorer event handler. The NewExplorer event handler adds the new Explorer to the sorted list used to wrap open Explorers and the new Explorer is assigned to the module level m_Explorer object.

Listing 6.14

```
#region explorer_related_events
    // NewExplorer event will be raised if there is UI
    private void m_Explorers_NewExplorer(Microsoft.Office.Interop.Outlook.Explorer
Explorer)
    {
        //assign ActiveExplorer
        m_Explorer = Explorer;
```

(continued)

Listing 6.14 *(continued)*

```
        if (m_Init == false)
        {
            //we didn't have UI before - initialize addin objects
            InitHandler();
        }

        if (m_Init == true)
        {
            OutExpl adder = new OutExpl();

            m_WrapperID = adder.AddExpl(Explorer, m_WrapperID, ref m_ExplWrap);

            adder = null;
        }
    }
}
```

The code in Listing 6.15 shows the event handler for the `Explorer.Close` event. When `Explorer.Close` fires, the module-level `m_Explorer` is assigned to `ActiveExplorer`. If that fails, and there are no open `Inspectors`, the `Teardown()` procedure is called to release all Outlook objects. The code in Listings 6.15 and 6.16 is only needed if you aren't using `Explorer` wrappers and aren't using VSTO 2005 SE. Similar code is used in the `Explorer` and `Inspector` wrappers to handle the `Close` events.

Listing 6.15

```
        // Monitor Explorer_Close to see when UI "disappears"
        private void m_Explorer_Close()
        {
            //release current reference
            m_Explorer = null;
            try
            {
                m_Explorer = m_Outlook.ActiveExplorer();
            }
            catch
            {
                if (m_Outlook.Inspectors.Count == 0)
                {
                    //release addin objects
                    if (m_Teardown == false) TearDown();
                }
            }
        }
#endregion
```

When a new `Inspector` is opened, it's checked to make sure it's not a Note `Inspector`, and if not a module level `m_InspectorClass` object is instantiated as the new `Inspector` for event-handling purposes as shown in Listing 6.16.

> `Inspector` *events that are overloaded by* `Inspector` *methods, such as* `Close`, *are handled not by the* `Inspector` *object but by the* `InspectorClass` *object in C#. This also applies to other objects where events are overloaded by methods with the same name.*

An event handler for the `Inspector.Close` event is created to allow the code to handle the closing of the new `Inspector`.

```
m_InspectorClass.InspectorEvents_Event_Close += new
Outlook.InspectorEvents_CloseEventHandler(molInspector_Close);
```

Then the new `Inspector` is added to the `Inspector` wrapper sorted list.

Listing 6.16

```csharp
#region inspector_related_events
    private void m_InspectorsClass_NewInspector(Outlook.Inspector Inspector)
    {
        //No handling of Inspectors for Notes, they are brain dead

        // set up to get the Class property of the item in the Inspector
        object item = Inspector.CurrentItem;

        Type _type;
        _type = item.GetType();

        object[] _args = new Object[] { };  // dummy argument array
        Outlook.OlObjectClass _class = Outlook.OlObjectClass.olNote;

        try // try to get the Class using reflection
        {
            _class = (Outlook.OlObjectClass)_type.InvokeMember("Class",
BindingFlags.Public | BindingFlags.GetField | BindingFlags.GetProperty, null, item,
_args);
        }
        catch (Exception ex)
        {
            //MessageBox.Show(ex.Message);
            _class = Outlook.OlObjectClass.olNote;
        }

        if (_class != Outlook.OlObjectClass.olNote)           {
            m_Inspector = Inspector;

a            try
            {
                m_InspectorClass = (Outlook.InspectorClass)m_Inspector;

                m_InspectorClass.InspectorEvents_Event_Close += new
Outlook.InspectorEvents_CloseEventHandler(molInspector_Close);

                OutInsp adder = new OutInsp();

                m_WrapperID = adder.AddInsp(Inspector, m_WrapperID, _class, ref
m_ExplWrap);

                adder = null;
            }
```

(continued)

Listing 6.16 *(continued)*

```
            catch (Exception ex)
            {
                MessageBox.Show(ex.Message);
            }
        }
    }
```

When the `Inspector` closes, the `Close` event handler assigns `ActiveInspector` to `m_Inspector`, and if that fails and there are no open `Explorers`, the `Teardown()` procedure is called to release the Outlook objects, as shown in Listing 6.17. The code in Listing 6.17 is used only if wrapper classes aren't being used.

Listing 6.17

```
    private void molInspector_Close()
    {
        m_Inspector = null;

        try
        {
            m_Inspector = m_Outlook.ActiveInspector();
        }
        catch
        {
            if (m_Inspector == null)
            {
                if (m_Outlook.Explorers.Count == 0)
                {
                    if (m_Teardown == false)
                    {
                        TearDown();
                    }
                }
            }
        }
    }
#endregion
```

C# with VSTO

The code for the C# with VSTO template is identical to the code for plain C#, except that the additional initialization code is placed in the `Startup` event handler, so it's not shown here. The module-level declarations and `Startup` event handler code for VSTO are almost identical to the plain C# code shown above and perform the same functions, so that code isn't shown here either.

Explorer and Inspector Wrappers

The `Explorer` and `Inspector` wrapper collections store classes that wrap `Explorer` and `Inspector` objects. This keeps the references alive, and also allows each `Explorer` and `Inspector` to have a different user interface and to respond differently and uniquely to events from the user interface or from some other source. The use of a wrapper class is a key concept when modifying the Outlook user interface and handling various events associated with specific Outlook items.

Here's an example of why using wrapper classes is such an important concept. Say that your company has business logic that says that every email item that goes to a recipient not within your organization must have a legal disclaimer appended to the email body. The company business logic also provides an added menu to `Explorers` that are displaying mail folders. This menu is used to open custom email templates that the company provides.

Wrapper classes make it possible to separately and uniquely handle each open `Inspector` to intercept the `MailItem.Send` event to see where the email is being sent to determine if the disclaimer must be added to the email. The `Explorer` wrapper makes it possible to maintain separate states of visibility for the templates menu for every open `Explorer`, based on what type of folder is being displayed in that `Explorer`. Wrapper classes also make it possible for a custom set of options provided by your addin to have separate options set for every open `Inspector` and `Explorer`, among many other uses.

The code to add a new `Explorer` to the `Explorer` wrapper collection, and to remove a wrapper class when an `Explorer` is closed is in a code module named `ExplWrap`. This module has two procedures, `AddExpl` and `KillExpl`. The corresponding module for `Inspectors` is named `InspWrap` and also has two procedures, `AddInsp` and `KillInsp`.

It's possible to set up one module or class that adds either `Inspectors` or `Explorers` to the appropriate collection or even to the same collection, but I prefer to use separate collections and modules to allow maximum flexibility in my addin coding. You can also set up a base class for a unified wrapper and wrapper class with classes that implement the base class and add specific functionality, depending on whether they are being used for `Explorers` or `Inspectors`.

Explorer Wrappers in VB.NET

The code for the `OutExpl` module is shown in Listings 6.18 and 6.19. The VSTO VB.NET addin template also uses this code.

The `AddExpl` procedure, in Listing 6.18, is passed the new `Explorer` and adds the `Explorer` to the `Explorer` property of the `ExplWrap` wrapper class. The value of a global ID variable for new wrapper class's `g_WrapperID` is stored in the wrapper class as the `Key` property, the new wrapper class is added to the `g_colExplWrap` global collection, and the `g_WrapperID` variable is then incremented for use in the next wrapper class. The `g_WrapperID` variable is shared between `Explorer` and `Inspector` wrappers.

Listing 6.18

```
Imports Outlook = Microsoft.Office.Interop.Outlook
Imports System.Windows.Forms

Friend Module OutExpl

    Public Sub AddExpl(ByVal Explorer As Outlook.Explorer)
        Dim objExplWrap As New ExplWrap

        Try
            objExplWrap.Explorer = Explorer

            objExplWrap.Key = g_WrapperID

            g_colExplWrap.Add(objExplWrap, CStr(g_WrapperID))
```

(continued)

Listing 6.18 *(continued)*

```
            g_WrapperID += 1

        Catch ex As Exception
            MessageBox.Show(ex.Message)
        End Try
        objExplWrap = Nothing
    End Sub
```

When the Explorer is closed, a Close event is handled by the wrapper class, which removes itself from the wrapper collection by calling KillExpl, as shown in Listing 6.19. Each wrapper class handles its own Close event, something that wouldn't be possible without a wrapper class.

Listing 6.19

```
    Public Sub KillExpl(ByVal WrapperID As Integer)
        Try
            g_colExplWrap.Remove(CStr(WrapperID))
        Catch ex As Exception
            MessageBox.Show(ex.Message)
        End Try
    End Sub
End Module
```

The code in Listings 6.20 and 6.21 show the ExplWrap class, used to handle Explorer events and user interface distinct to that wrapper class. A class-level Explorer object, m_objExpl, is declared WithEvents so that it can handle Explorer events, and is initialized when the public Explorer property is set to the Explorer being wrapped in the class.

Listing 6.20

```
Imports Outlook = Microsoft.Office.Interop.Outlook
Imports Office = Microsoft.Office.Core
Imports System.Windows.Forms

Friend Class ExplWrap
    Private WithEvents m_objExpl As Outlook.Explorer

    Private m_ID As Integer

    Private m_blnStartup As Boolean

    Private m_blnKilled As Boolean

    Public Property Explorer() As Outlook.Explorer
        Get
            Explorer = m_objExpl
        End Get

        Set(ByVal objExpl As Outlook.Explorer)
            m_objExpl = objExpl
```

Listing 6.20 *(continued)*

```
            m_blnStartup = True
        End Set
    End Property


    Public Property Key() As Integer
        Get
            Key = m_ID
        End Get

        Set(ByVal nID As Integer)
            m_ID = nID
        End Set
    End Property

    Public Sub New()
        m_blnKilled = False

        Try
            m_objExpl = Nothing
        Catch ex As Exception
            MessageBox.Show(ex.Message)
        End Try
    End Sub
```

Listing 6.21 shows what happens when the `Explorer` wrapped in a class is closed. The `Key` property, stored locally as `m_ID`, is used to remove the collection member with the same `Key` as the wrapper class from the wrapper class collection. This is done by calling `KillExpl` with the value of `m_ID`.

Listing 6.21

```
    Private Sub m_objExpl_Close() Handles m_objExpl.Close
        If Not m_blnKilled Then
            m_blnKilled = True
            KillExpl(m_ID)

            If m_objExpl IsNot Nothing Then
                m_objExpl = Nothing
            End If
        End If
    End Sub
End Class
```

Explorer Wrappers in C#

The code for the `OutExpl` class is shown in Listings 6.22 and 6.23. This code is also used by the VSTO C# addin template, but with a different `namespace` declaration.

The `AddExpl` procedure, in Listing 6.22, is passed the new `Explorer` and a wrapper ID value and adds the `Explorer` to the `Explorer` property of the `ExplWrap` wrapper class. The wrapper ID variable for the new wrapper class, `WrapperID`, is stored in the wrapper class as the `Key` property.

Because the sorted list used to store the wrapper classes isn't global in the C# code, the list is passed to the AddExpl procedure by reference, and the reference to the list is stored within the wrapper class. The WrapperID variable is then incremented for use in the next wrapper class and returned as the return value of the AddExpl procedure.

Listing 6.22

```
using System;
using System.Collections.Generic;
using System.Text;
using Outlook = Microsoft.Office.Interop.Outlook;
using System.Windows.Forms;

namespace CSAddinTemplate
{
    class OutExpl
    {
        public int AddExpl(Outlook.Explorer Explorer, int WrapperID,
ref System.Collections.SortedList WrapperCol)
        {
            ExplWrap objExplWrap = new ExplWrap();

            try
            {
                objExplWrap.Explorer = Explorer;

                objExplWrap.Key = WrapperID;

                objExplWrap.WrapperClass = WrapperCol;

                // add wrapper class to the collection to keep it alive
                WrapperCol.Add(WrapperID, ref objExplWrap);

                WrapperID += 1;
            }
            catch (Exception ex)
            {
                MessageBox.Show(ex.Message);
            }

            objExplWrap = null;

            return WrapperID;
        }
```

When the Explorer is closed, a Close event is handled by the wrapper class, which removes itself from the wrapper collection by calling KillExpl, as shown in Listing 6.23. Each wrapper class handles its own Close event, something that wouldn't be possible without a wrapper class.

Listing 6.23

```
        public void KillExpl(int WrapperID, System.Collections.SortedList WrapperCol)
        {
            try
```

Listing 6.23 *(continued)*

```
        {
                // remove wrapper class from wrapper collection
                WrapperCol.Remove(WrapperID);
        }
        catch (Exception ex)
        {
                MessageBox.Show(ex.Message);
        }
    }
  }
}
```

The code in Listings 6.24 and 6.25 show the `ExplWrap` class, used to handle `Explorer` events and user interface distinct to that wrapper class. A class-level `Explorer` object, `m_Expl`, is declared for use in handling `Explorer` events, and it is initialized when the public `Explorer` property is set to the `Explorer` being wrapped in the class.

When the `Explorer` property is initialized, the event handler for the `Close` event is created using this code:

```
m_ExplClass.ExplorerEvents_Event_Close += new
Outlook.ExplorerEvents_CloseEventHandler(m_Expl_Close);.
```

Listing 6.24

```
using System;
using System.Collections.Generic;
using System.Text;
using System.Runtime.InteropServices;
using Outlook = Microsoft.Office.Interop.Outlook;
using Office = Microsoft.Office.Core;
using System.Windows.Forms;

namespace CSAddinTemplate
{
    class ExplWrap
    {
        private Outlook.Explorer m_Expl = null;
        private Outlook.ExplorerClass m_ExplClass = null;

        private int m_ID = 0;

        private bool m_Startup = false;

        private bool m_Killed = false;

        private System.Collections.SortedList m_WrapperClass = null;

        public System.Collections.SortedList WrapperClass
        {
            get
            {
```

(continued)

Listing 6.24 *(continued)*

```
            return m_WrapperClass;
        }

        set
        {
            m_WrapperClass = value;
        }
    }

    public Outlook.Explorer Explorer
    {
        get
        {
            return m_Expl;
        }

        set
        {
            m_Expl = value;
```

The class-level Explorer *object is cast as an* ExplorerClass *object to allow handling of the* Explorer.Close *event.*

```
            m_ExplClass = (Outlook.ExplorerClass)m_Expl;

            // hook up the Close event handler
            m_ExplClass.ExplorerEvents_Event_Close += new
Outlook.ExplorerEvents_CloseEventHandler(m_Expl_Close);

            m_Killed = false;
            m_Startup = true;
        }
    }

    public int Key
    {
        get
        {
            return m_ID;
        }

        set
        {
            m_ID = value;
        }
    }
```

Listing 6.25 shows what happens when the Explorer wrapped in a class is closed. The Key property, stored locally as m_ID, is used to remove the collection member with the same Key as the wrapper class from the wrapper class collection. This is done by calling KillExpl in a new instance of the OutExpl class with the value of m_ID, and the stored instance of the sorted list used to store the wrapper class, m_WrapperClass. The Explorer.Close handler is released by removing it from the events handler so that the class can close cleanly.

Listing 6.25

```
        private void m_Expl_Close()
        {
            if (m_Killed == false)
            {
                m_Killed = true;

                OutExpl killer = new OutExpl();
                killer.KillExpl(m_ID, m_WrapperClass);
                killer = null;

                m_WrapperClass = null;

                // release the Close event handler
                m_ExplClass.ExplorerEvents_Event_Close -= new
Outlook.ExplorerEvents_CloseEventHandler(m_Expl_Close);

                if (m_Expl != null) {m_Expl = null;}
                if (m_ExplClass != null) {m_ExplClass = null;}
            }
        }
    }
}
```

Inspector Wrappers in VB.NET

The code for the OutInsp module is shown in Listings 6.26 and 6.27. This code is also used by the VSTO VB.NET addin template.

The AddInsp procedure, in Listing 6.26, is passed the new Inspector and adds the Inspector to the Inspector property of the InspWrap wrapper class if the Inspector is displaying a MailItem. A MailItem property in the wrapper class is used to store an instance of the item displayed in the Inspector. This MailItem is used to handle events for the item in the Inspector. The same method is used for handling events for other types of items, a ContactItem would be stored and its events handled for a contact in an Inspector, and so on.

Separate wrapper classes can be used for each type of Outlook item you are handling, which allows the handling of every property, method, and event of that type of item. An alternative approach is to use a base class that implements common properties, methods, and events of all types of items and to implement the base class in separate classes for specific types of items. A final approach is to use reflection to get and set properties and to call methods of items using late binding. This approach is not used here, because it's slower and not as intuitive as the approach used.

A global ID variable for the new wrapper class, g_WrapperID, is stored in the wrapper class as the Key property, the new wrapper class is added to the g_colInspWrap global collection, and the g_WrapperID variable is then incremented for use in the next wrapper class, the same way as in an Explorer wrapper.

Listing 6.26

```
Imports Outlook = Microsoft.Office.Interop.Outlook
Imports System.Windows.Forms

Friend Module OutInsp

    Public Sub AddInsp(ByVal Inspector As Outlook.Inspector)
        Dim objInspWrap As New InspWrap
        Dim oMail As Outlook.MailItem

        If (TypeOf (Inspector.CurrentItem) Is Outlook.MailItem) Then
            oMail = Nothing
            oMail = TryCast(Inspector.CurrentItem, Outlook.MailItem)
            If oMail IsNot Nothing Then
                Try
                        objInspWrap.Inspector = Inspector
                        objInspWrap.MailItem = oMail
                        objInspWrap.Key = g_WrapperID

                        g_colInspWrap.Add(objInspWrap, CStr(g_WrapperID))

                        g_WrapperID += 1

                Catch ex As Exception
                        MessageBox.Show(ex.Message)
                End Try
            End If
        End If

        objInspWrap = Nothing
        oMail = Nothing
    End Sub
```

When the `Inspector` is closed, the `Close` event is handled by the wrapper class, which removes itself from the wrapper collection by calling `KillInsp`, shown in Listing 6.27

Listing 6.27

```
    Public Sub KillInsp(ByVal WrapperID As Integer)
        Try
                g_colInspWrap.Remove(CStr(WrapperID))
        Catch ex As Exception
                MessageBox.Show(ex.Message)
        End Try
    End Sub

End Module
```

The code in Listings 6.28 to 6.30 show the `InspWrap` class, used to handle `Inspector` events and user interface distinct to that wrapper class. A class-level `Inspector` object, `m_objInsp`, is declared `WithEvents` so that it can handle `Inspector` events, and it is initialized when the public `Inspector` property is set to the `Inspector` being wrapped in the class.

Listing 6.28

```
Imports Outlook = Microsoft.Office.Interop.Outlook

Friend Class InspWrap
    Private WithEvents m_objInsp As Outlook.Inspector
    Private WithEvents m_objMail As Outlook.MailItem

    Private m_ID As Integer
    Private m_blnKilled As Boolean

    Public Property MailItem() As Outlook.MailItem
        Get
            MailItem = m_objMail
        End Get

        Set(ByVal objMail As Outlook.MailItem)
            m_objMail = objMail
        End Set
    End Property

    Public Property Inspector() As Outlook.Inspector
        Get
            Inspector = m_objInsp
        End Get

        Set(ByVal objInspector As Outlook.Inspector)
            m_objInsp = objInspector
        End Set
    End Property

    Public Property Key() As Integer
        Get
            Key = m_ID
        End Get

        Set(ByVal lngID As Integer)
            m_ID = lngID
        End Set
    End Property

    Private Sub m_objInsp_Activate() Handles m_objInsp.Activate

    End Sub
```

Listing 6.29 shows what happens when the `Inspector` wrapped in a class is closed. The `Key` property, stored locally as `m_ID`, is used to remove the collection member with the same `Key` as the wrapper class from the wrapper class collection. This is done by calling `KillInsp` with the value of `m_ID`.

Listing 6.29

```
    Private Sub m_objInsp_Close() Handles m_objInsp.Close
        If Not m_blnKilled Then
            m_blnKilled = True
            KillInsp(m_ID)

            If m_objMail IsNot Nothing Then
                m_objMail = Nothing
            End If

            If m_objInsp IsNot Nothing Then
                m_objInsp = Nothing
            End If
        End If
    End Sub
```

Listing 6.30 shows basic event handlers for the `MailItem` events in the wrapper class.

Listing 6.30

```
    Private Sub m_objMail_Close(ByRef Cancel As Boolean) Handles m_objMail.Close

    End Sub

    Private Sub m_objMail_Open(ByRef Cancel As Boolean) Handles m_objMail.Open

    End Sub

    Private Sub m_objMail_Send(ByRef Cancel As Boolean) Handles m_objMail.Send

    End Sub

    Private Sub m_objMail_Unload() Handles m_objMail.Unload

    End Sub

    Private Sub m_objMail_Write(ByRef Cancel As Boolean) Handles m_objMail.Write

    End Sub
End Class
```

Inspector Wrappers in C#

The code for the `OutInsp` class is shown below, in Listings 6.31 and 6.32. This code is also used by the VSTO C# addin template, but with a different `namespace` declaration.

The `AddInsp` procedure, in Listing 6.31, is passed the new `Inspector` and a wrapper ID value and adds the `Inspector` to the `Inspector` property of the `InspWrap` wrapper class. The wrapper ID variable for the new wrapper class, `WrapperID`, is stored in the wrapper class as the `Key` property if the `Inspector` is displaying a `MailItem`. A `MailItem` property in the wrapper class is used to store an instance of the item displayed in the `Inspector`. This `MailItem` is used to handle events for the item in the `Inspector`.

Because the sorted list used to store the wrapper classes isn't global in the C# code, the list is passed to the AddInsp procedure by reference, and the reference to the list is stored within the wrapper class. The WrapperID variable is then incremented for use in the next wrapper class and returned as the return value of the AddInsp procedure.

Listing 6.31

```
using Outlook = Microsoft.Office.Interop.Outlook;
using System.Windows.Forms;

namespace CSAddinTemplate
{
    class OutInsp
    {
        public int AddInsp(Outlook.Inspector Inspector, int WrapperID,
Outlook.OlObjectClass InspectorType, ref System.Collections.SortedList WrapperCol)
        {
            if (InspectorType == Outlook.OlObjectClass.olMail)
            {
                InspWrap objInspWrap = new InspWrap();
                Outlook.MailItem oMail = null;

                if (InspectorType == Outlook.OlObjectClass.olMail)
                {
                    try
                    {
                        oMail = (Outlook.MailItem)Inspector.CurrentItem;
                    }
                    catch (Exception ex)
                    {
                        MessageBox.Show(ex.Message);
                    }
                }

                if (oMail != null)
                {
                    try
                    {
                        objInspWrap.Inspector = Inspector;
                        objInspWrap.MailItem = oMail;
                        objInspWrap.Key = WrapperID;
                        objInspWrap.WrapperClass = WrapperCol;

                        // add wrapper class to the collection to keep it alive
                        WrapperCol.Add(WrapperID, objInspWrap);

                        WrapperID += 1;
                    }
                    catch (Exception ex)
                    {
                        MessageBox.Show(ex.Message);
                    }
                }
```

(continued)

175

Listing 6.31 *(continued)*

```
            objInspWrap = null;
            oMail = null;
        }
        return WrapperID;
    }
```

When the `Inspector` is closed, the `Close` event is handled by the wrapper class, which removes itself from the wrapper collection by calling `KillInsp`, shown in Listing 6.32.

Listing 6.32

```
        public void KillInsp(int WrapperID, System.Collections.SortedList WrapperCol)
        {
            // remove wrapper class from wrapper collection
            try {WrapperCol.Remove(WrapperID); }
            catch (Exception ex)
            {
                MessageBox.Show(ex.Message);
            }
        }
    }
}
```

The code in Listings 6.33 and 6.34 show the `InspWrap` class, used to handle `Inspector` events and user interface distinct to that wrapper class. A class-level `Inspector` object, `m_Insp`, is declared for use in handling `Inspector` events, and is initialized when the public `Inspector` property is set to the `Inspector` being wrapped in the class.

When the `Inspector` property is initialized, the event handler for the `Close` event is created using this code:

```
    m_InspClass.InspectorEvents_Event_Close +=
    newOutlook.InspectorEvents_CloseEventHandler(m_Insp_Close); .
```

`MailItem` event handling is added when the `MailItem` property is set. The following code is used to cast the `MailItem` to an event handling object m_events, declared as class `Outlook.ItemEvents_Event`.

```
        // hook up the Item.Close and Item.Send events
        m_events = (Outlook.ItemEvents_Event)m_Mail;
```

The code in Listing 6.33 hooks up event handlers only for the `Send` and `Close` events, using the `ItemEvents_Event` class.

```
        m_events.Send += new Outlook.ItemEvents_SendEventHandler(m_Mail_Send);

        m_events.Close += new Outlook.ItemEvents_CloseEventHandler(m_Mail_Close);
```

Events that aren't overloaded with methods of the same name can be handled using either an item reference, such as m_Mail.BeforeAttachmentAdd or as a `MailItemClass` object reference such as m_MailClass.BeforeAttachmentAdd.

176

Listing 6.33

```csharp
using System.Collections.Generic;
using System.Text;
using System.Runtime.InteropServices;
using Outlook = Microsoft.Office.Interop.Outlook;
using System.Windows.Forms;

namespace CSAddinTemplate
{
    class InspWrap
    {
        private Outlook.Inspector m_Insp = null;
        private Outlook.InspectorClass m_InspClass = null;

        private Outlook.MailItem m_Mail = null;

        private int m_ID = 0;

        private bool m_Startup = false;

        private bool m_blnKilled = false;

        private System.Collections.SortedList m_WrapperClass = null;

        private Outlook.ItemEvents_Event m_events;

        public System.Collections.SortedList WrapperClass
        {
            get
            {
                return m_WrapperClass;
            }

            set
            {
                m_WrapperClass = value;
            }
        }

        public Outlook.Inspector Inspector
        {
            get
            {
                return m_Insp;
            }

            set
            {
                m_Insp = value;
```

The class level Inspector *object is cast as an* InspectorClass *object to allow handling of the* Inspector.Close *event.*

```
                    m_InspClass = (Outlook.InspectorClass)m_Insp;

                    // hook up the Inspector Close event handler
                    m_InspClass.InspectorEvents_Event_Close += new
Outlook.InspectorEvents_CloseEventHandler(m_Insp_Close);


                    m_blnKilled = false;
                    m_Startup = true;
                }
            }

        public int Key
        {
            get
            {
                return m_ID;
            }

            set
            {
                m_ID = value;
            }
        }

        public Outlook.MailItem MailItem
        {
            get
            {
                return m_Mail;
            }

            set
            {
                m_Mail = value;
```

The class level `m_Mail` object is cast as an `ItemEvents_Event` object to allow handling of the `MailItem.Close` and `MailItem.Send` events.

```
                    // hook up the Item.Close and Item.Send events
                    m_events = (Outlook.ItemEvents_Event)m_Mail;

                    m_events.Send += new Outlook.ItemEvents_SendEventHandler(m_Mail_Send);

                    m_events.Close += new Outlook.ItemEvents_CloseEventHandler(m_Mail_Close);
                }
            }
```

Listing 6.34 shows what happens when the `Inspector` wrapped in a class is closed. The `Key` property, stored locally as `m_ID`, is used to remove the collection member with the same `Key` as the wrapper class from the wrapper class collection. This is done by calling `KillInsp` in a new instance of the `OutInsp` class with the value of `m_ID` and the stored instance of the sorted list used to store the wrapper class, `m_WrapperClass`. In addition to releasing all the class-level objects, the event handlers are removed so the class can cleanly close.

Listing 6.34

```
        private void m_Insp_Close()
        {
if (m_blnKilled == false)
        {
            m_blnKilled = true;

            // remove from the Inspector wrapper collection
            OutInsp killer = new OutInsp();
            killer.KillInsp(m_ID, m_WrapperClass);
            killer = null;

            m_WrapperClass = null;

            // release the Inspector.Close event handler
            m_InspClass.InspectorEvents_Event_Close -= new
Outlook.InspectorEvents_CloseEventHandler(m_Insp_Close);

            if (m_Insp != null) { m_Insp = null; }
            if (m_InspClass != null) { m_InspClass = null; }

            if (m_Mail != null) { m_Mail = null; }

            if (m_events != null) { m_events = null; };
        }
    }
```

The event handlers for MailItem.Close and MailItem.Send demonstrate displaying messages in modal MessageBox dialogs, but will be used for useful code later in the book. Setting the Boolean cancel to true cancels sending or closing the item.

```
        private void m_Mail_Close(ref bool Cancel)
        {
            MessageBox.Show("Item closing");
        }

        private void m_Mail_Send(ref bool cancel)
        {
            MessageBox.Show("MailItem_Send");
            //cancel = true;
        }
    }
}
```

Template Utility Code

This section shows the utility procedures, classes, and modules for this stage of the COM addin templates. There are differences in the handling of some things between standard and VSTO templates, mostly related to VSTO's ability to clean up after itself.

VB.NET Utility Code

The code in Listings 6.35 and 6.36 show the `InitHandler` and `Teardown` procedures called to initialize global objects and perform other initializations, and to release all objects when the addin is shutting down.

The `InitHandler` procedure is the same for both the standard and VSTO versions of the templates.

Listing 6.35

```
#Region "Utility procedures"
    Private Sub InitHandler()
        Dim sVerLeft2 As String

        Try
            g_objOL = m_objOutlook
            g_objNS = g_objOL.GetNamespace("MAPI")

            m_colInspectors = m_objOutlook.Inspectors

            '*********************************************************

            sVerLeft2 = Left(g_objOL.Version, 2)
            Select Case sVerLeft2
                Case "10"
                    g_OutlookVersion = 10
                Case "11"
                    g_OutlookVersion = 11
                Case "12"
                    g_OutlookVersion = 12
                Case Else
                    If Left(sVerLeft2, 1) = "9" Then
                        g_OutlookVersion = 9
                    Else
                        g_OutlookVersion = 0
                    End If
            End Select

            '*********************************************************

            m_blnInit = True
        Catch ex As Exception
            MessageBox.Show(ex.Message)

            If m_blnTeardown = False Then
                TearDown()
            End If
        End Try
    End Sub
```

The code in Listing 6.36 for the `Teardown` procedure unwraps the `Explorer` and `Inspector` collections to make sure that all wrapped objects are released; then it releases all other global and module-level objects.

The calls to the garbage collector usually aren't necessary for code only meant to run on Outlook 2007 or for VSTO code.

```
GC.Collect()
GC.WaitForPendingFinalizers()
```

Not calling the garbage collector speeds up code shutdown, but if orphaned objects remain in memory, Outlook can become hung.

Listing 6.36

```
Private Sub TearDown()
    Dim i As Integer
    Dim j As Integer

    If m_blnTeardown = False Then
        Try
            If g_colExplWrap IsNot Nothing Then
                j = g_colExplWrap.Count
                If j > 0 Then
                    For i = j To 1 Step -1
                        g_colExplWrap.Remove(i)
                    Next
                End If
                g_colExplWrap = Nothing
            End If

            If g_colInspWrap IsNot Nothing Then
                j = g_colInspWrap.Count
                If j > 0 Then
                    For i = j To 1 Step -1
                        g_colInspWrap.Remove(i)
                    Next
                End If
                g_colInspWrap = Nothing
            End If

        Catch ex As Exception
            MessageBox.Show(ex.Message)
        End Try

        If g_objNS IsNot Nothing Then
            g_objNS = Nothing
        End If

        If g_objOL IsNot Nothing Then
            g_objOL = Nothing
        End If

        Try
            'release reference to Outlook objects
            m_olExplorer = Nothing
```

(continued)

Listing 6.36 *(continued)*

```
            m_colExplorers = Nothing
            m_colInspectors = Nothing
            m_olInspector = Nothing
            m_objNS = Nothing
            m_objOutlook = Nothing
        Catch ex As Exception
            MessageBox.Show(ex.Message)
        End Try

        m_blnTeardown = True
        m_blnInit = False

        GC.Collect()
        GC.WaitForPendingFinalizers()
    End If
End Sub
```

The declarations in the `Globals` module are shown in Listing 6.37. The global `Outlook.Application` and `NameSpace` objects are derived from the addin application object, so they are trusted Outlook objects, and all objects derived from them are also trusted.

Listing 6.37

```
Imports Outlook = Microsoft.Office.Interop.Outlook

Friend Module Globals
    Public g_strProgID As String

    Public g_WrapperID As Integer

    Public g_OutlookVersion As Integer

    Public g_colExplWrap As New Collection
    Public g_colInspWrap As New Collection

    Public g_objOL As Outlook.Application
    Public g_objNS As Outlook.NameSpace
End Module
```

The C# templates don't use global declarations for Outlook.Application *and* NameSpace *objects; they use classes that are passed whatever objects the classes need. This approach can also be used in VB.NET code.*

C# Utility Code

The code in Listings 6.38 and 6.39 show the `InitHandler` and `Teardown` procedures that are called to initialize global objects and perform other initializations, and to release all objects when the addin is shutting down.

The `InitHandler` procedure is the same for both the standard and VSTO versions of the templates.

Listing 6.38

```
#region utility_procedures
public void InitHandler()
{
    string sVerLeft2 = "";
    string sVersion = "";

    //************************************************************

    sVersion = m_Outlook.Version;
    sVerLeft2 = sVersion.Substring(0, 2);
    switch( sVerLeft2)
    {
        case "10":
            m_OutlookVersion = 10;
    break;
        case "11":
            m_OutlookVersion = 11;
    break;
        case "12":
            m_OutlookVersion = 12;
    break;
        default:
            if ((sVerLeft2.Substring(0 , 1)) == "9")
            {
                m_OutlookVersion = 9;
            }
            else
            {
                m_OutlookVersion = 0;
            }
            break;
    }

    //set initialization flag
    m_Init = true;
}
```

The code in Listing 6.39 for the `Teardown` procedure clears the `Explorer` and `Inspector` sorted list collections to make sure that all wrapped objects are released; then it releases all other global and module level objects. Event handlers for `Inspectors`, `Explorers`, and property pages are removed from the event handler collection. The calls to the garbage collector usually aren't necessary for code only meant to run on Outlook 2007 or for VSTO code.

```
GC.Collect();
GC.WaitForPendingFinalizers();
```

Not calling the garbage collector speeds up code shutdown, but if orphaned objects remain in memory Outlook can become hung.

Listing 6.39

```
private void TearDown()
{
    if (m_Teardown == false)
    {
        try
        {
            if (m_ExplWrap != null)
            {
                m_ExplWrap.Clear();
                m_ExplWrap = null;
            }

            if (m_InspWrap != null)
            {
                m_InspWrap.Clear();
                m_InspWrap = null;
            }

            // remove the event handlers
            if (m_Explorers != null)
            {
                m_Explorers.NewExplorer -= new
                    Outlook.ExplorersEvents_NewExplorerEventHandler(
                    m_Explorers_NewExplorer);
            }

            if (m_InspectorsClass != null)
            {
                m_InspectorsClass.NewInspector -= new
                    Outlook.InspectorsEvents_NewInspectorEventHandler(
                    m_InspectorsClass_NewInspector);
            }

            //release reference to Outlook objects
            if (m_Explorer != null) m_Explorer = null;
            if (m_Explorers != null) m_Explorers = null;
            if (m_Inspectors != null) m_Inspectors = null;
            if (m_Inspector != null) m_Inspector = null;

            if (m_ExplorersClass != null) m_ExplorersClass = null;
            if (m_ExplorerClass != null) m_ExplorerClass = null;

            if (m_InspectorsClass != null) m_InspectorsClass = null;
            if (m_InspectorClass != null) m_InspectorClass = null;

            if (m_NameSpace != null) m_NameSpace = null;
            if (m_Outlook != null) m_Outlook = null;

            if (applicationObject != null) applicationObject = null;
            if (addInInstance != null) addInInstance = null;
```

Listing 6.39 (continued)

```
                m_Teardown = true;
                m_Init = false;

                GC.Collect();
                GC.WaitForPendingFinalizers();
            }
            catch (Exception ex)
            {
                MessageBox.Show(ex.Message);
            }
        }
    }
#endregion
```

Displaying Outlook Property Pages

Outlook property pages are displayed by a user in two ways:

❑   Select Tools ➪ Options in an Outlook folder menu to display the Options property page.

❑   Right-click a folder in the Navigation Pane and select Properties from the context menu to display the Folder property page.

The Options property page is used for application or general settings, while folder property pages are used for folder settings.

> *There's no way to access to individual tabs in the property pages in either the Options dialog or the folder Properties dialog using code.*

The `OptionsPagesAdd` event fires when Outlook is about to display the collection of built-in Options or folder property pages. This event is used to add a custom property page to the `Pages` collection by a COM addin. When folder property pages are about to display, the `OptionsPagesAdd` event fires on the `NameSpace` object. When the Tools ➪ Options property pages are about to display, the `OptionsPagesAdd` event fires on the Outlook `Application` object. Both events pass a `Pages` collection. The `NameSpace .OptionPagesAdd` event also passed a `Folder` object referencing the folder whose property page is about to be displayed.

Displaying Property Pages with VB.NET

The code in Listings 6.40 and 6.41 show how to display a property page using VB.NET code to display a `UserControl` object that provides the design surface for the property page. Listing 6.40 shows the code for a folder property page, which is executed when the `NameSpace.OptionsPagesAdd` event fires.

`FolderPP` is a `UserControl` object that you will design in the next chapter. An instance of the `FolderPP` object is created and passed to the `Add` method of the `Pages` collection passed in the event arguments.

The folder for which the property page is being displayed is also passed as an event argument, and it is used in the caption of the property page.

The Caption *property of the* FolderPP *object is set before the* Pages.Add *method is called. This is part of a workaround for a bug that occurs with Outlook 2003 property pages when added from .NET code, which is not needed if the addin is meant to only run in Outlook 2007.*

Listing 6.40

```
#Region "Property Page display events"
Private Sub m_objNS_OptionsPagesAdd(ByVal Pages As Outlook.PropertyPages,
ByVal Folder As Outlook.MAPIFolder) Handles m_objNS.OptionsPagesAdd

        Dim oPage As New FolderPP
        Dim caption As String

        caption = "VB Folder " & Folder.Name & " Property Page"
        oPage.Caption = caption

        Pages.Add(oPage, caption)

        oPage = Nothing
    End Sub
```

The code in Listing 6.41 is called when a user shows the Tools ⇨ Options dialog. This event handler is passed only one event argument, the Pages collection.

Listing 6.41

```
    Private Sub m_objOutlook_OptionsPagesAdd(ByVal Pages As_
        Outlook.PropertyPages) Handles m_objOutlook.OptionsPagesAdd

        Dim oPage As New ToolsOptionsPP
        Dim caption As String

        caption = "VB Outlook Property Page"
        oPage.Caption = caption

        Pages.Add(oPage, caption)

        oPage = Nothing
    End Sub
#End Region
```

Displaying Property Pages with C#

The code in Listings 6.42 and 6.43 show how to display a property page using C# code to display a UserControl object that provides the design surface for the property page. Listing 6.42 shows the code for a folder property page, which is executed when the NameSpace.OptionsPagesAdd event fires.

The initialization code for the C# templates shown in Listing 6.13 doesn't create event handlers for the `Outlook.Application` and `NameSpace Pages.Add` events. The code that creates these event handlers is added to the startup code just before the `Explorer` event handlers are created.

```
m_Outlook.OptionsPagesAdd += new
Outlook.ApplicationEvents_11_OptionsPagesAddEventHandler(m_objOutlook_OptionsPagesAdd);

m_NameSpace.OptionsPagesAdd += new
Outlook.NameSpaceEvents_OptionsPagesAddEventHandler(m_NameSpace_OptionsPagesAdd);
```

`FolderPP` is a `UserControl` object that you will design in the next chapter. An instance of the `FolderPP` object is created and passed to the `Add` method of the `Pages` collection passed in the event arguments. The folder for which the property page is being displayed is also passed as an event argument, and it is used in the caption of the property page.

The `Caption` property of the `FolderPP` object is set before the `Pages.Add` method is called. This is part of a workaround for a bug that occurs with Outlook 2003 property pages when added from .NET code, which is not needed if the addin is meant to only run in Outlook 2007.

Listing 6.42

```csharp
#region Property_Page_display_events
    private void m_NameSpace_OptionsPagesAdd(Outlook.PropertyPages Pages,
Outlook.MAPIFolder Folder)

    {
        FolderPP oPP = new FolderPP();
        string caption = "C# Outlook " + Folder.Name + " Property Page";

        oPP.Caption = caption;
        Pages.Add(oPP, caption);

        oPP = null;
    }
```

The code in Listing 6.43 is called when a user shows the Tools ⇨ Options dialog. This event handler is passed only one event argument, the `Pages` collection.

Listing 6.43

```csharp
    private void m_objOutlook_OptionsPagesAdd(Outlook.PropertyPages Pages)
    {
        ToolsOptionsPP oPP = new ToolsOptionsPP();
        string caption = "C# Outlook Property Page";

        oPP.Caption = caption;
        Pages.Add(oPP, caption);

        oPP = null;
    }
#endregion
```

Communicating with a COM Addin

In many cases, there's a need to communicate between an Outlook addin and some external program. This might be necessary to communicate with a property page compiled as a separate OCX control or to provide an external API (Application Programming Interface) between your addin's functionality and external programs.

In a classic COM addin written using VB 6, the hooks to set up an addin to talk to the outside world and to work with toolbars and menus takes two lines of code in the `OnConnection` event handler:

```
Private Sub IDTExtensibility2_OnConnection(ByVal Application As Object, _
   ByVal ConnectMode As AddInDesignerObjects.ext_ConnectMode, _
   ByVal AddInInst As Object, custom() As Variant)

   'put ProgID in a global variable
   gstrProgID = AddInInst.ProgId

   AddInInst.Object = Me
```

The `ProgID` of the addin instance is stored and used later for working with the `CommandBar` interfaces for custom menus and toolbars. The key to the communication with the addin from the outside is the setting of the addin instance's `Object` property to the addin object, represented as `Me`.

VB.NET

In VB.NET the process isn't much more complicated than in VB 6 code, the code for the VB.NET template adds the declaration in Listing 6.44 to the class-level declarations in the `Connect` class.

Listing 6.44

```
      Private addInInstance As Office.COMAddIn
```

Then the hook-up lines listed in Listing 6.45 are added to the code in the `OnConnection` event handler. Notice that in this case the addin object has to be cast to an `Office.COMAddIn` object due to the inherent late-binding when working with COM objects through the Interop with .NET code.

Listing 6.45

```
      Public Sub OnConnection(ByVal application As Object,_
       ByVal connectMode As Extensibility.ext_ConnectMode,_
       ByVal addInInst As Object, ByRef custom As _
       System.Array) Implements Extensibility.IDTExtensibility2.OnConnection
         m_blnTeardown = False

         addInInstance = Nothing
         addInInstance = TryCast(addInInst, Office.COMAddIn)

         If (addInInstance IsNot Nothing) Then
             'set module level reference to COMAddIn object
```

Listing 6.45 *(continued)*

```
        Try
            m_objOutlook = CType(application, Outlook.Application)

            'event-aware reference to Explorers collection
            'use NewExplorer event to watch for UI creation
            m_colExplorers = m_objOutlook.Explorers

            Try
                'put ProgID in a global variable
                g_strProgID = addInInstance.ProgId

                addInInstance.Object = Me
```

A publicly exposed method is added to the template in the `Connect` class that displays a `MessageBox` verifying that communication has been established, as shown in Listing 6.46. Any public `Sub`, `Function`, or `Property` can be added in the same way to the code in the `Connect` class to provide an interface between the Outlook addin and the outside world.

Listing 6.46

```
    Public Sub CalledFromOutside()
        MessageBox.Show("Test of an outside call to the COM addin")
    End Sub
```

Testing Addin Communications

The code in Listing 6.47 shows how the `CalledFromOutside` method is called from external code. The code is designed to run in the Outlook VBA project, but it can be modified to run from anywhere by instantiating an `Outlook.Application` object and using that instead of the Outlook VBA's `Application` object.

The code as shown will call the method in the VSTO VB.NET addin, uncomment the appropriate code line to call into the desired addin template code.

Listing 6.47

```
Sub TestCallToAddin()
  Dim oAddin As Office.COMAddIn

  Set oAddin = Application.COMAddIns.Item(" VSTO_VBOutlookTemplate") 'VSTO VB.NET
'   Set oAddin = Application.COMAddIns.Item("VBAddinTemplate.Connect") 'VB.NET
'   Set oAddin = Application.COMAddIns.Item("VSTO_CSOutlookTemplate") 'VSTO C#
'   Set oAddin = Application.COMAddIns.Item("CSAddinTemplate.Connect") 'C#
  If Not (oAddin Is Nothing) Then
    oAddin.Object.CalledFromOutside
  End If
End Sub
```

C#

The C# code for the new declarations in the Connect class are very similar to the VB.NET code, as shown in Listing 6.48.

Listing 6.48

```
public static string m_ProgID = "";

private Office.COMAddIn addInInstance = null;
```

The code to set the ProgID is also very similar to the VB.NET code, as shown in Listing 6.49. However, notice the major difference in the handling of setting the AddInInst.Object property, shown in the last line of Listing 6.49.

Listing 6.49

```
        public void OnConnection(object application,
Extensibility.ext_ConnectMode connectMode, object addInInst, ref System.Array
custom)
        {
            applicationObject = application;

            System.Windows.Forms.Application.EnableVisualStyles();

            try
            {
                addInInstance = (Office.COMAddIn)addInInst;
            }
            catch
            {
                addInInstance = null;
            }

            if (addInInstance != null)
            {
                //set module level reference to COMAddIn object
                try
                {
                    m_Outlook = (Outlook.Application)application;
                    m_NameSpace = m_Outlook.GetNamespace("MAPI");

                    //event-aware reference to Explorers collection
                    //use NewExplorer event to watch for UI creation
                    m_Explorers = m_Outlook.Explorers;

                    try
                    {
                        //put ProgID in a module level variable
                        m_ProgID = addInInstance.ProgId;

                        //addInInstance.Object = Me
                        addInInstance.GetType().InvokeMember(
```

Listing 6.49 *(continued)*

```
                            "Object",BindingFlags.Public |
                            BindingFlags.SetProperty, null,
                            addInInst, new object[] { this });
```

The generic `object` attribute of the `Object` property of the `AddInInst` object gives C# fits, and you can't just assign `this` to it. Instead, you must use `GetType().InvokeMember` on the `AddInInstance` object and supply the property (`Object`) and other arguments to set the `Object` property to `this`.

The code in Listing 6.50 shows the public method `CalledFromOutside` in C# code.

Listing 6.50

```
    public void CalledFromOutside()
    {
        MessageBox.Show("Call to C# addin from the outside world");
    }
```

VSTO with VB.NET

VSTO adds another level of complication to communicating with the outside world to Outlook addins. In VSTO code; you must use an override for the `RequestCOMAddInAutomationService` function to allow communication between the outside world and an Outlook addin. At the suggestion of my friend and colleague, Outlook MVP Jay B. Harlow of T.S. Bradley, I'm using an `AutomationObject` class to isolate the VSTO 2005 SE `ThisAddin` class from the outside world and funnel all communications between the addin and the ourtside world. Jay has an example of using an `AutomationClass` for this using VSTO 2003 and Outlook 2003 on his Web site at www.tsbradley.net.

The code in Listing 6.51 shows the `GlobalObjects` module in the VSTO VB.NET template that declares a public `AutomationObject`, `AddinObject`.

Listing 6.51

```
    Imports Microsoft.Office.Tools

    Friend Module GlobalObjects
        Public g_WrapperID As Integer

        Public g_OutlookVersion As Integer

        Public g_colExplWrap As New Collection
        Public g_colInspWrap As New Collection

        Public g_objOL As Outlook.Application
        Public g_objNS As Outlook.NameSpace

        Public g_ProgID As String

        Public AddinObject As AutomationObject

    End Module
```

The code in Listing 6.52 shows an implementation of the `AutomationObject` public class, which exposes a function `ExplCount` that returns the number of open Outlook Explorers to the calling code outside the addin.

Listing 6.52

```
Imports Outlook = Microsoft.Office.Interop.Outlook
Imports System
Imports System.Collections.Generic
Imports System.Text
Imports System.Windows.Forms

Public Class AutomationObject
    Private ReadOnly m_application As Outlook.Application

    Friend Sub New(ByVal application As ThisAddIn)
        Try
            m_application = application.Application
        Catch ex As Exception
            MessageBox.Show(ex.Message)
        End Try

    End Sub

    Public Function ExplCount() As String
        Dim RetVal As String = m_application.Explorers.Count.ToString
        Return RetVal
    End Function

End Class
```

The code in Listing 6.53 shows the startup code where the `AutomationObject` class is instantiated and the `ProgID` of the addin is stored in a global string variable for use with the `CommandBar` interface. VSTO 2005 SE provides access to the `Outlook.Application` object through the `Me.Application` property.

Listing 6.53

```
    Private Sub ThisAddIn_Startup(ByVal sender As Object, ByVal e As
System.EventArgs) Handles Me.Startup
        ' Store a reference to the Outlook.Application object.
        m_objOutlook = Me.Application

        Try
            AddinObject = New AutomationObject(Me)
        Catch ex As Exception
            MessageBox.Show(ex.Message)
        End Try

        g_ProgID = ThisAddIn.ProgId
```

In the same `ThisAddin` class, the override for `RequestCOMAddInAutomationService` is set up using a private instance of `AddinUtilities`, a COM visible interface that's actually what's called from outside the addin, as shown in Listing 6.54. This also requires that the interface expose a dual interface so that it's accessible both to the addin code and to the outside world.

Listing 6.54

```
        Private myUtilities As AddinUtilities

        Protected Overrides Function RequestCOMAddInAutomationService() As Object
            If (myUtilities Is Nothing) Then
                myUtilities = New AddinUtilities()
            End If

            Return myUtilities
        End Function

End Class 'Partial Public Class ThisAddIn

<ComVisibleAttribute(True), InterfaceType(ComInterfaceType.InterfaceIsDual)> _
Public Interface IAddinUtilities
    Sub CalledFromOutside()
End Interface

<ComVisibleAttribute(True), ClassInterface(ClassInterfaceType.None)> _
Public Class AddinUtilities
    Implements IAddinUtilities

    'Demonstrates a method that can be called from outside the addin.
    ' This technique can be used to call functions and to read/write properties.

    Sub CalledFromOutside() Implements IAddinUtilities.CalledFromOutside
        Dim myAddinObject As AutomationObject = AddinObject
        Dim Count As String = myAddinObject.ExplCount

        'MessageBox.Show("This is a test of an outside call to the COM addin")
        MessageBox.Show("There are currently " & Count & " Explorers open.")
    End Sub
End Class
```

In this case, the implementation of `AddinUtilities` exposes a method `CalledFromOutside` that allows access from the outside world and displays a `MessageBox` showing the number of open `Explorers`.

To add additional methods or properties to the exposed interface, you would add the name and type of the additional method or property to the `ClassInterface` and then implement the code for the method or property in the `AddinUtilities` class.

VSTO with C#

The C# VSTO code in Listing 6.55 is very similar to the VB.NET VSTO code, except in this case the ProgID, the Inspector wrapper, a SortedList object, and a reference to the Outlook.Application object are also exposed in the AutomationObject class. This is to expose those objects to other code in the addin, because C# has no true global objects as VB.NET does.

Listing 6.55

```csharp
using System;
using System.Collections.Generic;
using System.Text;
using System.Windows.Forms;
using Outlook = Microsoft.Office.Interop.Outlook;

public class AutomationObject
{
    private Outlook.Application m_application;
    private System.Collections.SortedList m_Wrapper; //Inspector wrapper
    private string m_ProgID;

    // class constructor
    public AutomationObject(ThisAddIn application,
    ref System.Collections.SortedList Wrapper, string ProgID)
    {
        m_application = application.Application;
        m_Wrapper = Wrapper;
        m_ProgID = ProgID;
    }

    public string ProgID()
    {
        return m_ProgID;
    }

    public string ExplCount()
    {
        string RetVal = m_application.Explorers.Count.ToString();
        return RetVal;
    }

    public System.Collections.SortedList InspectorWrapper()
    {
        return m_Wrapper;
    }

    public Outlook.Application App()
    {
        return m_application;
    }
}
```

The code in Listing 6.56 shows the `ThisAddin_Startup` procedure with the added code to get the `ProgID` and initialize the `AutomationObject` class. Getting the `ProgID` is more complex in C# than in VB.NET, you cannot directly access this property using the `ThisAddin` object as you can in VB.NET code. VSTO 2005 SE provides access to the `Outlook.Application` object through the `This.Application` property.

In VSTO C# code, the way to access the `ProgID` is to get the running assembly as an `AssemblyName` object using this code:

```
AssemblyName thisAssemblyName = null;
thisAssemblyName = Assembly.GetExecutingAssembly().GetName();
```

The `ProgID` is retrieved from the `thisAssemblyName` object as the `Name` property using this code:

```
m_ProgID = thisAssemblyName.Name;
```

Listing 6.56

```csharp
private void ThisAddin_Startup(object sender, System.EventArgs e)
{
    // allot space initially for 15 open Explorers at a time
    m_ExplWrap = new System.Collections.SortedList(15);

    // allot space initially for 15 open Inspectors at a time
    m_InspWrap = new System.Collections.SortedList(15);

    try
    {
        // get the ProgID of the addin to use later with buttons/toolbars
        AssemblyName thisAssemblyName = null;
        thisAssemblyName = Assembly.GetExecutingAssembly().GetName();
        m_ProgID = thisAssemblyName.Name; //ProgID for the addin
    }
    catch (Exception ex)
    {
        MessageBox.Show(ex.Message);
    }

    try
    {
        AddinObject = new AutomationObject(this, ref m_InspWrap, m_ProgID);
    }
    catch (Exception ex)
    {
        MessageBox.Show(ex.Message);
    }

    m_Outlook = this.Application;
```

The dual interface declaration for `AddinUtilities` as a COM visible interface is similar to the VB.NET code, given the syntactical differences between VB.NET and C#, as shown in Listing 6.57.

Listing 6.57

```
[ComVisible(true)]
[InterfaceType(ComInterfaceType.InterfaceIsDual)]
public interface IAddinUtilities
{
    void CalledFromOutside();
}


[ComVisible(true)]
[ClassInterface(ClassInterfaceType.None)]
public class AddinUtilities : IAddinUtilities
{
    // Demonstrates a method that can be called from outside the addin.
    // This technique is used to call functions and to read/write properties.
    public void CalledFromOutside()
    {
        AutomationObject myAddinObject = ThisAddIn.AddinObject;
        string Count = myAddinObject.ExplCount();
        string ID = myAddinObject.ProgID();

        //MessageBox.Show("This is a test of an outside call to the COM addin");
        MessageBox.Show("There are currently " + Count + " Explorers open.");
    }
}
```

Summary

In this chapter, you learned about creating Outlook COM addins and how to work with `Explorer` and `Inspector` wrappers. You also learned about some of the differences between shared and VSTO 2005 SE Outlook addins, and you learned how to communicate with a COM addin using external code.

In the next chapter, you will learn about working with the Outlook interface; including designing property pages, working with the `Inspector` Ribbons, `Explorer` `CommandBar` objects, and other elements such as views, custom task panes, and form regions.

7

COM Addins and the
Outlook User Interface

In this chapter, you learn how to use Outlook COM addins to work with the Outlook user interface. This includes using the `CommandBar` interface for Outlook `Explorers` for custom menus and toolbars, the Ribbon interface for Outlook `Inspectors`, `Explorer` and `Inspector` custom task panes, form regions, and custom Views. COM addins are required to work with the Ribbon and custom task panes, as well as to apply business logic to form regions.

These user interface techniques complete the Outlook addin templates that can be used as the foundation for all Outlook COM addin programming. As in the previous chapter, the code for the user interface portions of the addin templates are presented in VB.NET and C#, with variations for VSTO and shared addin templates. The templates are available for download from the Wrox Web site (www.wrox.com) as well as from my own Web site, www.slovaktech.com.

Deployment techniques for the addin templates are covered in Chapter 9.

Working with Menus and Toolbars

Outlook retains the older `CommandBar` interface for `Explorers`, while using the Ribbon interface for `Inspectors`. This doesn't mean that Outlook doesn't support the Ribbon; it actually has more Ribbon support than any other Office application because there are so many possible different `Inspector` types, such as email, appointments, tasks, and variations of types, such as read and compose `Inspectors`. There are also a number of different `Explorer` types, so the decision was made to support only `Inspector` Ribbons for Outlook 2007.

`Inspector` menus and toolbars will still work in Outlook 2007 using the old `CommandBar` interface, but those menus and toolbars and related menu or toolbar items are really second-class citizens in Outlook 2007. They are stripped from their original locations and placed in an Add-Ins tab, with each addin that uses the `CommandBar` interface having its own group in that tab. This makes discoverability of an addin's user interface difficult and separates it from the related functions for the user interface.

> *Inspector menus and toolbars aren't covered in this chapter, but the code for them is identical to the code for* `Explorer` *menus and toolbars, except that the code is applied to an* `Inspector` *instead of an* `Explorer`*. Menus and toolbars in an* `Inspector` *aren't valid until the first* `Activate` *event fires.*

Menus and Toolbars in Explorers

All menus and toolbars in Outlook are members of the `CommandBars` collection. In Outlook there is no set of application-wide `CommandBars`. The `CommandBars` collection is accessed from an individual `Explorer` or `Inspector` object, using `Explorer.CommandBars`, or `Inspector.CommandBars`.

Menu bars, such as the one that displays File and Tools, are the same objects as toolbars; they're all `CommandBar` objects. The main menu bar is the `Explorer.CommandBars.Item("Menu Bar")` object. This is a language-independent name and is the same in all localized versions of Outlook. The normal Standard toolbar in an `Explorer` is the `Explorer.CommandBars.Item("Standard")` object. Other default `CommandBar` objects in Outlook include the Advanced toolbar and the Web toolbar.

What are commonly referred to as "menus" in Outlook, such as File and Tools, are `CommandBarPopup` objects. When a `CommandBarPopup` object is clicked, it expands to show all controls added to that `CommandBarPopup` object, such as buttons or combo boxes and even other nested `CommandBarPopup` objects. All members of the `CommandBars` collection and associated controls are supplied by the Office library, not the Outlook library, and are common to all Office applications. Figure 7.1 shows the hierarchy of the `CommandBars` collection, which is used to create the menus and toolbars for Explorers and Inspectors.

Although other types of controls are listed in the `msoControlType` enumeration, only the `msoControlButton`, `msoControlEdit`, `msoControlDropdown`, `msoControlComboBox`, and `msoControlPopup` control types can be added to a `Controls` collection. There are no special object types for `Edit` and `Dropdown` controls, which you can only access through the generic `CommandBarControl` object. That limits the utility of `Edit` and `Dropdown` controls used in `CommandBar` applications.

The addin templates supply a set of helper functions for creating `CommandBar`, `CommandBarPopup`, `CommandBarButton`, and `CommandBarComboBox` objects, located in a `CommandBarsMaker` helper class. The following table shows how these controls are used in the Outlook user interface.

Control	Usage in the User Interface
CommandBar	Menu, toolbar
CommandBarPopup	Pop-up menu, drop-down control
CommandBarButton	Menu entry, toolbar button
CommandBarComboBox	ComboBox control

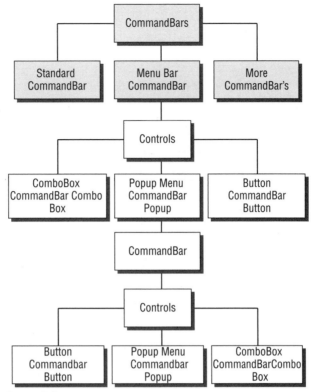

Figure 7.1

Where a control supports the `Temporary` attribute, `Temporary` is set to true to automatically remove the control when Outlook closes. Orphaned controls are deleted as a belt and suspenders precaution, if any exist. Controls become orphaned because of Outlook or addin crashes.

VB.NET

The code in Listing 7.1 creates a new `CommandBar` for Outlook, which normally is used as a new toolbar. The Office library is imported in the `CommandBarsMaker` class so access to the various `CommandBar` objects is available. First, the `CommandBars` collection is searched to see if an existing `CommandBar` has the same name as the `CommandBar` to be created. The assumption is an existing `CommandBar` is an orphan, left over from some previous run of the addin. If a matching `CommandBar` is found it's deleted and a new `CommandBar` is added to the `CommandBars` collection. The `NewBar` function returns an `Office.CommandBar` object.

Always delete items from a collection in a `For` loop using a down-counting loop; otherwise, you may end up deleting only one half of all items in the collection. This is because the index of items in the collection is being altered within the loop as items are deleted.

Listing 7.1

```vbnet
Imports System
Imports System.Collections.Generic
Imports System.Text
Imports Office = Microsoft.Office.Core
Imports System.Diagnostics

Public Class CommandBarsMaker

    Public Function NewBar(ByVal Bars As Office.CommandBars, ByVal barName As String, _
    ByVal Show As Boolean, ByVal Enabled As Boolean) As Office.CommandBar
        Dim _bar As Office.CommandBar = Nothing

        Try
            Dim j As Integer = Bars.Count
            Dim i As Integer

            For i = j To 1 Step -1
                _bar = Bars.Item(i)
                If (_bar.Name = barName) Then
                    _bar.Delete()
                End If
            Next

            _bar = TryCast(Bars.Add(barName, , , True), Office.CommandBar)

            If _bar IsNot Nothing Then
                _bar.Enabled = Enabled
                _bar.Visible = Show
            End If
        Catch
            _bar = Nothing
        End Try

        Return _bar
    End Function
```

The code in Listing 7.2 creates a new CommandBarPopup control in the specified CommandBar. If you add a CommandBarPopup to a horizontal menu, such as Menu Bar, the control works like the build-in File and Tools menus. If you add a CommandBarPopup to a vertical menu such as Tools, the control works like the built-in Send/Receive popup works, displaying an arrow to the right of the caption to indicate the control will expand when selected.

If an existing instance of the control is found using the FindControl method and using Tag as the search property, the instance is deleted. Then the control is added to the Controls collection of the specified CommandBar control. The BeginGroup property is used to set a dividing line before the control and is passed to NewMenu as a Boolean argument, ShowDivider.

Calling the FindControl method with the Recursive = True argument recursively looks for the specified control in all controls and subcontrols in the specified CommandBar.

Listing 7.2

```
Public Function NewMenu(ByVal Bar As Office.CommandBar, ByVal popName As String, _
ByVal Tag As Object, ByVal Show As Boolean, ByVal ProgID As String, _
ByVal ShowDivider As Boolean, ByVal TipText As String, ByVal Enabled As
Boolean) As Office.CommandBarPopup
    Dim _pop As Office.CommandBarPopup = Nothing

    Try
        _pop = TryCast(Bar.FindControl(Office.MsoControlType.msoControlPopup, ,
Tag, , True), Office.CommandBarPopup)

        If (_pop IsNot Nothing) Then
            _pop.Delete(False)
            _pop = Nothing
        End If

        _pop = TryCast(Bar.Controls.Add(Office.MsoControlType.msoControlPopup,
, , , True), Office.CommandBarPopup)

        If _pop IsNot Nothing Then
            With _pop
                .Tag = Tag.ToString()
                .Caption = popName
                .Visible = Show
                .Enabled = Enabled
                .BeginGroup = ShowDivider
                .OnAction = "<!" & ProgID & ">"
                .TooltipText = TipText
            End With
        End If
    Catch
        _pop = Nothing
    End Try

    Return _pop
End Function
```

The OnAction property is used to store an instance of the ProgID of the addin preceded by the required "<!" string and followed by the ">" string. This will activate the addin if a Click or Change event is detected and the addin is not already running. You can also specify the name of the event handler in the Parameter property of the control, although that's not done here.

> It's very important to use a unique Tag value for every CommandBarControl you create. A unique Tag guarantees that only the event handler for the specific control that fires an event will be called for that event. If a unique Tag is not used, every event handler for all instances of that control will be called when an event fires.

The code in Listing 7.3 creates a new CommandBarButton control. Aside from the type of control added, the code is similar to the code for creating a new CommandBarPopup control. The main difference in the two functions is the use of the `Style` property for a `CommandBarButton`. The style can be used to create a button with only a caption, only an icon or a button with both a caption and icon. The variations in the `MsoButtonStyle` enumeration for buttons with captions and icons set how and if captions are wrapped and where a caption is placed related to the icon. The icon isn't set in the `NewButton` function; the icon is set in the procedure that calls the `NewButton` function.

Listing 7.3

```
    Public Function NewButton(ByVal Bar As Office.CommandBar, _
    ByVal buttonName As String, ByVal Tag As String, ByVal Show As Boolean, ByVal
ProgID As String, _
    ByVal Style As Office.MsoButtonStyle, ByVal ShowDivider As Boolean, _
    ByVal TipText As String, ByVal Enabled As Boolean) As Office.CommandBarButton

        Dim _button As Office.CommandBarButton = Nothing

        Try
            _button = TryCast(Bar.FindControl(, , Tag, , True),
Office.CommandBarButton)

            If (_button IsNot Nothing) Then
                _button.Delete(False)
            End If
        Catch ex As Exception
            Debug.WriteLine(ex.Message)
        End Try

        Dim buttonType As Object = Office.MsoControlType.msoControlButton

        _button = TryCast(Bar.Controls.Add(buttonType, , , , True),
Office.CommandBarButton)

        If (_button IsNot Nothing) Then
            With _button
                .Caption = buttonName
                .Visible = Show
                .Enabled = Enabled
                .Style = Style
                .BeginGroup = ShowDivider
                .Tag = Tag
                .OnAction = "<!" & ProgID & ">"
                .TooltipText = TipText
            End With
        End If
        Return _button
    End Function
```

Listing 7.4 shows the `NewComboBox` function that's called to create a new `CommandBarComboBox` control in a `CommandBar`. `CommandBarComboBox` controls are used far less frequently in most addins than `CommandBarButton` and `CommandBarPopup` controls. The procedure that calls `NewComboBox` sets the list in the control.

Listing 7.4

```vb
    Public Function NewComboBox(ByVal Bar As Office.CommandBar, _
        ByVal comboName As String, ByVal Tag As String, ByVal Show As Boolean, _
        ByVal ProgID As String, ByVal Style As Office.MsoComboStyle, _
        ByVal ShowDivider As Boolean, ByVal TipText As String, _
        ByVal Enabled As Boolean) As Office.CommandBarComboBox

        Dim _combo As Office.CommandBarComboBox = Nothing

        Try
            _combo = TryCast(Bar.FindControl(, , Tag, , True),
Office.CommandBarComboBox)

            If (_combo IsNot Nothing) Then
                _combo.Delete(False)
            End If
        Catch ex As Exception
            Debug.WriteLine(ex.Message)
        End Try

        Dim controlType As Object = Office.MsoControlType.msoControlComboBox

        _combo = TryCast(Bar.Controls.Add(controlType, , , , True),
Office.CommandBarComboBox)

        If (_combo IsNot Nothing) Then
            With _combo
                .Caption = comboName
                .Visible = Show
                .Enabled = Enabled
                .Style = Style
                .BeginGroup = ShowDivider
                .Tag = Tag
                .OnAction = "<!" & ProgID & ">"
                .TooltipText = TipText
            End With
        End If

        Return _combo
    End Function
End Class
```

The creation of the controls is done in the `Explorer` wrapper class code. The `Activate` event for an `Explorer` is used to call the `DoStartup` procedure, where the class initialization code is executed. Because the first `Explorer` in Outlook may not fire an `Activate` event, the `SelectionChange` event is also used to check for a startup state. `SelectionChange` will fire when an initial selection is applied to a folder as well as when the selection changes.

It's always a good idea to back up use of the `Activate` event by using the `SelectionChange` event to account for differences in when and if `Activate` will fire, especially if you are supporting earlier versions of Outlook.

Class-level instances of a `CommandBarPopup` control and a `CommandBarButton` control are declared in Listing 7.5, with the `CommandBarButton` declared `WithEvents` so that it can handle the control's `Click` event. `ComboBox` controls fire a `Change` event instead of a `Click` event.

The `Explorer.Activate` and `SelectionChange` events both call `DoStartup` to initialize the user interface for the `Explorer` class and to perform any other startup initializations.

Listing 7.5

```
Private WithEvents m_button As Office.CommandBarButton

Private m_pop As Office.CommandBarPopup
Private Sub m_objExpl_Activate() Handles m_objExpl.Activate
    DoStartup()
End Sub

Private Sub m_objExpl_SelectionChange() Handles m_objExpl.SelectionChange
    DoStartup()
End Sub
```

The code in Listing 7.6 for `DoStartup` only executes the remainder of the startup code if both `m_blnStartup` is `True` (a condition set when the wrapper class is created) and the button hasn't been created yet. First, a `CommandBar` object is instantiated for the "Menu Bar" `CommandBar`, a language-independent name for the main Outlook menu.

The `Tag` properties for the `CommandBarPopup` and `CommandBarButton` are created by appending the string value of the `Key` property to unique strings. Every `Key` is unique to all `Explorers` and `Inspectors` for every Outlook session, and appending a `Key` value to a unique string is a good way to ensure that every `Tag` property is unique. It's also a good way to uniquely retrieve or identify that control in other code in the addin. An alternative to using a descriptive string with the `Key` appended is to create a GUID for each control you create and append the `Key` to that to create unique `Tag` properties.

Listing 7.6

```
    Private Sub DoStartup()
        If (m_blnStartup = True) Then
            If (m_button Is Nothing) Then
                Try
                    Dim bar As Office.CommandBar = m_objExpl.CommandBars.Item("Menu
    Bar")
                    Dim idMenu As String = "ExplTestMenu" & Key.ToString()
                    Dim id As String = "ExplTestButton" & Key.ToString()

                    Dim Style As Office.MsoButtonStyle =
    Office.MsoButtonStyle.msoButtonIconAndCaption

                    Dim buttonMaker As CommandBarsMaker = New CommandBarsMaker()

                    m_pop = buttonMaker.NewMenu(bar, "VBAddinTemplate", idMenu,
    True, g_strProgID, True, "Custom Menu", True)

                    If m_pop IsNot Nothing Then
```

Listing 7.6 *(continued)*

```
                m_button = buttonMaker.NewButton(m_pop.CommandBar, "Test
    Button", id, True, g_strProgID, Style, False, "Test", True)

                If (m_button IsNot Nothing) Then
                    ' add an icon to the button
                    Dim imgStreamPic As System.Drawing.Image
                    Dim oPic As IPictureDisp = Nothing
                    Dim ax As MyAxHost = New MyAxHost()

                    imgStreamPic = My.Resources.INFO.ToBitmap()

                    oPic = ax.IPictureDispFromImage(imgStreamPic)
                    m_button.Picture = oPic

                    imgStreamPic = Nothing
                    ax = Nothing
                    oPic = Nothing
                End If
            End If

            bar = Nothing
        Catch ex As Exception
            MessageBox.Show(ex.Message)
        End Try
    End If

    m_blnStartup = False
    End If
End Sub
```

An image is loaded from the project resources as an `Image` object, using a conversion from the stored BMP format to an `Image` format. Icons for `CommandBarButton` controls should be 256 colors (8-bit) in a 16 × 16 format. You can use a transparency mask for the icon by setting the `Mask` property of the button, although that isn't done in this sample code. The required `IPictureDisp` object for setting either the `Picture` or `Mask` properties is retrieved from the `AxHost` helper shown in Listing 7.16.

> The `PasteFace` *method of a* `CommandBarButton` *can be used to take an image from the Clipboard to supply a button icon, however that method isn't used in this code, so the contents of the Clipboard aren't disturbed. The* `FaceID` *property can also be used to set the button icon, but that property can only be set to one of the built-in icons, not a custom icon.*

The `Explorer.Close` event handler shown in Listing 7.7 releases all the class-level objects and removes the `Inspector` class from the wrapper collection.

Listing 7.7

```
    Private Sub m_objExpl_Close() Handles m_objExpl.Close
        If Not m_blnKilled Then
            m_blnKilled = True
            KillExpl(m_ID)
```

(continued)

Listing 7.7 *(continued)*

```
            If m_objExpl IsNot Nothing Then
                m_objExpl = Nothing
                m_button = Nothing
                m_pop = Nothing
            End If
        End If
    End Sub
```

The Click event handler in Listing 7.8 is a dummy handler that shows a MessageBox dialog and that fires when the VBAddinTemplate menu item (Popup control) is selected in the menu bar and the Test Button button is clicked.

Listing 7.8

```
    Private Sub m_button_Click(ByVal Ctrl As Microsoft.Office.Core.CommandBarButton,
  ByRef CancelDefault As Boolean) Handles m_button.Click
        MessageBox.Show(Ctrl.Caption & " clicked.")
    End Sub
```

C#

The C# code is very similar to the VB.NET code, differing only in language syntaxes. If you are coding your addin using C#, review the comments for the VB.NET code for information about creating the CommandBar objects and settings their properties.

The code in Listing 7.9 shows the function to create a new CommandBar object, NewBar. C# code doesn't recognize optional arguments for a procedure, so always fill in missing arguments in a procedure call using a System.Reflection.Missing.Value object when using C# code.

Listing 7.9

```
using System;
using System.Collections.Generic;
using System.Text;
using Office = Microsoft.Office.Core;
using System.Diagnostics;

    class CommandBarsMaker
    {
        private object missing = System.Reflection.Missing.Value;

        public Office.CommandBar NewBar(Office.CommandBars Bars,string barName,
            bool Show, bool Enabled)
        {
            Office.CommandBar _bar = null;
```

Listing 7.9 *(continued)*

```
        try
        {
            int j = 1;
            for (int i = Bars.Count; i >= j; i--)
            {
                _bar = Bars[i];
                if (_bar.Name == barName)
                {
                    _bar.Delete();

                    break;
                }
            }
            _bar = null;
            _bar = (Office.CommandBar)Bars.Add(barName, missing, missing, true);

            if (_bar != null)
            {
                _bar.Enabled = Enabled;
                _bar.Visible = Show;
            }
        }
        catch
        {
            _bar = null;
        }
        return _bar;
    }
```

The code in Listing 7.10 shows the function for creating a new Popup control, NewMenu. The call to the CommandBar.FindControl method is another example of using System.Reflection.Missing.Value objects when you are only using some optional arguments in the call to the method.

Listing 7.10

```
    public Office.CommandBarPopup NewMenu(Office.CommandBar Bar, string popName,
        object Tag, bool Show, string ProgID, bool ShowDivider, string TipText,
        bool Enabled)
    {
        Office.CommandBarPopup _pop = null;

        try
        {
            _pop = (Office.CommandBarPopup)Bar.FindControl(Microsoft.Office.Core.
MsoControlType.msoControlPopup, missing, Tag, missing, true);

            if (_pop != null)
            {
                _pop.Delete(false);
                _pop = null;
            }
```

(continued)

Listing 7.10 *(continued)*

```
            _pop = (Office.CommandBarPopup)Bar.Controls.Add(Office.
MsoControlType.msoControlPopup, missing, missing, missing, true);

            if (_pop != null)
            {
                _pop.Tag = Tag.ToString();
                _pop.Caption = popName;
                _pop.Visible = Show;
                _pop.Enabled = Enabled;
                _pop.BeginGroup = ShowDivider;
                _pop.OnAction = "<!" + ProgID + ">";
                _pop.TooltipText = TipText;
            }
        }
        catch
        {
            _pop = null;
        }
        return _pop;
    }
```

The code in Listing 7.11 shows the function for creating a new button control, `NewButton`.

Listing 7.11

```
    public Office.CommandBarButton NewButton(Office.CommandBar Bar,
        string buttonName, string Tag, bool Show, string ProgID,
        Office.MsoButtonStyle Style, bool ShowDivider,
        string TipText, bool Enabled)
    {
        Office.CommandBarButton _button = null;

        try
        {
            _button = (Office.CommandBarButton)Bar.FindControl(missing,
missing, Tag, missing, true);

            if (_button != null)
            {
                _button.Delete(false);
            }
        }
        catch (Exception ex)
        {
            Debug.WriteLine(ex.Message);
        }

        object buttonType = Office.MsoControlType.msoControlButton;

        _button = (Office.CommandBarButton)Bar.Controls.Add(buttonType,
missing, missing, missing, true);
```

Listing 7.11 *(continued)*

```
            if (_button != null)
            {
                _button.Caption = buttonName;
                _button.Visible = Show;
                _button.Enabled = Enabled;
                _button.Style = Style;
                _button.BeginGroup = ShowDivider;
                _button.Tag = Tag;
                _button.OnAction = "<!" + ProgID + ">";
                _button.TooltipText = TipText;
            }
            return _button;
    }
```

The code in Listing 7.12 shows the function for creating a new combobox control, NewComboBox.

Listing 7.12

```
        public Office.CommandBarComboBox NewComboBox(Office.CommandBar Bar,
            string comboName, string Tag, bool Show, string ProgID,
            Office.MsoComboStyle Style, bool ShowDivider,
            string TipText, bool Enabled)
        {
            Office.CommandBarComboBox _combo = null;

            try
            {
                _combo = (Office.CommandBarComboBox)Bar.FindControl(missing,
missing, Tag, missing, true);

                if (_combo != null)
                {
                    _combo.Delete(false);
                }
            }
            catch (Exception ex)
            {
                Debug.WriteLine(ex.Message);
            }

            object controlType = Office.MsoControlType.msoControlComboBox;

            _combo = (Office.CommandBarComboBox)Bar.Controls.Add(controlType,
missing, missing, missing, true);

            if (_combo != null)
            {
                _combo.Caption = comboName;
                _combo.Visible = Show;
                _combo.Enabled = Enabled;
```

(continued)

Listing 7.12 (continued)

```
            _combo.Style = Style;
            _combo.BeginGroup = ShowDivider;
            _combo.Tag = Tag;
            _combo.OnAction = "<!" + ProgID + ">";
            _combo.TooltipText = TipText;

            int i = 1;
            foreach (string Item in List)
            {
                _combo.AddItem(Item.ToString(), i++);
            }
        }
        return _combo;
    }
}
```

Listing 7.13 shows the code in the `Explorer` wrapper class that declares the class-level button and popup objects and creates the controls.

Listing 7.13

```
    private Office.CommandBarButton m_button = null;

    private Office.CommandBarPopup m_pop = null;
    private void m_Expl_Activate()
    {
        DoStartup();
    }

    private void m_Expl_SelectionChange()
    {
        DoStartup();
    }
```

Both the `Explorer.Activate` and `SelectionChange` events are used to ensure that the `CommandBar` user interface is created for all versions of Outlook and under all conditions. The `DoStartup` procedure creates the new pop-up and button controls and adds an icon to the button control.

```
    private void DoStartup()
    {
        string ProgID = CSAddinTemplate.Connect.m_ProgID;
        Office.CommandBar bar = m_Expl.CommandBars["Menu Bar"];
        CommandBarsMaker buttonMaker = new CommandBarsMaker();

        if (m_Startup == true)
        {
            if (m_button == null)
            {
                try
                {
```

```
                          string idMenu = "ExplTestMenu" + Key.ToString();
                          string id = "ExplTestButton" + Key.ToString();

                          Office.MsoButtonStyle Style =
Office.MsoButtonStyle.msoButtonIconAndCaption;

                          m_pop = buttonMaker.NewMenu(bar, "CSAddinTemplate", idMenu,
true, ProgID, true, "Custom Menu", true);
                          if (m_pop != null)
                          {
                              m_button = buttonMaker.NewButton(m_pop.CommandBar,
"Test Button", id, true, ProgID, Style, false, "Test", true);

                              if (m_button != null)
                              {
                                  m_button.Click += new
Office._CommandBarButtonEvents_ClickEventHandler(m_button_Click);
```

The `Click` event handler for the button is added to the `Explorer` wrapper class using the `CommandBarButtonEvents` interface. The `AxHost` helper class shown in Listing 7.17 is instantiated to provide the `IPictureDisp` object required for a button's `Picture` and `Mask` properties, which are used to show the button icons. Use only 256 color formatted as 16 × 16 images for `CommandBarButton` icons.

```
                                  // add an icon to the button
                                  System.Drawing.Image imgStreamPic;
                                  IPictureDisp oPic = null;
                                  MyAxHost ax = new MyAxHost();

                                  imgStreamPic = CSAddinTemplate.Properties.Resources
.INFO.ToBitmap();

                                  oPic = ax.IPictureDispFromImage(imgStreamPic);
                                  m_button.Picture = oPic;

                                  imgStreamPic = null;
                                  ax = null;
                                  oPic = null;
                              }
                          }
                      }
                      catch (Exception ex)
                      {
                          MessageBox.Show(ex.Message);
                      }
                  }
                  m_Startup = false;
              }
              bar = null;
              buttonMaker = null;
          }

          private void m_Expl_Close()
          {
```

```
            if (m_Killed == false)
            {
                m_Killed = true;

                OutExpl killer = new OutExpl();
                killer.KillExpl(m_ID, m_WrapperClass);
                killer = null;

                m_WrapperClass = null;

                // release the Close event handler
                m_ExplClass.ExplorerEvents_Event_Close -= new
Outlook.ExplorerEvents_CloseEventHandler(m_Expl_Close);

                // release the Activate handler
                m_ExplClass.ExplorerEvents_Event_Activate -= new
Outlook.ExplorerEvents_ActivateEventHandler(m_Expl_Activate);

                // release the SelectionChange handler
                m_Expl.SelectionChange -= new
Outlook.ExplorerEvents_10_SelectionChangeEventHandler(m_Expl_SelectionChange);

                if (m_pop != null)
                {
                    if (m_button != null)
                    {
                        m_button.Click -= new
Office._CommandBarButtonEvents_ClickEventHandler(m_button_Click);
                        m_button.Delete(false);
                    }
                    m_pop = null;
                }

                if (m_Expl != null) { m_Expl = null; }
                if (m_ExplClass != null) {m_ExplClass = null;}
                if (m_button != null) { m_button = null; }
            }
        }


        private void m_button_Click(Microsoft.Office.Core.CommandBarButton Ctrl,
ref bool CancelDefault)
        {
            MessageBox.Show(Ctrl.Caption + " was just clicked");
        }
    }
```

The `Close` event handler releases the class-level objects declared in the wrapper class and removes the class event handlers. The `Click` event handler in the template displays a `MessageBox` but is used in an addin to implement the business logic for the button and to perform any action the button calls for.

The `CommandBar` code in the template creates a new menu to the right of the Help menu in an `Explorer`, and creates one button for that menu. The result is shown in Figure 7.2

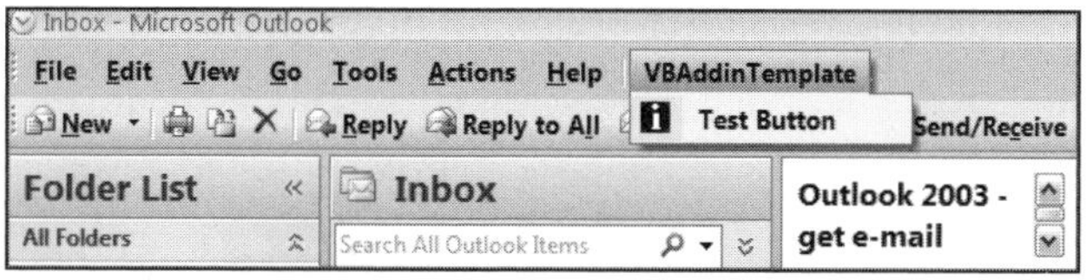

Figure 7.2

VSTO Interface Handlers

Setting up interface handlers for VSTO addins isn't as straightforward as it is in shared VB.NET or C# addins. In a VB.NET shared addin, you just add the required `Implements` statements for the Ribbon, Custom Task Pane, and Form Region interfaces:

```
' required implementation for handling IRibbon in Outlook 2007
Implements Office.IRibbonExtensibility

' required for CTP use
Implements Office.ICustomTaskPaneConsumer

' required for Form Region support
Implements Outlook.FormRegionStartup
```

In a C# shared addin, you add the interfaces to the class declaration:

```
public class Connect : Object, Extensibility.IDTExtensibility2,
        Office.IRibbonExtensibility, Office.ICustomTaskPaneConsumer,
        Outlook.FormRegionStartup
```

VSTO requires you to override the `RequestService` method and return a class that will implement the interface service request to handle the Ribbon, Custom Task Pane and Form Region interfaces.

VSTO provides a `CustomTaskPanes` *collection that you can use directly, without implementing Office* `CustomTaskPane` *objects. This is a very easy method of creating a custom task pane; the* `CustomTaskPanes.Add` *method is used to create the pane. However, the* `CustomTaskPane` *object provided by VSTO is limited. It doesn't have the* `Window` *property that in* `Office.CustomTaskPane` *objects is used to set the window where the task pane will be shown. VSTO* `CustomTaskPane` *objects are created in the active window, an* `Explorer`, *when the* `ThisAddin` *class starts up.*

VB.NET

The required code for adding Ribbon, Custom Task Pane, and Form Region interface support using VB.NET in a VSTO addin is shown in Listing 7.14. The override is added as a partial class addition to the `ThisAddin` class. The `GUID` of the interface requesting service is compared in turn with the `GUID` of each interface you are servicing, and the `ServiceRequest` handler is returned to the caller if that request is being handled.

The classes in the following table are used to implement the interface service request.

Interface	ServiceRequest Handler Class
IRibbonExtensibility	Ribbon
ICustomTaskPaneConsumer	CTPWrapper
FormRegionStartup	FormRegionWrapper

Listing 7.14

```
Partial Public Class ThisAddIn

    Private ribbon As Ribbon

    Private FormRegionWrapper As TimeTravelFormRegionWrapper

    Private TaskPaneWrapper As CTPWrapper
    Private Const CTP_PROGID As String = "VSTO_VBOutlookTemplate.EmailTaskPane"

    Protected Overrides Function RequestService(ByVal serviceGuid As System.Guid) _
As Object
        If serviceGuid = GetType(Office.IRibbonExtensibility).GUID Then
            If ribbon Is Nothing Then
                ribbon = New Ribbon()
            End If
            Return ribbon
        ElseIf serviceGuid = GetType(Outlook.FormRegionStartup).GUID Then
            If FormRegionWrapper Is Nothing Then
                FormRegionWrapper = New TimeTravelFormRegionWrapper()
                Return FormRegionWrapper
            End If
        ElseIf serviceGuid = GetType(Office.ICustomTaskPaneConsumer).GUID Then
            If TaskPaneWrapper Is Nothing Then
                TaskPaneWrapper = New CTPWrapper()
                Return TaskPaneWrapper
            End If
        End If

        Return MyBase.RequestService(serviceGuid)
    End Function

End Class
```

C#

The override for RequestService for C# is similar to the code for VB.NET, as shown in Listing 7.15.

Listing 7.15

```csharp
using System;
using System.Collections.Generic;
using System.Diagnostics;
using System.IO;
using System.Text;
using System.Reflection;
using System.Runtime.InteropServices;
using System.Windows.Forms;
using stdole;
using System.Drawing;
using Office = Microsoft.Office.Core;
using Outlook = Microsoft.Office.Interop.Outlook;
using Forms = Microsoft.Vbe.Interop.Forms;

using Resources = VSTO_CSOutlookTemplate.Properties.Resources;

public partial class ThisAddIn
{
    private Ribbon1 ribbon;
    private TimeTravelFormRegionWrapper FormRegionWrapper;

    private CTPWrapper TaskPaneWrapper;

    protected override object RequestService(Guid serviceGuid)
    {
        if (serviceGuid == typeof(Office.IRibbonExtensibility).GUID)
        {
            if (ribbon == null)
                ribbon = new Ribbon1();
            return ribbon;
        }
        if (serviceGuid == typeof(Outlook.FormRegionStartup).GUID)
        {
            if (FormRegionWrapper == null)
                FormRegionWrapper = new TimeTravelFormRegionWrapper();
            return FormRegionWrapper;
        }
        if (serviceGuid == typeof(Office.ICustomTaskPaneConsumer).GUID)
        {
            if (TaskPaneWrapper == null)
                TaskPaneWrapper = new CTPWrapper();
            return TaskPaneWrapper;
        }
        return base.RequestService(serviceGuid);
    }
}
```

AxHost

One problem in adding icons to buttons, which are the only CommandBar controls that support icons, is that the CommandBarButton and your code are in different processes if you wrote the addin using VB.NET or C#. An IPictureDisp object, which is required for setting the icon of a button, can't be passed across process boundaries. This problem doesn't apply to VB 6 COM addins, which run in-process with Outlook.

Using AxHost, which usually is used as a virtual host for ActiveX controls placed on Windows Forms, is an easy workaround for solving the problem of passing an IPictureDisp object across the process boundaries of the Interop. The following sections show AxHost implementations for both VB.NET and C#.

VB.NET

The code for using AxHost in VB.NET is pretty simple. A GUID is supplied to the New initialization procedure and a function is provided for converting an Image into an IPictureDisp object using the GetIPictureFromPicture function. A conversion function is used to convert the stored bitmap used as an icon into an Image object before GetIPictureFromPicture is called.

Listing 7.16

```
Public Class MyAxHost 'second class in Connect module
    Inherits System.Windows.Forms.AxHost

    Public Sub New()
        MyBase.New("{59EE46BA-677D-4d20-BF10-8D8067CB8B33}")
    End Sub

    Public Function IPictureDispFromImage(ByVal Image As System.Drawing.Image) As
stdole.IPictureDisp
        Dim oPic As stdole.IPictureDisp

        oPic = CType(System.Windows.Forms.AxHost.GetIPictureDispFromPicture(Image), _
            stdole.IPictureDisp)

        Return oPic
    End Function
End Class
```

C#

The C# code for using AxHost is shown in Listing 7.17.

Listing 7.17

```
using System;
using System.Collections.Generic;
using System.Text;
using System.Drawing;
using Office = Microsoft.Office.Core;
```

Listing 7.17 *(continued)*

```
using System.Diagnostics;
using System.IO;
using System.Windows.Forms;
using System.Reflection;
using stdole;

namespace CSAddinTemplate
{
    /// <summary>
    /// The MyAxHost is derived from AxHost to use the function
    /// AxHost.GetIPictureDispFromPicture(image);
    /// that returns an IPictureDisp interface from an Image.
    /// </summary>
    class MyAxHost : System.Windows.Forms.AxHost
    {

        /// <summary>
        /// Overloaded constructor with CLSID for the ribbon
        /// </summary>
        public MyAxHost()
            : base("{59EE46BA-677D-4d20-BF10-8D8067CB8B33}")
        {
        }

        public stdole.IPictureDisp IPictureDispFromImage(System.Drawing.Image image)
        {
            IPictureDisp oPic = null;

            try
            {
                // Convert the Resource bitmap to stdole.IPictureDisp
                oPic = (stdole.IPictureDisp)AxHost.GetIPictureDispFromPicture(image);
                return oPic;
            }
            catch (System.Exception ex)
            {
                Debug.WriteLine(ex.Message);
                return oPic;
            }
        }
    }
}
```

Working with the Ribbon

Working with the Ribbon is very different from working with CommandBars. Unlike the standard method of creating CommandBar user interface in the Explorer or Inspector wrapper, Ribbon control creation and event handling is performed in one set of procedures located in the class that implements the IDTExtensibility2 interface.

There are a number of limitations in working with the Ribbon compared to working with the `CommandBar` interface:

❑ Ribbon controls can't be enumerated, so there's no way to discover what controls are in the user interface.

❑ Control groups can be added to the built-in Ribbon tabs, but you can't add custom controls within a built-in control group.

❑ Built-in tabs, groups, and controls can't be selectively removed or replaced. To customize a built-in tab or group, you must replace the interface element, and replicate the context-sensitive user interface of that element.

❑ Ribbon control user interface is loaded once, the first time a Ribbon type is used in that addin session. The only Ribbon user interface that can be loaded dynamically is the *dynamicMenu* control.

Ribbon XML

Ribbon user interface is created using an XML description of the user interface. The Ribbon XML schema provides more types of controls than the `CommandBar` interface, allowing you to create custom tabs and groups, as well as the types of controls in the following table.

Control Type	Controls
Container	`box, buttonGroup, gallery`
Menu	`dynamicMenu, menu`
Control	`button, checkBox, comboBox, dialogBoxLauncher, dropdown, editBox, labelControl, splitButton, toggleButton`

In addition to working with tabs and groups, you can also work with the Office Menu, the new Office icon at the top left of Inspectors.

Listing 7.18 shows the XML for the sample Ribbon in the addin templates. The XML creates a new tab in mail compose Inspectors, inserted just after the built-in Message tab. The new tab has two groups of controls, three toggle buttons in one group and two buttons in a second group.

Ribbon controls can be normal or large size. There is room for three normal-sized or one large control in one column in the Ribbon. If a column of controls contains two controls, they are placed in the top two slots in the column. The XML uses a trick to separate the two buttons in the second group of controls, placing a third control between the two visible controls and giving it a label of one space. Making a control invisible moves other controls in that column up one slot, so a one space label is used to separate the two active controls.

Listing 7.18

```xml
<?xml version="1.0" encoding="utf-8" ?>
<customUI xmlns = "http://schemas.microsoft.com/office/2006/01/customui"
          onLoad = "Ribbon_OnLoad" >
```

Listing 7.18 *(continued)*

```
    <ribbon>
      <tabs>
        <tab id="VBAddinTab" label="VB Addin" visible="true"
  insertAfterMso="TabNewMailMessage" >
          <group id="GroupVBSettings" label="Settings for this e-mail"
  visible="true">
            <toggleButton id="VB1" size="normal" label="HTML" onAction="VBToggle"
  getPressed="VBPressed" getImage="VB_GetImage" />
            <toggleButton id="VB2" size="normal" label="Plain Text"
  onAction="VBToggle" getPressed="VBPressed" getSupertip="VB_GetSuperTip"
  getImage="VB_GetImage" />
            <toggleButton id="VB3" size="normal" label="Rich Text"
  getSupertip="VB_GetSuperTip" onAction="VBToggle" getPressed="VBPressed"
  getImage="VB_GetImage" />
          </group>
          <group id="GroupVBActions" label="Actions for this e-mail" visible="true">
            <button id="VB4" size="normal" label="Insert..."
  getSupertip="VB_GetSuperTip" onAction="VB_Action" getImage="VB_GetImage" />
            <button id="VB5" size="normal" label=" "  />
            <button id="VB6" size="normal" label="Configure..." onAction="VB_Action"
  getSupertip="VB_GetSuperTip" getImage="VB_GetImage" />
          </group>
        </tab>
      </tabs>
    </ribbon>
  </customUI>
```

The `onAction` *callback for* `button` *and* `toggleButton` *controls is the equivalent of a* `CommandBarButton`*'s* `Click` *event. The* `getPressed` *callback is fired when a* `toggleButton` *is invalidated and when the Ribbon XML is first instantiated.*

The Ribbon XML produces a Ribbon that looks like the one shown in Figure 7.3, for `Email.Compose` `Inspectors`.

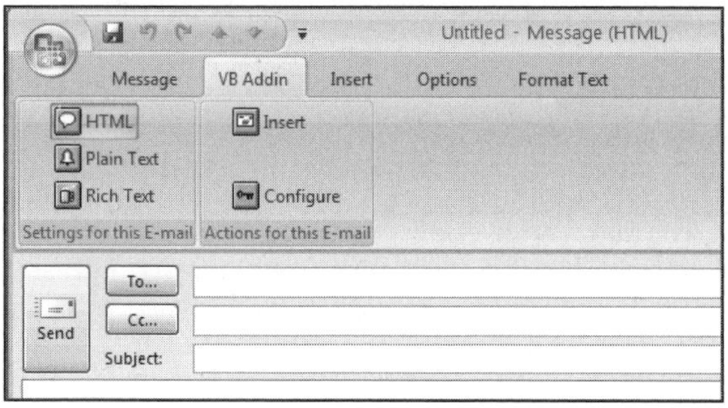

Figure 7.3

Ribbon Customization Rules

The following list shows the main rules to follow when creating or repurposing user interface for the Ribbon.

❑ To add controls to the Office Menu, use the `<officeMenu>` tag outside the `<tabs>` section:

```
<ribbon>
  <officeMenu>
    <button id="MyButton" visible="true" <!-- additional attributes -->
  </officeMenu>
  <tabs>
  </tabs>
```

❑ To repurpose built-in controls, use the `<commands>` tag. The `onAction` callback adds a `ByRef fCancelDefault As Boolean` argument to the callback for repurposed `button` and `toggleButton` controls. This allows you to intercept a built-in Ribbon button click, execute your own code, and cancel the default action if desired.

```
<commands>
  <command idMso="SendDefault" getEnabled="CheckSendEnabled"
    <onAction>="NewSend" />
</commsnds>
<ribbon>
```

❑ You can't add controls to built-in groups, except in the Office Menu.

❑ You can add groups to built-in tabs.

❑ You can't resize, reorder, rearrange, or otherwise modify built-in tabs, groups, or controls, except for adding your own groups to built-in tabs.

❑ You can't reorder built-in groups in built-in tabs, but if you add a built-in group to a different built-in tab, you can place it where you want.

❑ A contextual tab can only be used within its original tab set.

❑ You can only add supported controls to the Ribbon. If your user interface requires a control that the Ribbon does not support, you can add the control to a custom task pane.

Supplying Ribbon XML

The implementation of the `IRibbonExtensibility` interface is required to be in the class that implements the `IDTExtensibility` interface. The `IRibbonExtensibility` interface has one event, `Ribbon_OnLoad`, which passes an `IRibbonUI` object. The `IRibbonUI` object has two methods, `Invalidate` and `InvalidateControl`. All control over Ribbon controls is exercised using those two methods and various callbacks.

Outlook supports many different Ribbon types; in fact, there are more Outlook Ribbons than for any other Office application. The first time an `Inspector` is opened for a specific type of item the `GetCustomUI` callback method is called to get the XML for that Ribbon type. The XML is cached for the remainder of that Outlook session for other instances of that Ribbon type.

VB.NET

Listing 7.19 shows the implementation of the `IRibbonExtensibility` interface. A class-level `IRibbonUI` object is declared to hold the `Ribbon` object passed in `Ribbon_OnLoad` and the event handler for `GetCustomUI` returns the XML for the `Inspector` type that is about to be opened.

Listing 7.19

```
' required implementation for handling IRibbon in Outlook 2007
Implements Office.IRibbonExtensibility

' Ribbon UI declarations
Private m_Ribbon As Office.IRibbonUI
```

Outlook has 19 different types of `Inspectors` that are supported by 19 different Ribbons. The sample code returns Ribbon XML for a `Microsoft.Outlook.Mail.Compose Inspector`. You can write different XML for each type of `Inspector`, or supply the same XML for several different `Inspector` types.

```
#Region "Ribbon Stuff"
#Region "Ribbon Initializer"
    Function GetCustomUI(ByVal RibbonID As String) As String Implements
Microsoft.Office.Core.IRibbonExtensibility.GetCustomUI
        'RibbonID indicates type of Inspector that is about to be displayed,
        '   valid RibbonID values are as follows:
        'Microsoft.Outlook.Mail.Read
        'Microsoft.Outlook.Mail.Compose
        'Microsoft.Outlook.MeetingRequest.Read
        'Microsoft.Outlook.MeetingRequest.Send
        'Microsoft.Outlook.Appointment
        'Microsoft.Outlook.Contact
        'Microsoft.Outlook.Journal
        'Microsoft.Outlook.Task
        'Microsoft.Outlook.DistributionList
        'Microsoft.Outlook.Report
        'Microsoft.Outlook.Resend
        'Microsoft.Outlook.Response.Read
        'Microsoft.Outlook.Response.Compose
        'Microsoft.Outlook.Response.CounterPropose
        'Microsoft.Outlook.RSS
        'Microsoft.Outlook.Post.Read
        'Microsoft.Outlook.Post.Compose
        'Microsoft.Outlook.Sharing.Read
        'Microsoft.Outlook.Sharing.Compose

        'In this sample only new mail Inspector is handled for a button.

        Select Case RibbonID
            Case "Microsoft.Outlook.Mail.Compose"
                ' Return the RibbonX markup stored as a resource in the project
                Return My.Resources.CustomRibbon
            Case Else
                Return String.Empty
        End Select
    End Function
#End Region
```

The following table shows the `RibbonID` passed by `GetCustomUI` and the Outlook `MessageClass` that corresponds to the `RibbonID`. Custom message classes will be initialized with the same Ribbon XML, so you may have to show or hide your controls for custom message classes where you don't want your user interface to show, using a `getVisible` callback.

RibbonID	Corresponding MessageClass
Microsoft.Outlook.Mail.Read	IPM.Note.
Microsoft.Outlook.Mail.Compose	IPM.Note.
Microsoft.Outlook.MeetingRequest.Read	IPM.Schedule.Meeting.Request, IPM.Schedule.Meeting.Canceled
Microsoft.Outlook.MeetingRequest.Send	IPM.Schedule.Meeting.Request
Microsoft.Outlook.Appointment	IPM.Appointment.
Microsoft.Outlook.Contact	IPM.Contact.
Microsoft.Outlook.Journal	IPM.Activity.
Microsoft.Outlook.Task	IPM.Task. and IPM.TaskRequest.
Microsoft.Outlook.DistributionList	IPM.DistList.
Microsoft.Outlook.Report	IPM.Report.
Microsoft.Outlook.Resend	IPM.Resend.
Microsoft.Outlook.Response.Read	IPM.Schedule.Meeting.Response
Microsoft.Outlook.Response.Compose	IPM.Schedule.Meeting.Response
Microsoft.Outlook.Response.CounterPropose	IPM.Schedule.Meeting.Response
Microsoft.Outlook.RSS	IPM.Post.Rss
Microsoft.Outlook.Post.Read	IPM.Post.
Microsoft.Outlook.Post.Compose	IPM.Post.
Microsoft.Outlook.Sharing.Read	IPM.Sharing.
Microsoft.Outlook.Sharing.Compose	IPM.Sharing.

C#

The C# code shown in Listing 7.20 implements the `IRibbonExtensibility` interface class, instantiates an `IRibbonUI` object, and handles the `GetCustomUI` callback to provide the Ribbon XML for a `Mail.Compose` Inspector.

Listing 7.20

```
    public class Connect : Object, Extensibility.IDTExtensibility2,
        Office.IRibbonExtensibility, Office.ICustomTaskPaneConsumer,
Outlook.FormRegionStartup

        //Ribbon UI object
        private Office.IRibbonUI m_Ribbon;

#region Ribbon_Stuff
#region Ribbon_Initializer
    public string GetCustomUI(string RibbonID)
    {
        //Implements Microsoft.Office.Core.IRibbonExtensibility.GetCustomUI

        //RibbonID indicates type of Inspector that is about to be displayed,
        //   valid RibbonID values are as follows:
        //Microsoft.Outlook.Mail.Read
        //Microsoft.Outlook.Mail.Compose
        //Microsoft.Outlook.MeetingRequest.Read
        //Microsoft.Outlook.MeetingRequest.Send
        //Microsoft.Outlook.Appointment
        //Microsoft.Outlook.Contact
        //Microsoft.Outlook.Journal
        //Microsoft.Outlook.Task
        //Microsoft.Outlook.DistributionList
        //Microsoft.Outlook.Report
        //Microsoft.Outlook.Resend
        //Microsoft.Outlook.Response.Read
        //Microsoft.Outlook.Response.Compose
        //Microsoft.Outlook.Response.CounterPropose
        //Microsoft.Outlook.RSS
        //Microsoft.Outlook.Post.Read
        //Microsoft.Outlook.Post.Compose
        //Microsoft.Outlook.Sharing.Read
        //Microsoft.Outlook.Sharing.Compose

        //In this sample only new mail Inspector is handled for a button.

        switch(RibbonID)
        {
            case "Microsoft.Outlook.Mail.Compose":
                // Return the RibbonX markup stored as a resource in the project
                return Properties.Resources.CustomRibbon;
            default:
            {
                return String.Empty;
```

(continued)

Listing 7.20 *(continued)*

```
            }
        }
    }
#endregion
```

Ribbon Callbacks

The code in Listing 7.21 shows callbacks for onAction, getPressed, getImage, getlabel, getVisible, and getSuperTip for button and toggleButton Ribbon controls.

The first onAction callback tests the control.Id property to make sure that the callback is for a control with an Id of "VB6", which is the Configure button, and then iterates through the Inspector wrapper collection to match the control.Context with the Inspector in the wrapper class so that it can act on the correct Inspector. The control.Context of an Outlook Ribbon is always an Inspector and can be compared with other Inspector objects to see if they are the same object. When the onAction handler finds the correct Inspector, it toggles the visibility of a custom task pane. This isolates the button action to a specific Inspector and toggles the visibility of only that Inspector's custom task pane.

Listing 7.21

```
#Region "Ribbon Callbacks"
    Public Sub VB_Action(ByVal control As Office.IRibbonControl)
        Debug.Print("VB_Action")

        Dim myInsp As Outlook.Inspector = CType(control.Context, Outlook.Inspector)
        Dim oInspWrap As InspWrap = Nothing

        If (control.Id = "VB6") Then
            Try
                For Each oInspWrap In g_colInspWrap
                    If (oInspWrap.Inspector Is myInsp) Then
                        If oInspWrap.TaskPane IsNot Nothing Then
                            oInspWrap.TaskPane.Visible = True
                        End If
                    Else
                        If oInspWrap IsNot Nothing Then
                            oInspWrap.TaskPane.Visible = False
                        End If
                    End If
                Next
            Catch ex As Exception
                MessageBox.Show(ex.Message)
            End Try
        End If

        oInspWrap = Nothing
        myInsp = Nothing
    End Sub
```

When the custom task pane is made visible by clicking the `Configure` Ribbon `button`, the result looks like Figure 7.4, showing a custom task pane in the `Inspector`.

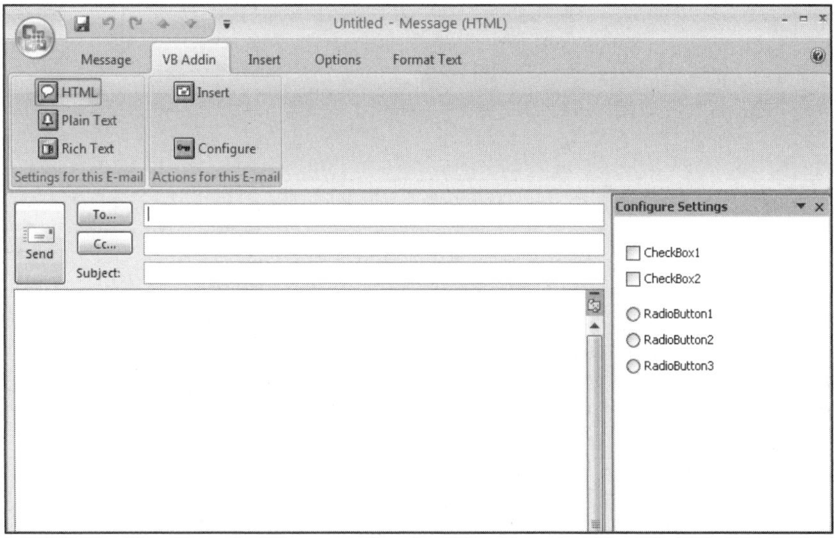

Figure 7.4

The second `onAction` callback handles clicks on any one of three `toggleButtons`. After checking for the correct `Inspector`, the code tests to see which `toggleButton` was clicked:

❑ If the `HTML toggleButton` was clicked, the code sets the `HTML` property in the `Inspector` wrapper `True`, changes the mail item's format to HTML and invalidates all three controls using the `InvalidateControl` method.

❑ If the `Plain Text toggleButton` was clicked, the code sets the `PT` property in the `Inspector` wrapper `True`, changes the mail item's format to Plain Text, and invalidates all three controls, using the `InvalidateControl` method.

❑ If the `Rich Text toggleButton` was clicked, the code sets the `RTF` property in the `Inspector` wrapper `True`, changes the mail item's format to RTF, and invalidates all three controls, using the `InvalidateControl` method.

When a control is invalidated using `InvalidateControl`, every callback declared by that control is called. Invalidating a control is the only way to make changes to that control, such as changing a label or icon. The `Invalidate` method is used to invalidate all custom controls created by that addin.

```
Public Sub VBToggle(ByVal control As Office.IRibbonControl, ByVal pressed As Boolean)
    Dim myInsp As Outlook.Inspector = CType(control.Context, Outlook.Inspector)
    Dim oInspWrap As InspWrap = Nothing

    Try
        For Each oInspWrap In g_colInspWrap
            If (oInspWrap.Inspector Is myInsp) Then
```

```
                Select Case control.Id
                    Case "VB1"
                        oInspWrap.HTML = True
                        oInspWrap.PT = False
                        oInspWrap.RTF = False
                        oInspWrap.MailItem.BodyFormat =
Outlook.OlBodyFormat.olFormatHTML
                        m_Ribbon.InvalidateControl("VB1")
                        m_Ribbon.InvalidateControl("VB2")
                        m_Ribbon.InvalidateControl("VB3")
                    Case "VB2"
                        oInspWrap.PT = True
                        oInspWrap.HTML = False
                        oInspWrap.RTF = False
                        oInspWrap.MailItem.BodyFormat =
Outlook.OlBodyFormat.olFormatPlain
                        m_Ribbon.InvalidateControl("VB1")
                        m_Ribbon.InvalidateControl("VB2")
                        m_Ribbon.InvalidateControl("VB3")
                    Case "VB3"
                        oInspWrap.RTF = True
                        oInspWrap.HTML = False
                        oInspWrap.PT = False
                        oInspWrap.MailItem.BodyFormat =
Outlook.OlBodyFormat.olFormatRichText
                        m_Ribbon.InvalidateControl("VB1")
                        m_Ribbon.InvalidateControl("VB2")
                        m_Ribbon.InvalidateControl("VB3")
                    Case Else
                End Select
            End If
        Next
    Catch ex As Exception
        MessageBox.Show(ex.Message)
    End Try

    oInspWrap = Nothing
    myInsp = Nothing
End Sub
```

The result of clicking the `Rich Text toggleButton` in the HTML email shown in Figure 7.3 is shown in Figure 7.5. The Rich Text button is selected, and the email format has been changed to Rich Text.

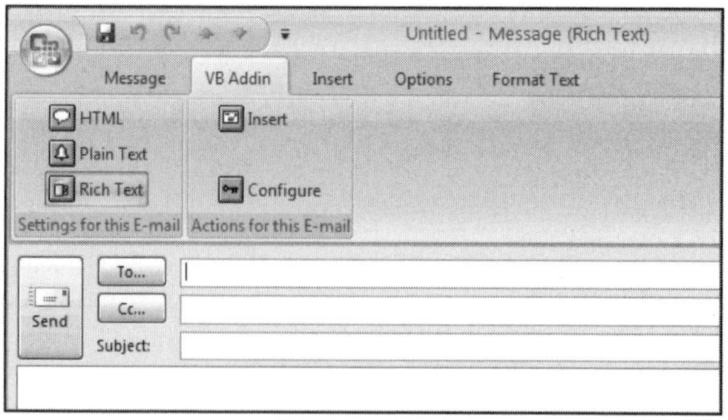

Figure 7.5

The `getPressed` callback function fires for a `toggleButton` when the control is first shown and when it's invalidated. This callback is used to return the toggled state for the `toggleButton`. When the control is invalidated in the second `onAction` handler, the `getPressed` function is called again to set the state to the value of the appropriate property in the `Inspector` wrapper.

```
Public Function VBPressed(ByVal control As Office.IRibbonControl) As Boolean
    Debug.Print("VB_GetPressed " & control.Id.ToString)

    Dim myInsp As Outlook.Inspector = CType(control.Context, Outlook.Inspector)
    Dim oInspWrap As InspWrap = Nothing

    Try
        For Each oInspWrap In g_colInspWrap
            If (oInspWrap.Inspector Is myInsp) Then
                Select Case control.Id
                    Case "VB1"
                        Return oInspWrap.HTML
                    Case "VB2"
                        Return oInspWrap.PT
                    Case "VB3"
                        Return oInspWrap.RTF
                    Case Else
                End Select
            End If
        Next
    Catch ex As Exception
        MessageBox.Show(ex.Message)
    End Try

    oInspWrap = Nothing
    myInsp = Nothing
End Function
```

The `getImage` callback is used to supply the icon for `button`, `toggleButton`, and other controls that can display an image. The function returns an `IPictureDisp` object that's used as the image for the icon. If you use an image format that supports transparency, such as PNG, you can supply icons with a transparent background in the Ribbon. In the template code, BMP images stored as resources in the addin are used to provide the icon images. The `AxHost` class shown in Listing 7.16 is used to convert the image into an `IPictureDisp` object.

```
    Public Function VB_GetImage(ByVal control As Office.IRibbonControl) As
stdole.IPictureDisp
        Dim imgStreamPic As System.Drawing.Bitmap
        Dim oPic As IPictureDisp
        Dim ax As MyAxHost

        Select Case control.Id
            Case "VB1"
                imgStreamPic = My.Resources.BALLOON
            Case "VB2"
                imgStreamPic = My.Resources.BELL
            Case "VB3"
                imgStreamPic = My.Resources.CUP
            Case "VB4"
                imgStreamPic = My.Resources.ENVELOPE
```

```
            Case "VB6"
                   imgStreamPic = My.Resources.KEY
            Case Else
                   imgStreamPic = My.Resources.HAPPY
       End Select

       ax = New MyAxHost

       oPic = ax.IPictureDispFromImage(imgStreamPic)

       imgStreamPic = Nothing
       ax = Nothing

       Return oPic

End Function
```

The `getVisible` and `getEnabled` callback functions are called when a control is first made visible and when it's invalidated. The `getVisible` callback is shown here:

```
Public Function VB_GetVisible(ByVal control As Office.IRibbonControl) As Boolean
       Debug.Print("VB_GetVisible")


       Return True

End Function
```

The `getLabel` callback enables you to set the label of a control on startup and whenever the control is invalidated:

```
Public Function VB_GetLabel(ByVal control As Office.IRibbonControl) As String
       Debug.Print("VB_GetLabel")

       Dim Name As String = "Control_" & control.Id
       Return Name

End Function
```

The `getSuperTip` callback enables you to set the text of the SuperTip that's shown when the mouse cursor is hovered over a control:

```
Public Function VB_GetSuperTip(ByVal control As Office.IRibbonControl) As String
       Debug.Print("VB_GetSuperTip")

       Dim Name As String = "Tip_" & control.Id
       Return Name

End Function
```

The `Ribbon_OnLoad` event fires when the Ribbon XML is first loaded, when the first `Inspector` of a particular Ribbon type is added. The template code uses this callback to store the `IRibbonUI` object in a class-level variable and sets the Ribbon wrapper in the first `Inspector` wrapper class to the `IRibbonUI` object. When the first `Inspector` is loaded for that type of Ribbon, the related Ribbon wrapper object is null, it usually doesn't become valid until the first `Activate` event fires in the `Inspector`.

If the template is handling more than one Ribbon type, you should use a different method of making sure the correct `IRibbonUI` object is stored in the wrapper. In that case, the code might check for a specific `control.Id` in the `getVisible` callback fired when the control is first displayed and determine the Ribbon type from a list of IDs. The `Inspector.CurrentItem` could then be compared to the list of Ribbon types to make sure the correct `Inspector` wrapper was storing the correct `IRibbonUI` object.

The code in Listing 7.22 shows the `Ribbon_OnLoad` callback handler and a property that returns the current `IRibbonUI` object.

Listing 7.22

```
Public Sub Ribbon_OnLoad(ByVal Ribbon As Office.IRibbonUI)
    Debug.Print("Ribbon_OnLoad")

    m_Ribbon = Ribbon

    Dim wrap As InspWrap = Nothing

    For Each wrap In g_colInspWrap
        If wrap.Ribbon Is Nothing Then
            wrap.Ribbon = m_Ribbon
        End If
    Next

    wrap = Nothing

End Sub
#End Region

#Region "Ribbon Properties"
    Friend ReadOnly Property Ribbon() As Office.IRibbonUI
        Get
            Return m_Ribbon
        End Get
    End Property
#End Region

#End Region
```

C#

The C# code in Listing 7.23 is very similar to the VB.NET code in Listing 7.36. Two `onAction` callbacks are shown, one for `button` controls and one for `toggleButton` controls. Additional callback handlers are shown for `getPressed`, `getImage`, `getLabel`, `getVisible`, and `getSuperTip`.

The `Inspector` wrapper `SortedList` is searched to retrieve the `Inspector` that matches the control `.Context` object. When the matching `Inspector` is found, its task pane visibility is toggled.

Listing 7.23

```
#region Ribbon_Callbacks
    public void CS_Action(Office.IRibbonControl control)
    {
        Debug.WriteLine("CS_Action " + control.Id.ToString());

        if (control.Id == "CS6")
        {
            try
            {
                Outlook.Inspector myInsp = (Outlook.Inspector)control.Context;

                int j = m_InspWrap.Count;

                for (int i = 0; i < j; i++)
                {
                    InspWrap wrapped = (InspWrap)m_InspWrap.GetByIndex(i);

                    if (wrapped.Inspector == myInsp)
                    {
                        wrapped.TaskPane.Visible = true;
                    }
                    else
                    {
                        wrapped.TaskPane.Visible = false;
                    }
                }
            }
            catch (Exception ex)
            {
                MessageBox.Show(ex.Message);
            }
        }
    }
```

The CSToggle onAction callback handler toggles the email body format and invalidates the toggleButton controls to force firing the getPressed callback and the toggleButtons are set to the correct state:

```
    public void CSToggle(Office.IRibbonControl control, bool pressed)
    {
        Debug.WriteLine("CSToggle " + control.Id.ToString());
        // pressed is True if the new button state is On.

        try
        {
            Outlook.Inspector myInsp = (Outlook.Inspector)control.Context;

            int j = m_InspWrap.Count;

            for (int i = 0; i < j; i++)
            {
```

```
            InspWrap wrapped = (InspWrap)m_InspWrap.GetByIndex(i);

            if (wrapped.Inspector == myInsp)
            {
                switch (control.Id)
                {
                    case "CS1":
                        wrapped.HTML = true;
                        wrapped.PT = false;
                        wrapped.RTF = false;
                        wrapped.MailItem.BodyFormat =
Outlook.OlBodyFormat.olFormatHTML;
                        m_Ribbon.InvalidateControl("CS1");
                        m_Ribbon.InvalidateControl("CS2");
                        m_Ribbon.InvalidateControl("CS3");
                        // m_Ribbon.Invalidate();
                        break;
                    case "CS2":
                        wrapped.HTML = false;
                        wrapped.PT = true;
                        wrapped.RTF = false;
                        wrapped.MailItem.BodyFormat =
Outlook.OlBodyFormat.olFormatPlain;
                        m_Ribbon.InvalidateControl("CS1");
                        m_Ribbon.InvalidateControl("CS2");
                        m_Ribbon.InvalidateControl("CS3");
                        // m_Ribbon.Invalidate();
                        break;
                    case "CS3":
                        wrapped.HTML = false;
                        wrapped.PT = false;
                        wrapped.RTF = true;
                        wrapped.MailItem.BodyFormat =
Outlook.OlBodyFormat.olFormatRichText;
                        m_Ribbon.InvalidateControl("CS1");
                        m_Ribbon.InvalidateControl("CS2");
                        m_Ribbon.InvalidateControl("CS3");
                        break;
                    default:
                        {
                            break;
                        }
                }
                break;
            }
        }
    }
    catch (Exception ex)
    {
        MessageBox.Show(ex.Message);
    }

}
```

The getPressed callback is used for the toggleButtons to return a Boolean indicating what state they should assume. A return value of true for a control shows that the control as selected; a return value of false deselects the control.

```csharp
public bool CSPressed(Office.IRibbonControl control)
{
    Debug.WriteLine("CS_GetPressed " + control.Id.ToString());

    bool retVal = false;

    try
    {
        Outlook.Inspector myInsp = (Outlook.Inspector)control.Context;

        int j = m_InspWrap.Count;

        for (int i = 0; i < j; i++)
        {
            InspWrap wrapped = (InspWrap)m_InspWrap.GetByIndex(i);

            if (wrapped.Inspector == myInsp)
            {
                switch (control.Id)
                {
                    case "CS1":
                        retVal = wrapped.HTML;
                        break;
                    case "CS2":
                        retVal = wrapped.PT;
                        break;
                    case "CS3":
                        retVal = wrapped.RTF;
                        break;
                    default:
                    {
                        retVal = false;
                        break;
                    }
                }
                break;
            }
        }
    }
    catch (Exception ex)
    {
        MessageBox.Show(ex.Message);
    }

    return retVal;
}
```

The AxHost class in Listing 7.17 is used to convert a bitmap format resource into an IPictureDisp object, which is returned by the getImage callback to serve as the icon for the specified control:

```csharp
public stdole.IPictureDisp CS_GetImage(Office.IRibbonControl control)
{
```

```
        System.Drawing.Image imgStreamPic;
        IPictureDisp oPic = null;
        MyAxHost ax = new MyAxHost();

        switch(control.Id)
        {
            case "CS1":
                imgStreamPic = Properties.Resources.BALLOON;
                break;
            case "CS2":
                imgStreamPic = Properties.Resources.BELL;
                break;
            case "CS3":
                imgStreamPic = Properties.Resources.CUP;
                break;
            case "CS4":
                imgStreamPic = Properties.Resources.ENVELOPE;
                break;
            case "CS6":
                imgStreamPic = Properties.Resources.KEY;
                break;
            default:
            {
                imgStreamPic = Properties.Resources.HAPPY;
                break;
            }
        }

        oPic = ax.IPictureDispFromImage(imgStreamPic);

        imgStreamPic = null;
        ax = null;

        return oPic;
    }
```

The getVisible callback is used to set the visibility of a control, and fires when a control is first displayed and when it's invalidated. The getLabel callback provides a label for a control, and the getSuperTip callback provides SuperTip text for a control.

```
public bool CS_GetVisible(Office.IRibbonControl control)
{
    Debug.WriteLine("Control_" + control.Id);
    return true;
}
public string CS_GetLabel(Office.IRibbonControl control)
{
    string Name = "CS_GetLabel Control_" + control.Id;
    Debug.WriteLine(Name);
    return Name;
}
public string CS_GetSuperTip(Office.IRibbonControl control)
{
    string Name = "Tip_" + control.Id;
    Debug.WriteLine(Name);
    return Name;
}
```

The code in Listing 7.24 shows the `Ribbon_OnLoad` event that passes an `IRibbonUI` object used for invalidating controls with the `Invalidate` and `InvalidateControl` methods.

Listing 7.24

```
public void Ribbon_OnLoad(Office.IRibbonUI Ribbon)
{
    Debug.WriteLine("Ribbon_OnLoad");
    m_Ribbon = Ribbon;

    int j = m_InspWrap.Count;

    for (int i = 0; i < j; i++)
    {
        InspWrap wrapped = (InspWrap)m_InspWrap.GetByIndex(i);

        if (wrapped.Ribbon == null)
        {
            wrapped.Ribbon = m_Ribbon;
        }
    }
}
#endregion

#region Ribbon_Properties
    public Office.IRibbonUI Ribbon
    {
        get
        {
            return m_Ribbon;
        }
    }
#endregion

#endregion
```

VSTO

The VSTO template code for working with the Ribbon is identical to the shared addin code, except that it's placed in an `InterfaceHandler` class instead of in the `Connect` class. The `RequestService` code used for interface handling was shown in Listing 7.14 for VB.NET and in Listing 7.15 for C#.

Custom Task Panes

Outlook has had task panes such as the built-in Help and Research panes, but for the first time in Outlook 2007 your code can create custom task panes for `Inspectors` and `Explorers`. Custom task panes can be used to provide a design surface that's more flexible to work with than Ribbon controls because it allows you to design the user interface in a larger frame that can display any ActiveX control or .NET User Control that's made COM visible. This allows you to use many controls that aren't provided by the Ribbon for your user interface.

The task panes in this chapter use the `ICustomTaskPaneConsumer` interface, an `ICTPFactory` object used to create task panes, and `CustomTaskPane` objects, all supplied by the Office 2007 library.

VSTO provides a `CustomTaskPanes` collection that can be used to easily add a task pane, but the task panes added using the `CustomTaskPanes` collection are limited because they don't have the `Window` property used to set the `Inspector` or `Explorer` that shows the task pane. VSTO task panes are shown in the first `Explorer` window.

In addition to providing a design surface for controls that take immediate action, such as buttons, task panes can be used as configuration screens for setting options for a specific `Inspector` or `Explorer`.

Creating Custom Task Panes

To create a custom task pane, you first implement the `ICustomTaskPaneConsumer` interface. This interface provides an event, `CTPFactoryAvailable`, which provides a `ICTPFactory` object used to create all your custom task panes. Make sure to save this object so that it remains in scope for the lifetime of your COM addin. When the task pane is created, the `Window` property is set to bind the task pane to a specific `Inspector` or `Explorer`.

The VSTO implementation of `ICustomTaskPaneConsumer` uses the `InterfaceHandler` class shown in Listing 7.14 and Listing 7.15. The code in their `CTPWrapper` classes is the same as the VB.NET and C# code shown below.

VB.NET

The code in Listing 7.25 shows the implementation of the `CTPFactoryAvailable` event fired by the `ICustomTaskPaneConsumer` implementation class. A class-level `ICTPFactory` object is instantiated, which is used to create all the task panes created by the addin. The `CTPFactoryAvailable` event fires asynchronously with Outlook events but has fired by the time the `OnStartupComplete` event fires. The first time you can create a task pane in Outlook is during the `OnStartupComplete` event. VSTO 2005 SE code can use the `Startup` event to create task panes. That event is delayed in VSTO 2005 SE until `OnStartupComplete` fires.

Listing 7.25

```
' required for CTP use
Implements Office.ICustomTaskPaneConsumer

' Task Pane declarations
Private m_CTP As Office.ICTPFactory
Private CTP As Office.CustomTaskPane
Private Const CTP_PROGID As String = "VBAddinTemplate.EmailTaskPane"

    Public Sub CTPFactoryAvailable(ByVal CTPFactoryInst As Office.ICTPFactory)
Implements Office.ICustomTaskPaneConsumer.CTPFactoryAvailable
        ' store the Custom Task Pane factory instance
        m_CTP = CTPFactoryInst
    End Sub

    Public Sub OnStartupComplete(ByRef custom As System.Array) Implements
```

(continued)

Listing 7.25 *(continued)*

```
Extensibility.IDTExtensibility2.OnStartupComplete
        ' for an Explorer task pane
        'Try
        'CTP = m_CTP.CreateCTP("VBAddinTemplate.EmailTaskPane", "VB.NET Config",
m_olExplorer)
        'CTP.DockPositionRestrict =
Microsoft.Office.Core.MsoCTPDockPositionRestrict.msoCTPDockPositionRestrictNoChange
        'CTP.DockPosition =
Microsoft.Office.Core.MsoCTPDockPosition.msoCTPDockPositionRight
        'CTP.Visible = True
        'Catch ex As Exception
        'MessageBox.Show(ex.Message)
        'End Try
    End Sub
```

To display a task pane in the first Outlook `Explorer`, uncomment the `OnStartupComplete` code. This code displays a dummy task pane that's docked to the right of the `Explorer`, locked to prevent the user from moving the task pane.

The Explorer custom task pane displayed when the code above is uncommented is shown in Figure 7.6

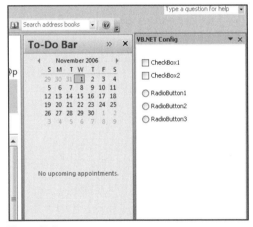

Figure 7.6

The code in Listing 7.26 adds a custom task pane to an `Inspector` in the `NewInspector` event handler. Setting the `Window` property of the task pane to the `Inspector` in `NewInspector` binds the task pane to that window. The initial state of the task pane is set to not visible. The task pane is shown by clicking the `Configure` button in the `Email.Compose Inspector` custom Ribbon. The Configure button acts as a toggle for the task pane's visibility.

Listing 7.26

```
#Region "Inspector (item window) related events"
    Private Sub m_colInspectors_NewInspector(ByVal Inspector As
```

Listing 7.26 (continued)

```
Microsoft.Office.Interop.Outlook.Inspector) Handles m_colInspectors.NewInspector
        'No handling of Inspectors for Notes, they are brain dead
        If Not (TypeOf (Inspector.CurrentItem) Is Outlook.NoteItem) Then
            m_olInspector = Inspector

            If TypeOf (Inspector.CurrentItem) Is Outlook.MailItem Then
                CTP = m_CTP.CreateCTP(CTP_PROGID, "Configure Settings", Inspector)
                CTP.DockPositionRestrict =
Microsoft.Office.Core.MsoCTPDockPositionRestrict.msoCTPDockPositionRestrictNoChange
                CTP.DockPosition =
Microsoft.Office.Core.MsoCTPDockPosition.msoCTPDockPositionRight
                CTP.Visible = False
            Else
                CTP = Nothing
            End If

            'wrap and m_Ribbon are dummies, filled in when Ribbon_OnLoad and
BeforeFormRegionShow fire
            Dim wrap As New TimeTravelFormRegionWrapper()
            AddInsp(Inspector, CTP, wrap, m_Ribbon)
            wrap = Nothing
        End If
    End Sub
```

C#

The C# code in Listing 7.27 implements the `ICustomTaskPaneConsumer` interface and handles the `CTPFactoryAvailable` event to get an `ICTPFactory` object used to create your custom tasks. Make sure that this object retains scope during execution of your COM addin.

Listing 7.27

```
    public class Connect : Object, Extensibility.IDTExtensibility2,
        Office.IRibbonExtensibility, Office.ICustomTaskPaneConsumer,
Outlook.FormRegionStartup

        //CTP objects
        private Office.ICTPFactory m_CTP;
        private Office.CustomTaskPane CTP;
        private const string CTP_PROGID = "CSAddinTemplate.EmailTaskPane";
        private const string CTP_EXPL_PROGID = "CSAddinTemplate.CustomTaskPane";
        private const string CTP_TITLE = "CS Config";
        private const string CTP_EXPL_TITLE = "CS WEB";

    public void CTPFactoryAvailable(Office.ICTPFactory CTPFactoryInst)
    {
        //Implements Office.ICustomTaskPaneConsumer.CTPFactoryAvailable

        // store the Custom Task Pane factory instance
        m_CTP = CTPFactoryInst;
    }
```

(continued)

Listing 7.27 (continued)

```
        public void OnStartupComplete(ref System.Array custom)
        {
            // uncomment for an Explorer task pane
            //if (m_CTP != null)
            //{
            //    try
            //    {
            //        CTP = m_CTP.CreateCTP(CTP_EXPL_PROGID, CTP_EXPL_TITLE,
m_Explorer);
            //        CTP.DockPositionRestrict =
Office.MsoCTPDockPositionRestrict.msoCTPDockPositionRestrictNoChange;
            //        CTP.DockPosition =
Office.MsoCTPDockPosition.msoCTPDockPositionRight;
            //        CTP.Visible = true;
            //    }
            //    catch (Exception ex)
            //    {
            //        MessageBox.Show(ex.Message);
            //    }
            //}

        }
```

Uncomment the code in `OnStartupComplete` to create the task pane when the event fires.

The code snippet below shows the part of the `NewInspector` event handler that adds a custom task pane to the `Inspector`.

```
            switch (_class)
            {
                case Outlook.OlObjectClass.olMail:
                    CTP = m_CTP.CreateCTP(CTP_PROGID, CTP_TITLE, Inspector);
                    CTP.DockPositionRestrict =
Office.MsoCTPDockPositionRestrict.msoCTPDockPositionRestrictNoChange;
                    CTP.DockPosition =
Office.MsoCTPDockPosition.msoCTPDockPositionRight;
                    CTP.Visible = false;
                    break;
                case Outlook.OlObjectClass.olAppointment:
                    m_RegionWrap = new TimeTravelFormRegionWrapper();
                    break;
                default:
                {
                    break;
                }
            }

            // m_RegionWrap and m_Ribbon are dummies, filled in when
Ribbon_OnLoad and BeforeFormRegionShow fire
            m_WrapperID = adder.AddInsp(Inspector, m_WrapperID, _class, ref
m_InspWrap, CTP, m_RegionWrap, m_Ribbon);
```

Working with Custom Task Panes

The user can close custom task panes. Every task pane has a close control as well as a drop-down that has a Close command. The user interface doesn't provide a method of displaying a custom task pane unless you create that method yourself. The Ribbon code in Listings 7.21 and 7.23 show one method of controlling visibility of a task pane by providing a Ribbon button to open the task pane or to close it when it's already visible. For `Explorers`, where there is no Ribbon, create a button in the `CommandBars` interface to control visibility for an `Explorer` task pane.

Task panes can be used to set configuration options for specific `Inspectors` or `Explorers`, or as an alternate to an added tab in the Tools ⇨ Options dialog for general application settings. What you display in a task pane is limited only by the available space, the controls available to you and your imagination. Some other examples of uses for task panes are:

❑ Using a Web browser control to have a task pane display Web pages and content.

❑ Using a Web service to populate controls or information displays in the task pane.

❑ Displaying grids or data bound controls to show information from a database, such as sales order information.

❑ Displaying aggregated information from a number of different Outlook folders to show information in the same way that the Activities tab does in a contact form.

Custom task panes provide two events, `DockPositionStateChange` and `VisibleStateChange`, that can be used to handle changes in position and visibility. Both events pass the `CustomTaskPane` object that is changing state. If you handle task pane events in your `Inspector` wrapper class, you can separately handle those events for each open `Inspector`.

For VB.NET code, the declaration in the `Inspector` wrapper would include a `WithEvents` statement, such as `Private WithEvents m_Pane As Office.CustomTaskPane`.

For C# code, the declaration of the task pane object would be the normal declaration and the event handlers would be added when the task pane object was instantiated:

```
private Office.CustomTaskPane m_Pane;

     public Office.CustomTaskPane TaskPane
     {
         get
         {
             return m_Pane;
         }

         set
         {
             m_Pane = value;

             if (m_Pane != null)
             {
                 // hook up the CTP event
                 m_Pane.VisibleStateChange += new
Office._CustomTaskPaneEvents_VisibleStateChangeEventHandler(m_Pane_VisibleStateChange);
```

```
                        m_Pane.DockPositionStateChange += new
    Microsoft.Office.Core._CustomTaskPaneEvents_DockPositionStateChangeEventHandler(m_
    Pane_DockPositionStateChange);
                    }
            }
        }
```

If the task pane is being used to set configuration options, the VisibleStateChange event can be used to save the settings in the task pane when the Visible property of the CustomTaskPaneInst object passed in VisibleStateChange is false.

Form Regions

Form regions use OFS files designed with the Outlook forms designer, as you saw in Chapter 5, as the design surface for the form region. All business logic for a form region is implemented using a COM addin. The definition for the form region is supplied using XML, which is usually read when the GetFormRegionStorage event of the FormRegionStartup interface fires.

The FormRegionStartup interface requires four event handlers, which fire in the following order:

❑   GetFormRegionManifest

❑   GetFormRegionIcon

❑   GetFormRegionStorage

❑   BeforeFormRegionShow

GetFormRegionManifest and GetFormRegionIcon are only called if the registry entry for the form region has a special format; otherwise, only GetFormRegionStorage and BeforeFormRegionShow are called. All form regions require a registry entry for the MessageClass that the form region is designed to supplement. You can use a standard MessageClass, such as IPM.Appointment, to handle all items of that MessageClass and custom MessageClasses derived from that standard MessageClass, or you can specify a custom MessageClass to only handle that specific class of items.

There are two formats that can be used for the registry value, which determines whether the GetFormRegionManifest and GetFormRegionIcon events are called. For example, a form region for all appointment items would use the registry key HKCU\Software\Microsoft\Office\Outlook\ FormRegions\IPM.Appointment.

In that registry key a string value is added for the form region, using the form region name. The Time Travel form region uses the name "TimeTravel", so that would be the string value name. The string value would have either of the two formats in the following table.

Registry Value	Type	Data
TimeTravel	REG_SZ	File path and file name for TimeTravelDefinition.XML
TimeTravel	REG_SZ	=VBAddinTemplate.Connect

The first format provides the name for the XML file that defines the form region. This format is used also for form regions that aren't controlled by COM addins. The second format precedes the `ProgID` of the COM addin with an "=". The XML supplied to define the form region uses different tags depending on the format of the registry entry.

For the first format, where only `GetFormRegionStorage` and `BeforeFormRegionShow` are called, the XML looks like Listing 7.28. In this format the `ProgID` of the addin is supplied using the `<addin>` tag. If a `<layoutFile>` tag is used instead of `<addin>`, the form region is a standalone form region not controlled by a COM addin.

Listing 7.28

```xml
<?xml version="1.0" encoding="utf-8"?>
<FormRegion xmlns="http://schemas.microsoft.com/office/outlook/12/formregion.xsd">
    <!-- Internal name for the form region OFS file -->
    <name>TimeTravel</name>

    <!-- Either adjacent or separate -->
    <!-- Separate has an icon in the Pages section of the Ribbon to open the region -->
    <formRegionType>separate</formRegionType>

    <!-- Title for the form region -->
    <formRegionName>Travel Time</formRegionName>

    <!-- Show in preview pane -->
    <showReadingPane>false</showReadingPane>

    <!-- Show for Inspector read mode for -->
    <showInspectorRead>true</showInspectorRead>

    <!-- Show for Inspector compose mode -->
    <showInspectorCompose>true</showInspectorCompose>

    <!-- The addin that controls the Form Region -->
    <addin>VSTO_VBOutlookTemplate</addin>
</FormRegion>
```

When the second registry format is used, any `<addin>` and `<layoutFile>` tags are ignored. Outlook already knows the `ProgID` of the addin from the registry value. The name of the form region is known from the name of the registry entry, so the `<name>` tag in the XML is also ignored.

The `GetFormRegionManifest` event handler receives a `FormRegionName` string and an `LCID` 32-bit integer. The event handler must return a string with the XML form region definition. The XML can be retrieved from a resource in the addin or from a file.

The `GetFormRegionIcon` event handler receives a `FormRegionName` string, an `LCID` 32-bit integer and an `Icon` value from the `OlFormRegionIcon` enumeration. It returns either an `IPictureDisp` object or a byte array representing the icon file.

When the `GetFormRegionManifest` event handler is used, all icons must come from the `GetFormRegionIcon` event handler, and any `<icons>` `<page>` nodes in the XML must be empty nodes or contain the word `addin` if an icon is supplied by the addin. Icons supplied in `GetFormRegionIcon` must be either `IPictureDisp` objects or byte arrays with the bytes representing the original bytes in the icon file.

Creating Custom Form Regions

Whichever format is used to provide the form region XML to Outlook, the `GetFormRegionStorage` event handler is called to provide the OFS file used as the form region design and display surface. A pointer to the OFS file location is returned by this event handler, as shown in Listing 7.29. The `GetFormRegionStorage` event handler must be located in the class that implements `IDTExtensibility2`, and it is called the first time a particular form region is loaded in Outlook. This happens not only when an item is opened but also when it's displayed in the preview pane or menu actions cause a form of that `MessageClass` to be loaded. Menu actions that can cause `GetFormRegionStorage` to fire are opening the Actions menu or opening the New Form dialog.

VB.NET

The code in Listing 7.29 shows the implementation of form region support in VB.NET. When `GetFormRegionStorage` is called, it passes `FormRegionName`, `Item`, `LCID`, `FormRegionMode`, and `FormRegionSize`. `Item` is the Outlook item that's requesting the form region and can be checked to see what form region storage should be returned based on the `MessageClass` of the `Item`. `FormRegionMode` is either `olFormRegionRead`, `olFormRegionCompose`, or `olFormRegionPreview`. If you are supporting only some of those modes, this value can be checked to see whether or not to return a form region storage object. `FormRegionSize` is either `olFormRegionTypeAdjoining` or `olFormRegionTypeSeparate`, which also can be checked to see what mode to support or what XML to supply.

Listing 7.29

```
    ' required for Form Region support
    Implements Outlook.FormRegionStartup

    ' Form Region declarations
    Private Const TIME_TRAVEL_FORM_REGION As String = "TimeTravel" ' use the value
in the <name> tag in the Region XML
    Private m_FormRegion As Outlook.FormRegion

    Function GetFormRegionStorage(ByVal FormRegionName As String, ByVal Item As
Object, ByVal LCID As Integer, ByVal FormRegionMode As Outlook.OlFormRegionMode,
ByVal FormRegionSize As Outlook.OlFormRegionSize) As Object Implements
Outlook.FormRegionStartup.GetFormRegionStorage
        ' FormRegionName is the name of the region being loaded, can be returned as
an OFS file as a Resource or as an OFS file.
        ' Item is the Outlook item looking for the form region. Based on the
registry entry for that MessageClass.
        ' LCID is the locale setting for internationalization usage
        ' FormRegionMode is either read, compose or preview
        ' FormRegionSize is either adjoining or separate
        Try
            If FormRegionName = TIME_TRAVEL_FORM_REGION Then
                ' return the name of the Resources file that's the Form Region OFS file
                Return My.Resources.TimeTravel
            Else
                ' if it's not for us return Nothing
                Return Nothing
            End If
        Catch ex As Exception
            Debug.WriteLine(ex.Message)
            Return Nothing
        End Try
    End Function
```

`BeforeFormRegionShow` fires when the form region is about to be displayed. In the template code, it's used to initialize the form region controls.

```
    Sub BeforeFormRegionShow(ByVal FormRegion As Outlook.FormRegion) Implements
Outlook.FormRegionStartup.BeforeFormRegionShow
        m_FormRegion = FormRegion

        Dim wrap As InspWrap = Nothing

        For Each wrap In g_colInspWrap
            If wrap.Inspector Is FormRegion.Inspector Then
                wrap.Region.Init(FormRegion)
            End If
        Next

        wrap = Nothing
    End Sub
```

C#

The C# code in Listing 7.30 shows the implementation of `FormRegionStartup` and the `GetFormRegionStorage` event handler.

Listing 7.30

```
    public class Connect : Object, Extensibility.IDTExtensibility2,
        Office.IRibbonExtensibility, Office.ICustomTaskPaneConsumer,
Outlook.FormRegionStartup
    {

        // Form Region declarations
        // use the value in the <name> tag in the Region XML
        private const string TIME_TRAVEL_FORM_REGION = "TimeTravel";
        private Outlook.FormRegion m_FormRegion;
        private TimeTravelFormRegionWrapper m_RegionWrap;

    public object GetFormRegionStorage(string FormRegionName,
        object Item, int LCID, Outlook.OlFormRegionMode FormRegionMode,
        Outlook.OlFormRegionSize FormRegionSize)
    {
        //Implements Outlook.FormRegionStartup.GetFormRegionStorage

        // FormRegionName is the name of the region being loaded, can be returned
as an OFS file as a Resource or as an OFS file.
        // Item is the Outlook item looking for the form region. Based on the
registry entry for that MessageClass.
        // LCID is the locale setting for internationalization usage
        // FormRegionMode is either read, compose or preview
        // FormRegionSize is either adjoining or separate
        try
        {
            if (FormRegionName == TIME_TRAVEL_FORM_REGION)
            {
```

(continued)

Listing 7.30 *(continued)*

```
                //m_RegionWrap = new TimeTravelFormRegionWrapper();
                // return the name of the Resources file that's the Form Region OFS
file
                return Properties.Resources.TimeTravel;
            }
            else
            {
                // if it's not for us return Nothing
                return null;
            }
        }
        catch (Exception ex)
        {
            Debug.WriteLine(ex.Message);
            return null;
        }
    }
```

When the `BeforeFormRegionShow` event handler fires, the controls on the form region design surface are initialized:

```
    public void BeforeFormRegionShow(Outlook.FormRegion FormRegion)
    {
        //Implements Outlook.FormRegionStartup.BeforeFormRegionShow
        m_FormRegion = FormRegion;

        int j = m_InspWrap.Count;

        for (int i = 0; i < j; i++)
        {
            InspWrap wrapped = (InspWrap)m_InspWrap.GetByIndex(i);

            if (wrapped.Inspector == FormRegion.Inspector)
            {
                wrapped.Region.Init(FormRegion, m_Outlook);
                break;
            }
        }
    }
```

VSTO

VSTO code uses the `InterfaceHandler` code shown in Listings 7.14 and 7.15 to implement the `TimeTravelFormRegionWrapper` class in response to the `RequestService` method. The `GetFormRegionStorage` and `BeforeFormRegionShow` event handlers are the same as the code shown in Listings 7.29 and 7.30 for those events.

Working with Custom Form Regions

The shared addin templates use a `TimeTravelFormRegionWrapper` class to interface between the form region and Outlook. The VSTO templates put the same interface code into a COM visible class in the

`InterfaceHandler` module. When the `FormRegion` object is passed to the code, the `FormRegion.Form` property is cast to a `Forms.UserForm` object from the MS Forms 2.0 library, which is the Outlook form hosting the form region.

Most ActiveX controls can be used with a form region, but some may be more compatible than others. Microsoft only tests the controls in the Forms 2.0 library for compatibility; other controls may work but not fire all their events or expose all of their native properties when placed on a form region. This is the same limitation that Outlook forms have with untested ActiveX controls. Only ActiveX controls should be placed on a form region, .NET controls should never be used.

Most of the native Forms 2.0 library controls are automatically proxied in form regions with Windows theme-aware controls. For example, the `CheckBox` control is replaced by the `OlkCheckBox` control. This behavior is controlled by the `FormRegion.SuppressControlReplacement` Boolean property.

If the data in the form region controls is persistent, it makes sense to store the data with the item. If there isn't too much data to store, it can be stored in `UserProperty`'s. For larger amounts of data, it's better to store it in hidden attachments on the item. Setting the `Position` property of an `Attachment` to 0 in a Rich Text item hides it from the user interface. Most items such as appointments and tasks have Rich Text bodies by default. Mail items can be made Rich Text by setting the `BodyFormat` property to `olFormatRichText`.

VB.NET

The code in Listing 7.31 shows part of the form region initialization code and how the form and controls are cast to object variables. The only event exposed by a `FormRegion` object are `Close` and `Expanded`.

Changes in controls are detected by handling control events. Declare a control object `WithEvents` to handle events on that control, for example `Private WithEvents TravelToStartDate As Outlook.OlkDateControl` enables you to handle `Change` and other date control events.

The `FormRegion.Form` object is a `Forms.UserForm` object, which enables you to access pages and controls on the form as you would in Outlook forms code. Cast each control on the control to its corresponding `Olk` control to work with its properties, methods, and events.

The `Close` event fires when the form region is being closed; the event can't be canceled. The `Expanded` event fires when the expansion state of an adjoining form region changes. You can't change the expanded status of a form region using code.

Listing 7.31

```
Public Class TimeTravelFormRegionWrapper
    Private WithEvents m_Region As Outlook.FormRegion
    Private WithEvents m_Form As Forms.UserForm

    Private oAppt As Outlook.AppointmentItem

    Private TravelToStartDate As Outlook.OlkDateControl
    Private TravelToStartTime As Outlook.OlkTimeControl
    Private TravelToStartTimeZone As Outlook.OlkTimeZoneControl
```

(continued)

Listing 7.31 *(continued)*

```
    ' Other control variables
    Public Sub Init(ByVal Region As Outlook.FormRegion)
        m_Region = Region
        oAppt = TryCast(Region.Item, Outlook.AppointmentItem)
        m_Form = CType(m_Region.Form, Forms.UserForm)

        InitializeControls()
    End Sub
    Private Sub InitializeControls()
        Dim oZone As Outlook.TimeZone = Nothing

        Try
            TravelToStartDate =
TryCast(m_Form.Controls.Item("olkTravelToStartDate"), Outlook.OlkDateControl)
            TravelToStartTime =
TryCast(m_Form.Controls.Item("olkTravelToStartTime"), Outlook.OlkTimeControl)
            TravelToStartTimeZone =
TryCast(m_Form.Controls.Item("olkTravelToStartTimeZone"), Outlook.OlkTimeZoneControl)

' Other control initializations
    Private Sub m_Region_Close() Handles m_Region.Close

    End Sub

    Private Sub m_Region_Expanded(ByVal Expand As Boolean) Handles m_Region.Expanded

    End Sub
```

C#

The C# code to initialize the form region wrapper class and some of the class level control objects is shown in Listing 7.32. Add event handlers for the `FormRegion.Close` and `Expanded` events, and add event handlers for any control events you want to handle. Cast the `FormRegion.Form` object to a `Forms.UserForm` object to work with the properties, methods, and events of the form. Cast controls on the form region to the corresponding `Olk` Outlook control. `Close` and `Expanded` are the only events exposed by the `FormRegion` object.

Listing 7.32

```
    public class TimeTravelFormRegionWrapper
    {
        #region Class_Declarations
        private Outlook.Application m_Outlook = null;

        private  Outlook.FormRegion m_Region;
        private  Forms.UserForm m_Form;

        private Outlook.AppointmentItem oAppt;

        private Outlook.OlkDateControl TravelToStartDate;
```

Listing 7.32 *(continued)*

```
        private Outlook.OlkTimeControl TravelToStartTime;
        private Outlook.OlkTimeZoneControl TravelToStartTimeZone;

// Other control variables
        public void Init(Outlook.FormRegion Region, Outlook.Application OL)
        {
            try
            {
                m_Region = Region;
                // hook up Close and Expanded event handlers
                m_Region.Close+=new
Outlook.FormRegionEvents_CloseEventHandler(m_Region_Close);
                m_Region.Expanded += new
Outlook.FormRegionEvents_ExpandedEventHandler(m_Region_Expanded);

                oAppt = (Outlook.AppointmentItem)m_Region.Item;

                m_Outlook = OL;

                m_Form = (Forms.UserForm)m_Region.Form;

                InitializeControls();
            }
            catch (Exception ex)
            {
                Debug.WriteLine(ex.Message);
            }
        }
        private void InitializeControls()
        {
            Outlook.TimeZone oZone = null;

            try
            {
                TravelToStartDate =
(Outlook.OlkDateControl)m_Form.Controls.Item("olkTravelToStartDate");
                TravelToStartTime =
(Outlook.OlkTimeControl)m_Form.Controls.Item("olkTravelToStartTime");
                TravelToStartTimeZone =
(Outlook.OlkTimeZoneControl)m_Form.Controls.Item("olkTravelToStartTimeZone");
                // Other initializations
        void m_Region_Expanded(bool Expand)
        {
            // handles m_Region.Expanded
            Debug.WriteLine("Form Region expanded");
        }


        private void m_Region_Close()
        {
            //handles m_Region.Close
        }
```

Custom Views

Since Outlook 2002 you've been able to create custom views using XML placed into the `View.XML` property. It was a limited custom view; the many autoformatting options available when creating a custom view in the user interface can't be added in an XML view description, and view filtering is also not possible when supplying an XML view description.

Outlook 2007 adds a more complete way to create a custom view using code, although for many views the best starting point is still to create a custom view using the user interface tools and then reading the XML for the view and applying it using code.

Types of Custom Views

The following table lists the members of the `OlViewType` enumeration returned by the `View.Type` property. Once you know the view type you can cast a generic `View` object to the more specialized view object for that type of view. The `DailyTaskListView` type only applies to the To-Do Bar.

View type	OLViewTypes member
BusinessCardView	olBusinessCardView
CalendarView	olCalendarView
CardView	olCardView
IconView	olIconView
TableView	olTableView
TimelineView	olTimelineView
DailyTaskListView	olDailyTaskListView

Each specialized type of `View` object has properties that provide a way to duplicate in code the properties that you can assign to a view using the view designer in the user interface, such as allowing in-cell editing and formatting rules.

Creating Custom Views

Each `Folder` object has a `Views` collection, to which you can add a custom view using the `Add` method. When you add a new view to a `Folder` object, you select the view name, type, and save option. The save option allows you to save the view for all folders of that type, for that folder only for all users, or for that folder only for you.

You aren't limited to creating only certain types of views for certain types of folders. You can create just about any view you want for any type of folder. For example, the most commonly used view type for the Inbox folder is a table view. You can create a timeline view for the Inbox even though timeline views are usually used with Journal and Tasks folders. Once the view has been created and a view type assigned to the view, your formatting choices are limited by what's available for that view type. You can't have in-cell editing in a timeline view; in-cell editing is available only for table and card views. You can only work with the available types of views; you cannot create a completely new type of view.

To create a custom timeline view for the Inbox, the following code could be used. This example uses VBA code:

```
Dim oFolder As Outlook.Folder
Dim oView As Outlook.View
Dim oTimeLine As Outlook.TimelineView

Set oFolder = Application.Session.GetDefautlFolder(olFolderInbox)
Set oView = oFolder.Views.Add("My View", olTimelineView, _
  olViewSaveOptionAllFoldersOfType)

Set oTimeLine = oView
```

This code creates a new timeline view named "My View" that is available for all email folders. This view is temporary until it's saved. By casting the generic `View` object to a `TimelineView` object, the special properties of a timeline view are now available for use in filtering and formatting the new view.

> *To retrieve and work with a previously created view, access the view from the* `Views` *collection of a folder like this:* `Set oTimeLine = oFolder.Views.Item("My View")`.

Filtering and Formatting Custom Views

After a view is created, you can apply filtering and formatting to the view. The filter for a view is a DASL filter, the same type of filter used for searching. In this case, the timeline view will be filtered for only unread items in the folder, using the DASL filter `"urn:schemas:httpmail:read" = 0`. The available formatting for a timeline view includes grouping fields, the font for the item and upper and lower scales, maximum label width, start and end date fields, options for showing labels and week numbers, and expansion settings.

The following code sets up filtering and formatting for the custom timeline view:

```
With oTimeLine
    .Filter = "urn:schemas:httpmail:read" = 0
    .StartField = "ReceivedTime"
    .EndField = "LastModificationTime"
    .DefaultExpandCollapseSetting = olAllExpanded
    .ItemFont.Name = "Tahoma"
    .ItemFont.Size = 10
    .UpperScaleFont.Name = "Segoe"
    .UpperScaleFont.Size = 12
    .UpperScaleFont.Bold = True
    .LowerScaleFont.Name = "Segoe"
    .LowerScaleFont.Size = 10
    .UpperScaleFont.Italic = True
    .MaxLabelWidth = 40
    .ShowLabelWhenViewingByMonth = True
```

```
        .ShowWeekNumbers = True
        .TimelineViewMode = olTimelineViewWeek

        Dim colOrderFields As Outlook.OrderFields
        Dim oOrderField As Outlook.OrderField
        Set colOrderFields = .GroupByFields
        Set oOrderField = colOrderFields.Add("ReceivedTime", True) 'descending
        .Save
        .Apply
    End With
```

When you add an OrderField *to a view, it's appended to the* OrderFields *collection for that view. To insert an* OrderField *in a specific place in the grouping order, use the* Insert *method of the* OrderFields *collection.*

As the previous code sample shows, the filtering and formatting you can apply to a view using code is now equal to the filtering and formatting you can apply to a view using the view designer in the user interface.

The fields you can display in a view depend on the type of view you are creating. Timeline views only allow StartField and EndField fields, which were set in the sample code. Other view types that allow many more fields in the view expose a ViewFields collection where you can add, insert, and remove fields to design your view.

View XML

If you are designing a view with a large number of fields, it may be easier to design parts of the view using the view designer in the user interface and capture the generated XML for the view than to use only code to add every ViewField you want. You can then apply the captured XML to the custom View object when you create it using code.

To open the view designer select View ➪ Current View ➪ Define Views. Click New to create a new view, and select the type of view to create. Name the view, and click OK to start designing view XML for the custom view. The Fields button is used to set up fields for the view, which become the custom view's XML. The other buttons available in the designer depend on the type of view and mirror the properties you can set from code.

Use the controls in the Fields designer to add, remove, and order the fields shown in the view. When the view is designed with the fields you want, save and apply the view and then use code to capture that view XML. The View.XML can then be saved as a file or resource in your project to add to the XML property for the view you create. If you create a table view named "TestTable" in the Tasks folder, you can capture its XML as shown here:

```
Dim oFolder As Outlook.Folder
Dim oView As Outlook.View

Set oFolder = Application.Session.GetDefautlFolder(olFolderTasks)
Set oView = oFolder.Views.Item("TestTable")

Debug.Print oView.XML
```

This code prints the XML for the view in the Immediate window in the VBA project. You can copy that XML and paste it into a Notepad file and save the file with an XML file extension to make it available to your code. Other methods of outputting and saving the XML can be used. When you create the view in code, you retrieve the persisted XML and store it in the `View.XML` property to set the fields you want for your view.

Summary

In this chapter, you learned about working with the Outlook user interface and how to create your own customizations to the Outlook user interface. The techniques you learned in this chapter for working with `CommandBars`, the Ribbon, custom task panes, form regions, and custom views allow you to make significant changes and additions to the user interface, and with the property page controls you learned about in Chapter 6, they allow you to display configuration dialogs in a number of different ways. These techniques will be used in the case studies for actual COM addins later in this book.

In the next chapter, you will learn how to interface Outlook with other applications.

8

Interfacing Outlook with Other Applications

In this chapter, you will learn how to interface Outlook with other applications such as Word, Excel, and Access. An Outlook programming book can't cover every application that can be interfaced with Outlook; the list includes any application that works with data and exposes an object model or can read or write data using any interface such as ADO or ADO.NET or an intermediate object such as a Web service. This chapter serves as an introduction to the topic of interfacing with other applications, a topic that merits a book of its own.

> *If the application you want to interface with has a macro recorder, such as Word or Excel, use the macro recorder to capture keystrokes for various actions and to create the VBA code that is the macro. This makes learning how to work with those object models easier than starting to write code from scratch.*

The location used to save the templates, worksheets and databases used for the examples in this chapter is C:\Pro_Outlook. If you change the location where these files are stored, change the file paths in the code samples in this chapter to match where you saved the files. The code and templates for this chapter can be downloaded from the Wrox web site (www.wrox.com). The code files for the chapter are Chapter_8_Database.bas, Chapter_8_Excel.bas, Chapter_8_Word.bas, Chapter_8_IE.bas, and the modules for the Browser form BrowserForm.frm and BrowserForm.frx.

The examples are written to run as Outlook macros in the Outlook VBA project and use the intrinsic Application object to refer to the Outlook.Application object. If the code is used in another context such as a COM add-in or standalone code, use an instantiated Outlook.Application object instead of Application.

Microsoft Word

Interfacing Outlook data with Word is an excellent way of being able to format your data for printing, avoiding the limited printing functionality of Outlook, and using Outlook data in form letters and formatted data presentations. The Word code in this example requires a reference set to the Microsoft Word 12 object model. Select Tools ➪ References, and add a reference to the Microsoft Word 12.0 Object Library.

The code in this section creates a Word `Table` object and fills it with a list of incomplete tasks. The table is created entirely in code, but you can also work with Word templates that contain preformatted tables and access those objects through the `Document.Tables` collection. To add a document to Word based on a predesigned template, use the `Add` method of the `Documents` collection:

```
Set objDoc = objWord.Documents.Add(strTemplate)
```

In addition to displaying Outlook data in tables, you can also use `Bookmarks`, `CustomProperties`, and `FormFields` to display Outlook data in Word documents created from templates. `Bookmarks`, `CustomProperties`, and `FormFields` can also be read, allowing data in Word documents to be used by Outlook. You can create as many `Bookmark` fields as you need for information that you want to merge into the document, up to a maximum of 16,379 per document. You also can have up to 32,000 fields in any one document.

Access the data in a `Bookmark` as follows:

```
objDoc.Bookmarks("FullName").Range.Text = strFullName
```

Make sure to update the `Fields` collection to save the data in the document after setting the `Bookmark` value:

```
objDoc.Fields.Update
```

Access the data in a `CustomProperty` as follows:

```
objDoc.CustomDocumentProperties("Full Name").Value = strFullName
```

Figure 8-1 shows the result of running the code in Listing 8-1.

Subject	Due Date	Start Date	Status	% Complete	
			7/15/2007		
Chapter 9	7/16/2007	7/9/2007	Not Started	0%	
finalize installer for Marty	7/23/2007	7/18/2007	In Progress	50%	
Final AR for book	7/24/2007	7/15/2007	Not Started	0%	
Finalize for WZ addin beta release	7/31/2007	5/1/2007	In Progress	90%	
Casey heartworm pill	8/8/2007	8/8/2007	Not Started	0%	
Test newly discovered ActiveInspector bug	10/8/2007	7/15/2007	Not Started	0%	

Figure 8-1

The code gets a filtered collection of incomplete tasks using the `Restrict` filter `"[Status] <> " &
olTaskComplete)`. The date is inserted into a new document added to a Word `Documents` collection in
a header line before two paragraph marks. A `Table` is added, with columns for `Subject`, `StartDate`,
`DueDate`, `Status`, and `PercentComplete`. The table is created with one row for each item in the filtered
`Tasks` collection, plus one row for column headers.

The data for each column in the table is set using `Cells(n).Range.Text` to access the column contents.
The table is sorted on the `DueDate` property, with the header row excluded from the sort. Finally, the
`Document` is made active and visible.

Listing 8-1

```
Sub TasksToWordTable()
  Dim objNS As Outlook.NameSpace
  Dim objFolder As Outlook.MAPIFolder
  Dim objTask As Outlook.TaskItem
  Dim colItems As Outlook.Items
  Dim objWord As Word.Application
  Dim objRange As Word.Range
  Dim objTable As Word.Table
  Dim objDoc As Word.Document
  Dim strStatus As String
  Dim lngRowCount As Long
  Dim lngColCount As Long

  Set objNS = Application.GetNamespace("MAPI")
  Set objFolder = objNS.GetDefaultFolder(olFolderTasks)

  Set colItems = objFolder.Items.Restrict("[Status] <> " & olTaskComplete)

  ' add 1 row for each item, 1 row for headers
  lngRowCount = colItems.Count + 1

  ' 5 columns: subject, due date, start date, status, %complete
  lngColCount = 5

  Set objWord = CreateObject("Word.Application")

  Set objDoc = objWord.Documents.Add()

  With objDoc
    .Content.InsertBefore CStr(Date)

    .Range.Bold = True
    .Range.ParagraphFormat.Alignment = wdAlignParagraphCenter

    .Paragraphs.Add
    .Paragraphs.Add
  End With

  objWord.Selection.Goto wdGoToLine, wdGoToAbsolute, 3
```

(continued)

255

Listing 8-1 *(continued)*

```
Set objRange = objDoc.Range(Start:=objWord.Selection.Start)
objRange.Bold = False

Set objTable = objDoc.Tables.Add(objRange, lngRowCount, lngColCount)

objTable.Borders.InsideLineStyle = wdLineStyleSingle
objTable.Borders.OutsideLineStyle = wdLineStyleSingle

lngRowCount = 1

With objTable.Rows(lngRowCount)
  .Cells(1).Range.Text = "Subject"
  .Cells(1).Range.Bold = True

  .Cells(2).Range.Text = "Due Date"
  .Cells(2).Range.Bold = True

  .Cells(3).Range.Text = "Start Date"
  .Cells(3).Range.Bold = True

  .Cells(4).Range.Text = "Status"
  .Cells(4).Range.Bold = True

  .Cells(5).Range.Text = "% Complete"
  .Cells(5).Range.Bold = True
End With

objTable.ApplyStyleHeadingRows = True

For Each objTask In colItems
  lngRowCount = lngRowCount + 1

  With objTable.Rows(lngRowCount)
    .Cells(1).Range.Text = objTask.Subject
    .Cells(2).Range.Text = CStr(objTask.DueDate)
    .Cells(3).Range.Text = CStr(objTask.StartDate)

    Select Case objTask.Status
    Case olTaskNotStarted
      strStatus = "Not Started"
    Case olTaskInProgress
      strStatus = "In Progress"
    Case olTaskWaiting
      strStatus = "Waiting"
    Case olTaskDeferred
      strStatus = "Deferred"
    End Select
    .Cells(4).Range.Text = strStatus

    .Cells(5).Range.Text = CStr(objTask.PercentComplete) & "%"
```

Listing 8-1 *(continued)*

```
    End With
  Next

  objTable.Sort ExcludeHeader:=True, FieldNumber:=2, _
    SortFieldType:=wdSortFieldDate

  objWord.Visible = True
  objDoc.Activate
  objDoc.ActiveWindow.Visible = True

  Set objTask = Nothing
  Set colItems = Nothing
  Set objFolder = Nothing
  Set objNS = Nothing
  Set objDoc = Nothing
  Set objRange = Nothing
  Set objTable = Nothing
  Set objWord = Nothing
End Sub
```

Microsoft Excel

Using Outlook data in Excel provides a way to do analysis of the data using Excel's spreadsheet functions and to make use of Excel's graphing ability. You can also use Excel to format Outlook data for printing; Excel's printing abilities are much better than Outlook's although Word provides even better print formatting abilities than Excel does. The Excel code in this example requires a reference set to the Microsoft Excel 12 object model. Select Tools ➪ References, and add a reference to the Microsoft Excel 12.0 Object Library.

When you open Excel Workbooks that contain an Auto_Open macro using code, the macro will not run automatically. To run the Auto_Open macro, you can use the RunAutoMacros method. The RunAutoMacros method has one argument that specifies which macro to run. The parameter can be anyone of the xlRunAutoMacro constants listed in the following table:

xlRunAutoMacro Value	When it runs
xlAutoOpen	Workbook.Open
xlAutoClose	Workbook.Close
xlAutoActivate	Workbook.Activate
xlAutoDeactivate	Workbook.Deactivate

Figure 8-2 shows an Excel Worksheet contacts list created by the code in Listing 8-2.

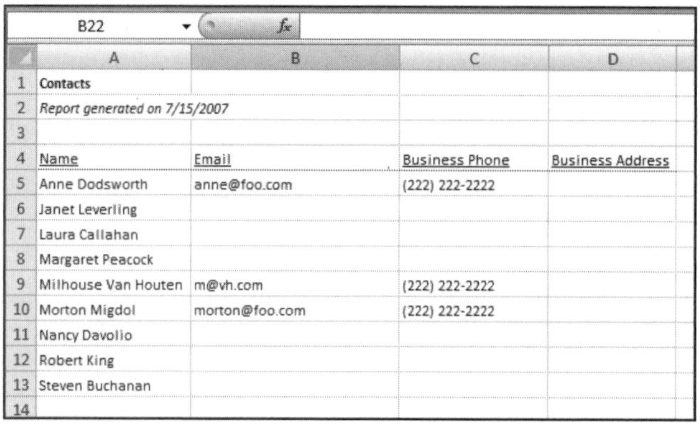

	A	B	C	D
1	**Contacts**			
2	*Report generated on 7/15/2007*			
3				
4	Name	Email	Business Phone	Business Address
5	Anne Dodsworth	anne@foo.com	(222) 222-2222	
6	Janet Leverling			
7	Laura Callahan			
8	Margaret Peacock			
9	Milhouse Van Houten	m@vh.com	(222) 222-2222	
10	Morton Migdol	morton@foo.com	(222) 222-2222	
11	Nancy Davolio			
12	Robert King			
13	Steven Buchanan			
14				

Figure 8-2

The `ContactToExcel` and `AllContactsToExcel` methods shown in Listing 8-2 take the first or all contacts in the default `Contacts` folder and use some of the data from the contacts to populate an Excel `Worksheet`.

Listing 8-2

```
Private m_objExcel As Excel.Application
Private m_objSheet As Excel.Worksheet
Private m_lngSheets As Long

Sub ContactToExcel()
  Dim objContact As Outlook.ContactItem
  Dim objFolder As Outlook.Folder

  Call SetupExcel

  Set objFolder = Application.Session.GetDefaultFolder(olFolderContacts)
  Set objContact = objFolder.Items(1)

  Call OneOutlookContactToExcel(objContact)

  Set m_objExcel = Nothing
  Set m_objSheet = Nothing

  Set objContact = Nothing
  Set objFolder = Nothing
End Sub

Sub AllContactsToExcel()
  Dim colContacts As Outlook.Items
  Dim objFolder As Outlook.Folder

  Call SetupExcel

  Set objFolder = Application.Session.GetDefaultFolder(olFolderContacts)
  Set colContacts = objFolder.Items
```

Listing 8-2 *(continued)*

```
    Call OutlookContactsToExcel(colContacts)

    Set m_objExcel = Nothing
    Set m_objSheet = Nothing

    Set colContacts = Nothing
    Set objFolder = Nothing
End Sub
```

The code in Listing 8-3 sets up Excel by creating an `Excel.Application` object and adding a new `Workbook` with one `Worksheet` to the `Workbooks` collection. The margins and page orientation are also set for the `Worksheet`.

Listing 8-3

```
Private Sub SetupExcel()
    'Get an Excel Application object
    Set m_objExcel = CreateObject("Excel.Application")

    With m_objExcel
        'Initialize Excel items
        'Save the previous setting for the number of Sheets
        'in a new WorkBook
        m_lngSheets = .SheetsInNewWorkbook
        'Only 1 sheet in this WorkBook
        .SheetsInNewWorkbook = 1
        'Create a new WorkBook and make it active
        .Workbooks.Add
        'Activate Sheet 1
        Set m_objSheet = .ActiveWorkbook.Sheets(1)
        m_objSheet.Activate
        .Visible = True

        'left and right margins at 0.25"
        m_objSheet.PageSetup.LeftMargin = .InchesToPoints(0.25)
        m_objSheet.PageSetup.RightMargin = .InchesToPoints(0.25)

        'top and bottom margins at 0.50"
        m_objSheet.PageSetup.TopMargin = .InchesToPoints(0.5)
        m_objSheet.PageSetup.BottomMargin = .InchesToPoints(0.5)
    End With

    m_objSheet.PageSetup.Orientation = xlLandscape 'landscape display
End Sub
```

Listing 8-4 shows the `OneOutlookContactToExcel` and `OutlookContactsToExcel` methods used to do the actual work of taking the Outlook contact data and putting it in the Excel `Worksheet`. First, the sheet titles are set by calling `ExcelSheetTitlesSettings`, then `ExcelSetData` is called to add the data for one contact to the `Worksheet`. In `OutlookContactsToExcel`, where all the default contacts are being used for `Worksheet` data, the `ExcelSetData` method is called once for each contact. Finally, the `ExcelFinalProcessing` method is called to format the `Worksheet`.

Listing 8-4

```
Private Sub OneOutlookContactToExcel(objContact As Outlook.ContactItem)
  Dim intRow As Integer

  Call ExcelSheetTitlesSettings(m_objSheet)

  'Start adding data at Column A, Row 5
  intRow = 4 'this number will be incremented in ExcelSetData

  Call ExcelSetData(objContact, intRow, m_objSheet)

  Call ExcelFinalProcessing(m_objSheet, intRow)

  'Restore the old setting for number of Sheets
  'in a new WorkBook
  m_objExcel.SheetsInNewWorkbook = m_lngSheets
End Sub
Private Sub OutlookContactsToExcel(colContacts As Outlook.Items)
  Dim objContact As Outlook.ContactItem
  Dim obj As Object
  Dim intRow As Integer
  Dim lngNumber As Long
  Dim i As Long

  Call ExcelSheetTitlesSettings(m_objSheet)

  'Start adding data at Column A, Row 5
  intRow = 4 'this number will be incremented in ExcelSetData

  lngNumber = 0
  For i = 1 To colContacts.Count
    Set obj = colContacts.Item(i)
    If obj.Class = olContact Then
      Set objContact = obj
      lngNumber = lngNumber + 1
      Call ExcelSetData(objContact, intRow, m_objSheet)
    End If
  Next i

  Call ExcelFinalProcessing(m_objSheet, intRow)

  'Restore the old setting for number of Sheets
  'in a new WorkBook
  m_objExcel.SheetsInNewWorkbook = m_lngSheets

  Set objContact = Nothing
  Set obj = Nothing
End Sub
```

The code in Listing 8-5 is used to set the Worksheet titles for the data columns. A title and subtitle are added to the Worksheet; then the column headings are added. Data is added to the Worksheet using objSheet.Range, which is used to place the data in specific cells for the title, subtitle, and column headers.

Listing 8-5

```
Private Sub ExcelSheetTitlesSettings(m_objSheet As Excel.Worksheet)
  Dim objRange As Excel.Range
  Dim strSubtitle As String

  'Column A, Row 1 Sheet Title - Bold, 9 pt
  Set objRange = m_objSheet.Range("A1")
  SetSheetTitles objRange, "Contacts", True, 9, _
    xlUnderlineStyleNone, False, 1

  strSubtitle = "Report generated on " & Date

  'Column A, Row 2 Sheet Subtitle - Italic, 9 pt
  Set objRange = m_objSheet.Range("A2")
  SetSheetTitles objRange, strSubtitle, False, 9, _
    xlUnderlineStyleNone, True, 1

  'Column headings - Underlined, 9 pt, thick bottom border
  'Column A heading
  Set objRange = m_objSheet.Range("A4")
  SetSheetHeadings objRange, "Name", False, 9, xlHairline, _
    xlContinuous, xlUnderlineStyleSingle, False, 1

  'Column B heading
  Set objRange = m_objSheet.Range("B4")
  SetSheetHeadings objRange, "Email", False, 9, xlHairline, _
    xlContinuous, xlUnderlineStyleSingle, False, 1

  'Column C heading
  Set objRange = m_objSheet.Range("C4")
  SetSheetHeadings objRange, "Business Phone", False, 9, xlHairline, _
    xlContinuous, xlUnderlineStyleSingle, False, 1

  'Column D heading
  Set objRange = m_objSheet.Range("D4")
  SetSheetHeadings objRange, "Business Address", False, 9, xlHairline, _
    xlContinuous, xlUnderlineStyleSingle, False, 1

  Set objRange = Nothing
End Sub
```

The code in Listing 8-6 is used to set the Outlook contact data in the Worksheet, to do the final processing of sorting the Worksheet by name, and to fit the Worksheet cells to the data. The SetRangeData method is called once for each column of data placed in the Worksheet with parameters passed to SetRangeData for the Worksheet, column, row, data, bold face font, cell alignment, and format.

Listing 8-6

```
Private Sub ExcelSetData(objContact As Outlook.ContactItem, _
  intRow As Integer, m_objSheet As Excel.Worksheet)

  Dim strCol As String
```

(continued)

Listing 8-6 *(continued)*

```
    With objContact
      'start at column A.
      strCol = "A"
      strCol = Chr(Asc(strCol) - 1)

      'Start a new data Row
      intRow = intRow + 1

      SetRangeData m_objSheet, strCol, intRow, _
        .FullName, False, 2, ""

      SetRangeData m_objSheet, strCol, intRow, _
        .Email1Address, False, 2, ""

      SetRangeData m_objSheet, strCol, intRow, _
        .BusinessTelephoneNumber, False, 2, ""

      SetRangeData m_objSheet, strCol, intRow, _
        .BusinessAddress, False, 2, ""
    End With
End Sub

Private Sub ExcelFinalProcessing(m_objSheet As Excel.Worksheet, _
  intRow As Integer)

  Dim strCol As String
  Dim strRange As String
  Dim objRange As Excel.Range

  'Set up a string variable for the last cell
  strCol = "D"
  strRange = strCol & CStr(intRow)

  'Set a Range covering all the data in the Sheet
  Set objRange = m_objSheet.Range("A5", strRange)

  'Sort the Sheet by column "A" that has contact name.
  objRange.Sort Key1:=m_objSheet.Range("A5")

  'Set a Range covering all the headings and data in the Sheet
  strRange = "A4:" & strRange

  'AutoFit the Rows
  m_objSheet.Range(strRange).Rows.AutoFit

  'AutoFit the Columns
  m_objSheet.Range(strRange).Columns.AutoFit

  Set objRange = Nothing
End Sub
```

Listing 8-7 shows the code used to set the `Worksheet` headings, titles, and data. In each case, a `Range` object is used as the location for the information, with properties of the cell such as format and alignment set for each cell.

Listing 8-7

```
Private Sub SetSheetHeadings(objRange As Excel.Range, _
   strValue As String, blnBold As Boolean, lngFontSize As Long, _
   lngBorderWeight As Long, lngLineStyle As Long, _
   lngUnderLine As Long, blnItalic As Boolean, lngAlign As Long)

   Select Case lngAlign
   Case 1
      lngAlign = xlHAlignGeneral
   Case 2
      lngAlign = xlHAlignLeft
   Case 3
      lngAlign = xlHAlignRight
   Case 4
      lngAlign = xlHAlignCenter
   Case Else
      lngAlign = xlHAlignGeneral
   End Select

   With objRange
      .Value = strValue
      .HorizontalAlignment = lngAlign
      .Font.Bold = blnBold
      .Font.Italic = blnItalic
      .Font.Size = lngFontSize
      .Font.Underline = lngUnderLine
      .Borders(xlEdgeBottom).LineStyle = lngLineStyle
      .Borders(xlEdgeBottom).Weight = lngBorderWeight
   End With
End Sub

Private Sub SetSheetTitles(objRange As Excel.Range, _
   strValue As String, blnBold As Boolean, lngFontSize As Long, _
   lngUnderLine As Long, blnItalic As Boolean, lngAlign As Long)

   Select Case lngAlign
   Case 1
      lngAlign = xlHAlignGeneral
   Case 2
      lngAlign = xlHAlignLeft
   Case 3
      lngAlign = xlHAlignRight
   Case 4
      lngAlign = xlHAlignCenter
   Case Else
      lngAlign = xlHAlignGeneral
   End Select

   With objRange
      .Value = strValue
      .HorizontalAlignment = lngAlign
      .Font.Bold = blnBold
      .Font.Italic = blnItalic
```

(continued)

Listing 8-7 *(continued)*

```
      .Font.Size = lngFontSize
      .Font.Underline = lngUnderLine
   End With
End Sub

Private Sub SetRangeData(m_objSheet As Excel.Worksheet, _
   strColumn As String, intRow As Integer, _
   strValue As String, blnBold As Boolean, _
   lngAlign As Long, strFormat As String)

   Dim objRange As Excel.Range
   Dim strRange As String

   Select Case lngAlign
   Case 1
      lngAlign = xlHAlignGeneral
   Case 2
      lngAlign = xlHAlignLeft
   Case 3
      lngAlign = xlHAlignRight
   Case 4
      lngAlign = xlHAlignCenter
   Case Else
      lngAlign = xlHAlignGeneral
   End Select

   strColumn = Chr(Asc(strColumn) + 1)
   strRange = strColumn & CStr(intRow)
   Set objRange = m_objSheet.Range(strRange)
   With objRange
      .NumberFormat = strFormat
      .Value = strValue
      .BorderAround
      .Font.Bold = blnBold
      .HorizontalAlignment = lngAlign
      .Font.Size = 9
   End With

   Set objRange = Nothing
End Sub
```

Microsoft Access

The examples in this section use data in Access databases, but you can work with any database that supports standard query language, such as SQL (Structured Query Language), and standard data access methods, such as ADO in the COM world and ADO.NET in the managed code world. These examples all read data from a database using SQL query strings, but Outlook data also can be written to databases by using SQL Insert and Update queries.

Databases such as Access expose functions in addition to access to their data. Among other things, you can use code to open filtered or unfiltered reports, forms, and print data.

To open an unfiltered report, pass the report name to the `OpenReport` method of the `DoCmd` object:

```
objAccess.DoCmd.OpenReport strReport, acViewPreview ' open unfiltered report
```

To open a filtered report, pass the report name and SQL filter string to the `OpenReport` method of the `DoCmd` object:

```
objAccess.DoCmd.OpenReport strReport, acViewPreview, , strSQL ' open filtered
report
```

To open a filtered form, pass the form name and the filter string to the `OpenForm` method of the `DoCmd` object:

```
objAccess.DoCmd.OpenForm "Employees", , , "[Title]='Manager'" ' open form
```

To print data, call the `RunCommand` method of the `DoCmd` object with the `acCmdPrint` argument:

```
objAccess.DoCmd.RunCommand acCmdPrint ' print data
```

The code in these examples requires references to be set to the Microsoft Access 12, ActiveX Data Objects (ADO), and DAO (Data Access Objects) object models. Select Tools ⇨ References, and add references to the Microsoft Access 12.0 Object Library, Microsoft ActiveX Data Objects 2.8 Library, and Microsoft DAO 3.6 Object Library.

ADO

The code in Listing 8-8 uses ADO (ActiveX Data Objects) to read data from an Access database and create a monthly report email addressed to each person in the Contacts table of the database. ADO can be used to read and write data from many different types of databases such as SQL Server, Oracle, and MySQL, its use isn't limited to Access. The related ADO.NET is available for use with managed code.

An ADO `Connection` can be created with both `mdb` and `accdb` databases by specifying the appropriate `OLEDB` provider, or by using a DSN as a `ConnectionString`. The `OLEDB` providers to use for the `mdb` and `accdb` database formats are:

❏   For `mdb` files use `"Microsoft.Jet.OLEDB.4.0"` as the `ConnectionProvider` property.

❏   For `accdb` files use `"Microsoft.ACE.OLEDB.12.0"` as the `ConnectionProvider` property.

After the `ConnectionProvider` or `ConnectionString` is set, the `Connection` is opened and a `Recordset` object is created. A SQL statement is used to retrieve the `First Name` and `e-mail Address` columns from the `Contacts` table. The `Recordset` is iterated and the information in each record in the `Recordset` is used to address the email monthly report.

Listing 8-8

```
Sub OpenDatabase_ADO()
    Dim objConnection As ADODB.Connection
    Dim objRecordset As ADODB.Recordset
    Dim objMail As Outlook.MailItem
```

(continued)

Listing 8-8 *(continued)*

```
      Dim strDBPath As String
      Dim strSql As String

      'strDBPath = "C:\Pro_Outlook\Contacts.mdb"
      strDBPath = "C:\Pro_Outlook\Contacts.accdb"

      Set objConnection = New ADODB.Connection

      'Set the ConnectionString
      'objConnection.ConnectionString = "dsn=Pro Outlook 2007" 'with a DSN
      'objConnection.Provider = "Microsoft.Jet.OLEDB.4.0" 'using an MDB file
      objConnection.Provider = "Microsoft.ACE.OLEDB.12.0" 'using an ACCDB file

      'Open a Connection to the Database
      objConnection.Open strDBPath

      If objConnection.State = adStateOpen Then
        Set objRecordset = New ADODB.Recordset

        'Build the Select Statement
        strSql = "SELECT [First Name], [e-mail Address] FROM Contacts;"

        'Open the Recordset
        objRecordset.Open strSql, objConnection, adOpenForwardOnly

        If Not (objRecordset Is Nothing) Then
          objRecordset.MoveFirst
          Do While Not objRecordset.EOF
            Set objMail = Application.CreateItem(olMailItem)

            With objMail
              .Recipients.Add objRecordset("e-mail Address")
              .Subject = "Monthly Report " & Date
              .Body = "Dear " & objRecordset("First Name") & "," & vbCrLf
              .Display
            End With

            objRecordset.MoveNext
          Loop

          objRecordset.Close
          Set objRecordset = Nothing
        End If

        objConnection.Close
        Set objConnection = Nothing
      Else
        MsgBox "Unable to open connection to database", , "Pro Outlook 2007"
      End If

      Set objMail = Nothing
    End Sub
```

Access DAO

DAO is an older, now more rarely used way of working with Access and other Microsoft Jet databases that still is useful in some situations. DAO can only work with mdb databases; it hasn't been updated to work with newer database format such as accdb type databases.

The code in Listing 8-9 uses the Access object model to open a Database object, which is used to open in a Recordset, which is iterated through to create monthly report emails addressed to each record in the Recordset.

Listing 8-9

```
Sub OpenDatabase_Access()
  Dim objAccess As Access.Application
  Dim objDB As DAO.Database
  Dim objRecordset As DAO.Recordset
  Dim objMail As Outlook.MailItem
  Dim strDBPath As String

  strDBPath = "C:\Pro_Outlook\Contacts.mdb"

  'Get a Database object using the Access CurrentDb() method.

  Set objAccess = CreateObject("Access.Application")
  objAccess.OpenCurrentDatabase strDBPath
  Set objDB = objAccess.CurrentDb()

  'Work with the retrieved DAO Database object.
  If Not (objDB Is Nothing) Then
    Set objRecordset = objDB.OpenRecordset _
    ("SELECT [First Name], [e-mail Address] FROM Contacts;")

    If Not (objRecordset Is Nothing) Then
      objRecordset.MoveFirst
      Do While Not objRecordset.EOF
        Set objMail = Application.CreateItem(olMailItem)

        With objMail
          .Recipients.Add objRecordset("[e-mail Address]")
          .Subject = "Monthly Report " & Date
          .Body = "Dear " & objRecordset("[First Name]") & "," & vbCrLf
          .Display
        End With

        objRecordset.MoveNext
      Loop

      objRecordset.Close
      Set objRecordset = Nothing
    End If

    objDB.Close
    Set objDB = Nothing
  End If
```

(continued)

Listing 8-9 *(continued)*

```
      objAccess.Quit
      Set objAccess = Nothing

      Set objMail = Nothing
End Sub
```

DAO DBEngine

The code in Listing 8-10 uses DAO to create a DBEngine object, which is used to open the Contacts database. The First Name and e-mail Address fields of the Contacts table are retrieved in a Recordset, which is iterated to create monthly report emails addressed to each record in the Recordset.

Listing 8-10

```
'This will work with an Access MDB database,
'but not with an Access ACCDB database.
Sub OpenDatabase_DAO()
  Dim objDB As DAO.Database
  Dim objEngine As DAO.DBEngine
  Dim objRecordset As DAO.Recordset
  Dim objMail As Outlook.MailItem
  Dim strDBPath As String

  On Error Resume Next

  strDBPath = "C:\Pro_Outlook\Contacts.mdb"

  'Get a DAO Database object using the DAO DBEngine object.
  Set objEngine = CreateObject("DAO.DBEngine.36")
  Set objDB = objEngine.OpenDatabase(strDBPath)

  'Work with the DAO Database object.
  If Not (objDB Is Nothing) Then
    Set objRecordset = objDB.OpenRecordset _
    ("SELECT [First Name], [e-mail Address] FROM Contacts;")

    If Not (objRecordset Is Nothing) Then
      objRecordset.MoveFirst
      Do While Not objRecordset.EOF
        Set objMail = Application.CreateItem(olMailItem)
        objMail.Recipients.Add objRecordset("[e-mail Address]")
        objMail.Subject = "Monthly Report " & Date
        objMail.Body = "Dear " & objRecordset("[First Name]") & "," & vbCrLf
        objMail.Display

        objRecordset.MoveNext
      Loop

      objRecordset.Close
      Set objRecordset = Nothing
    End If
```

Listing 8-10 *(continued)*

```
        objDB.Close
        Set objDB = Nothing
    End If

    Set objEngine = Nothing
    Set objMail = Nothing
End Sub
```

Web Browser

Outlook data can be displayed in a Web browser or in a form that contains a Web browser control. If you have Outlook data formatted as HTML, it can be useful to bypass Outlook's HTML display capabilities, which are provided by Word and use different HTML display engines. Word in Office 12 has some limitations on the HTML tags it permits, so some emails may also display with better formatting using a Web browser than using Outlook to display the emails. This workaround addresses a common complaint about Outlook's HTML rendering, the tag limitations imposed on things such as CSS (Cascading Style Sheets) for security reasons.

The code in the next example shows how to use a Web browser control in a `UserForm` to display an email and how to display an email using Internet Explorer.

Browser Control Form

The Browser Control Form uses a `WebBrowser` control to display emails, bypassing the Word HTML rendering that Outlook uses. Select Insert ➪ Form to insert a `UserForm` in the VBA project, and name the form `BrowserForm`.

The `WebBrowser` control used in the form isn't in the standard Controls Toolbox, so it must be added so it can be used. Select the form and open the Control Toolbox by selecting View@@Toolbox or by clicking the Control Toolbox icon on the Standard toolbar. Right-click the Control Toolbox and select Additional Controls to display the controls list and scroll the controls list until you see `Microsoft Web Browser`. Check the `Microsoft Web Browser` control, and click OK to add the `WebBrowser` control to the Controls Toolbox.

1. Set the properties of the form as shown in the following table:

Form Property	Value
Name	BrowserForm
Caption	Browser Previewer
Height	325
Width	325

2. Add a `WebBrowser` control to the form. Place and size the control so that it looks like the control shown in Figure 8-3. Leave the control properties at their default settings.

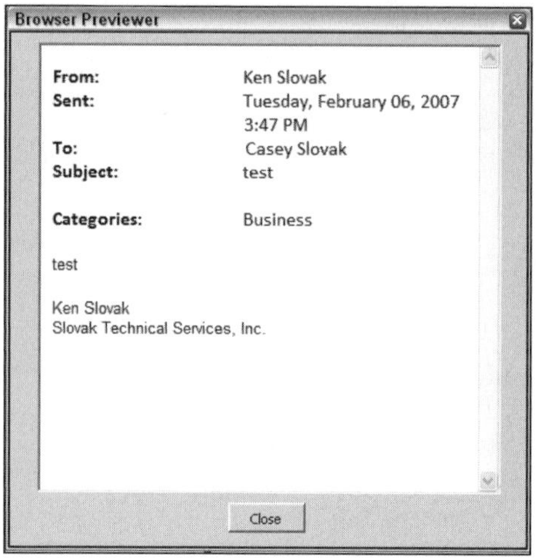

Figure 8-3

3. Add a `CommandButton` control and set its properties as shown:

CommandButton Property	Value
Caption	Close
Height	18
Left	136
Top	282
Width	48

The code in Listing 8-11 uses a file path stored in the `FileAddress` public string variable to display an HTML email saved as an HTM document in the file system. The `Navigate` method of the `WebBrowser` control is used to display the HTM file in the `UserForm`.

Listing 8-11

```
Public FileAddress As String
Private m_blnStartup As Boolean

Private Sub CommandButton1_Click()
  Unload Me
End Sub
```

Listing 8-11 *(continued)*

```
Private Sub UserForm_Activate()
  On Error Resume Next

  If m_blnStartup Then
    WebBrowser1.Navigate FileAddress

    m_blnStartup = False
  End If
End Sub

Private Sub UserForm_Initialize()
  m_blnStartup = True
End Sub
```

The code in Listing 8-12 saves the selected email item to the file system at `C:\Pro_Outlook`, using the email's `Subject` as the file name with the file type `htm`. The `SaveAs` method of the `MailItem` is used with the `olHTML Type` argument to save the email as an HTML document. The `FileAddress` public variable in the `BrowserForm` is set to the path and file name of the HTML file, and the `BrowserForm` is displayed. The HTML document file is deleted after it's displayed in the `BrowserForm`.

Listing 8-12

```
Public Sub ViewInBrowserForm()
  Dim oForm As New BrowserForm
  Dim omail As Outlook.MailItem
  Dim colSelection As Outlook.Selection
  Dim sPath As String

  Set colSelection = Application.ActiveExplorer.Selection

  If colSelection.Count = 1 Then
    Set omail = colSelection.Item(1)
    sPath = "c:\Pro_Outlook\" & omail.Subject & ".htm"
    omail.SaveAs sPath, olHTML

    oForm.FileAddress = sPath
    oForm.Show

    Kill sPath
  End If

  Set oForm = Nothing
  Set omail = Nothing
  Set colSelection = Nothing
End Sub
```

The code in Listing 8-13 automates Internet Explorer to display the currently selected email item. The `MailItem` is saved to the file system as an HTML document just as in Listing 8-12, but instead of displaying the HTML document in a `UserForm`, an instance of Internet Explorer is created and used to display the

HTML document. The HTML document in the file system isn't deleted, because the browser's Refresh action would fail if the source document wasn't still available.

The code in Listing 8-13 requires a reference set to the Internet Explorer object model. Select Tools ⇨ References, and click Browse to open the Add Reference dialog. In the Add Reference dialog, scroll the file list in the System32 folder and select shdocvw.dll, the Internet Explorer object library. Click Open to add Microsoft Internet Controls to the references list. Click OK to add the reference to Microsoft Internet Controls.

Listing 8-13

```
Private m_objIE As InternetExplorer

Public Sub ShowIE()
  Dim omail As Outlook.MailItem
  Dim colSelection As Outlook.Selection

  Set colSelection = Application.ActiveExplorer.Selection

  If colSelection.Count = 1 Then
    Set omail = colSelection.Item(1)
    Call ViewInIE(omail)
  End If

  Set omail = Nothing
  Set colSelection = Nothing
End Sub

Private Sub ViewInIE(objMail As Outlook.MailItem)
  Dim strURL As String
  Dim strPath As String

  strPath = "c:\Pro_Outlook\" & objMail.Subject & ".htm"
  objMail.SaveAs strPath, olHTML

  strURL = "File://" & strPath

  Set m_objIE = New InternetExplorer

  m_objIE.Visible = True
  m_objIE.Navigate strURL
End Sub
```

Figure 8-4 shows an email displayed in an Internet Explorer Browser window.

Summary

In this chapter, you learned about using automation code to interface Outlook with other applications such as Word, Excel, and Access. In the next chapter you will learn about various tips and tricks to use when programming Outlook so that your code runs faster and better, how to write Outlook applications that support multiple versions of Outlook, and how to work around Outlook programming limitations.

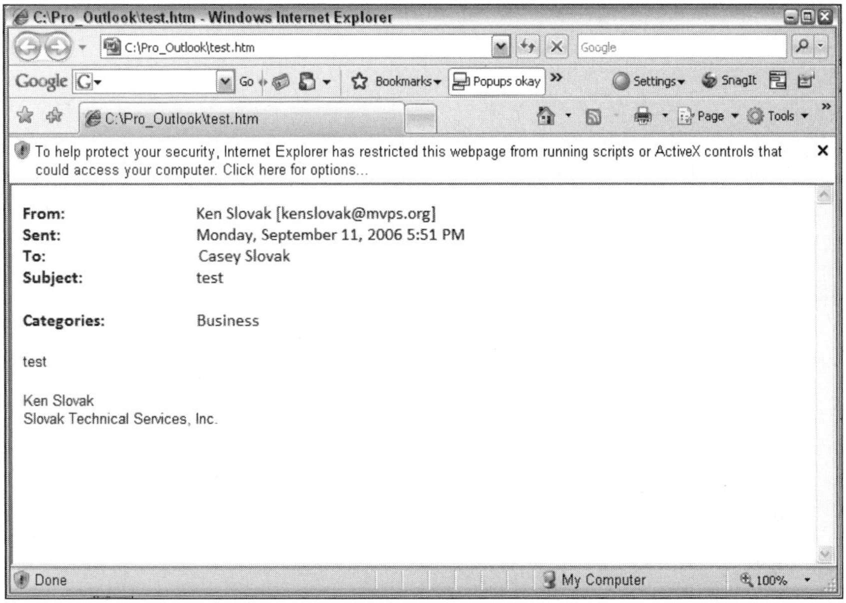
C:\Pro_Outlook\test.htm - Windows Internet Explorer
C:\Pro_Outlook\test.htm
Google
Bookmarks
Popups okay
Settings
SnagIt
C:\Pro_Outlook\test.htm
Page
Tools
To help protect your security, Internet Explorer has restricted this webpage from running scripts or ActiveX controls that could access your computer. Click here for options...
From: Ken Slovak [kenslovak@mvps.org]
Sent: Monday, September 11, 2006 5:51 PM
To: Casey Slovak
Subject: test
Categories: Business
test
Ken Slovak
Slovak Technical Services, Inc.
Done
My Computer
100%

Figure 8-4

9

Real-World Outlook Programming

In this chapter, you learn about real-world Outlook programming and how to make the best use of Outlook code to support multiple versions of Outlook. You also learn about coding to work around known problems for Outlook developers, how to deploy managed code addins, and how to use different APIs, such as Redemption, to accomplish tasks that still can't be accomplished using the Outlook object model. The tricks and tips presented in this chapter are things I've learned and discovered in my years of Outlook programming and should be helpful in your Outlook coding projects.

Supporting Multiple Versions of Outlook

Microsoft would like everyone to only use the latest versions of their software, but in the real world people run older versions of their software for as long as they can. Most people don't upgrade to the latest version of software such as Outlook until they get a new computer, and sometimes not even then. I've seen questions about running Outlook 2000 on Windows Vista, certainly a mismatch between a seven-year-old version of Outlook and the newest version of Windows.

When writing an Outlook addin, one problem is deciding what Outlook versions to support. If you support versions from Outlook 2000 on, the first version to support COM addins, you increase possible market share for your addin. If you only support Outlook 2007, you have a much smaller potential market for your addin, but there's no need for maintaining code compatibility with older versions.

The rule of thumb when developing an addin is to develop it on a computer with the oldest version of the software you plan to support and to use the Outlook object library from that version of Outlook. Of course, that means you can't use all the nice, new features such as `PropertyAccessor`, but there are ways to work around that problem. You also can't use any of the new events added to the Outlook object model, such as the new context menu events, and that limitation is something you generally have to accept.

For managed code, addins you can only install one version of an application's PIAs in the GAC (Global Assembly Cache), so unless you can place a PIA in some folder on the computer, you must use a computer where the oldest version of Outlook that you plan to support is installed. Otherwise, you can't reference the correct PIA and won't be able to build your code.

Managed code addins also have problems with PIAs for versions older than Outlook 2003, the PIAs are specific to a particular Outlook version. For example, an addin that installs the Outlook 2002 PIAs won't be able to run on Outlook 2000 or on versions of Outlook newer than Outlook 2002. Addins developed using the Outlook 2003 PIAs will run on Outlook 2007, but not on versions of Outlook older than Outlook 2003.

Microsoft's answer to all this is to maintain separate versions of your addin for different versions of Outlook, something that's not very practical for most developers. For that reason, you should generally try not to use managed code for addins if the addin has to support Outlook 2000 or Outlook 2002. For such cases it's recommended that you develop the addin using unmanaged code. If the addin only has to support Outlook 2003 and Outlook 2007, then it's a good candidate for a managed code addin, if other considerations also tilt towards a managed code addin.

Coding for Compatibility

In unmanaged code such as VB 6 or VBA code, you can use an Object declaration instead of using a typed declaration such as Dim oMail As Outlook.MailItem. A declaration like this is known as using late binding, meaning that the Object is reconciled with the actual object that's assigned to it at runtime, not at compile time. This is slower than using early binding, where a typed declaration is used, but it provides the flexibility of being able to use properties and methods that were added to the object in a later version of Outlook.

Here's an example of an early bound declaration in unmanaged code compiled on a computer with Outlook 2003 installed. This example can access any property or method available in Outlook 2003 but will fail to compile if any property or method added in Outlook 2007 is referenced:

```
Dim oMail As Outlook.MailItem
If g_lngVersion > 11 Then ' look for Outlook 2007
  If oMail.IsMarkedAsTask Then ' this line will fail to compile
```

This example will compile and run correctly on a computer with Outlook 2003 and will use the new property if the code is running on a computer with Outlook 2007:

```
Dim oMail As Object
If g_lngVersion > 11 Then ' look for Outlook 2007
  If oMail.IsMarkedAsTask Then ' this line will compile
```

In managed code, you can use reflection to access late-bound properties and methods, as shown in the following code from the C# addin template. This code uses reflection to get the value of the Class property from an Inspector.CurrentItem object:

```
Type _type;
_type = item.GetType();
```

```
        object[] _args = new Object[] { };  // dummy argument array

        try // try to get the Class using reflection
        {
            _class = (Outlook.OlObjectClass)_type.InvokeMember("Class",
BindingFlags.Public | BindingFlags.GetField | BindingFlags.GetProperty, null, item,
_args);
        }
        catch (Exception ex)
        {
            //MessageBox.Show(ex.Message);
            _class = Outlook.OlObjectClass.olNote;
        }
```

Similar code can be used with properties and methods added in a later version of Outlook than the code was compiled against.

When you use late-binding, the code runs slower than early-bound code because the object references have to be resolved at runtime. Managed code is intrinsically late bound, the passage of the COM objects through the COM Interop returns `Objects`, not typed objects such as `MailItem`. That's why you have to cast the objects retrieved through the COM Interop to their typed equivalents. Using reflection to work with properties and methods with managed code `Objects` slows things down even more, but sometimes you have to use reflection to do what you need to do.

Ribbon Considerations and Workarounds

The Ribbon in Outlook 2007 `Inspectors` adds more complications to your life if you have to support Outlook 2003 and Outlook 2007 in the same addin. The Ribbon implementation interface is required to be in the same class that implements `IDTExtensibility2`, the interface that's needed for all COM addins. The `IRibbonExtensibility` interface is defined in the Office 2007 object library, and is not present in older versions of the Office object library. Things would be a lot easier if you could put all the Ribbon code in a child DLL that was loaded and used only if the Ribbon was needed, but the current architecture makes that impossible.

Possible Ribbon Workaround Problems

No workarounds for the limitations on Ribbon usage in unified addins compiled under Outlook 2003 are supported by Microsoft, and all are subject to possible breakage. If Microsoft changes any of the signatures in the Office object library for Ribbon objects, all workarounds for the Ribbon version limitations will probably break and not work or throw an exception. Of course, if Microsoft does change the Ribbon signatures or the Office object library signature, it will break most existing code that follows the current guidelines, so for the moment it's possible to work with the Ribbon in an addin compiled with the Outlook 2003 object library. The Ribbon control and its properties and methods should never be accessed when running on Outlook 2003; that will throw a runtime exception.

The Ribbon workaround that is best suited for both managed and unmanaged code is an extraction of the Ribbon interface and objects into a separate tlb (type library) for the Ribbon. This has already been done by Dennis Wallentin, known as XL-Dennis. A download of a Ribbon tlb is available on his Web site. The articles describing the tlb extraction and the Ribbon interface are at http://xldennis.wordpress.com/2006/12/22/using-iribbonextensibilitys-type-library-with-com-add-ins.

The advantage of using a Ribbon tlb is that you can reference it as a separate project reference apart from any reference to the Office object library. This allows you to reference the Office and Outlook 2003 PIAs or object libraries and also the Ribbon tlb in the same project and to compile the project on a computer with Office and Outlook 2003 installed. The following C# example shows how to use the Ribbon tlb in the class that implements IDTExtensibility2:

```
using XLIRibbonExtensibility; // ribbon interface

public class Connect : Object, IDTExtensibility2, IRibbonExtensibility
  {
    // Ribbon for Outlook 2007
    IRibbonUI ribbon;


    // The one required Ribbon callback
    public void Ribbon_OnLoad(IRibbonUI Ribbon)
    {
      Debug.WriteLine("Ribbon_OnLoad");
      this.ribbon = Ribbon;
    }
```

The code first references the XLIRibbonExtensibility tlb that is added to the project references. The tlb does not have to be deployed with your addin to the target computer. The implementation declaration for the IRibbonExtensibility interface is added to the Connect class declaration, then an IRibbonUI object is declared in the class. The one event handler required by the IRibbonExtensibility interface is handled by the Ribbon_OnLoad method, which sets the class level IRibbonUI ribbon object.

The Ribbon callbacks declared in the Ribbon XML manifest and the GetCustomUI callback are all placed in the same Connect class that handles the IDTExtensibility2 events such as OnConnection, and are only called if the addin is running on Outlook 2007. For Outlook 2003, the code handles the user interface for Inspectors as usual, with CommandBar objects. Explorers in Outlook 2007 don't use the Ribbon, so Explorer user interface handling for Outlook 2003 and Outlook 2007 is identical.

Ribbon-related code in other classes in the addin, such as calls to the Invalidate or InvalidateControl methods of an IRibbonUI object are contained in test blocks to ensure that they are only executed if the code is running on Outlook 2007:

```
if (version == 12)
{
  this.ribbon.Invalidate();
}
```

Addin Deployment

It often seems easier to create and build an addin than it is to successfully deploy it to users. That's especially the case with managed code addins, where CAS (Code Access Security) considerations, AppDomain concerns, project requirements, and prerequisites are added to the normal addin deployment considerations. The following sections show how to successfully deploy COM addins developed in different environments.

Unmanaged Code Addins

Deployment of unmanaged code addins is pretty easy, especially if you use a commercial installer such as Wise or InstallShield. The minimal deployment consists of your addin DLL, and any subsidiary DLLs and OCXs (ActiveX Controls). If you reference any object libraries in your addin, you must either deploy those libraries if they aren't installed by Windows or Office, or check that the dependencies are installed by your installer.

If you don't use a Designer class that self-registers as an Outlook COM addin, you must also include a registry file or other means of writing the required registry keys for the addin.

All COM addins must create the following registry values for the class that implements IDTExtensibility2:

Registry Value	Value Type	Value
LoadBehavior	REG_DWORD	3
Description	REG_SZ	Description of the addin
FriendlyName	REG_SZ	The name of the addin
CommandLineSafe	REG_DWORD	0

These registry values are placed in either the HKEY_CURRENT_USER or HKEY_LOCAL_MACHINE hives of the registry in the \Software\Microsoft\Office\Outlook\Addins\<ProgID> registry path, where <ProgID> is the ProgID of the addin, for example MyAddin.Connect.

Installing an addin in the HKEY_CURRENT_USER hive of the registry is the normal installation location for a COM addin. The addin is visible in the COM Addins dialog and may be connected and disconnected by the user. Installation in HKEY_LOCAL_MACHINE is considered an administrative installation, and the addin is not visible in the Outlook 2003 COM Addins dialog. It is visible in the Outlook 2007 COM Addins dialog, but users without administrative permissions can't change the connected status of the addin.

Administrative installations prevent users from changing the addin status in the COM Addins dialog if they are even visible in the dialog and are installed for all users on that computer, not only for the user who installed the addin. This type of installation can only be performed by a user with administrative permissions.

Installations in HKEY_CURRENT_USER are only available for the user who installed the addin, that user's registry is the only one where the addin is registered. A repair of the installation or a re-registration of the addin DLL by each user is required to make the addin available for that user.

The only other consideration for deploying unmanaged code addins is whether or not to sign the addin DLL and any subsidiary DLLs and OCXs. Signing is recommended for security reasons, but code signing certificates can be expensive if purchased from a certificate authority that's widely recognized such as VeriSign or Thawte. Using self-created code signing certificates are better than not signing code, but aren't traceable back to a certificate authority and may not be recognized by many organizations.

Managed Code Addins

The three biggest problems facing managed code developers are:

1. Requirements
2. Prerequisites
3. Security

The only requirement for a managed code addin is usually the correct version of the Framework. Setup project code written in managed code won't even run unless the correct Framework version is installed. Installing the Framework as part of your installation is usually impractical due to its large size of over 20 MB and the Framework has to be installed using an administrative logon to Windows. Installers usually check for the presence of the correct version of the Framework and display a message to the user to install the Framework before proceeding with installation of the addin and then abort the installation if the Framework isn't installed.

> *Code that was written for Framework 1.1 will usually run under Framework 2.0, but it's wise to always check for usages that were deprecated in Framework 2.0 and to see if any alternatives exist for those usages.*

The prerequisites for an addin are usually installed during installation if they aren't already present. These prerequisites usually include:

❑ Outlook 2003 or Outlook 2007 PIA

❑ Office 2003 or Office 2007 PIA

❑ Extensibility.DLL for Outlook 2003 addins

❑ Stdole.DLL for Outlook 2003 addins

If the Framework was installed before Office 2007 was installed, all of the above prerequisites are installed with Office, but the installer should always check that the prerequisites were installed and install them if they weren't. The deployment walkthroughs for shared managed code addins provide enough information about checking and installing the prerequisites for successful deployment if they are followed carefully.

Security for managed code addins is very important; managed code addins will fail to load when Outlook starts if their security is incorrect. There are two levels to managed code security for a developer, CAS security and AppDomain namespace. These levels of security are handled differently for shared addins and VSTO addins.

Setting CAS security for shared addins isn't required, but all shared addins share the same `AppDomain` unless a shim is used. Sharing an `AppDomain` with another addin is not a good idea, if that addin crashes Outlook, your addin will be disabled along with the problem addin. A shim is code written in unmanaged C++ that sets up a separate `AppDomain` for your addin when the addin is installed. This isolates your addin from any other addin that is also running. VSTO addins don't need separate shims, they contain their own code to set up a separate `AppDomain` for themselves.

All managed code addins should use strong naming and signing with a code certificate as a security measure. Setting the project properties for code signing and strong naming don't actually sign the addin DLL. You must sign the DLL after it's compiled with the signing and strong naming settings to actually add a signature to the DLL. If you are obfuscating your addin, you must sign it after obfuscation, other the obfuscation corrupts the signature. Follow the directions for your code certificate to sign your DLL. It may be necessary in most installation projects to add build actions to sign the compiled DLL before it's packaged by the Setup project into an installation MSI file.

The following sections show the deployment differences for shared addins and VSTO addins.

VSTO 2005 SE Addins

The critical thing with deploying VSTO addins is to follow to the letter the deployment walkthrough available at `http://msdn2.microsoft.com/en-us/library/bb332051.aspx`. One thing that's especially important is with the custom action in the `SetSecurity` project. This custom action should all be on one line, with spaces separating the command switches.

The other important thing with VSTO deployments is to ensure that the VSTO Runtime and possibly the VSTO Language Pack are installed. These runtime components are covered in the deployment walkthrough. Things will get easier for VSTO deployments when Visual Studio 2008 ships, with VSTO addins using `ClickOnce` deployment technology, but until then the only deployment route is the `SetSecurity` project and the deployment walkthrough.

One disadvantage with the ClickOnce technology and VSTO addins is they will require installation of Framework 3.0 or higher.

Shared Managed Code Addins

Shared addins must use shims to have their own `AppDomains`. Almost nine months after the release of Office 2007, Microsoft has finally released a shim wizard that works with Office 2007, the Ribbon and other new features of Office 2007 such as custom task panes. There are technical reasons shim support for the Ribbon is problematic, and Microsoft recommends not using shared addins and using VSTO addins instead. However, VSTO addins have problems when you're supporting multiple versions of Outlook. The link for the download for the shim wizard and an article about the wizard is at `http://msdn2.microsoft.com/en-us/library/bb508939.aspx`.

The Outlook team has released three sample addins that include shims that support the Ribbon. There are no instructions for customizing the shims in the sample projects, but it's not hard to figure out how to change the `GUID` referenced in the sample shim to your addin's `GUID` and to change the referenced addin `ProgID` to your own `ProgID`. The techniques shown in these shims can be used with the workaround for Ribbon support shown in the Ribbon Considerations and Workarounds section of this chapter to add Ribbon support to a shim written for Outlook 2003. This allows shimming Ribbon support for an addin supporting both Outlook 2003 and Outlook 2007.

The link for the download of the sample projects is `http://www.microsoft.com/downloads/details` `.aspx?familyid=f871c923-3c42-485d-83c7-10a54a92e8a2&displaylang=en`. Make sure that you comply with the requirements for the sample addins before you download them, especially the requirement for Visual Studio 2005 Standard Edition or above.

Outlook Programming Limitations

Even with all the enhancements to the Outlook object model in Outlook 2007, there are limitations and bugs that can cause problems with using some of the enhancements. Longstanding problems with code for Outlook 2003 and earlier still remain. The next two sections discuss some problems with Outlook 2007 and possible workarounds for the problems, and show how to work around the major problem facing developers in Outlook 2003 and earlier, which is working with WordMail items.

Outlook 2007

You've learned about limitations of some of the new Outlook properties and methods in the sections of the book where these properties and methods are discussed. The following list shows what I consider the most important limitations and those most likely to cause severe problems for your addin:

❑ Creating hidden items in folders other than mail folders causes the hidden items to be created as visible items in the Inbox folder. This serious bug is scheduled to be fixed in Outlook 2007 SP1, but developers still won't be able to trust this functionality unless they are assured that their addins will only be running on computers where Outlook 2007 SP1 is installed. Probably the best workaround for using hidden items for configurations with the Outlook object model is to create the hidden items in the Inbox and use a `MessageClass` that describes the configurations the hidden item is storing, such as `IPM.Note.ContactSettings`.

❑ The rounding of times to the nearest minute in uses of the local time to UTC and UTC to local time can cause inaccurate results from time comparisons. There really is no workaround with the Outlook object model unless you take this limitation into account and use time comparisons that test for a range of time plus or minus one minute. Another way to work around this problem is to perform your own time zone conversions and not use the Outlook methods.

❑ The `NewMailEx` event sometimes skips incoming items when large numbers of items come in at one time. The `NewMail` and `ItemAdd` events also can miss incoming items, in the case of `ItemAdd` if more than 16 items come in at one time. This is a MAPI limitation, so there's not much you can do to work around this problem other than scanning the folder at intervals looking for unprocessed items.

❑ Accessing the `item.SendUsingAccount` object property anywhere except in a `Send` event handler returns an exception, and setting the property to `null` or `Nothing` does not set the sending account to the default account. A rather ugly workaround for the limitations on setting or reading the sending account is to create an email and send it, intercepting the `Send` event and reading `SendUsingAccount` to find the default sending account. This information can be used later to set the sending account to the default account in other emails.

❑ The `PropertyAccessor` object has a number of limitations that can cause problems if you're not aware of them. Reading of binary and string properties is pretty much limited to about 4 KB of data, anything larger than that runs the risk of being truncated. You can write larger amounts of data but you can't read it back. A workaround for this problem would be to store large amounts of data as either an attachment on a hidden item, a hidden attachment on a visible item or as the `Body` property of a hidden item, although that doesn't address a need to store data for an item in the item as a named property. Other problems with `PropertyAccessor` are that you can't delete any named properties that weren't created by your code and you can't delete any properties that Outlook creates in the named properties namespaces. Another problem with using `PropertyAccessor` is that some properties are blocked and will return an exception or null data if accessed, the blocked properties include `PR_ATTACH_DATA_BIN` (the binary data making up an attachment) and `PR_RTF_COMPRESSED` (the raw Rich Text–formatted strings making up a Rich Text message).

❑ The `GetStorage` method to retrieve hidden items has two major limitations: you can only retrieve the most recently modified or created instance of a hidden item stored in a folder for any given `MessageClass`, and you can't create or access hidden items in Exchange Public Folders. The workaround for the first problem is to use the `Table` object for the folder and filter the `Table` to only include hidden items of the desired `MessageClass`. There is no workaround for the second problem when using the Outlook object model.

Many of these problems also can be worked around by using an alternate API such as Redemption or CDO 1.21, but that involves using either a third-party library in the case of Redemption or an optional library that has to be downloaded and has severe security limitations in the case of CDO.

Outlook 2003 and Earlier

Probably the biggest problem facing developers in Outlook 2003 and earlier versions of Outlook is creating and maintaining a `CommandBar` interface for WordMail. These problems have been fixed in Outlook 2007 WordMail. The problems with WordMail stem from how Outlook sets up and uses WordMail. Outlook actually subclasses an instance of `msword.exe`, the full Word application, which then runs as a process of Outlook, although it also runs as its own Word process. This makes controlling a WordMail item and separating any Word document user interface from any Outlook user interface a particular problem and introduces various Word considerations into your Outlook code. Outlook 2007 uses a separate DLL that's a subset of the full Word application that avoids these problems, that instance of WordMail runs completely in-process with Outlook.

The out of process state of the WordMail thread relative to the Outlook process prevents using the `Picture` *and* `Mask` *properties of a* `CommandBarButton`. *Those object properties take an* `IPictureDisp` *object as the button picture, and mask and* `IPictureDisp` *objects cannot be passed across process boundaries, a COM limitation of* `IPictureDisp`. *The workaround for this problem is to use the Clipboard to create the masked picture and to use the* `PasteFace` *method of the button to add an image to a WordMail* `CommandBarButton`. *This problem doesn't exist for Ribbon images in Outlook 2007 WordMail items because in Outlook 2007 WordMail is running in the same process as Outlook.*

The following blocks of VB/VBA code show how to work around the problems caused by WordMail in Outlook 2003 or earlier when creating and maintaining a `CommandBar` user interface in WordMail items. The first block shows the declarations in an `Inspector` wrapper class of the Word objects needed to work with a WordMail `CommandBar` interface. Word objects for `Application`, `Window`, and `Document` are declared, with the `Application` object declared to handle events.

```
Private WithEvents m_objInsp As Outlook.Inspector
```

```
Private WithEvents oWord As Word.Application
Private oWindow As Word.Window
Private m_oDoc As Word.Document

Private m_ButtonSetupHandled As Boolean
Private m_blnStartup As Boolean
Private m_blnWordMail As Boolean

Private m_lngID As Long ' Inspector Wrapper Key value
```

The following code shows simplified `Inspector Activate` and `Close` event handlers. If the `Inspector
.IsWordMail` property is `True`, the Word objects are instantiated. In the case of Outlook 2007, `IsWordMail`
is always `True`. These objects should be instantiated in the first `Activate` event to fire in the `Inspector`;
before that event, the Word object model for the objects won't be fully available. Never use the
`NewInspector` event handler to instantiate these objects or to test for `IsWordMail`, the weak object reference passed in `NewInspector` doesn't provide the fully instantiated objects needed. The `Close` event
handler kills any user interface that was created and forces the WordMail `Document` window to close,
which prevents "ghost" `Inspector` windows from remaining as artifacts in the display. The Word
`CustomizationContext`, where any user interface is stored is manipulated to set the `Saved` property to
`True` after any user interface has been deleted. Word doesn't honor the `Temporary = True` argument
for user interface, so if you don't delete any user interface you created, it will remain as an artifact in Word
documents. Setting `CustomizationContext.Saved = True` restores the `CustomizationContext` to a
saved state and prevents any dialogs from being shown to prompt the user to save changes to Normal.dot.

```
Private Sub m_objInsp_Activate()
  If blnStartup Then
    If objInsp.IsWordMail Then
      m_blnWordMail = True

      Set m_oDoc = objInsp.WordEditor
      Set oWord = m_oDoc.Application
      Set oWindow = oWord.ActiveWindow

      CreateButtons
    End If
    m_blnStartup = False
  End If
End Sub

Private Sub m_objInsp_Close()
  KillButtons

  If g_lngVersion < 12 Then
    m_oDoc.Close wdDoNotSaveChanges
  End If

  oWord.CustomizationContext.Saved = True
End Sub
```

User interface is added to WordMail items the same way that a user interface is added to an Outlook
editor item. You get the `Inspector.CommandBars` collection and add your own user interface to the
`CommandBars` collection, as new menus or toolbars and as buttons in existing menus and toolbars. One
limitation of WordMail is that you can't add to the Standard toolbar, if your Outlook editor code adds user

interface to the Standard toolbar, use a test for WordMail and create the user interface in a custom toolbar when WordMail is being used instead of using the Standard toolbar. At the end of the `CreateButtons` method the `Word.CustomizationContext.Saved` property is set to `True` to always keep `CustomizationContext` in a saved state. This is repeated each time the WordMail user interface is manipulated by creating or deleting user interface or by changing the visibility or enabled status of the user interface.

```
Private Sub CreateButtons()
  'Create CommandBar UI here

  ' At end of Sub
  m_ButtonSetupHandled = True
  oWord.CustomizationContext.Saved = True
End Sub
```

The Word `WindowActivate` event handler is the key part of handling WordMail `Inspector` user interface visibility and enabling. You don't want your user interface to show up in Word documents, and in cases where multiple Inspectors are open, you want each `Inspector` to have separate user interface so that you don't see multiple copies of the user interface in any one `Inspector`. When the `WindowActivate` event fires, the code tests for Outlook 2003 and earlier, and if Outlook 2007 isn't running, then it checks for the `EnvelopeVisible` property of the active Word window. If `EnvelopeVisible` is `True`, the window is a WordMail window, if it is `False`, the window is a Word `Document` window. In the case of a `Document` window, you want your user interface to be invisible; in the case of a WordMail window, you want the correct user interface for that `Inspector` to be shown.

```
Private Sub oWord_WindowActivate(ByVal Doc As Word.Document, _
  ByVal Wn As Word.Window)

  On Error Resume Next

  If g_lngVersion < 12 Then
    If (oWindow Is Nothing) Then
      Set oWindow = Wn
    End If

    If Not (Wn.EnvelopeVisible) Then 'this is Word, not a WordMail window
      Call SetupButtonsForThisInspector(False)
    Else
      If Not m_ButtonSetupHandled Then
        Call SetupButtonsForThisInspector(True)
        m_ButtonSetupHandled = True
      End If
    End If
  End If

  m_ButtonSetupHandled = False
End Sub
```

The `SetupButtonsForThisInspector` method takes care of setting the visibility and enabled state for any user interface. It's called with the `blnShow` argument set to `True` for WordMail windows and with `blnShow` set to `False` for Word `Document` windows. The `Inspector.CommandBars` collection is iterated through and each `CommandBar` is tested to see if it's a built-in `CommandBar` or a nonstandard `CommandBar`. Built-in `CommandBar` objects are left alone to be controlled by Word or Outlook. All other toolbars are tested to see if they were created by the code in the addin or by some other application. When a `CommandBar` is created, the `Name` is set to a unique string concatenated with the `Key` property for that `Inspector` wrapper class. If the `CommandBar` `Name` starts with the unique string, it was created by the code, if not it was created by something else and is ignored. If the code created the `CommandBar`, the complete `Name` is then tested to see if that `CommandBar` belongs to that `Inspector` wrapper class. If so, the `Visible` and `Enabled` properties of the `CommandBar` are set `True`. If the `CommandBar` doesn't belong to that `Inspector` wrapper class, the `Visible` and `Enabled` properties are set `False` to hide that `CommandBar` from the user interface. Similar code would be used to control the `Visible` and `Enabled` state of any buttons added to existing toolbars or menus.

```
Private Sub SetupButtonsForThisInspector(blnShow As Boolean)
    Dim strKey As String
    Dim strName As String
    Dim strMenuName As String
    Dim colBars As Office.CommandBars
    Dim oBar As Office.CommandBar

    On Error Resume Next

    If g_lngVersion < 12 Then
        strKey = CStr(m_lngID)

        strMenuName = "MyCustomToolbar" & strKey

        Set colBars = m_objInsp.CommandBars
        For Each oBar In colBars
            With oBar
                strName = ""
                strName = .Name
                If Err Then
                    Err.Clear
                Else
                    If Not (.BuiltIn) Then
                        If InStr(1, strName, " MyCustomToolbar ", vbTextCompare) > 0 Then
                            If strName = strMenuName Then
                                .Enabled = blnShow
                                .Visible = blnShow
                            Else
                                .Enabled = False
                                .Visible = False
                            End If
                        End If
                    End If
                End If
            End With
        Next
    End If

    Set colBars = Nothing
    Set oBar = Nothing
End Sub
```

One thing to be aware of with WordMail user interface objects such as CommandBarButton *objects is that even in their* Click *event handlers attempts to access other properties or methods of the* CommandBarButton *object will usually return automation errors when accessed. The workaround for this problem is to reinstantiate the* CommandBarButton *object just before you access the properties or methods. This applies even in a* Click *event handler for the button where you might want to perform actions such as changing the* State *property of the button to cause it to be depressed or in an up state. This workaround also applies if you need to change the* Visible *and* Enabled *states of any* CommandBarButton *object.*

Things We Still Don't Have in Outlook 2007

The goal for enhancements to the Outlook 2007 object model was to achieve parity with the CDO object model in the richness of the available properties and methods and to achieve performance improvements to speed up time-consuming processes in Outlook. The goal of speeding up time-consuming processes has largely been achieved with the addition of the Table object. Using a Table instead of using an iteration of an Items collection provides speed gains of up to an order of magnitude, an impressive achievement. You've learned about many of the existing limitations in the Outlook 2007 object model throughout this book and especially in this chapter. This section shows how to use the PropertyAccessor object to work around what's still missing from the Outlook object model that's available when using CDO code.

The DeliveryReceipt and ReadReceipt properties available for CDO Message objects are evaluated by using the MAPI properties for DeliveryReceipt and ReadReceipt. These properties are Boolean properties and are accessed as follows:

❑   DeliveryReceipt is accessed as the PR_ORIGINATOR_DELIVERY_REPORT_REQUESTED property using the property tag 0x0023000B (&H23000B in VB code).

❑   ReadReceipt is accessed as the PR_READ_RECEIPT_REQUESTED property using the property tag 0x0029000B (&H29000B in VB code).

Other properties missing from the Outlook object model are accessed as follows:

❑   The Encrypted and Signed properties are accessed using the property tag PR_SECURITY (0x00340003 or &H340003), a 32-bit Long flags property. To read the state of the Encrypted flag, And the value from PR_SECURITY with 2. To read the state of the Signed flag, And the value from PR_SECURITY with 1.

❑   The OutOfOffice state can be read by using the PR_OOF_STATE property using the property tag 0x661D000B (&H661D000B in VB code) on the default Store object.

❑   The OutOfOfficeText property, the message sent by an Out of Office reply, is stored in the Inbox as a hidden message with the MessageClass IPM.Note.Rules.OofTemplate.Microsoft. The text is stored in the Body of the message, which can be retrieved using the GetStorage method.

There are no guides that I know of that provide a complete list of all properties and flags used by Outlook. The most useful tool to find these properties and their property tags is a MAPI viewer, such as OutlookSpy or MFCMAPI. There are also MAPI header files in C format available in both the Windows and Exchange SDKs (Software Development Kits), which are also very useful for finding things.

Using Alternate APIs

The need for using alternate APIs with Outlook code has been lessened with the changes to the Outlook 2007 object model, but the need hasn't disappeared completely. There are still things you just can't do with the Outlook object model that you can do with alternate APIs, and if you're developing for earlier versions of Outlook, the need to use alternate APIs is the same as it was before Outlook 2007. The need for using an alternate API usually had one of two drivers, either a need to do something that can't be done using the Outlook object model or a need to bypass the security in earlier versions of Outlook.

CDO

Before the Outlook object model security guard was added to Outlook 2000 SP2, there were no security problems and the need for using alternate APIs was only to do things that couldn't be done using only the Outlook object model. CDO 1.21 was usually the best answer for developers who didn't know Extended MAPI or were unable to use C++ or Delphi for Extended MAPI, the only languages supported for use with Extended MAPI.

The security changes made use of CDO impractical in many cases, and using CDO is not supported at all for use with managed code. Many things will work with CDO in managed code but not all the time. Things will break or fail to work unexpectedly and there's no way to make them work again. I strongly recommend avoiding all use of CDO in managed code.

There were already handicaps to using CDO, which was an optional installation for Office. A demand installation of CDO could be done by calling the Office installer from code; however, the user needed to have the Office CD or network share available to be able to install CDO in those cases. CDO is now only available as a download from the Microsoft Web site. and is considered to be deprecated by Microsoft, so it's now even harder to ensure that CDO is installed if needed.

The security in CDO is even stricter than the security on the Outlook object model. In Outlook code security is a limitation only on properties and methods that can be used to send items, harvest email addresses, and perform possibly compromising actions. In CDO, security comes into play even when just accessing a Contacts folder, among other limitations.

There is a workaround for the CDO security when using the security form stored in an Exchange Public Folder, but many organizations haven't used that method and it's very hard to maintain and keep working when multiple versions of Outlook are being used in an organization. The security form also doesn't work if Exchange isn't being used or if Public Folders aren't being used.

For these reasons most developers have stopped using CDO as an alternate API and have switched to other alternatives to the Outlook object model.

If you want to experiment with CDO, you can download the version for Outlook 2007 from `http://www.microsoft.com/downloads/details.aspx?familyid=2714320d-c997-4de1-986f-24f081725d36&displaylang=en`. Each version of Outlook has a tightly coupled version of CDO, and you shouldn't try to mix and match Outlook and CDO versions. You also shouldn't try using the security-free server-side version of CDO for Exchange server in a client context from Outlook code. The best reference Web site for CDO is located at `www.cdolive.com`, with useful code samples at `www.cdolive`

site is mostly dormant, it hasn't been updated in many years, and mistakes in some of the code samples have remained there for years. However, it's still the best online resource for CDO that's available.

Redemption

The rest of this chapter is devoted to examples of working with Redemption code to perform Outlook programming tasks. I emphasize Redemption in this book because it's the most complete of the options available for doing things not available in the Outlook object model and as a way to bypass the Outlook security. Redemption is also the alternate API that I've used most often during the last seven years since CDO use became impractical, and I've been involved with the development and testing of Redemption since before it was released, from the original specifications on. The author of Redemption, Dmitry Streblechenko, is also a long-time Outlook MVP colleague and friend. The following code listings show Redemption use for a number of common tasks, some of which can also now be performed with the Outlook 2007 object model.

Redemption is a COM wrapper around Extended MAPI and can be used from both managed and unmanaged code. The original set of Redemption objects was an answer to the Outlook security and included Safe objects that aren't limited at all by the security, such as SafeMailItem, SafeContactItem, and SafeRecipient. Those objects are dependent on Outlook objects and have an Item property that is set to the Outlook object by using code such as safeMail.Item = oMail.

The specification for Redemption was later expanded to be a complete replacement for CDO, providing a library that's not limited by security and can be used in managed code, unlike CDO, and in services, unlike the Outlook object model. The CDO replacement project culminated in the addition of the RDO class of objects to Redemption, RDO standing for Redemption Data Objects.

The first Redemption code sample in Listing 9-1 creates an RDOSession object and assigns its MAPIOBJECT property, which represents an IUnknown object to the hidden MAPIOBJECT property of the Outlook NameSpace object. To see the NameSpace.MAPIOBJECT property, added to the Outlook object model in Outlook 2002, in the Object Browser right-click in the Object Browser pane that shows the properties, methods, and events and select Show Hidden Members. The code gets the default Calendar folder and iterates through its contents as an RDOItems collection, clearing the Private property of each item in the folder. The Private property is set by setting the Sensitivity property using the PR_SENSITIVITY property tag to 2, which is the SENSITIVITY_PRIVATE value.

At the end of the procedure, the RDOSession.Logoff method is called to log off from the Extended MAPI session established by the Logon method or assignment of RDOSession.MAPIOBJECT. Cleaning up after an Extended MAPI session is very important so that Outlook isn't hung when it closes and can close cleanly.

Listing 9-1

```
Sub ClearPrivacy()
   Dim rdmSession As Redemption.rdoSession
   Dim rdmFolder As Redemption.rdoFolder
   Dim colMessages As Redemption.rdoItems
   Dim rdmMessage As Redemption.rdoMail
```

(continued)

Listing 9-1 *(continued)*

```
    Const PR_SENSITIVITY = &H360003
    Const SENSITIVITY_PRIVATE = 2
    Const SENSITIVITY_NONE = 0

    Set rdmSession = CreateObject("Redemption.RDOSession")
    rdmSession.MAPIOBJECT = Application.Session.MAPIOBJECT

    Set rdmFolder = rdmSession.GetDefaultFolder(olFolderCalendar)
    Set colMessages = rdmFolder.Items
    For Each rdmMessage In colMessages
      With rdmMessage
        If .Fields(PR_SENSITIVITY) = SENSITIVITY_PRIVATE Then
          .Fields(PR_SENSITIVITY) = SENSITIVITY_NONE
          .Save
        End If
      End With
    Next

    rdmSession.Logoff

    Set colMessages = Nothing
    Set rdmMessage = Nothing
    Set rdmSession = Nothing
    Set rdmFolder = Nothing
End Sub
```

There are two ways to tell an RDOSession object how to connect to an Outlook session, if one is available. The first is to use the RDOSession.MAPIOBJECT property, as shown in Listing 9-1. That method is used when the RDOSession is running in-process with Outlook as part of code in a COM addin or in the Outlook VBA project. The other way is to use the Logon method. This method is similar to the CDO Session.Logon method and must be used when running standalone Redemption code or when your Outlook code is running out of process with Outlook in standalone code or code running in another application, such as in the Word VBA project.

For code running in an Outlook 2000 addin, the way to use the Logon method is:

```
    session.Logon "", "", False, False
```

This sets the RDOSession to use the same session as Outlook is using and to use the same logon used by the Outlook session. The default in Redemption for the NewSession argument, the third argument, is True, which opens the Redemption session in a new session apart from the Outlook session. For in-process code or code where Outlook is already running this forces the RDO objects to be marshaled across process boundaries, something MAPI doesn't like to do, so always use NewSession = False in any Redemption code running along side Outlook code.

The code in Listing 9-2 shows how to use an RDOAddressEntry object to retrieve the SMTP email address equivalent for an Exchange distinguished name email address. The code creates an Outlook Recipient object using a name in the Exchange Active Directory and resolving that name for the Recipient. The Recipient object's ID property is used with the RDOSession.GetAddressEntryFromID method to retrieve an RDOAddressEntry. The SMTPAddress property of the RDOAddressEntry is used to retrieve the SMTP address.

Listing 9-2

```
Sub SMTPFromEX()
  Dim objRecip As Outlook.Recipient
  Dim objNS As Outlook.NameSpace
  Dim rdmAE As Redemption.RDOAddressEntry
  Dim rdmSession As Redemption.rdoSession

  Set objNS = Application.Session

  Set rdmSession = CreateObject("Redemption.RDOSession")
  rdmSession.MAPIOBJECT = objNS.MAPIOBJECT

  Set objRecip = objNS.CreateRecipient("Casey Slovak")
  objRecip.Resolve

  If objRecip.Resolved Then
    Set rdmAE = rdmSession.GetAddressEntryFromID(objRecip.AddressEntry.id)

    MsgBox "SMTP address for " & rdmAE.Name & ": " & rdmAE.SMTPAddress
  End If

  rdmSession.Logoff

  Set objRecip = Nothing
  Set objNS = Nothing
  Set rdmAE = Nothing
  Set rdmSession = Nothing
End Sub
```

The code in Listing 9-3 shows how to use a method of the MAPIUtils object to convert local time to UTC time. A date/time value is passed to the HrLocalToGMT method and returns the UTC time converted from the local time. This method preserves the seconds of a time value without rounding or truncation, so it can be used as a substitute for the Outlook time conversion methods. The Cleanup method called at the end of the procedure is used to clean up the Extended MAPI session used by the MAPIUtils object.

Listing 9-3

```
Sub GetGMT()
  Dim rdmUtils As Redemption.MAPIUtils
  Dim datTime As Date
  Dim strReturn As String
  Dim datReturn As Date

  Set rdmUtils = CreateObject("Redemption.MAPIUtils")
  datReturn = rdmUtils.HrLocalToGMT(Time)
  strReturn = CStr(datReturn)

  rdmUtils.Cleanup
  Set rdmUtils = Nothing
End Sub
```

The code in Listing 9-4 uses the RDOStores collection to find the Exchange Public Folders Store with the FindExchangePublicFoldersStore method. If this store is found the PR_IPM_FAVORITES_ENTRYID property, which only exists in that Store object is read to retrieve the EntryID of the Public Folder Favorites folder. MAPI stores EntryIDs as binary properties, using the property type PT_BINARY. Retrieving this value returns an array of binary bytes. Outlook (and CDO) take care of this for you by treating the EntryID property as a string value, doing the conversion from binary array to string behind the scenes. When using a MAPI wrapper such as Redemption this isn't done; Redemption treats each property as its MAPI type, so the MAPIUtilities.HrArrayToString method is called to convert the binary array for EntryID into a string value. The EntryID string is then used to retrieve the Public Folder Favorites folder as an RDOFolder object.

Listing 9-4

```
Sub GetPFFavs()
  Dim rdmSession As Redemption.rdoSession
  Dim colInfoStores As Redemption.RDOStores
  Dim rdmInfoStore As Redemption.rdoStore
  Dim rdmFavFolder As Redemption.rdoFolder
  Dim rdmUtils As Redemption.MAPIUtils
  Dim strFavID As String

  Const PR_IPM_FAVORITES_ENTRYID = &H66300102
  Const PR_IPM_PUBLIC_FOLDERS_ENTRYID = &H66310102

  Set rdmSession = CreateObject("Redemption.RDOSession")
  rdmSession.MAPIOBJECT = Application.Session.MAPIOBJECT

  Set rdmUtils = CreateObject("Redemption.MAPIUtils")
  rdmUtils.MAPIOBJECT = rdmSession.MAPIOBJECT

  ' Get InfoStore collection
  Set colInfoStores = rdmSession.Stores
  Set rdmInfoStore = colInfoStores.FindExchangePublicFoldersStore

  If Not (rdmInfoStore Is Nothing) Then
    strFavID = rdmUtils.HrArrayToString(rdmInfoStore.Fields(PR_IPM_FAVORITES_ENTRYID))
    If strFavID <> "" Then
      Debug.Print strFavID
      ' Get favorites folder
      Set rdmFavFolder = rdmSession.GetFolderFromID(strFavID, rdmInfoStore.EntryID)
      If Not (rdmFavFolder Is Nothing) Then
        MsgBox "Favorites folder is " & rdmFavFolder.Name
      End If
    End If
  End If

  rdmUtils.Cleanup
  rdmSession.Logoff

  Set rdmSession = Nothing
  Set colInfoStores = Nothing
  Set rdmInfoStore = Nothing
  Set rdmFavFolder = Nothing
  Set rdmUtils = Nothing
End Sub
```

The code in Listing 9-5 is used to create an X-header for an email item. When the X-header is created it's created as a named MAPI property using the special GUID {00020386-0000-0000-C000-000000000046} and only exists as a named MAPI property until the email is sent. The transport mechanism then takes that MAPI property and adds it to the headers created for the email. Although mail headers don't exist in intraorganizational Exchange emails the MAPI named properties are preserved, so they can be retrieved even if an email is sent only within an Exchange organization. In this case, the X-header just consists of 5000 "A" characters, but it can contain any text you want. The X-header, along with any other mail headers, can be retrieved using the PR_TRANSPORT_MESSAGE_HEADERS (0x007D001E) property tag, and the headers can be parsed out of this string property.

Listing 9-5

```
Sub Create_XHeader()
  Dim objMail As Outlook.MailItem
  Dim rdmMail As Redemption.SafeMailItem
  Dim tag As Long

  Const MAPI_XHEADER_GUID = "{00020386-0000-0000-C000-000000000046}"
  Const PT_STRING8 = &H1E

  Set objMail = Application.CreateItem(olMailItem)
  With objMail
    .Recipients.Add "caseyslovak@mvps.org"
    .Subject = "test headers"
    .Body = "test"
    .Save
  End With

  Set rdmMail = CreateObject("Redemption.SafeMailItem")

  With rdmMail
    .Item = oMail

    tag = .GetIDsFromNames(MAPI_XHEADER_GUID, "Custom X-Header")
    tag = tag Or PT_STRING8 'the type is PT_STRING8

    .Fields(tag) = String(5000, "A")
    .Save

    ' trick Outlook into thinking that something has changed
    .Subject = .Subject
    .Save
  End With

  objMail.Display

  ' send the email to let Outlook turn the MAPI named property
  ' into an x-header

  Set rdmMail = Nothing
  Set objMail = Nothing
End Sub
```

The code in Listing 9-6 shows how to get the Free/Busy information for a member of the Exchange Global Address List. An RDOAddressEntry object is retrieved using RDOSession.AddressBook.GAL .ResolveName, which uses the GAL property of the AddressBook collection of Address Lists to retrieve the Global Address List. The ResolveName method available for all RDOAddressList objects is used to resolve the name into an RDOAddressEntry object. The GetFreeBusy method of the RDOAddressEntry object is used to retrieve three months of Free/Busy data for that RDOAddressEntry.

Listing 9-6

```
Sub GetFB()
  Dim rdmSession As Redemption.rdoSession
  Dim rdmUser As Redemption.RDOAddressEntry

  Set rdmSession = CreateObject("Redemption.RDOSession")
  rdmSession.MAPIOBJECT = Application.Session.MAPIOBJECT

  Set rdmUser = rdmSession.AddressBook.GAL.ResolveName("Casey Slovak")

  MsgBox rdmUser.GetFreeBusy(#8/1/2007#, 90, True)

  rdmSession.Logoff

  Set rdmSession = Nothing
  Set rdmUser = Nothing
End Sub
```

The code in Listing 9-7 iterates through the RDOStores collection, checking each loaded RDOStore for its type, using the StoreKind property. An Exchange store is recognized as one of the skPrimaryExchangeMailbox, skDelegateExchangeMailbox or skPublicFolders types, and if one of those store types is found, the store is assigned to an RDOExchangeStore object. The ServerDN property of the RDOExchangeStore object is used to display the distinguished name of the Exchange server.

Listing 9-7

```
Sub CheckStores()
  Dim rdmSession As New rdoSession
  Dim rdmStore As Redemption.rdoStore
  Dim colStores As Redemption.RDOStores
  Dim rdmEX As Redemption.RDOExchangeStore

  Set rdmSession = CreateObject("Redemption.RDOSession")
  rdmSession.MAPIOBJECT = Application.Session.MAPIOBJECT

  For Each rdmStore In rdmSession.Stores
    With rdmStore
      If (.StoreKind = skPrimaryExchangeMailbox) Or _
          (.StoreKind = skDelegateExchangeMailbox) Or _
          (.StoreKind = skPublicFolders) Then
```

Listing 9-7 (continued)

```
        Set rdmEX = rdmStore
        MsgBox rdmEX.ServerDN
    End If
  End With
Next

rdmSession.Logoff

Set rdmSession = Nothing
Set rdmStore = Nothing
Set colStores = Nothing
Set rdmEX = Nothing
End Sub
```

The code in Listing 9-8 uses a `MAPITable` object to retrieve all items where the sender name starts with the case-insensitive name "John." This filter will return emails with sender names starting with John, Johnny, and Johnson but not Johanna. Working with `MAPITable` filters is the most difficult thing to understand with Redemption code for developers who aren't familiar with Extended MAPI filters. Redemption uses the same filter terms as Extended MAPI, not the familiar Jet property syntax used for Items collections filters or restrictions.

The filter in Listing 9-8 uses a content filter (`RES_CONTENT`) to test the contents of the specified property `PR_SENDER_NAME` (`ulPropTag`). The "fuzzy level" for the filter (`ulFuzzyLevel`) is set to ignore case for a case-insensitive filter and to check for the test string assigned to the `lpProp` at the beginning of the property. Just as with an Outlook 2007 `Table` object the `Columns` for the table are added, in this case to return values for `SenderName` and `Subject`. After a `Restrict` is applied to the filter the returned `MAPITable` is retrieved one `Row` at a time, using the `GetRow` method and sender and subject values are retrieved from the `MAPITable`.

Listing 9-8

```
Sub GetJohnsFromTableRestricted()
  Dim strDisplayName As String
  Dim rdmSession As Redemption.rdoSession
  Dim rdmFolder As Redemption.rdoFolder
  Dim rdmTable As Redemption.MAPITable
  Dim rdmFilter As Redemption.TableFilter
  Dim rdmRestr As Redemption.RestrictionContent
  Dim rdmItems As Redemption.rdoItems

  Dim Columns(1) As Variant
  Dim Row As Variant

  Const PR_SENDER_NAME = &HC1A001E
  Const PR_SUBJECT = &H37001E

  strDisplayName = "John"
```

(continued)

Listing 9-8 *(continued)*

```
   Set rdmSession = CreateObject("Redemption.RDOSession")
   rdmSession.MAPIOBJECT = Application.Session.MAPIOBJECT

   Set rdmFolder = rdmSession.GetDefaultFolder(olFolderInbox)
   Set rdmItems = rdmFolder.Items
   Set rdmTable = rdmItems.MAPITable
   Set rdmFilter = rdmTable.Filter

   'set up the filter on the MAPITable
   With rdmFilter
     .Clear

     Set rdmRestr = .SetKind(RES_CONTENT)
     With rdmRestr
       rdmRestr.ulPropTag = PR_SENDER_NAME
       rdmRestr.ulFuzzyLevel = FL_IGNORECASE + FL_PREFIX
       rdmRestr.lpProp = strDisplayName
     End With

     'filter is done, restrict and read the data
     .Restrict

     Columns(0) = PR_SENDER_NAME
     Columns(1) = PR_SUBJECT
   End With

   With rdmTable
     .Columns = Columns
     .GoToFirst

     Do
       Row = .GetRow
       If Not IsEmpty(Row) Then
         MsgBox "Sender is " & Row(0) & vbCrLf & "Subject: " & Row(1)
       End If
     Loop Until IsEmpty(Row)
   End With

   rdmSession.Logoff

   Set rdmSession = Nothing
   Set rdmFolder = Nothing
   Set rdmTable = Nothing
   Set rdmFilter = Nothing
   Set rdmRestr = Nothing
   Set rdmItems = Nothing
End Sub
```

A filter for a `MAPITable` *can be applied using either* `Restrict` *or by using the* `FindFirst`, `FindNext`, *and* `FindLast` *methods of the* `TableFilter` *object. A* `Restrict` *is faster because only rows that meet the filter conditions are returned in the table, but the entire table is searched to return the requested subset of the collection. However, restrictions are cached on the Exchange server normally for eight days and can build up if they are used for nonconstant restrictions. Over time, this can slow down an Exchange server and data access from it to an enormous degree. A filter is applied to the table only when the* `FindFirst`, `FindNext` *or* `FindLast` *methods are called; only one row at a time is returned from the table, and the filter isn't cached, so it has no effect on performance of the server. The rule of thumb is to use* `Restrict` *for filters that are constant and likely to be used over and over again. If the filter is not constant, for example a filter on today, where the condition changes every day, use a filter and not a restriction.*

The code in Listing 9-9 uses the same filter as the code in Listing 9-8, but instead of a `Restrict`, the `FindFirst` and `FindNext` methods are used to traverse the `MAPITable`. `FindFirst(True)` is used before the loop to traverse the table to make sure that at least one `Row` was returned in the `MAPITable`. After each pass through the loop, the `FindNext(True)` method is called to ensure there is another `Row` of data to read. `FindFirst`, `FindNext`, and `FindLast` all take arguments for the direction of the find, with `True` being forward and `False` meaning a search backwards.

Listing 9-9

```
Sub GetJohnsFromTable()
  Dim strDisplayName As String
  Dim rdmSession As Redemption.rdoSession
  Dim rdmFolder As Redemption.rdoFolder
  Dim rdmTable As Redemption.MAPITable
  Dim rdmFilter As Redemption.TableFilter
  Dim rdmRestr As Redemption.RestrictionContent
  Dim rdmItems As Redemption.rdoItems

  Dim Columns(1) As Variant
  Dim Row As Variant

  Const PR_SENDER_NAME = &HC1A001E
  Const PR_SUBJECT = &H37001E

  strDisplayName = "John"

  Set rdmSession = CreateObject("Redemption.RDOSession")
  rdmSession.MAPIOBJECT = Application.Session.MAPIOBJECT

  Set rdmFolder = rdmSession.GetDefaultFolder(olFolderInbox)
  Set rdmItems = rdmFolder.Items
  Set rdmTable = rdmItems.MAPITable
  Set rdmFilter = rdmTable.Filter

  'set up the filter on the MAPITable
  With rdmFilter
    .Clear

    Set rdmRestr = .SetKind(RES_CONTENT)
```

(continued)

Listing 9-9 *(continued)*

```
    With rdmRestr
        rdmRestr.ulPropTag = PR_SENDER_NAME
        rdmRestr.ulFuzzyLevel = FL_IGNORECASE + FL_PREFIX
        rdmRestr.lpProp = strDisplayName
    End With

    Columns(0) = PR_SENDER_NAME
    Columns(1) = PR_SUBJECT
End With

With rdmTable
    .Columns = Columns

    If rdmFilter.FindFirst(True) Then
        Do
            Row = .GetRow
            If Not IsEmpty(Row) Then
                MsgBox "Sender is " & Row(0) & vbCrLf & "Subject: " & Row(1)
            End If
        Loop Until Not (rdmFilter.FindNext(True))
    End If
End With

rdmSession.Logoff

Set rdmSession = Nothing
Set rdmFolder = Nothing
Set rdmTable = Nothing
Set rdmFilter = Nothing
Set rdmRestr = Nothing
Set rdmItems = Nothing
End Sub
```

The code in Listing 9-10 uses a table search to return a Boolean property created in the PS_PUBLIC_STRINGS namespace, demonstrating how to access properties in the range above 0x80000000 hex. Properties in this range will have different property tags in each different store and with different store providers. This is unlike properties below that address range, where the property tags are constant from store to store, such as PR_SENDER_NAME, which always has a property tag of 0x0C1A001E. To get the correct property tag for properties above the 0x80000000 range, including properties created by Outlook such as FlagRequest or BusinessAddress, the GetIdsFromNames method is called. GetIdsFromNames returns the correct property tag for the store in which the item is located, no matter what type of store or if the item was moved from one store to another. To create the correct property tag you, supply GetIdsFromNames with a GUID and either a name or an ID for the property and then Or the result with the property type. In this case, the GUID is PS_PUBLIC_STRINGS, the name is "MyCustomProp" and the property type is PT_BOOLEAN.

Listing 9-10

```
Sub GetItemsWithCustomProp()
  Dim rdmSession As Redemption.rdoSession
  Dim rdmUtils As Redemption.MAPIUtils
```

Listing 9-10 *(continued)*

```
Dim rdmFolder As Redemption.rdoFolder
Dim rdmTable As Redemption.MAPITable
Dim rdmFilter As Redemption.TableFilter
Dim rdmRestrictProp As Redemption.RestrictionAnd
Dim rdmRes1 As Redemption.RestrictionProperty
Dim rdmRes2 As Redemption.RestrictionNot
Dim rdmRes3 As Redemption.RestrictionContent
Dim rdmExist1 As Redemption.RestrictionExist
Dim rdmItems As Redemption.rdoItems
Dim rdmMail As Redemption.rdoMail

Dim tag As Long
Dim strPropName As String

Dim Columns(4) As Variant
Dim Row As Variant

Const PS_PUBLIC_STRINGS As String = "{00020329-0000-0000-C000-000000000046}"

Const PR_ENTRYID = &HFFF0102
Const PR_LONGTERM_ENTRYID_FROM_TABLE = &H66700102

Const PT_BOOLEAN = &HB

strPropName = "MyCustomProp"

Set rdmSession = CreateObject("Redemption.RDOSession")
rdmSession.MAPIOBJECT = Application.Session.MAPIOBJECT

Set rdmUtils = CreateObject("Redemption.MAPIUtils")
rdmUtils.MAPIOBJECT = rdmSession.MAPIOBJECT

Set rdmFolder = rdmSession.GetDefaultFolder(olFolderSentMail)
Set rdmItems = rdmFolder.Items
Set rdmTable = rdmItems.MAPITable
Set rdmFilter = rdmTable.Filter

tag = rdmFolder.GetIDsFromNames(PS_PUBLIC_STRINGS, strPropName)
tag = tag Or PT_BOOLEAN

'set up the filter on the MAPITable
With rdmFilter
  .Clear

  Set rdmRestrictProp = .SetKind(RES_AND)
  With rdmRestrictProp
    Set rdmExist1 = .Add(RES_EXIST)
    With rdmExist1
      .ulPropTag = tag
    End With

    Set rdmRes1 = .Add(RES_PROPERTY)
```

(continued)

Listing 9-10 *(continued)*

```
   With rdmRes1
      .ulPropTag = tag
      .relop = RELOP_EQ
      .lpProp = True
   End With

   Set rdmRes2 = .Add(RES_NOT)

   Set rdmRes3 = rdmRes2.SetKind(RES_CONTENT)
   With rdmRes3
      .ulFuzzyLevel = FL_IGNORECASE + FL_SUBSTRING
      .ulPropTag = PR_SUBJECT
      .lpProp = "Test"
   End With
  End With

  Columns(0) = tag
  Columns(1) = PR_SUBJECT
  Columns(2) = PR_ENTRYID
  Columns(3) = PR_LONGTERM_ENTRYID_FROM_TABLE
End With

With rdmTable
  .Columns = Columns

  If rdmFilter.FindFirst(True) Then
    Do
      Row = .GetRow
      If Not IsEmpty(Row) Then

        If VarType(Row(0)) <> vbError Then
          strEntryID = rdmUtils.HrArrayToString(Row(3))
          If strEntryID = "" Then
            strEntryID = rdmUtils.HrArrayToString(Row(2))
          End If

          Set rdmMail = rdmSession.GetMessageFromID(strEntryID, _
            rdmFolder.StoreID)

          rdmMail.Display
        End If
      End If
    Loop Until Not (rdmFilter.FindNext(True))
  End If
End With

rdmUtils.Cleanup

rdmSession.Logoff
```

Listing 9-10 *(continued)*

```
    Set rdmSession = Nothing
    Set rdmFolder = Nothing
    Set rdmTable = Nothing
    Set rdmFilter = Nothing
    Set rdmUtils = Nothing
    Set rdmItems = Nothing
    Set rdmRestrictProp = Nothing
    Set rdmRes1 = Nothing
    Set rdmRes2 = Nothing
    Set rdmRes3 = Nothing
    Set rdmExist1 = Nothing
End Sub
```

The code in Listing 9-10 requests both an PR_ENTRYID and PR_LONGTERM_ENTRYID_FROM_TABLE as columns in the MAPITable. Some store providers, notably Exchange, will return a short-term EntryID for an item, which is only valid for that Outlook or MAPI session. The property may be different in a different session. Store providers, such as the PST file provider, only supply long-term EntryIDs, which are the same from session to session but return them in the PR_ENTRYID property. In cases where Exchange is being used, you always should retrieve both properties and check first to see if the long-term property is present. If it's not present then fall back to using the value from PR_ENTRYID.

The code in Listing 9-11 locates and enumerates the contents of the Personal Forms Library. This isn't really a separate object, the Personal Forms Library consists of hidden items in the hidden Common Views folder shown in MAPI viewers as IPM_COMMON_VIEWS. Published forms in this folder are identified by a MessageClass of IPM.Microsoft.FolderDesign.FormsDescription. The code finds the IPM_COMMON_VIEWS folder in the default Store and uses a MAPITable filter returning only items with that MessageClass. The custom form's MessageClass is in the oddly named property PR_MAILBEAT _BOUNCE_SERVER and the display name of the form is in the PR_DISPLAY_NAME property. Both properties are retrieved and a list of all forms published in the Personal Forms Library is then displayed.

Listing 9-11

```
Sub ListPersonalFormsLibrary()
  Dim rdmStore As Redemption.rdoStore
  Dim rdmFolder As Redemption.rdoFolder
  Dim colItems As Redemption.rdoItems
  Dim rdmMail As Redemption.rdoMail
  Dim rdmSession As Redemption.rdoSession
  Dim rdmUtils As Redemption.MAPIUtils
  Dim rdmTable As Redemption.MAPITable
  Dim rdmFilter As Redemption.TableFilter
  Dim rdmRestr As Redemption.RestrictionContent

  Dim commonViewsID As String
  Dim customForms As String

  Dim Columns(4) As Variant
```

(continued)

Listing 9-11 *(continued)*

```
Dim Row As Variant

Const CUSTOM_FORM_DESIGN_MESSAGECLASS = "IPM.Microsoft.FolderDesign.FormsDescription"

Const PR_COMMON_VIEWS_ENTRYID = &H35E60102
Const PR_MAILBEAT_BOUNCE_SERVER = &H6800001E
Const PR_MESSAGE_CLASS = &H1A001E
Const PR_DISPLAY_NAME = &H3001001E

Set rdmSession = CreateObject("Redemption.RDOSession")
rdmSession.MAPIOBJECT = Application.Session.MAPIOBJECT

Set rdmUtils = CreateObject("Redemption.MAPIUtils")
rdmUtils.MAPIOBJECT = rdmSession.MAPIOBJECT

Set rdmStore = rdmSession.Stores.DefaultStore

commonViewsID = rdmUtils. _
  HrArrayToString(rdmStore.Fields(PR_COMMON_VIEWS_ENTRYID))

If commonViewsID <> "" Then
  Set rdmFolder = rdmSession.GetFolderFromID(commonViewsID, rdmStore.EntryID)
  Set colItems = rdmFolder.HiddenItems
  Set rdmTable = colItems.MAPITable
  Set rdmFilter = rdmTable.Filter

  With rdmFilter
    .Clear

    Set rdmRestr = .SetKind(RES_CONTENT)
    With rdmRestr
      rdmRestr.ulPropTag = PR_MESSAGE_CLASS
      rdmRestr.ulFuzzyLevel = FL_IGNORECASE + FL_FULLSTRING
      rdmRestr.lpProp = CUSTOM_FORM_DESIGN_MESSAGECLASS
    End With

    'filter is done, restrict and read the data
    .Restrict

    Columns(0) = PR_MAILBEAT_BOUNCE_SERVER ' the custom MessageClass
    Columns(1) = PR_DISPLAY_NAME ' custom form display name

    With rdmTable
      If rdmTable.RowCount > 0 Then
        customForms = "Your Personal Forms Library includes:" & vbCrLf

        .Columns = Columns
        .GoToFirst

        Do
          Row = .GetRow
          If Not IsEmpty(Row) Then
```

Listing 9-11 *(continued)*

```
            customForms = customForms & "Display Name: " & Row(1) & vbTab & _
                "Custom MessageClass: " & Row(0) & vbCrLf
          End If
        Loop Until IsEmpty(Row)
      Else
        customForms = "Your Personal Forms Library is empty"
      End If
    End With
  End With
End If

MsgBox customForms

rdmUtils.Cleanup

rdmSession.Logoff

Set rdmStore = Nothing
Set rdmFolder = Nothing
Set colItems = Nothing
Set rdmMail = Nothing
Set rdmUtils = Nothing
Set rdmSession = Nothing
End Sub
```

The preceding examples of using Redemption code show the power of Redemption code and its similarities and differences with both Outlook and CDO code.

Summary

In this chapter, you learned about coding for Outlook in the real world and how to work around different Outlook problems and limitations. You also learned how to deploy managed code addins for Outlook and how to use alternate APIs to accomplish tasks that still cannot be accomplished using the Outlook object model.

The next chapter provides a case study of a real Outlook COM addin, the Task Management System, that is provided as both VB.NET and C# shared addin projects.

10

Task Management System

In this chapter you will learn how to use an Outlook COM addin to extend tasks to create a hierarchical task system. The Task Management System addin lets you add child tasks to an existing task, and uses a custom task pane to display related tasks in a treeview control.

Outlook tasks have always been isolated items, only suitable for use as a to-do list. A task can be linked to a contact but you can't relate one task to another to provide for parent-child relationships, something necessary for use as a task manager. The Task Management System adds the basic essentials for a task manager and can be used as the basis for a more sophisticated set of task management features.

The code is provided as two addin projects, one in VB.NET and the other in C#. Both are specific to Outlook 2007, using the `PropertyAccessor` object and the Ribbon, which aren't available in earlier versions of Outlook. Both projects require Visual Studio 2005 and Framework 2.0 or higher.

The projects are available for download from the Wrox web site (`www.wrox.com`) as well as from `www.slovaktech.com`. These projects also include setup projects configured to create debug installations. Shims used to provide unique application domains for shared addins are not provided for the projects.

Task Management System Features

The user interface for adding child tasks and displaying related tasks is provided by a custom Ribbon tab with two controls, shown in Figure 10-1.

The Show Related Tasks control displays the custom task pane shown at the right of Figure 10-1 and populates the treeview control nodes with the parents and children of the currently open task.

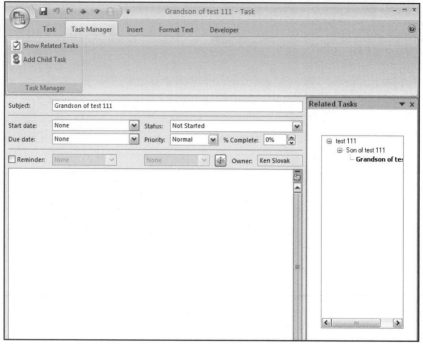

Figure 10-1

One limitation of the projects is they only go one level deep when displaying child tasks. The code doesn't display grandchild tasks. The code displays parent tasks of the current task up to the original parent task.

The Add Child Task control opens a new task item as a child task of the current task. Two named properties are added to each task item, `ParentTask` and `ChildTasks`. The `ParentTask` property is used to store the `EntryID` of a task's parent task, serving as a link field, allowing the retrieval of the parent task at any time. Because any task can have many child tasks the `ChildTasks` property is created as a multi-valued string property that can store the `EntryID`'s of multiple tasks.

The simple task manager enabled by adding two link fields to task items can be expanded to create a powerful task management system. A few of the ways the task manager can be expanded are:

1. Add code to search for all levels of child tasks, and to display the child tasks of sibling tasks and related tasks.

2. Add a Form Region to display and set task priorities to allow for task prioritization.

3. Add additional Ribbon controls and task panes to display task family timelines, graphs of tasks status, displays of outstanding tasks and other analytical displays.

The code for each class in the addin is shown in the following sections, first as VB.NET code and then as C# code.

The Connect Class

The Connect class is the class that's exposed to Outlook and to COM. Any managed code addin must expose at least one class to COM for the addin to be recognized by Outlook. This class implements the Office IRibbonExtensibility and ICustomTaskPaneConsumer interfaces to handle Ribbon callbacks and custom task panes, in addition to the IDTExtensibility2 interface needed for COM addins to connect with their hosts. Office 2007 requires that the IRibbonExtensibility interface for handling the Ribbon is declared in the same class that declares the IDTExtensibility2 interface.

The Connect class is also used to handle the NewExplorer and NewInspector events, as well as the ExplorerClose and InspectorClose events. These events are used to wrap new Explorers and Inspectors in collections to allow event handling in multiple open Explorers and Inspectors as well as to handle shutdown code when Outlook is closing or the user has disconnected the addin. Ribbon callbacks and initializations are handled in the Connect class, in addition to the events and initializations for the custom task panes.

The VB Connect Class

The code in Listing 10-1 declares the Connect class GUID and ProgID and sets the Connect class visible to COM. The implementations for Extensibility, the Ribbon and custom task panes are declared and then module-level declarations are made for objects, variables, and constants used throughout the class.

Some objects are declared WithEvents, allowing them to handle the events exposed for those object types. Objects that are declared WithEvents are Outlook.Application, NameSpace, Explorers, Inspectors, Explorer, and Inspector.

Listing 10-1

```
Imports Extensibility
Imports System.Runtime.InteropServices
Imports Outlook = Microsoft.Office.Interop.Outlook
Imports Office = Microsoft.Office.Core
Imports System.Windows.Forms
Imports System.Text
Imports System.Reflection
Imports System.Drawing
Imports stdole

<GuidAttribute("C4AF1D53-1F7B-4e17-87E9-D44198617FFC"), _
ProgIdAttribute("TaskManager.Connect"), ComVisible(True)> _
Public Class Connect

#Region "Interface implementations"
    Implements Extensibility.IDTExtensibility2

    ' required implementation for handling IRibbon in Outlook 2007
    Implements Office.IRibbonExtensibility

    ' required for CTP use
    Implements Office.ICustomTaskPaneConsumer
#End Region
```

(continued)

Listing 10-1 *(continued)*

```vb
#Region "Module level declarations"

    Private addInInstance As Office.COMAddIn

    Private WithEvents m_objOutlook As Outlook.Application
    Private WithEvents m_objNS As Outlook.NameSpace

    ' Event-aware references to Explorers collection & ActiveExplorer
    Private WithEvents m_colExplorers As Outlook.Explorers
    Private WithEvents m_olExplorer As Outlook.Explorer

    ' Event-aware references to Inspectors collection & ActiveInspector
    Private WithEvents m_colInspectors As Outlook.Inspectors
    Private WithEvents m_olInspector As Outlook.Inspector

    ' State flags
    Private m_blnTeardown As Boolean
    Private m_blnInit As Boolean

    ' Ribbon UI declarations
    Private m_Ribbon As Office.IRibbonUI

    ' Task Pane declarations
    Private m_CTP As Office.ICTPFactory
    Private CTP As Office.CustomTaskPane

    Private Const CTP_PROGID As String = "TaskManager.TaskPane"
    Private Const CTP_TITLE As String = "Related Tasks"
#End Region
```

The code in Listing 10-2 is used to handle the `IDTExtensibility2` events declared in that interface. The `OnBeginShutdown`, `OnAddInsUpdate` and `OnStartupComplete` events aren't used in this addin. The `OnConnection` event handler instantiates module-level objects and variables, and initializes event handlers. The `OnDisconnection` event is used to shut down the addin when the user disconnects the addin or when Outlook is shutting down.

Listing 10-2

```vb
#Region "IDTExtensibility events"
    Public Sub OnBeginShutdown(ByRef custom As System.Array) _
      Implements Extensibility.IDTExtensibility2.OnBeginShutdown

    End Sub

    Public Sub OnAddInsUpdate(ByRef custom As System.Array) _
      Implements Extensibility.IDTExtensibility2.OnAddInsUpdate

    End Sub

    Public Sub OnStartupComplete(ByRef custom As System.Array) _
      Implements Extensibility.IDTExtensibility2.OnStartupComplete
```

Listing 10-2 *(continued)*

```vb
            ' for an Explorer task pane
            'Try
            '   CTP = m_CTP.CreateCTP("TaskManager.TaskTaskPane", _
            '     "VB.NET Config", m_olExplorer)

            '   CTP.DockPositionRestrict = Microsoft.Office.Core. _
            '     MsoCTPDockPositionRestrict.msoCTPDockPositionRestrictNoChange

            '   CTP.DockPosition = Microsoft.Office.Core. _
            '     MsoCTPDockPosition.msoCTPDockPositionRight

            '   CTP.Visible = True
            'Catch ex As Exception
            '   MessageBox.Show(ex.Message)
            'End Try
    End Sub

    Public Sub OnDisconnection(ByVal RemoveMode As _
      Extensibility.ext_DisconnectMode, _
      ByRef custom As System.Array) Implements _
      Extensibility.IDTExtensibility2.OnDisconnection

        If m_blnTeardown = False Then
            TearDown()
        End If
    End Sub

    Public Sub OnConnection(ByVal application As Object, _
      ByVal connectMode As Extensibility.ext_ConnectMode, _
      ByVal addInInst As Object, ByRef custom As System.Array) _
      Implements Extensibility.IDTExtensibility2.OnConnection

        m_blnTeardown = False

        addInInstance = Nothing
        addInInstance = TryCast(addInInst, Office.COMAddIn)

        System.Windows.Forms.Application.EnableVisualStyles()

        If (addInInstance IsNot Nothing) Then
            'set module level reference to COMAddIn object
            Try
                m_objOutlook = CType(application, Outlook.Application)

                'event-aware reference to Explorers collection
                'use NewExplorer event to watch for UI creation
                m_colExplorers = m_objOutlook.Explorers

                Try
                    'put ProgID in a global variable
                    g_strProgID = addInInstance.ProgId
```

(continued)

Listing 10-2 *(continued)*

```
                addInInstance.Object = Me

                'Are we starting with UI?
                If m_colExplorers.Count > 0 Then
                    m_olExplorer = m_objOutlook.Explorers.Item(1)

                    'we have UI
                    InitHandler()

                    If m_blnInit = True Then
                        AddExpl(m_olExplorer)
                    End If

                    m_objNS = m_objOutlook.GetNamespace("MAPI")

                    m_colInspectors = m_objOutlook.Inspectors
                Else
                    'do nothing
                    'monitor Explorers collection (in this module)
                    'if NewExplorer event is raised then we have UI
                End If
            Catch ex As Exception
                TearDown()
            End Try

        Catch ex As Exception
            TearDown()
        End Try
    Else
        TearDown()
    End If
    End Sub
#End Region
```

The code in Listing 10-3 is used to handle the `CTPFactoryAvailable` event which is the one event required by the `ICustomTaskPaneConsumer` interface, and is fired when the COM TaskPane factory is available to create new task pane instances. This factory instance is stored in a module-level object, so it can be made available whenever a new task pane has to be created.

Listing 10-3

```
#Region "Task Panes"
    Public Sub CTPFactoryAvailable(ByVal CTPFactoryInst _
      As Office.ICTPFactory) Implements _
      Office.ICustomTaskPaneConsumer.CTPFactoryAvailable

        ' store the Custom Task Pane factory instance
        m_CTP = CTPFactoryInst
    End Sub
#End Region
```

Listing 10-4 shows the code used to provide the Ribbon XML for the addin's Ribbon user interface. The XML is only provided for a `RibbonID` of `Microsoft.Outlook.Task` and is only called for the first time a task item is opened. The Ribbon XML is shown in Listing 10-38.

Listing 10-4

```
#Region "Ribbon Stuff"
#Region "Ribbon Initializer"
    Function GetCustomUI(ByVal RibbonID As String) As String _
        Implements Microsoft.Office.Core.IRibbonExtensibility.GetCustomUI

        'RibbonID indicates type of Inspector about to be displayed,
        '   valid RibbonID values are as follows:
        'Microsoft.Outlook.Mail.Read
        'Microsoft.Outlook.Mail.Compose
        'Microsoft.Outlook.MeetingRequest.Read
        'Microsoft.Outlook.MeetingRequest.Send
        'Microsoft.Outlook.Appointment
        'Microsoft.Outlook.Contact
        'Microsoft.Outlook.Journal
        'Microsoft.Outlook.Task
        'Microsoft.Outlook.DistributionList
        'Microsoft.Outlook.Report
        'Microsoft.Outlook.Resend
        'Microsoft.Outlook.Response.Read
        'Microsoft.Outlook.Response.Compose
        'Microsoft.Outlook.Response.CounterPropose
        'Microsoft.Outlook.RSS
        'Microsoft.Outlook.Post.Read
        'Microsoft.Outlook.Post.Compose
        'Microsoft.Outlook.Sharing.Read
        'Microsoft.Outlook.Sharing.Compose

        'In this sample only new Task Inspector is handled for a button.

        Select Case RibbonID
            Case "Microsoft.Outlook.Task"
                ' Return the RibbonX markup stored as a resource
                '    in the project
                Return My.Resources.CustomRibbon
            Case Else
                Return String.Empty
        End Select
    End Function
#End Region
```

The code in Listing 10-5 shows the Ribbon callbacks used in the addin and the `IRibbonUI` property declared in Listing 10-1 as `m_Ribbon`. This property is declared as `Friend` to expose it only internally in the addin, and not expose it to COM.

The `VB_Action` callback is called when the user clicks either of the Ribbon controls. The `control` object passed to `VB_Action` contains `Context` and `Id` properties that are essential in knowing which control was clicked and in which `Inspector`. The `Inspector` where the control was clicked is contained in the `Context` property, and the control's XML `id` attribute is contained in the `Id` property.

The `Inspector` wrapper collection is iterated through to find the `Inspector` where the Ribbon control click occurred. This is possible because the wrapper class stores a reference to the `Inspector` it's wrapping. After the `Inspector` is found, either the task pane visibility is toggled if the `Id` is `Tasks1` or a child task is created if the `Id` is `Tasks2`. A child task is created by calling the `AddChildTask` method exposed in the `Inspector` wrapper.

The `VB_GetImage` callback is called when the Ribbon requests an image for a control. A `Case` block is used to test the `control.Id` property to see which PNG file to return from the project resources. The file is converted into an `IPictureDisp` object, which is required by the Ribbon, using the `AxHost` class implementation that's part of the `Connect` module.

The `Ribbon_OnLoad` event fires when the Ribbon is loading. This event fires on the first `Inspector` opened in an Outlook Session some time after the `NewInspector` event fires, so this event is used to update the Ribbon property in each open `Inspector` when the event fires.

Listing 10-5

```
#Region "Ribbon Callbacks"
    Public Sub VB_Action(ByVal control As Office.IRibbonControl)
        Debug.Print("VB_Action")

        Dim myInsp As Outlook.Inspector = CType(control.Context, _
            Outlook.Inspector)

        Dim oInspWrap As InspWrap = Nothing

        If (control.Id = "Tasks1") Then
            Try
                For Each oInspWrap In g_colInspWrap
                    If (oInspWrap.Inspector Is myInsp) Then
                        If oInspWrap.TaskPane IsNot Nothing Then
                            oInspWrap.TaskPane.Visible = True
                        End If
                    Else
                        If oInspWrap IsNot Nothing Then
                            oInspWrap.TaskPane.Visible = False
                        End If
                    End If
                Next
            Catch ex As Exception
                MessageBox.Show(ex.Message)
            End Try
        ElseIf (control.Id = "Tasks2") Then
            Try
                For Each oInspWrap In g_colInspWrap
                    If (oInspWrap.Inspector Is myInsp) Then
                        oInspWrap.AddChildTask()
```

Listing 10-5 *(continued)*

```vb
                    Exit For
                End If
            Next
        Catch ex As Exception
            MessageBox.Show(ex.Message)
        End Try
    End If

    oInspWrap = Nothing
    myInsp = Nothing
End Sub

Public Function VB_GetImage(ByVal control As _
    Office.IRibbonControl) As stdole.IPictureDisp

    Dim imgStreamPic As System.Drawing.Bitmap
    Dim oPic As IPictureDisp
    Dim ax As MyAxHost

    'Return Nothing

    Select Case control.Id
        Case "Tasks1"
            imgStreamPic = My.Resources.Task
        Case "Tasks2"
            imgStreamPic = My.Resources.Related
        Case Else
            imgStreamPic = Nothing
    End Select

    ax = New MyAxHost

    oPic = ax.IPictureDispFromImage(imgStreamPic)

    imgStreamPic = Nothing
    ax = Nothing

    Return oPic

End Function

Public Sub Ribbon_OnLoad(ByVal Ribbon As Office.IRibbonUI)
    Debug.Print("Ribbon_OnLoad")

    m_Ribbon = Ribbon

    Dim wrap As InspWrap = Nothing

    For Each wrap In g_colInspWrap
        If wrap.Ribbon Is Nothing Then
            wrap.Ribbon = m_Ribbon
        End If
    Next
```

(continued)

Listing 10-5 *(continued)*

```
        wrap = Nothing

    End Sub
#End Region

#Region "Ribbon Properties"
    Friend ReadOnly Property Ribbon() As Office.IRibbonUI
        Get
            Return m_Ribbon
        End Get
    End Property
#End Region

#End Region
```

The code in Listing 10-6 contains the `InitHandler` and `Teardown` utility methods. The `InitHandler` method is used to instantiate global `Outlook.Application` and `NameSpace` objects, and to test for the currently running version of Outlook. The `Teardown` method releases all unmanaged code objects and calls the garbage collector to ensure an immediate release of those resources so that Outlook can close cleanly.

Listing 10-6

```
#Region "Utility procedures"
    Private Sub InitHandler()
        Dim sVerLeft2 As String

        Try
            g_objOL = m_objOutlook
            g_objNS = g_objOL.GetNamespace("MAPI")

            '***********************************************************

            sVerLeft2 = Left(g_objOL.Version, 2)
            Select Case sVerLeft2
                Case "10"
                    g_OutlookVersion = 10
                Case "11"
                    g_OutlookVersion = 11
                Case "12"
                    g_OutlookVersion = 12
                Case Else
                    If Left(sVerLeft2, 1) = "9" Then
                        g_OutlookVersion = 9
                    Else
                        g_OutlookVersion = 0
                    End If
            End Select

            '***********************************************************

            m_blnInit = True
```

Listing 10-6 *(continued)*

```
        Catch ex As Exception
            MessageBox.Show(ex.Message)

            If m_blnTeardown = False Then
                TearDown()
            End If
        End Try
    End Sub

    Private Sub TearDown()
        Dim i As Integer
        Dim j As Integer

        If m_blnTeardown = False Then
            Try
                If g_colExplWrap IsNot Nothing Then
                    j = g_colExplWrap.Count
                    If j > 0 Then
                        For i = j To 1 Step -1
                            g_colExplWrap.Remove(i)
                        Next
                    End If
                    g_colExplWrap = Nothing
                End If

                If g_colInspWrap IsNot Nothing Then
                    j = g_colInspWrap.Count
                    If j > 0 Then
                        For i = j To 1 Step -1
                            g_colInspWrap.Remove(i)
                        Next
                    End If
                    g_colInspWrap = Nothing
                End If

            Catch ex As Exception
                MessageBox.Show(ex.Message)
            End Try

            If g_objNS IsNot Nothing Then
                g_objNS = Nothing
            End If


            If g_objOL IsNot Nothing Then
                g_objOL = Nothing
            End If

            Try
                'release Ribbon reference
                m_Ribbon = Nothing
```

(continued)

Listing 10-6 (continued)

```
            'release CTP references
            m_CTP = Nothing
            CTP = Nothing

            'release reference to Outlook objects
            m_olExplorer = Nothing
            m_colExplorers = Nothing
            m_colInspectors = Nothing
            m_olInspector = Nothing
            m_objNS = Nothing
            m_objOutlook = Nothing
        Catch ex As Exception
            MessageBox.Show(ex.Message)
        End Try

        m_blnTeardown = True
        m_blnInit = False

        GC.Collect()
        GC.WaitForPendingFinalizers()
    End If
End Sub

#End Region
```

Listing 10-7 shows the code for the `NewExplorer` and `Explorer.Close` event handlers. When `NewExplorer` is called the new `Explorer` is added to the `Explorer` wrappers collection. This enables references to the `Explorer` and the class used to handle `Explorer` events to stay alive and not be removed by the garbage collector. The class-level `m_olExplorer` object is set to the new `Explorer`, allowing the code to monitor the closing of the most recently opened `Explorer`.

If the `m_blnInit` variable is `False` when the `NewExplorer` event fires, that indicates that Outlook has previously been started with no user interface and a user interface is being added. This condition usually occurs when code starts Outlook using automation and the user later starts a normal Outlook session. The `InitHandler` method is called in this case to initialize the addin.

When the `Explorer.Close` event fires, an attempt is made to set the class-level `Explorer` object to `ActiveExplorer`. If this attempt fails, the code checks to see if there are no more `Explorers` or `Inspectors`, to see if the `Teardown` method should be called to release the addin's objects. This check is more necessary in earlier versions of Outlook than in Outlook 2007, but it doesn't hurt. This allows you to handle cases where Outlook was started using automation and a user interface was added later and then closed, leaving the automation code keeping the Outlook session open.

Listing 10-7

```
#Region "Explorer (folder window) related events"

    ' NewExplorer event will be raised if there is UI
    Private Sub m_colExplorers_NewExplorer(ByVal Explorer As _
      Microsoft.Office.Interop.Outlook.Explorer) _
      Handles m_colExplorers.NewExplorer
```

Listing 10-7 (continued)

```
        'assign ActiveExplorer
        m_olExplorer = Explorer

        If m_blnInit = False Then
            'we didn't have UI before - initialize add-in objects
            InitHandler()
        End If

        If m_blnInit = True Then
            AddExpl(Explorer)
        End If
    End Sub

    ' Monitor Explorer_Close to see when UI "disappears"
    Private Sub m_olExplorer_Close() Handles m_olExplorer.Close
        'release current reference
        m_olExplorer = Nothing

        Try
            m_olExplorer = m_objOutlook.ActiveExplorer
        Catch ex As Exception
            Err.Clear()
            If m_objOutlook.Inspectors.Count = 0 Then
                'release add-in objects
                If m_blnTeardown = False Then
                    TearDown()
                End If
            End If
        End Try
    End Sub
#End Region
```

The code in Listing 10-8 handles the NewInspector and Inspector.Close events. When the NewInspector event fires, the Inspector is checked to make sure that it isn't showing a Note item. If it is a Note item the item is ignored. Handling Inspector events for Note items can lead to Outlook crashes. The class-level m_olInspector object is set to the new Inspector. If the item is a Task item a new instance of a custom task pane is created and set to assume a fixed position at the right side of its parent window, the new Inspector. The Inspector is added to the Inspector wrapper collection to keep references to it alive and allow handling of events fired in that Inspector.

When the Inspector.Close event fires, an attempt is made to assign ActiveInspector to the m_olInspector object. If that fails and there are no open Explorers, the Teardown method is called to release the addin's objects.

Listing 10-8

```
#Region "Inspector (item window) related events"

    Private Sub m_colInspectors_NewInspector(ByVal Inspector _
        As Microsoft.Office.Interop.Outlook.Inspector) _
        Handles m_colInspectors.NewInspector
```

(continued)

Listing 10-8 *(continued)*

```
            'No handling of Inspectors for Notes, they are brain dead
        If Not (TypeOf (Inspector.CurrentItem) Is Outlook.NoteItem) Then
            m_olInspector = Inspector

            Try
                If TypeOf (Inspector.CurrentItem) Is TaskItem Then
                    CTP = m_CTP.CreateCTP(CTP_PROGID, _
                      CTP_TITLE, Inspector)

                    CTP.DockPositionRestrict = Microsoft.Office.Core. _
                      MsoCTPDockPositionRestrict. _
                      msoCTPDockPositionRestrictNoChange

                    CTP.DockPosition = Microsoft.Office.Core. _
                      MsoCTPDockPosition.msoCTPDockPositionRight

                    CTP.Visible = False
                Else
                    CTP = Nothing
                End If

                'm_Ribbon is a dummy, filled in when Ribbon_OnLoad fires
                AddInsp(Inspector, CTP, m_Ribbon)
            Catch ex As Exception
                Debug.WriteLine(ex.Message)
                'm_Ribbon is a dummy, filled in when Ribbon_OnLoad fires
                AddInsp(Inspector, CTP, m_Ribbon)
            End Try
        End If
    End Sub

    Private Sub m_olInspector_Close() Handles m_olInspector.Close
        m_olInspector = Nothing

        Try
            m_olInspector = m_objOutlook.ActiveInspector
        Catch ex As Exception
            MessageBox.Show(ex.Message)

            If m_olInspector Is Nothing Then
                If m_objOutlook.Explorers.Count = 0 Then
                    If m_blnTeardown = False Then
                        TearDown()
                    End If
                End If
            End If
        End Try
    End Sub
#End Region

End Class
```

The code in Listing 10-9 shows the implementation of the AxHost class used to convert an image file into an IPictureDisp object to be passed to the Ribbon as the image for the button control.

Listing 10-9

```
#Region "AxHost"
Public Class MyAxHost 'second class in Connect module
    Inherits System.Windows.Forms.AxHost

    Public Sub New()
        MyBase.New("{59EE46BA-677D-4d20-BF10-8D8067CB8B33}")
    End Sub

    Public Function IPictureDispFromImage(ByVal Image As System.Drawing.Image) As
stdole.IPictureDisp
        Dim oPic As stdole.IPictureDisp

        oPic = CType(System.Windows.Forms.AxHost.GetIPictureDispFromPicture(Image), _
        stdole.IPictureDisp)

        Return oPic
    End Function
End Class
#End Region
```

The C# Connect Class

The C# Connect class performs the same functions as the VB `Connect` class, implementing the
`IDTExtensibility2`, `IRibbonExtensibility`, and `ICustomTaskPaneConsumer` interfaces. It also
initializes the class-level event handling for `Explorers`, `Inspectors`, and callback functions for the Ribbon.
One difference is the C# `Connect` class module doesn't include an `AxHost` implementation, which is in a
separate class in the C# code. Another difference is that instead of a global code module containing objects
available anywhere in the addin global objects in the C# code are referenced as `public` properties and
constants in the `Connect` class.

The code in Listing 10-10 shows the implementation declarations for the interfaces, and class- and addin-
level objects and variables. The `m_ProgID`variable is declared as a `public static string`, `m_Outlook`,
and `m_NameSpace` are declared as `public static objects`, making them accessible to other classes in
the code.

The `public ParentTag` and `ChildTag` string constants are used for the parent and child properties in
the `http://schemas.microsoft.com/mapi/string` namespace. The addin `GUID` is used to qualify
the namespace, eliminating any possibility of property naming collisions. The C# code uses `SortedList`
objects instead of Visual Basic `Collections` to store the `Explorer` and `Inspector` wrapper classes,
keeping them alive and safe from the garbage collector.

Listing 10-10

```
namespace TaskManagerCS
{
    using System;
    using Extensibility;
    using System.Runtime.InteropServices;
```

(continued)

Listing 10-10 *(continued)*

```csharp
using System.Reflection;
using System.Windows.Forms;
using Outlook = Microsoft.Office.Interop.Outlook;
using Office = Microsoft.Office.Core;
using Microsoft.Vbe.Interop.Forms;
using stdole;
using System.Drawing;
using System.Text;
using System.Diagnostics;

/// <summary>
///    The object for implementing an Add-in.
/// </summary>
/// <see also class='IDTExtensibility2' />
[GuidAttribute("D5CAD45F-2995-43e4-8121-327A3C9E0C65"),
  ProgId("TaskManagerCS.Connect")]
public class Connect : Object, Extensibility.IDTExtensibility2,
    Office.IRibbonExtensibility, Office.ICustomTaskPaneConsumer
{
    #region Module_level_declarations
    public static string m_ProgID = "";

    public const string ParentTag =
      "http://schemas.microsoft.com/mapi/string/"
      + "{D5CAD45F-2995-43e4-8121-327A3C9E0C65}/ParentTask";

    public const string ChildTag =
      "http://schemas.microsoft.com/mapi/string/"
      + "{D5CAD45F-2995-43e4-8121-327A3C9E0C65}/ChildTasks";

    // start of COM objects
    private object applicationObject = null;

    public static Outlook.Application m_Outlook = null;
    public static Outlook.NameSpace m_NameSpace = null;

    private Office.COMAddIn addInInstance = null;

    // References to Explorers collection & ActiveExplorer
    private Outlook.Explorers m_Explorers = null;

    private Outlook.Explorer m_Explorer = null;
    private Outlook.ExplorerClass m_ExplorerClass = null;

    // References to Inspectors collection & ActiveInspector
    private Outlook.Inspectors m_Inspectors = null;

    private Outlook.Inspector m_Inspector = null;
    private Outlook.InspectorClass m_InspectorClass = null;

    // end of COM objects
```

Listing 10-10 *(continued)*

```
// Explorer Wrapper Collection
private System.Collections.SortedList m_ExplWrap = null;

// Inspector Wrapper Collection
private System.Collections.SortedList m_InspWrap = null;

private int m_WrapperID = 0;

private int m_OutlookVersion = 0;

//Initialization flags
private bool m_Teardown = false;

private bool m_Init = false;

//Ribbon UI object
private Office.IRibbonUI m_Ribbon;

//CTP objects
private Office.ICTPFactory m_CTP;
private Office.CustomTaskPane CTP;

private const string CTP_PROGID = "TaskManagerCS.TaskPane";
private const string CTP_TITLE = "Related Tasks";

#endregion
```

The code in Listing 10-11 is used for the IDTExtensibility2 events. The OnBeginShutdown, OnAddInsUpdate, and OnStartupComplete events aren't used in this addin. The OnConnection event handler instantiates module-level objects and variables, and initializes event handlers. The OnDisconnection event is used to shut down the addin when the user disconnects the addin or when Outlook is shutting down.

Listing 10-11

```
/// <summary>
/// Implements the constructor for the Add-in object.
/// Place your initialization code within this method.
/// </summary>
public Connect()
{
}

#region Startup_Shutdown
/// <summary>
///      Implements the OnConnection method of the IDTExtensibility2 interface.
///      Receives notification that the Add-in is being loaded.
/// </summary>
/// <param term='application'>
///      Root object of the host application.
/// </param>
```

(continued)

Listing 10-11 *(continued)*

```csharp
        /// <param term='connectMode'>
        ///      Describes how the Add-in is being loaded.
        /// </param>
        /// <param term='addInInst'>
        ///      Object representing this Add-in.
        /// </param>
        /// <seealso class='IDTExtensibility2' />
        public void OnConnection(object application,
          Extensibility.ext_ConnectMode connectMode,
          object addInInst, ref System.Array custom)
        {
            applicationObject = application;

            System.Windows.Forms.Application.EnableVisualStyles();

            try
            {
                addInInstance = (Office.COMAddIn)addInInst;
            }
            catch
            {
                addInInstance = null;
            }

            if (addInInstance != null)
            {
                //set module level reference to COMAddIn object
                try
                {
                    m_Outlook = (Outlook.Application)application;
                    m_NameSpace = m_Outlook.GetNamespace("MAPI");

                    //event-aware reference to Explorers collection
                    //use NewExplorer event to watch for UI creation
                    m_Explorers = m_Outlook.Explorers;

                    try
                    {
                        //put ProgID in a module level variable
                        m_ProgID = addInInstance.ProgId;

                        //addInInstance.Object = Me
                        addInInstance.GetType().InvokeMember(
                          "Object", BindingFlags.Public |
                          BindingFlags.SetProperty, null,
                          addInInst, new object[] { this });

                        m_Teardown = false;

                        //Are we starting with UI?
                        if (m_Explorers.Count > 0)
                        {
```

Listing 10-11 *(continued)*

```
                m_Explorer = m_Outlook.Explorers[1];

                //we have UI - initialize base class
                InitHandler();

                if (m_Init == true)
                {
                    // allot space initially for
                    // 15 open Explorers at a time
                    m_ExplWrap = new
                        System.Collections.SortedList(15);

                    OutExpl adder = new OutExpl();

                    m_WrapperID = adder.AddExpl(
                        m_Explorer, m_WrapperID,
                        ref m_ExplWrap);

                    adder = null;

                    // allot space initially for
                    // 15 open Inspectors at a time
                    m_InspWrap = new
                        System.Collections.SortedList(15);
                }

                m_Inspectors = m_Outlook.Inspectors;

                m_Explorers.NewExplorer += new
                    Microsoft.Office.Interop.Outlook.
                    ExplorersEvents_NewExplorerEventHandler(
                    m_Explorers_NewExplorer);

                m_ExplorerClass =
                    (Outlook.ExplorerClass)m_Explorer;

                m_ExplorerClass.ExplorerEvents_Event_Close +=
                    new Microsoft.Office.Interop.Outlook.
                    ExplorerEvents_CloseEventHandler(
                    m_Explorer_Close);

                m_Inspectors.NewInspector += new
                    Microsoft.Office.Interop.Outlook.
                    InspectorsEvents_NewInspectorEventHandler(
                    m_Inspectors_NewInspector);
            }
            else
            {
                //do nothing
                //monitor Explorers collection
                //if NewExplorer event is raised
                //then we have UI
            }
        }
```

(continued)

Listing 10-11 *(continued)*

```
                catch (Exception ex)
                {
                    MessageBox.Show(ex.Message);
                    TearDown();
                }
            }
            catch (Exception ex)
            {
                MessageBox.Show(ex.Message);
                TearDown();
            }
        }
        else TearDown();
}


/// <summary>
///     Implements the OnDisconnection method of the
/// IDTExtensibility2 interface.
///     Receives notification that the Add-in is being unloaded.
/// </summary>
/// <param term='disconnectMode'>
///     Describes how the Add-in is being unloaded.
/// </param>
/// <param term='custom'>
///     Array of parameters that are host application specific.
/// </param>
/// <see also class='IDTExtensibility2' />
public void OnDisconnection(
  Extensibility.ext_DisconnectMode
  disconnectMode, ref System.Array custom)
{
    if (m_Teardown == false) TearDown();
}


/// <summary>
///     Implements the OnAddInsUpdate method of the
///  IDTExtensibility2 interface.
///     Receives notification that the collection of
///  Add-ins has changed.
/// </summary>
/// <param term='custom'>
///     Array of parameters that are host application specific.
/// </param>
/// <seealso class='IDTExtensibility2' />
public void OnAddInsUpdate(ref System.Array custom)
{
}


/// <summary>
///     Implements the OnStartupComplete method of the
///  IDTExtensibility2 interface.
```

Listing 10-11 *(continued)*

```
///        Receives notification that the host application has
///   completed loading.
/// </summary>
/// <param term='custom'>
///        Array of parameters that are host application specific.
/// </param>
/// <seealso class='IDTExtensibility2' />
public void OnStartupComplete(ref System.Array custom)
{
}

/// <summary>
///        Implements the OnBeginShutdown method of the
///   IDTExtensibility2 interface.
///        Receives notification that the host application
///   is being unloaded.
/// </summary>
/// <param term='custom'>
///        Array of parameters that are host application specific.
/// </param>
/// <seealso class='IDTExtensibility2' />
public void OnBeginShutdown(ref System.Array custom)
{
}

#endregion
```

The code in Listing 10-12 shows the `InitHandler` and `Teardown` methods. The `InitHandler` method doesn't do anything other than storing the Outlook version and setting the initialization flag, but it can be used for any startup initializations. The `Teardown` method clears the `SortedList` objects used as wrapper collections to release the referenced wrapper classes, releases the event handlers and class-level objects, and calls the garbage collector to release the COM objects and allow Outlook to close cleanly.

Listing 10-12

```
#region utility_procedures
public void InitHandler()
{
    string sVerLeft2 = "";
    string sVersion = "";

    //**********************************************************

    sVersion = m_Outlook.Version;
    sVerLeft2 = sVersion.Substring(0, 2);
    switch (sVerLeft2)
    {
        case "10":
            m_OutlookVersion = 10;
            break;
```

(continued)

Listing 10-12 *(continued)*

```
            case "11":
                m_OutlookVersion = 11;
                break;
            case "12":
                m_OutlookVersion = 12;
                break;
            default:
                if ((sVerLeft2.Substring(0, 1)) == "9")
                {
                    m_OutlookVersion = 9;
                }
                else
                {
                    m_OutlookVersion = 0;
                }
                break;
        }

        //set initialization flag
        m_Init = true;
    }

    private void TearDown()
    {
        if (m_Teardown == false)
        {
            try
            {
                if (m_ExplWrap != null)
                {
                    m_ExplWrap.Clear();
                    m_ExplWrap = null;
                }

                if (m_InspWrap != null)
                {
                    m_InspWrap.Clear();
                    m_InspWrap = null;
                }

                // remove the event handlers
                if (m_Explorers != null)
                {
                    m_Explorers.NewExplorer -=
                        new Microsoft.Office.Interop.Outlook.
                        ExplorersEvents_NewExplorerEventHandler(
                        m_Explorers_NewExplorer);
                }

                if (m_InspectorClass != null)
                {
                    new Microsoft.Office.Interop.Outlook.
                    InspectorEvents_CloseEventHandler(
```

Listing 10-12 *(continued)*

```
                            m_InspectorClass_Close);
              }

              if (m_Inspectors != null)
              {
                  m_Inspectors.NewInspector -=
                  new Microsoft.Office.Interop.Outlook.
                  InspectorsEvents_NewInspectorEventHandler(
                  m_Inspectors_NewInspector);
              }

              //release Ribbon reference
              m_Ribbon = null;

              //release CTP references
              m_CTP = null;
              CTP = null;

              //release reference to Outlook objects
              if (m_Explorer != null) m_Explorer = null;
              if (m_Explorers != null) m_Explorers = null;

              if (m_Inspectors != null) m_Inspectors = null;
              if (m_Inspector != null) m_Inspector = null;

              if (m_ExplorerClass != null) m_ExplorerClass = null;

              if (m_InspectorClass != null) m_InspectorClass = null;

              if (m_NameSpace != null) m_NameSpace = null;
              if (m_Outlook != null) m_Outlook = null;

              if (applicationObject != null) applicationObject = null;
              if (addInInstance != null) addInInstance = null;

              m_Teardown = true;
              m_Init = false;

              GC.Collect();
              GC.WaitForPendingFinalizers();
          }
          catch (Exception ex)
          {
              MessageBox.Show(ex.Message);
          }
      }
  }
#endregion
```

Listing 10-13 shows the code for the `NewExplorer` and `Explorer_Close` event handlers. When `NewExplorer` is called the new `Explorer` is added to the `Explorer` wrappers collection. This enables references to the `Explorer` and the class used to handle `Explorer` events to stay alive and not be removed by the garbage collector. The class-level `m_Explorer` object is set to the new `Explorer`, allowing the code to monitor the closing of the most recently opened Explorer. If the m_Init variable is false when the NewExplorer event fires, the InitHandler method is called to initialize the addin.

When the Explorer_Close event fires, an attempt is made to set the class-level m_Explorer object to ActiveExplorer. If this attempt fails, the code checks to see if there are no more Explorers or Inspectors, to see if the Teardown method should be called to release the addin's objects. This check is more necessary in earlier versions of Outlook than in Outlook 2007, but it doesn't hurt. This allows you to handle cases where Outlook was started using automation and a user interface was added later and then closed, leaving the automation code keeping the Outlook session open.

Listing 10-13

```
#region explorer_related_events
// NewExplorer event will be raised if there is UI
private void m_Explorers_NewExplorer(
  Microsoft.Office.Interop.Outlook.Explorer Explorer)
{
    //assign ActiveExplorer
    m_Explorer = Explorer;

    if (m_Init == false)
    {
        //we didn't have UI before - initialize add-in objects
        InitHandler();
    }

    if (m_Init == true)
    {
        OutExpl adder = new OutExpl();

        m_WrapperID = adder.AddExpl(Explorer, m_WrapperID,
          ref m_ExplWrap);

        adder = null;
    }
}

// Monitor Explorer_Close to see when UI "disappears"
private void m_Explorer_Close()
{
    //release current reference
    m_Explorer = null;
    try
    {
        m_Explorer = m_Outlook.ActiveExplorer();
    }
    catch
    {
        if (m_Outlook.Inspectors.Count == 0)
        {
            //release add-in objects
            if (m_Teardown == false) TearDown();
        }
    }
}
#endregion
```

The code in Listing 10-14 handles the `NewInspector` and `m_InspectorClass_Close` events. When the `NewInspector` event fires, the `Inspector` is checked to make sure that it isn't showing a `Note` item. If it is a `Note` item, the item is ignored. Handling `Inspector` events for `Note` items can lead to Outlook crashes. The class-level `m_Inspector` object is set to the new `Inspector`, and a `Close` event handler is added to the `Inspector`. If the item is a `Task` item, a new instance of a custom task pane is created and set to assume a fixed position at the right side of its parent window, the new `Inspector`. The `Inspector` is added to the `Inspector SortedList` wrapper collection to keep references to it alive and allow handling of events fired in that `Inspector`.

The `Class` of the `Inspector` is retrieved using reflection with the following code:

```
object item = Inspector.CurrentItem;

Type _type;
_type = item.GetType();

object[] _args = new Object[] { };  // dummy argument array
Outlook.OlObjectClass _class = Outlook.OlObjectClass.olNote;

try // try to get the Class using reflection
{
    _class = (Outlook.OlObjectClass)_type.InvokeMember(
        "Class", BindingFlags.Public |
        BindingFlags.GetField | BindingFlags.GetProperty,
        null, item, _args);
}
catch (Exception ex)
{
    MessageBox.Show(ex.Message);
    _class = Outlook.OlObjectClass.olNote;
}
```

When the `m_InspectorClass_Close` event fires, an attempt is made to assign `ActiveInspector` to the `m_Inspector` object. If that fails and there are no open `Explorers`, the `Teardown` method is called to release the addin's objects.

Listing 10-14

```
#region inspector_related_events
private void m_Inspectors_NewInspector(
  Microsoft.Office.Interop.Outlook.Inspector Inspector)
{
    //No handling of Inspectors for Notes, they are brain dead

    // set up to get the Class property of the item in the Inspector
    object item = Inspector.CurrentItem;

    Type _type;
    _type = item.GetType();

    object[] _args = new Object[] { };  // dummy argument array
    Outlook.OlObjectClass _class = Outlook.OlObjectClass.olNote;
```

(continued)

Listing 10-14 *(continued)*

```
try // try to get the Class using reflection
{
    _class = (Outlook.OlObjectClass)_type.InvokeMember(
      "Class", BindingFlags.Public |
      BindingFlags.GetField | BindingFlags.GetProperty,
      null, item, _args);
}
catch (Exception ex)
{
    MessageBox.Show(ex.Message);
    _class = Outlook.OlObjectClass.olNote;
}

if (_class != Outlook.OlObjectClass.olNote)
{
    m_Inspector = Inspector;

    try
    {
        m_InspectorClass = (Outlook.InspectorClass)m_Inspector;
        m_InspectorClass.InspectorEvents_Event_Close +=
          new Microsoft.Office.Interop.Outlook.
          InspectorEvents_CloseEventHandler(
          m_InspectorClass_Close);

        OutInsp adder = new OutInsp();

        switch (_class)
        {
            case Outlook.OlObjectClass.olTask:
                CTP = m_CTP.CreateCTP(CTP_PROGID,
                  CTP_TITLE, Inspector);

                CTP.DockPositionRestrict =
                  Office.MsoCTPDockPositionRestrict.
                  msoCTPDockPositionRestrictNoChange;

                CTP.DockPosition =
                  Office.MsoCTPDockPosition.
                  msoCTPDockPositionRight;

                CTP.Visible = false;
                break;
            default:
                {
                    break;
                }
        }

        // m_Ribbon is a dummy, filled in when
        // Ribbon_OnLoad fires
```

Listing 10-14 *(continued)*

```
                m_WrapperID = adder.AddInsp(Inspector,
                    m_WrapperID, _class, ref m_InspWrap,
                    CTP, m_Ribbon);

                adder = null;
            }
            catch (Exception ex)
            {
                MessageBox.Show(ex.Message);
            }
        }
    }

    private void m_InspectorClass_Close()
    {
        m_Inspector = null;

        try
        {
            m_Inspector = m_Outlook.ActiveInspector();
        }
        catch
        {
            if (m_Inspector == null)
            {
                if (m_Outlook.Explorers.Count == 0)
                {
                    if (m_Teardown == false)
                    {
                        TearDown();
                    }
                }
            }
        }
    }
#endregion
```

The code in Listing 10-15 shows the Ribbon callbacks used in the addin and the `IRibbonUI` property declared in Listing 10-10 as `m_Ribbon`.

The `CS_Action` callback is called when the user clicks either of the Ribbon controls. The `control` object passed to `CS_Action` contains `Context` and `Id` properties that are essential in knowing which control was clicked and in which `Inspector`. The `Inspector` where the control was clicked is contained in the `Context` property, and the control's XML `id` attribute is contained in the `Id` property.

The `Inspector` wrapper collection is iterated through to find the `Inspector` where the Ribbon control click occurred. This is possible because the wrapper class stores a reference to the `Inspector` it's wrapping. After the `Inspector` is found either the task pane visibility is toggled if the `Id` is `Tasks1` or a child task is created if the `Id` is `Tasks2`. A child task is created by calling the `AddChildTask` method exposed in the `Inspector` wrapper.

The CS_GetImage callback is called when the Ribbon requests an image for a control. A Switch block is used to test the control.Id property to see which PNG file to return from the project resources. The file is converted into an IPictureDisp object, which is required by the Ribbon, using the AxHost class implementation shown in Listing 10-17.

The Ribbon_OnLoad event fires when the Ribbon is loading. This event fires on the first Inspector opened in an Outlook Session some time after the NewInspector event fires, so this event is used to update the Ribbon property in each open Inspector when the event fires.

Listing 10-15

```
#region Ribbon_Stuff
#region Ribbon_Initializer
public string GetCustomUI(string RibbonID)
{
    //Implements IRibbonExtensibility.GetCustomUI

    //RibbonID indicates type of Inspector about to be displayed,
    //   valid RibbonID values are as follows:
    //Microsoft.Outlook.Mail.Read
    //Microsoft.Outlook.Mail.Compose
    //Microsoft.Outlook.MeetingRequest.Read
    //Microsoft.Outlook.MeetingRequest.Send
    //Microsoft.Outlook.Appointment
    //Microsoft.Outlook.Contact
    //Microsoft.Outlook.Journal
    //Microsoft.Outlook.Task
    //Microsoft.Outlook.DistributionList
    //Microsoft.Outlook.Report
    //Microsoft.Outlook.Resend
    //Microsoft.Outlook.Response.Read
    //Microsoft.Outlook.Response.Compose
    //Microsoft.Outlook.Response.CounterPropose
    //Microsoft.Outlook.RSS
    //Microsoft.Outlook.Post.Read
    //Microsoft.Outlook.Post.Compose
    //Microsoft.Outlook.Sharing.Read
    //Microsoft.Outlook.Sharing.Compose

    //In this sample only new Task Inspector is handled.

    switch (RibbonID)
    {
        case "Microsoft.Outlook.Task":
            // Return the RibbonX markup stored as a resource
            return Properties.Resources.CustomRibbon;
        default:
            {
                return String.Empty;
            }
    }
}
#endregion
```

Listing 10-15 *(continued)*

```
#region Ribbon_Callbacks
public void CS_Action(Office.IRibbonControl control)
{
    if (control.Id == "CSTasks1")
    {
        try
        {
            Outlook.Inspector myInsp =
                (Outlook.Inspector)control.Context;

            int j = m_InspWrap.Count;

            for (int i = 0; i < j; i++)
            {
                InspWrap wrapped =
                    (InspWrap)m_InspWrap.GetByIndex(i);

                if (wrapped.Inspector == myInsp)
                {
                    wrapped.TaskPane.Visible = true;
                }
                else
                {
                    wrapped.TaskPane.Visible = false;
                }
            }
        }
        catch (Exception ex)
        {
            MessageBox.Show(ex.Message);
        }
    }
    else
    {
        if (control.Id == "CSTasks2")
        {
            try
            {
                Outlook.Inspector myInsp =
                    (Outlook.Inspector)control.Context;

                int j = m_InspWrap.Count;

                for (int i = 0; i < j; i++)
                {
                    InspWrap wrapped =
                        (InspWrap)m_InspWrap.GetByIndex(i);

                    if (wrapped.Inspector == myInsp)
                    {
                        wrapped.AddChildTask();
                    }
                }
            }
```

(continued)

Listing 10-15 *(continued)*

```
                catch (Exception ex)
                {
                    MessageBox.Show(ex.Message);
                }
            }
        }
    }

    public stdole.IPictureDisp CS_GetImage(
      Office.IRibbonControl control)
    {
        System.Drawing.Image imgStreamPic;
        IPictureDisp oPic = null;
        MyAxHost ax = new MyAxHost();

        switch (control.Id)
        {
            case "CSTasks1":
                imgStreamPic = Properties.Resources.Task;
                break;
            case "CSTasks2":
                imgStreamPic = Properties.Resources.Related;
                break;
            default:
                {
                    imgStreamPic = null;
                    break;
                }
        }

        if (imgStreamPic != null)
        {
            oPic = ax.IPictureDispFromImage(imgStreamPic);
        }

        imgStreamPic = null;
        ax = null;

        return oPic;
    }

    public void Ribbon_OnLoad(Office.IRibbonUI Ribbon)
    {
        m_Ribbon = Ribbon;

        int j = m_InspWrap.Count;

        for (int i = 0; i < j; i++)
        {
            InspWrap wrapped = (InspWrap)m_InspWrap.GetByIndex(i);
```

Listing 10-15 *(continued)*

```
            if (wrapped.Ribbon == null)
            {
                wrapped.Ribbon = m_Ribbon;
            }
        }
    }
#endregion

#region Ribbon_Properties
public Office.IRibbonUI Ribbon
{
    get
    {
        return m_Ribbon;
    }
}
#endregion

#endregion
```

The code in Listing 10-16 is used to handle the CTPFactoryAvailable event, which is the one event required by the ICustomTaskPaneConsumer interface and is fired when the COM TaskPane factory is available to create new task pane instances. This factory instance is stored in a module-level object so that it is available whenever a new task pane has to be created.

Listing 10-16

```
#region TaskPane
public void CTPFactoryAvailable(Office.ICTPFactory CTPFactoryInst)
{
    //Implements Office.ICustomTaskPaneConsumer.CTPFactoryAvailable

    // store the Custom Task Pane factory instance
    m_CTP = CTPFactoryInst;
}
#endregion
    }
}
```

C# MyAxHost

The MyAxHost class is used in the C# code to convert the PNG file images stored as resources in the project into IPictureDisp objects to pass to the Ribbon for use as button images. The Ribbon requires that any button image is passed to the getImage callback as an IPictureDisp object. IPictureDisp objects can only be passed within the same process, an IPictureDisp object cannot be passed across process boundaries. This means that the code will work in a COM addin, which runs in-process with Outlook but wouldn't work in a standalone application or other out-of-process code that automates Outlook.

Listing 10-17

```csharp
using System;
using System.Collections.Generic;
using System.Text;
using System.Drawing;
using Office = Microsoft.Office.Core;
using System.Diagnostics;
using System.IO;
using System.Windows.Forms;
using System.Reflection;
using stdole;

namespace TaskManagerCS
{
    /// <summary>
    /// The MyAxHost is derived from AxHost to use the function
    /// AxHost.GetIPictureDispFromPicture(image);
    /// that returns an IPictureDisp interface from an Image.
    /// </summary>
    class MyAxHost : System.Windows.Forms.AxHost
    {

        /// <summary>
        /// Overloaded constructor with CLSID for the ribbon
        /// </summary>
        public MyAxHost()
            : base("{59EE46BA-677D-4d20-BF10-8D8067CB8B33}")
        {
        }

        public stdole.IPictureDisp IPictureDispFromImage(
          System.Drawing.Image image)
        {
            IPictureDisp oPic = null;

            try
            {
                // Convert the Resource bitmap to stdole.IPictureDisp
                oPic = (stdole.IPictureDisp)
                  AxHost.GetIPictureDispFromPicture(image);
                return oPic;
            }
            catch (System.Exception ex)
            {
                Debug.WriteLine(ex.Message);
                return oPic;
            }
        }
    }
}
```

VB Globals

The VB code uses a Globals code module declared with Friend scope, which makes the objects and variables available to the code in the addin but not to outside code. The wrapper collections for Explorers and Inspectors as well as Outlook.Application and NameSpace objects are declared as Public to make them available anywhere in the addin code.

The constant declarations for ParentTag and ChildTag used for the ParentTask and ChildTasks named properties are constructed by using the http://schemas.microsoft.com/mapi/string namespace concatenated with the GUID of the addin, {C4AF1D53-1F7B-4e17-87E9-D44198617FFC}, and the name of the named property. This creates a unique namespace for the properties that prevents any possible property naming collisions with other code.

Listing 10-18

```
Imports Outlook = Microsoft.Office.Interop.Outlook

Friend Module Globals
    Public g_strProgID As String

    Public g_WrapperID As Integer

    Public g_OutlookVersion As Integer

    Public g_colExplWrap As New Collection
    Public g_colInspWrap As New Collection

    Public g_objOL As Outlook.Application
    Public g_objNS As Outlook.NameSpace

    Public Const ParentTag As String = _
       "http://schemas.microsoft.com/mapi/string/" _
       & "{C4AF1D53-1F7B-4e17-87E9-D44198617FFC}/ParentTask"

    Public Const ChildTag As String = _
       "http://schemas.microsoft.com/mapi/string/" _
       & "{C4AF1D53-1F7B-4e17-87E9-D44198617FFC}/ChildTasks"

End Module
```

VB OutExpl

The code in Listing 10-19 shows the methods used to add and remove instances of the Explorer wrapper class ExplWrap to and from the global g_colExplWrap collection. The code sets the Explorer property of the wrapper class to the Explorer passed to the AddExpl method and sets the Key property to the next key value used to retrieve the Explorer from its wrapper collection. When the Explorer is closed, the KillExpl method is called from within the Explorer.Close event handler to remove the ExplWrap class from the wrapper collection, which allows the class and the objects declared in it to be released when they go out of scope.

Listing 10-19

```vb
Imports Outlook = Microsoft.Office.Interop.Outlook
Imports System.Windows.Forms

Friend Module OutExpl

    Public Sub AddExpl(ByVal Explorer As Outlook.Explorer)
        Dim objExplWrap As New ExplWrap

        Try
            objExplWrap.Explorer = Explorer

            objExplWrap.Key = g_WrapperID

            g_colExplWrap.Add(objExplWrap, CStr(g_WrapperID))

            g_WrapperID += 1

        Catch ex As Exception
            MessageBox.Show(ex.Message)
        End Try

        objExplWrap = Nothing
    End Sub

    Public Sub KillExpl(ByVal WrapperID As Integer)
        Try
            g_colExplWrap.Remove(CStr(WrapperID))
        Catch ex As Exception
            MessageBox.Show(ex.Message)
        End Try
    End Sub
End Module
```

C# OutExpl

The code in Listing 10-20 shows the methods used to add and remove instances of the `Explorer` wrapper class `ExplWrap` to the global `SortedList` wrapper collection. The code sets the `Explorer` property of the wrapper class to the `Explorer` passed to the `AddExpl` method and sets the `Key` property to the next key value used to retrieve the `Explorer` from its wrapper collection. A reference to the `SortedList` wrapper collection is also stored in the `Explorer` wrapper class to allow the code in the class to reference itself within the `SortedList` collection. When the `Explorer` is closed, the `KillExpl` method is called from within the `Explorer.Close` event handler to remove the `ExplWrap` class from the wrapper collection, which allows the class and the objects declared in it to be released when they go out of scope.

Listing 10-20

```csharp
using System;
using System.Collections.Generic;
using System.Text;
```

Listing 10-20 *(continued)*

```csharp
using Outlook = Microsoft.Office.Interop.Outlook;
using System.Windows.Forms;

namespace TaskManagerCS
{
    class OutExpl
    {
        public int AddExpl(Outlook.Explorer Explorer, int WrapperID,
          ref System.Collections.SortedList WrapperCol)
        {
            ExplWrap objExplWrap = new ExplWrap();

            try
            {
                objExplWrap.Explorer = Explorer;

                objExplWrap.Key = WrapperID;

                objExplWrap.WrapperClass = WrapperCol;

                // add wrapper class to the collection to keep it alive
                WrapperCol.Add(WrapperID, objExplWrap);

                WrapperID += 1;
            }
            catch (Exception ex)
            {
                MessageBox.Show(ex.Message);
            }

            objExplWrap = null;

            return WrapperID;
        }

        public void KillExpl(int WrapperID,
          System.Collections.SortedList WrapperCol)
        {
            try
            {
                // remove wrapper class from wrapper collection
                WrapperCol.Remove(WrapperID);
            }
            catch (Exception ex)
            {
                MessageBox.Show(ex.Message);
            }
        }
    }
}
```

VB ExplWrap

The code in Listing 10-21 shows the Explorer wrapper class ExplWrap. This class is used to handle events fired by the Explorer within that Explorer, allowing event handling to be specific to only that one Explorer instance. In this addin, the Explorer events that are handled are the Activate, SelectionChange, and Close events. The Activate and SelectionChange events aren't used here but usually are used to create any CommandBar user interface required for the Explorer.

> When a new Explorer is opened, the NewExplorer event provides a weak object reference to the new Explorer. Many of the properties of the Explorer aren't populated when NewExplorer fires; they only become populated when the first Activate event fires. Activate events are usually used to add user interface elements to an Explorer. If Outlook is started with a user interface, the initial Activate event may not fire on the original Explorer opened by Outlook. In that case, as the startup folder receives focus, the SelectionChange event fires, so that is also used to create user interface for the Explorer, usually by checking a flag value that is set True when the user interface is created. This flag is tested in both the Activate and SelectionChange event handlers so that duplicate user interfaces aren't created in the Explorer.

When the Explorer.Close event fires, the code removes that instance of ExplWrap from the Explorer wrapper collection by calling the KillExpl method to allow the wrapper class to go out of scope and be released.

Listing 10-21

```vb
Imports Outlook = Microsoft.Office.Interop.Outlook
Imports Office = Microsoft.Office.Core
Imports System.Windows.Forms
Imports System.Diagnostics
Imports System
Imports System.Collections.Generic
Imports System.Text
Imports System.Runtime.InteropServices
Imports stdole

Friend Class ExplWrap
    Private WithEvents m_objExpl As Outlook.Explorer

    Private m_ID As Integer

    Private m_blnStartup As Boolean

    Private m_blnKilled As Boolean

    Public Property Explorer() As Outlook.Explorer
        Get
            Explorer = m_objExpl
        End Get

        Set(ByVal value As Outlook.Explorer)
            m_objExpl = value
            m_blnStartup = True
        End Set
```

Listing 10-21 *(continued)*

```vbnet
        End Property

        Public Property Key() As Integer
            Get
                Key = m_ID
            End Get

            Set(ByVal value As Integer)
                m_ID = value
            End Set
        End Property

        Public Sub New()
            m_blnKilled = False

            Try
                m_objExpl = Nothing
            Catch ex As Exception
                MessageBox.Show(ex.Message)
            End Try
        End Sub

        Private Sub m_objExpl_Activate() Handles m_objExpl.Activate
        End Sub

        Private Sub m_objExpl_SelectionChange() Handles m_objExpl.SelectionChange
        End Sub

        Private Sub m_objExpl_Close() Handles m_objExpl.Close
            If Not m_blnKilled Then
                m_blnKilled = True
                KillExpl(m_ID)

                If m_objExpl IsNot Nothing Then
                    m_objExpl = Nothing
                End If
            End If
        End Sub
    End Class
```

C# ExplWrap

The code in Listing 10-22 shows part of the Explorer wrapper class ExplWrap. This class is used to handle events fired by the Explorer within that Explorer, allowing event handling to be specific to only that one Explorer instance. In this addin, the Explorer events that are handled are the Activate, SelectionChange, and Close events. The Activate and SelectionChange events aren't used here but usually are used to create any CommandBar user interface required for the Explorer. When the Explorer property of the wrapper class is set, the event handlers for the Explorer are added to the wrapper class.

Listing 10-22

```
using System;
using System.Collections.Generic;
using System.Text;
using System.Runtime.InteropServices;
using Outlook = Microsoft.Office.Interop.Outlook;
using Office = Microsoft.Office.Core;
using System.Windows.Forms;
using stdole;

namespace TaskManagerCS
{
    class ExplWrap
    {
        private Outlook.Explorer m_Expl = null;
        private Outlook.ExplorerClass m_ExplClass = null;

        private int m_ID = 0;

        private bool m_Killed = false;

        private System.Collections.SortedList m_WrapperClass = null;

        public System.Collections.SortedList WrapperClass
        {
            get
            {
                return m_WrapperClass;
            }

            set
            {
                m_WrapperClass = value;
            }
        }

        public Outlook.Explorer Explorer
        {
            get
            {
                return m_Expl;
            }

            set
            {
                m_Expl = value;

                m_ExplClass = (Outlook.ExplorerClass)m_Expl;

                // hook up the Close event handler
                m_ExplClass.ExplorerEvents_Event_Close +=
                  new Outlook.ExplorerEvents_CloseEventHandler(
                  m_Expl_Close);
```

Listing 10-22 *(continued)*

```
                // hook up the Activate event handler
                m_ExplClass.ExplorerEvents_Event_Activate +=
                new Outlook.ExplorerEvents_ActivateEventHandler(
                m_Expl_Activate);

                // hook up the SelectionChange event handler
                m_Expl.SelectionChange += new
                    Outlook.ExplorerEvents_10_SelectionChangeEventHandler(
                    m_Expl_SelectionChange);

                m_Killed = false;
            }
        }

        public int Key
        {
            get
            {
                return m_ID;
            }

            set
            {
                m_ID = value;
            }
        }
    }
```

The code in Listing 10-23 shows the unused `Activate` and `SelectionChange` event handlers as well as the `Close` event handler. When the `Close` event fires, the code removes that instance of `ExplWrap` from the `Explorer` wrapper collection by calling the `KillExpl` method to allow the wrapper class to go out of scope and be released.

Listing 10-23

```
        private void m_Expl_Activate()
        {
        }

        private void m_Expl_SelectionChange()
        {
        }

        private void m_Expl_Close()
        {
            if (m_Killed == false)
            {
                m_Killed = true;

                OutExpl killer = new OutExpl();
                killer.KillExpl(m_ID, m_WrapperClass);
                killer = null;
```

(continued)

Listing 10-23 (continued)

```
            m_WrapperClass = null;

            // release the Close event handler
            m_ExplClass.ExplorerEvents_Event_Close -= new
              Outlook.ExplorerEvents_CloseEventHandler(
              m_Expl_Close);

            // release the Activate handler
            m_ExplClass.ExplorerEvents_Event_Activate -= new
              Outlook.ExplorerEvents_ActivateEventHandler(
              m_Expl_Activate);

            // release the SelectionChange handler
            m_Expl.SelectionChange -= new
              Outlook.ExplorerEvents_10_SelectionChangeEventHandler(
              m_Expl_SelectionChange);

            if (m_Expl != null) { m_Expl = null; }
            if (m_ExplClass != null) { m_ExplClass = null; }
        }
    }
  }
}
```

VB OutInsp

The code in Listing 10-24 shows the methods used to add and remove instances of the Inspector wrapper class InspWrap to the global g_colInspWrap collection. The code sets the Inspector property of the wrapper class to the Inspector passed to the AddInsp method and sets the Key property to the next key value used to retrieve the Inspector from its wrapper collection if the item in the Inspector is a Task item. The TaskItem property of the Inspector wrapper class is set to the TaskItem in the Inspector .CurrentItem, and a copy of the IRibbonUI and CustomTaskPane objects used for the Ribbon and custom task pane in the Inspector are also set.

When the first Inspector is opened in an Outlook session, the IRibbonUI object hasn't been instantiated yet, which happens when the Ribbon_OnLoad event fires, some time after NewInspector fires and before the first Inspector.Activate event fires in that Inspector. When Ribbon_OnLoad fires, the event handler code iterates through the Inspector wrapper collection and sets the IRibbonUI object reference in the wrapper class to the instance of the Ribbon passed to Ribbon_OnLoad.

When the Inspector is closed, the KillInsp method is called from within the Inspector.Close event handler to remove the InspWrap class from the wrapper collection, which allows the class and the objects declared in it to be released when they go out of scope.

Listing 10-24

```
Imports Outlook = Microsoft.Office.Interop.Outlook
Imports Office = Microsoft.Office.Core
Imports System.Windows.Forms
```

Listing 10-24 *(continued)*

```
Friend Module OutInsp

    Public Sub AddInsp(ByVal Inspector As Outlook.Inspector, _
        ByVal Pane As Office.CustomTaskPane, _
        ByVal Ribbon As Office.IRibbonUI)

        Dim objInspWrap As New InspWrap
        Dim oTask As Outlook.TaskItem = Nothing

        If (TypeOf (Inspector.CurrentItem) Is Outlook.TaskItem) Then
            oTask = TryCast(Inspector.CurrentItem, Outlook.TaskItem)
            If oTask IsNot Nothing Then
                Try
                    With objInspWrap
                        .Inspector = Inspector
                        .TaskItem = oTask
                        .Ribbon = Ribbon
                        .TaskPane = Pane

                        .Key = g_WrapperID
                    End With

                    g_colInspWrap.Add(objInspWrap, CStr(g_WrapperID))

                    g_WrapperID += 1

                Catch ex As Exception
                    MessageBox.Show(ex.Message)
                End Try
            End If
        End If

        objInspWrap = Nothing
        oTask = Nothing
    End Sub

    Public Sub KillInsp(ByVal WrapperID As Integer)
        Try
            g_colInspWrap.Remove(CStr(WrapperID))
        Catch ex As Exception
            MessageBox.Show(ex.Message)
        End Try
    End Sub

End Module
```

C# OutInsp

The code in Listing 10-25 shows the methods used to add and remove instances of the Inspector wrapper class InspWrap to and from the SortedList Inspector wrapper collection. The code sets the Inspector property of the wrapper class to the Inspector passed to the AddInsp method and sets the Key property to the next key value used to retrieve the Inspector from its wrapper collection if the item in the

Inspector is a Task item. The TaskItem property of the Inspector wrapper class is set to the TaskItem in the Inspector.CurrentItem, and a copy of the IRibbonUI and CustomTaskPane objects used for the Ribbon and custom task pane in the Inspector are also set. A reference to the SortedList wrapper collection is also set in the InspWrap wrapper class to allow referencing of the Inspector wrapper class in the wrapper collection.

When the first Inspector is opened in an Outlook session, the IRibbonUI object hasn't been instantiated yet, which happens when the Ribbon_OnLoad event fires, some time after NewInspector fires and before the first Inspector.Activate event fires in that Inspector. When Ribbon_OnLoad fires the event handler code iterates through the Inspector wrapper collection and sets the IRibbonUI object reference in the wrapper class to the instance of the Ribbon passed to Ribbon_OnLoad.

When the Inspector is closed the KillInsp method is called from within the Inspector.Close event handler to remove the InspWrap class from the wrapper collection, which allows the class and the objects declared in it to be released when they go out of scope.

Listing 10-25

```csharp
using System;
using System.Collections.Generic;
using System.Text;
using Outlook = Microsoft.Office.Interop.Outlook;
using System.Windows.Forms;
using Office = Microsoft.Office.Core;

namespace TaskManagerCS
{
    class OutInsp
    {
        public int AddInsp(Outlook.Inspector Inspector, int WrapperID,
            Outlook.OlObjectClass InspectorType,
            ref System.Collections.SortedList WrapperCol,
            Office.CustomTaskPane Pane, Office.IRibbonUI Ribbon)
        {
            InspWrap objInspWrap = new InspWrap();
            Outlook.TaskItem oTask = null;

            switch (InspectorType)
            {
                case Outlook.OlObjectClass.olTask:
                    try
                    {
                        oTask = (Outlook.TaskItem)Inspector.CurrentItem;
                    }
                    catch (Exception ex)
                    {
                        MessageBox.Show(ex.Message);
                    }

                    if (oTask != null)
                    {
```

Listing 10-25 *(continued)*

```
                    try
                    {
                        objInspWrap.Inspector = Inspector;
                        objInspWrap.TaskItem = oTask;
                        objInspWrap.Key = WrapperID;
                        objInspWrap.WrapperClass = WrapperCol;
                        objInspWrap.TaskPane = Pane;
                        objInspWrap.Ribbon = Ribbon;

                        // add wrapper class to the collection
                        // to keep it alive
                        WrapperCol.Add(WrapperID, objInspWrap);

                        WrapperID += 1;
                    }
                    catch (Exception ex)
                    {
                        MessageBox.Show(ex.Message);
                    }
                }
                break;
        }

        objInspWrap = null;
        oTask = null;

        return WrapperID;
    }

    public void KillInsp(int WrapperID,
      System.Collections.SortedList WrapperCol)
    {
        // remove wrapper class from wrapper collection
        try { WrapperCol.Remove(WrapperID); }
        catch (Exception ex)
        {
            MessageBox.Show(ex.Message);
        }
    }
}
}
```

VB InspWrap

The declarations part of the `Inspector` wrapper class `InspWrap` is shown in Listing 10-26. Event-aware declarations are made for the `Inspector`, `TaskItem`, and `CustomTaskPane` objects, and local instances of the `IRibbonUI` and `TaskPane` objects are declared. Public properties for the `Ribbon`, `TaskPane`, `TaskItem`, `Inspector`, and `Key` are also declared in this section of the wrapper class code.

Listing 10-26

```
Imports Outlook = Microsoft.Office.Interop.Outlook
Imports Office = Microsoft.Office.Core
Imports System.Windows.Forms

Friend Class InspWrap
    Private WithEvents m_objInsp As Outlook.Inspector
    Private WithEvents m_objTask As Outlook.TaskItem

    Private WithEvents m_Pane As Office.CustomTaskPane = Nothing
    Private m_Control As TaskPane = Nothing

    Private m_Ribbon As Office.IRibbonUI

    Private m_ID As Integer
    Private m_blnKilled As Boolean

    Private m_Startup As Boolean

    Public Property Ribbon() As Office.IRibbonUI
        Get
            Return m_Ribbon
        End Get

        Set(ByVal value As Office.IRibbonUI)
            m_Ribbon = value
        End Set
    End Property

    Public Property TaskPane() As Office.CustomTaskPane
        Get
            Return m_Pane
        End Get

        Set(ByVal value As Office.CustomTaskPane)
            m_Pane = value
        End Set
    End Property

    Public Property TaskItem() As Outlook.TaskItem
        Get
            Return m_objTask
        End Get

        Set(ByVal value As Outlook.TaskItem)
            m_objTask = value
        End Set
    End Property

    Public Property Inspector() As Outlook.Inspector
        Get
            Return m_objInsp
```

Listing 10-26 *(continued)*

```
        End Get

        Set(ByVal value As Outlook.Inspector)
            m_objInsp = value

            m_Startup = True
        End Set
    End Property

    Public Property Key() As Integer
        Get
            Return m_ID
        End Get

        Set(ByVal value As Integer)
            m_ID = value
        End Set
    End Property
```

Listing 10-27 shows the code for the AddChildTask method. This is called when the user clicks the Ribbon button Add Child Task, and is declared as a Public method, so it can be called from the Ribbon onAction callback in the Connect class. Adding a child task requires three steps:

1. Create a new task that will be the child task, and save it so that it has a valid EntryID property.

2. Add a property to the child task ParentTask that holds the EntryID of the parent task, to allow retrieval of the parent from the child.

3. Add a property named ChildTasks to the parent task, if it doesn't already exist. This property is used to hold the EntryIDs of all child tasks of a parent task.

The parent property is a simple string property, because each task can have only one parent. The child property is a multi-valued property, because each task can have many child tasks. The values of the child tasks property are read and written using an array of strings, where each array element represents one child task.

The GUID of the addin is used as the GUID of the named properties. This ensures that there are no naming collisions with other addins or Outlook code, as might occur if the PS_PUBLIC_STRINGS namespace were used. The PS_PUBLIC_STRINGS namespace is used for properties added to the UserProperties collection and also by many addins. Common properties added to Outlook items only if they contain data, such as FlagRequest, also use the PS_PUBLIC_STRINGS namespace.

The properties are created using the http://schemas.microsoft.com/mapi/string namespace, so they aren't visible in the Outlook user interface, as they would be if they were created as properties added to the UserProperties collection.

After the child task is created and the parent and child properties are set in the parent and child tasks, the new child task is displayed.

Listing 10-27

```
Public Sub AddChildTask()
    If m_objTask IsNot Nothing Then
        Try
            If m_Pane IsNot Nothing Then
                If m_objTask.EntryID <> "" Then
                    Dim _Task As Outlook.TaskItem = Nothing

                    _Task = CType(g_objOL.CreateItem( _
                      Outlook.OlItemType.olTaskItem), _
                      Outlook.TaskItem)

                    If (_Task IsNot Nothing) Then
                        _Task.Save()

                        Dim ItemID As String = m_objTask.EntryID

                        Dim _Accessor As _
                          Outlook.PropertyAccessor = Nothing

                        Dim sParent() As String = {ItemID}

                        _Accessor = _Task.PropertyAccessor
                        If (_Accessor IsNot Nothing) Then
                            Try
                                _Accessor.SetProperty(ParentTag, _
                                  sParent)

                            Catch ex As Exception
                            End Try

                        End If

                        _Task.Save()
                        ItemID = _Task.EntryID

                        Dim count As Integer

                        Dim oAccessor As _
                          Outlook.PropertyAccessor = Nothing

                        oAccessor = m_objTask.PropertyAccessor
                        If (oAccessor IsNot Nothing) Then
                            Dim children() As String
                            Try
                                children = _
                                  oAccessor.GetProperty(ChildTag)

                                Try
                                    Dim result As Boolean = False
                                    count = children.GetLength(0)
                                    For i As Integer = 0 To count - 1
                                        If children(i) = ItemID Then
                                            result = True
```

Listing 10-27 *(continued)*

```
                                                Exit For
                                        End If
                                Next
                                If Not result Then
                                        Dim ChildrenCopy(count) _
                                          As String

                                        children.CopyTo(ChildrenCopy, 0)
                                        ChildrenCopy(count) = ItemID
                                        oAccessor. _
                                          SetProperty(ChildTag, _
                                          ChildrenCopy)

                                        m_objTask.Save()
                                End If
                        Catch ex As Exception
                                MessageBox.Show(ex.Message)
                        End Try
                Catch ex As Exception
                        Dim ChildrenCopy() As String = {ItemID}

                        oAccessor._
                          SetProperty(ChildTag, ChildrenCopy)

                        m_objTask.Save()
                End Try
            End If

            _Task.Display()

            _Task = Nothing

                    End If
                End If
            End If
        Catch ex As Exception
                MessageBox.Show(ex.Message)
        End Try
    End If
End Sub
```

The code in Listing 10-28 shows the event handlers encapsulated in the Inspector wrapper class. The class handles the Inspector's Activate and Close events and the Close, Open, Unload, and Write events for the TaskItem in the Inspector. The task events are blanks, not used in this addin.

The Activate event is used to call the Init method of the task pane UserControl if the Inspector is first being activated. The m_Pane TaskPane object declared at class level is used to instantiate the m_Control object that represents the ContentControl of the UserControl. The ContentControl exposes any public properties, methods, and events in the UserControl object, and is used when calling the Init method. Finally, the Ribbon control is invalidated, which forces an update of the Ribbon and fires the getImage callback for each Ribbon control.

The `Inspector.Close` event is used to release all the class-level objects in the wrapper class and to remove the wrapper class from the `Inspector` wrapper collection by calling the `KillInsp` method.

Listing 10-28

```
    Private Sub m_objInsp_Activate() Handles m_objInsp.Activate
        If m_Startup Then
            If m_objTask IsNot Nothing Then
                If (m_Ribbon IsNot Nothing) Then
                    If (m_Pane IsNot Nothing) Then
                        m_Control = CType(m_Pane.ContentControl, TaskPane)
                        If m_Control IsNot Nothing Then
                            m_Control.Init(Me.m_objTask.EntryID)
                        End If
                        m_Ribbon.Invalidate()

                        m_Startup = False
                    End If
                End If
            End If
        End If
    End Sub

    Private Sub m_objInsp_Close() Handles m_objInsp.Close
        If Not m_blnKilled Then
            m_blnKilled = True
            KillInsp(m_ID)

            If m_objTask IsNot Nothing Then
                m_objTask = Nothing
            End If

            If m_objInsp IsNot Nothing Then
                m_objInsp = Nothing
            End If

            If m_Pane IsNot Nothing Then
                m_Pane.Delete()
                m_Pane = Nothing
            End If

            If m_Ribbon IsNot Nothing Then
                m_Ribbon = Nothing
            End If

        End If
    End Sub

    Private Sub m_objTask_Close(ByRef Cancel As Boolean) _
      Handles m_objTask.Close

    End Sub
```

Listing 10-28 *(continued)*

```
    Private Sub m_objTask_Open(ByRef Cancel As Boolean) _
      Handles m_objTask.Open

    End Sub

    Private Sub m_objTask_Unload() Handles m_objTask.Unload

    End Sub

    Private Sub m_objTask_Write(ByRef Cancel As Boolean) _
      Handles m_objTask.Write

    End Sub
```

The code in Listing 10-29 completes the code for the InspWrap Inspector wrapper class. This code shows the event handlers for the two events exposed by the CustomTaskPane object, DockPositionStateChange and VisibleStateChange. The task pane position is fixed at the right side of the Inspector window when the task pane is created, so the DockPositionStateChange event handler isn't used in the addin. The VisibleStateChange event handler is used to test for the visibility of the task pane. If it's visible, the Init method of the task pane UserControl is called to initialize the treeview control of the task pane. The Init method is passed the EntryID of the TaskItem displayed in the Inspector so that it can retrieve that item and work with its ParentTask and ChildTasks properties.

Listing 10-29

```
    Private Sub m_Pane_DockPositionStateChange(ByVal _
      CustomTaskPaneInst As Microsoft.Office.Core.CustomTaskPane) _
      Handles m_Pane.DockPositionStateChange

    End Sub

    Private Sub m_Pane_VisibleStateChange(ByVal CustomTaskPaneInst _
      As Microsoft.Office.Core.CustomTaskPane) _
      Handles m_Pane.VisibleStateChange

      If CustomTaskPaneInst.Visible = True Then
          m_Control.Init(Me.m_objTask.EntryID)
      End If
    End Sub
  End Class
```

C# InspWrap

The declarations part of the Inspector wrapper class InspWrap is shown in Listing 10-30. Declarations are made for the Inspector, TaskItem, and CustomTaskPane objects, and local instances of the IRibbonUI and TaskPane objects are declared. Public properties for the Ribbon, TaskPane, TaskItem, Inspector, SortedList wrapper collection, and Key are also declared in this section of the wrapper class code. Event handlers are added for the CustomTaskPane.VisibleStateChange, CustomTaskPane.DockPositionStateChange, Inspector.Activate Inspector.Close, and TaskItem.Close events.

Listing 10-30

```
using System;
using System.Collections.Generic;
using System.Text;
using System.Diagnostics;
using System.Runtime.InteropServices;
using Outlook = Microsoft.Office.Interop.Outlook;
using Office = Microsoft.Office.Core;
using System.Windows.Forms;

namespace TaskManagerCS
{
    class InspWrap
    {
        private Outlook.Inspector m_Insp = null;
        private Outlook.InspectorClass m_InspClass = null;

        private Outlook.TaskItem m_Task = null;

        private Office.IRibbonUI m_Ribbon = null;

        private int m_ID = 0;

        private bool m_Startup = false;

        private bool m_blnKilled = false;

        private System.Collections.SortedList m_WrapperClass = null;

        private Outlook.ItemEvents_Event m_events = null;

        private Office.CustomTaskPane m_Pane = null;
        private TaskPane m_Control = null;

        public Office.IRibbonUI Ribbon
        {
            get
            {
                return m_Ribbon;
            }

            set
            {
                m_Ribbon = value;
            }
        }

        public Office.CustomTaskPane TaskPane
        {
            get
            {
                return m_Pane;
            }
```

Listing 10-30 *(continued)*

```
            set
            {
                m_Pane = value;

                if (m_Pane != null)
                {
                    // hook up the CTP event
                    m_Pane.VisibleStateChange += new
                        Office.
                        _CustomTaskPaneEvents_VisibleStateChangeEventHandler(
                        m_Pane_VisibleStateChange);

                    m_Pane.DockPositionStateChange += new
                        Microsoft.Office.Core.
_CustomTaskPaneEvents_DockPositionStateChangeEventHandler(
m_Pane_DockPositionStateChange);
                }
            }
        }

        public System.Collections.SortedList WrapperClass
        {
            get
            {
                return m_WrapperClass;
            }

            set
            {
                m_WrapperClass = value;
            }
        }

        public Outlook.Inspector Inspector
        {
            get
            {
                return m_Insp;
            }

            set
            {
                m_Insp = value;

                m_InspClass = (Outlook.InspectorClass)m_Insp;

                // hook up the Inspector Close event handler
                m_InspClass.InspectorEvents_Event_Close += new
                    Microsoft.Office.Interop.Outlook.
                    InspectorEvents_CloseEventHandler(m_Insp_Close);

                // hook up the Inspector Activate event handler
```

(continued)

Listing 10-30 (continued)

```
                    m_InspClass.InspectorEvents_Event_Activate += new
                        Microsoft.Office.Interop.Outlook.
                        InspectorEvents_ActivateEventHandler(m_Insp_Activate);

                    m_blnKilled = false;
                    m_Startup = true;
                }
            }

        public int Key
        {
            get
            {
                return m_ID;
            }

            set
            {
                m_ID = value;
            }
        }


        public Outlook.TaskItem TaskItem
        {
            get
            {
                return m_Task;
            }

            set
            {
                m_Task = value;

                if (m_Task != null)
                {
                    // hook up the Item.Close event
                    m_events = (Outlook.ItemEvents_Event)m_Task;

                    m_events.Close += new
                        Microsoft.Office.Interop.Outlook.
                        ItemEvents_CloseEventHandler(m_Task_Close);
                }
            }
        }
    }
```

The code in Listing 10-31 shows the event handlers encapsulated in the Inspector wrapper class. The class handles the Inspector's Activate and Close events and the Close event for the TaskItem in the Inspector. The task event is blank and not used in this addin.

The Activate event is used to call the Init method of the task pane UserControl if the Inspector is first being activated. The m_Pane TaskPane object declared at class level is used to instantiate the m_Control object that represents the ContentControl of the UserControl. The ContentControl exposes any public properties, methods and events in the `UserControl` object, and is used when calling the `Init` method. Finally, the Ribbon control is invalidated, which forces an update of the Ribbon and fires the `getImage` callback for each Ribbon control.

The `Inspector.Close` event is used to release all the class-level objects in the wrapper class and to remove the wrapper class from the `Inspector` wrapper collection by calling the `KillInsp` method. All the event handlers added to the `Inspector` wrapper class are dereferenced in the `Close` event.

Listing 10-31

```
void m_Insp_Activate()
{
    if (m_Startup == true)
    {
        if (m_Task != null)
        {
            if (m_Ribbon != null)
            {
                if (m_Pane != null)
                {
                    try
                    {
                        m_Control = (TaskPane)m_Pane.ContentControl;
                        if (m_Control != null)
                        {
                            m_Control.Init(this.m_Task.EntryID);
                        }
                    }
                    catch (Exception ex)
                    {
                        MessageBox.Show(ex.Message);
                    }

                    m_Ribbon.Invalidate();
                    m_Startup = false;
                }
            }
        }
    }
}

private void m_Insp_Close()
{
    if (m_blnKilled == false)
    {
        m_blnKilled = true;

        // remove from the Inspector wrapper collection
        OutInsp killer = new OutInsp();
        killer.KillInsp(m_ID, m_WrapperClass);
        killer = null;

        m_WrapperClass = null;
```

(continued)

Listing 10-31 *(continued)*

```
            m_Control = null;

            // release the Inspector.Close event handler
            m_InspClass.InspectorEvents_Event_Close -= new
              Microsoft.Office.Interop.Outlook.
              InspectorEvents_CloseEventHandler(m_Insp_Close);

            // release the Inspector Activate event handler
            m_InspClass.InspectorEvents_Event_Activate -= new
              Microsoft.Office.Interop.Outlook.
              InspectorEvents_ActivateEventHandler(m_Insp_Activate);

            if (m_Insp != null) { m_Insp = null; }
            if (m_InspClass != null) { m_InspClass = null; }

            if (m_Task != null)
            {
                if (m_events != null)
                {
                    m_events.Close -= new
                        Microsoft.Office.Interop.Outlook.
                        ItemEvents_CloseEventHandler(m_Task_Close);

                    m_events = null;
                }
            if (m_Task != null)
                m_Task = null;
            }

            if (m_Pane != null)
            {
                m_Pane.VisibleStateChange -= new Office.
_CustomTaskPaneEvents_VisibleStateChangeEventHandler(
m_Pane_VisibleStateChange);

                m_Pane.DockPositionStateChange -= new
                    Microsoft.Office.Core.
_CustomTaskPaneEvents_DockPositionStateChangeEventHandler(
m_Pane_DockPositionStateChange);

                m_Pane.Delete();
                m_Pane = null;
            }

            if (m_Ribbon != null) { m_Ribbon = null; }
        }
    }

    private void m_Task_Close(ref bool Cancel)
    {
        Debug.WriteLine("Item closing");
    }
```

Listing 10-32 shows the code for the AddChildTask method. This is called when the user clicks the Ribbon button Add Child Task, and is declared as a public method so that it can be called from the Ribbon onAction callback in the Connect class. Adding a child task requires three steps:

1. Create a new task that will be the child task, and save it so that it has a valid EntryID property.

2. Add a property to the child task ParentTask that holds the EntryID of the parent task to allow retrieval of the parent from the child.

3. Add a property named ChildTasks to the parent task, if it doesn't already exist. This property is used to hold the EntryIDs of all child tasks of a parent task.

The parent property is a simple string property, because each task can have only one parent. The child property is a multi-valued property, because each task can have many child tasks. The values of the child tasks property are read and written using an array of strings, where each array element represents one child task. After the child task is created, and the parent and child properties are set in the parent and child tasks, the new child task is displayed.

Listing 10-32

```
public void AddChildTask()
{
    if (m_Task != null)
    {
        try
        {
            if (m_Pane != null)
            {
                if (m_Task.EntryID != null)
                {
                    Outlook.TaskItem _Task = null;
                    _Task = (Outlook.TaskItem)
                        Connect.m_Outlook.CreateItem(
                            Outlook.OlItemType.olTaskItem);


                    if (_Task != null)
                    {
                        _Task.Save();

                        string ItemID = m_Task.EntryID;

                        Outlook.PropertyAccessor _Accessor = null;
                        string [] sParent = {ItemID};

                        _Accessor = _Task.PropertyAccessor;
                        if (_Accessor != null)
                        {
                            try
                            {
                                _Accessor.SetProperty(
                                    Connect.ParentTag, sParent);
                            }
```

(continued)

Listing 10-32 *(continued)*

```
                    catch (Exception ex)
                    {
                    }
        }

        _Task.Save();
        ItemID = _Task.EntryID;

        int count;

        Outlook.PropertyAccessor oAccessor = null;
        oAccessor = m_Task.PropertyAccessor;
        if (oAccessor != null)
        {
            string [] children;
            try
            {
                children = (
                  string [])oAccessor.GetProperty(
                  Connect.ChildTag);

                try
                {
                    bool result = false;
                    count = children.GetLength(0);
                    for (int i = 0; i <= (count - 1);
                      i++)
                    {
                        if (children[i] == ItemID)
                        {
                            result = true;
                            break;
                        }
                    }
                    if (result == false)
                    {
                        string[] ChildrenCopy =
                          new string[count];

                        children.CopyTo(
                          ChildrenCopy, 0);

                        ChildrenCopy[count] = ItemID;
                        oAccessor.SetProperty(
                          Connect.ChildTag,
                          ChildrenCopy);

                        m_Task.Save();
                    }
                }
                catch (Exception ex)
                {
```

Listing 10-32 (continued)

```
                            MessageBox.Show(ex.Message);
                        }
                    }
                    catch (Exception ex)
                    {
                        string [] ChildrenCopy = {ItemID};
                        oAccessor.SetProperty(
                          Connect.ChildTag,
                          ChildrenCopy);

                        m_Task.Save();
                    }
                }

                _Task.Display(false);

                _Task = null;

            }
          }
        }
        catch (Exception ex)
        {
            MessageBox.Show(ex.Message);
        }
    }
}
```

The code in Listing 10-33 completes the code for the C# InspWrap Inspector wrapper class. This code shows the event handlers for the two events exposed by the CustomTaskPane object, DockPositionStateChange and VisibleStateChange. The task pane position is fixed at the right side of the Inspector window when the task pane is created, so the DockPositionStateChange event handler isn't used in the addin. The VisibleStateChange event handler is used to test for the visibility of the task pane. If it's visible, the Init method of the task pane UserControl is called to initialize the treeview control of the task pane. The Init method is passed the EntryID of the TaskItem displayed in the Inspector, so it can retrieve that item and work with its ParentTask and ChildTasks properties.

Listing 10-33

```
void m_Pane_VisibleStateChange(
  Office.CustomTaskPane CustomTaskPaneInst)
{
    Debug.WriteLine("Task Pane Visibility: " +
      CustomTaskPaneInst.Visible.ToString());

    if (CustomTaskPaneInst.Visible == true)
    {
        m_Control.Init(this.m_Task.EntryID);
```

(continued)

Listing 10-33 *(continued)*

```
            }
    }

    void m_Pane_DockPositionStateChange(
      Microsoft.Office.Core.CustomTaskPane CustomTaskPaneInst)
    {
        Debug.WriteLine("Task Pane Position Change: " +
          " " + CustomTaskPaneInst.DockPosition.ToString());
    }
  }
}
```

VB TaskPane

The task pane is a `UserControl` with one control on it, a treeview control. A treeview control was selected for the task pane because it can easily display a hierarchical view of different items, such as parent and child tasks.

The code in Listing 10-34 shows the `Init` method of the task pane, which takes the `EntryID` of a task item and searches up the chain of links from the task's `ParentTask` property to the ultimate parent of the task item. All child tasks, including the current task, are children or otherwise descended from that top-level parent task. Each task that's retrieved is stored in a `Stack` object, which allows the pushing and popping of items in a last in, first out order.

When a node is added to the treeview control in the task pane, the text for the node is set to the task's `Subject` and the key value is set to the task's `EntryID`, allowing any task displayed in a node in the treeview to be easily retrieved.

Listing 10-34

```
Imports Outlook = Microsoft.Office.Interop.Outlook
Imports Office = Microsoft.Office.Core
Imports System.Windows.Forms
Imports System.Drawing
Imports System.Collections.Generic

Public Class TaskPane
    Public TaskID As String

    Public Sub New()

        ' This call is required by the Windows Form Designer.
        InitializeComponent()

        ' Add any initialization after the InitializeComponent() call.
    End Sub

    Public Sub Init(ByVal inID As String)
        Dim oTask As Outlook.TaskItem = Nothing
        Dim oTopNode As TreeNode = Nothing
```

Listing 10-34 *(continued)*

```
Dim ParentTask As Outlook.TaskItem = Nothing
Dim tempTask As Outlook.TaskItem = Nothing
Dim i As Integer
Dim listCount As Integer
Dim sID As String

Dim list As New System.Collections.Generic.Stack(Of String)

Me.TreeView1.Nodes.Clear()
list.Clear()

If inID <> "" Then
    Try
        TaskID = inID
        oTask = CType(g_objNS.GetItemFromID(inID), Outlook.TaskItem)
    Catch ex As Exception
        oTask = Nothing
        MessageBox.Show(ex.Message)
    End Try

    If oTask IsNot Nothing Then
        If oTask.EntryID <> "" Then
            Dim ItemID As String = oTask.EntryID

            Dim oAccessor As Outlook.PropertyAccessor = Nothing

            oAccessor = oTask.PropertyAccessor
            If (oAccessor IsNot Nothing) Then
                Try
                    Dim sParent() As String
                    Dim sParentID As String

                    tempTask = oTask
                    Do
                        oAccessor = Nothing
                        oAccessor = tempTask.PropertyAccessor
                        If (oAccessor IsNot Nothing) Then
                            sParent = _
                            oAccessor.GetProperty(ParentTag)

                            Try
                                sParentID = sParent(0)
                                ParentTask = _
                                GetParentTask(sParentID)

                                If (ParentTask IsNot Nothing) Then
                                    list.Push(sParentID)
                                    tempTask = ParentTask
                                End If
                            Catch ex As Exception
                                Exit Do
                            End Try
```

(continued)

363

Listing 10-34 *(continued)*

```
                Else
                    Exit Do
                End If
            Loop Until (ParentTask Is Nothing)
        Catch ex As Exception
            'MessageBox.Show(ex.Message)
        End Try

        Dim ChildTask As Outlook.TaskItem
        Dim oChildNode As TreeNode
        Dim oMeNode As TreeNode

        Dim count As Integer
        Dim sChildID As String
        Dim children() As String

        listCount = list.Count
        If listCount > 0 Then
            sID = list.Pop()
            listCount -= 1

            ParentTask = CType(g_objNS.GetItemFromID(sID), _
                Outlook.TaskItem)

            oTopNode = Me.TreeView1.Nodes.Add( _
                ParentTask.EntryID, ParentTask.Subject)

            For i = listCount To 1 Step -1
                sID = list.Pop()

                ParentTask = CType(g_objNS. _
                    GetItemFromID(sID), Outlook.TaskItem)

                oTopNode = oTopNode.Nodes.Add( _
                    ParentTask.EntryID, ParentTask.Subject)
            Next
        End If

        If oTopNode Is Nothing Then
            oMeNode = Me.TreeView1.Nodes.Add( _
                oTask.EntryID, oTask.Subject)
        Else
            oMeNode = oTopNode.Nodes.Add( _
                oTask.EntryID, oTask.Subject)
        End If

        oMeNode.NodeFont = New Font(Me.TreeView1.Font, _
            Me.TreeView1.Font.Style Or FontStyle.Bold)

        Try
            oAccessor = oTask.PropertyAccessor
            children = oAccessor.GetProperty(ChildTag)
```

Listing 10-34 *(continued)*

```
                    Try
                        count = children.GetLength(0)
                        If count > 0 Then
                            For j As Integer = 0 To count - 1
                                ChildTask = Nothing

                                sChildID = children(j)
                                ChildTask = GetParentTask(sChildID)

                                If ChildTask IsNot Nothing Then
                                    oChildNode = oMeNode. _
                                    Nodes.Add(ChildTask. _
                                    EntryID, ChildTask.Subject)
                                End If
                            Next
                        End If
                    Catch ex As Exception
                        'MessageBox.Show(ex.Message)
                    End Try
                Catch ex As Exception
                End Try
            End If
        End If
    End If
    Me.TreeView1.ExpandAll()
End If

oTask = Nothing
oTopNode = Nothing
ParentTask = Nothing
tempTask = Nothing
list = Nothing
End Sub
```

Listing 10-35 shows the code for retrieving a task item from its `EntryID` property and for handling a mouse double-click on any task displayed in the task relationships treeview control.

When a task or any other Outlook item is retrieved using managed code, the object retrieved is really a late-bound object. To use it as a task item (or other specific type of Outlook item), you must cast the object to its specific type, as shown in the code that uses the `CType` method to cast the object as an `Outlook.TaskItem`.

When a node in the treeview is double-clicked, the code in `NodeMouseDoubleClick` retrieves the key value of the selected node, which is the `EntryID` of that task. The selected task is then retrieved and displayed.

Listing 10-35

```
Private Function GetParentTask(ByVal id As String) _
    As Outlook.TaskItem
```

(continued)

Listing 10-35 *(continued)*

```
            Dim oParent As Outlook.TaskItem

            Try
                oParent = CType(g_objNS.GetItemFromID(id), _
                    Outlook.TaskItem)

            Catch ex As Exception
                oParent = Nothing
            End Try

            Return oParent
        End Function

        Private Sub TreeView1_NodeMouseDoubleClick(ByVal sender As Object, _
            ByVal e As System.Windows.Forms.TreeNodeMouseClickEventArgs) _
            Handles TreeView1.NodeMouseDoubleClick

            Dim sID As String = e.Node.Name
            If sID <> "" Then
                If TaskID = sID Then
                    MessageBox.Show("This task is already open.")
                Else
                    Dim oTask As Outlook.TaskItem = Nothing
                    Try
                        oTask = CType(g_objNS.GetItemFromID(sID), _
                            Outlook.TaskItem)

                    Catch ex As Exception
                    End Try

                    If oTask IsNot Nothing Then
                        oTask.Display()
                    End If
                End If
            End If
        End Sub
    End Class
```

C# TaskPane

The code in Listing 10-36 shows the Init method of the task pane, which takes the EntryID of a task item and searches up the chain of links from the task's ParentTask property to the ultimate parent of the task item. All child tasks, including the current task, are children or otherwise descended from that top-level parent task. Each task that's retrieved is stored in a Stack object, which allows the pushing and popping of items in a last in, first out order.

When a node is added to the treeview control in the task pane, the text for the node is set to the task's Subject, and the key value is set to the task's EntryID, allowing any task displayed in a node in the treeview to be easily retrieved.

Listing 10-36 shows how the objects declared as `public static` in the `Connect` class can be referenced from other classes in the addin. The `Connect` class is always in scope for the lifetime of the addin, so `public static` objects in `Connect`, such as `m_NameSpace`, are referenced using the following syntax:

```
Connect.m_NameSpace
```

Listing 10-36

```csharp
namespace TaskManagerCS
{
    public partial class TaskPane : UserControl
    {
        public string TaskID;
        private object missing = System.Reflection.Missing.Value;

        public TaskPane()
        {
            InitializeComponent();

            treeView1.NodeMouseDoubleClick +=
                new TreeNodeMouseClickEventHandler(
                treeView1_NodeMouseDoubleClick);
        }

        public void Init(string inID)
        {
            Outlook.TaskItem oTask = null;
            TreeNode oTopNode = null;
            Outlook.TaskItem ParentTask = null;
            Outlook.TaskItem tempTask = null;
            int i;
            int listCount;
            string sID;

            Stack<string> list = new Stack<string>();

            this.TreeView1.Nodes.Clear();
            list.Clear();

            if (inID != null)
            {
                try
                {
                    TaskID = inID;
                    oTask = (Outlook.TaskItem)Connect.
                        m_NameSpace.GetItemFromID(TaskID,
                        missing);
                }
                catch (Exception ex)
                {
                    oTask = null;
                    MessageBox.Show(ex.Message);
                }
```

(continued)

Listing 10-36 *(continued)*

```
                if (oTask != null)
                {
                    if (oTask.EntryID != "")
                    {
                        string ItemID = oTask.EntryID;

                        Outlook.PropertyAccessor oAccessor = null;

                        oAccessor = oTask.PropertyAccessor;
                        if (oAccessor != null)
                        {
                            try
                            {
                                string [] sParent;
                                string sParentID;

                                tempTask = oTask;
                                do
                                {
                                    oAccessor = null;
                                    oAccessor = tempTask.PropertyAccessor;
                                    if (oAccessor != null)
                                    {
                                        sParent = oAccessor.GetProperty(
                                          Connect.ParentTag);

                                        try
                                        {
                                            sParentID = sParent[0];
                                            ParentTask = GetParentTask(
                                              sParentID);

                                            if (ParentTask != null)
                                            {
                                                list.Push(sParentID);
                                                tempTask = ParentTask;
                                            }
                                        }
                                        catch (Exception ex)
                                        {
                                            break;
                                        }
                                    }
                                    else
                                    {
                                        break;
                                    }
                                }
                                while (ParentTask != null);
                            }
                            catch (Exception ex)
                            {
```

Listing 10-36 *(continued)*

```csharp
            //MessageBox.Show(ex.Message);
        }

        Outlook.TaskItem ChildTask;
        TreeNode oChildNode;
        TreeNode oMeNode;

        int count;
        string sChildID;
        string [] children;

        listCount = list.Count;
        if (listCount > 0)
        {
            sID = list.Pop();
            listCount -= 1;

            ParentTask = (Outlook.TaskItem)Connect.
                m_NameSpace.GetItemFromID(sID);

            oTopNode = this.TreeView1.Nodes.Add(
              ParentTask.EntryID,

                ParentTask.Subject);

            for (i = listCount; i >= 1; i--)
            {
                sID = list.Pop();

                ParentTask = (Outlook.TaskItem)
                  Connect.m_NameSpace.GetItemFromID(
                  sID);

                oTopNode = oTopNode.Nodes.Add(
                  ParentTask.EntryID, ParentTask.Subject);
            }
        }

        if (oTopNode == null)
        {
            oMeNode = this.TreeView1.Nodes.Add(
              oTask.EntryID, oTask.Subject);
        }
        else
        {
            oMeNode = oTopNode.Nodes.Add(
              oTask.EntryID, oTask.Subject);
        }

        oMeNode.NodeFont = new Font(this.TreeView1.Font,
          this.TreeView1.Font.Style | FontStyle.Bold);
```

(continued)

Listing 10-36 (continued)

```
                    try
                    {
                        oAccessor = oTask.PropertyAccessor;
                        children = oAccessor.GetProperty(
                          Connect.ChildTag);

                        try
                        {
                            count = children.GetLength[0];
                            if (count > 0)
                            {
                                for (int j = 0; j <= (count - 1); j++)
                                {
                                    ChildTask = null;

                                    sChildID = children[j];
                                    ChildTask = GetParentTask(sChildID);

                                    if (ChildTask != null)
                                    {
                                        oChildNode = oMeNode.
                                          Nodes.Add(ChildTask.
                                          EntryID, ChildTask.Subject);
                                    }
                                }
                            }
                        }
                        catch (Exception ex)
                        {
                            //MessageBox.Show(ex.Message);
                        }
                    }
                    catch (Exception ex)
                    {
                    }
                }
            }
        }
        this.TreeView1.ExpandAll();
    }

    oTask = null;
    oTopNode = null;
    ParentTask = null;
    tempTask = null;
    list = null;
}
```

Listing 10-37 shows the code for retrieving a task item from its `EntryID` property and for handling a mouse double-click on any task displayed in the task relationships treeview control. When a task or any other Outlook item is retrieved using managed code, the object retrieved is really a late-bound object. To use it as a task item (or other specific type of Outlook item), you must cast the object to its specific type, as shown in the code that casts the retrieved task item as an `Outlook.TaskItem` object.

When a node in the treeview is double-clicked, the code in `NodeMouseDoubleClick` retrieves the `key` value of the selected node, which is the `EntryID` of that task. The selected task is then retrieved and displayed.

Listing 10-37

```
Outlook.TaskItem GetParentTask(string id)
{
    Outlook.TaskItem task = null;
    try
    {
        task = (Outlook.TaskItem)
          Connect.m_NameSpace.GetItemFromID(
          sParentID, missing);
    }
    catch (Exception ex)
    {
        //MessageBox.Show(ex.Message);
        task = null;
    }

    return task;
}

void  treeView1_NodeMouseDoubleClick(object sender,
    TreeNodeMouseClickEventArgs e)
{
    string sID = e.Node.Name;
    if (sID != "")
    {
        if (TaskID == sID)
        {
            MessageBox.Show("This task is already open.");
        }
        else
        {
            Outlook.TaskItem oTask = null;
            try
            {
                oTask = (Outlook.TaskItem)
                  Connect.m_NameSpace.GetItemFromID(
                  sID, missing);
            }
            catch (Exception ex)
            {
                //MessageBox.Show(ex.Message);
            }

            if (oTask != null)
            {
                oTask.Display(false);
            }
        }
    }
}
```

VB Ribbon XML

As you saw in Chapter 5 when learning how to use COM addins to work with the Ribbon, the Ribbon design is provided using XML tags. The XML for the Task Manager user interface is shown in Listing 10-38, which provides a custom Ribbon tab, one group in the custom tab, and two button controls for adding a child task and displaying the family relationships of the current task.

The Ribbon XML shown in Listing 10-38 is very similar to the XML code shown in Listing 10-39, except that it uses different id values for the tab, group, and buttons. You should always use unique id values for each addin you write so that your user interface is completely independent of any other addin's user interface. You can also use an XML namespace to qualify the user interface objects in your custom Ribbon to provide further isolation between the controls in your addin and those in other addins.

Listing 10-38

```xml
<?xml version="1.0" encoding="utf-8" ?>
<customUI xmlns = "http://schemas.microsoft.com/office/2006/01/customui"
          onLoad = "Ribbon_OnLoad" >
  <ribbon>
    <tabs>
      <tab id="TaskManTab" label="Task Manager" visible="true"
          insertAfterMso="TabTask" >
        <group id="GroupTask" label="Task Manager" visible="true">
          <button id="Tasks1" size="normal" label="Show Related Tasks"
            onAction="VB_Action" getImage="VB_GetImage" />
          <button id="Tasks2" size="normal" label="Add Child Task"
            onAction="VB_Action" getImage="VB_GetImage" />
        </group>
      </tab>
    </tabs>
  </ribbon>
</customUI>
```

There are two primary methods of ensuring that your ids are unique to your own application: using an id value that's guaranteed to be unique or adding a namespace definition to your XML declarations and then using the idQ tag instead of an id tag. The addins in this chapter use a string value for the id properties that should be unique but aren't guaranteed to be unique.

One way to guarantee a unique id value is to use GUID as part of your id. This GUID can be the GUID of your addin; in the case of the VB.NET addin, the GUID would be C4AF1D53-1F7B-4e17-87E9-D44198617FFC. Concatenating the tab, group, or control id with the GUID will guarantee an awkward but unique id value for each tag in the Ribbon XML.

An alternative to the unique GUID-based tag value is to use the idQ tag with an XML namespace. This method also allows easy sharing of custom tabs and groups within a family of addins. To use the idQ tag, you must first declare a namespace using the following syntax. The xmlns keyword is used to define an XML namespace myAddin.

```xml
<customUI xmlns = "http://schemas.microsoft.com/office/2006/01/customui
    xmlns:myAddin="TaskManager.Connect" onLoad = "Ribbon_OnLoad" >
```

The name of your XML namespace should be the `ProgID` of your COM addin, in this case `TaskManager`
`.Connect`. The variable assigned to the namespace definition is then used to qualify all tab, control, and
group references to this namespace, as shown in the code below that declares a new tab labeled "Task
Manager" using the `idQ` value of `myAddin.TaskManTab`.

```
<tab idQ="myAddin.TaskManTab" label="Task Manager" visible="true"
    insertAfterMso="TabTask" >
```

C# Ribbon XML

The Ribbon XML shown in Listing 10-39 is very similar to the XML code shown in Listing 10-38, except for
using different `id` values for the tab, group, and buttons. You should always use unique `id` values for each
addin you write so that your user interface is completely independent of any other addin's user interface.

Listing 10-39

```xml
<?xml version="1.0" encoding="utf-8" ?>
<customUI xmlns = "http://schemas.microsoft.com/office/2006/01/customui"
        onLoad = "Ribbon_OnLoad" >
  <ribbon>
    <tabs>
      <tab id="CSTaskManTab" label="Task Manager" visible="true"
          insertAfterMso="TabTask" >
        <group id="CSGroupTask" label="Task Manager" visible="true">
          <button id="CSTasks1" size="normal" label="Show Related Tasks"
              onAction="CS_Action" getImage="CS_GetImage" />
          <button id="CSTasks2" size="normal" label="Add Child Task"
              onAction="CS_Action" getImage="CS_GetImage" />
        </group>
      </tab>
    </tabs>
  </ribbon>
</customUI>
```

Summary

In this chapter, you learned about the code for the Task Management System addin that provides a hierarchical task management system. You learned how to work with custom task panes in `Inspectors`, how
to create the Ribbon controls for the addin, and how to create linkages between different tasks to enable
sets of parent and child relationships between different task items.

The code for the VB.NET and C# versions of the TaskManager addins are available for downloading from
the Wrox web site (`www.wrox.com`) and from `www.slovaktech.com`.

Outlook 2007 Object Model Summary

Outlook 2007 introduces many new objects and collections to the Outlook object model, each with associated methods, properties, and events. Many existing objects and collections are also enhanced with new methods, properties, and events. This appendix lists all new objects and collections in Outlook 2007, with their associated methods, properties, and events as well as methods, properties, and events added to previously existing objects and collections in the Outlook object model. These include:

❑ The new Table objects in Outlook and the increased importance of DASL syntax in Outlook coding also require familiarity with the various DASL property tags for Outlook items, and many common DASL property tags are also listed in this appendix. DASL is the search syntax (DAV Searching and Locating) used in WEBDav (Web Distributed Authoring and Versioning) and also for Exchange and Outlook access based on schemas defined by Microsoft.

❑ All new objects and collections in the Outlook 2007 object model, with their associated methods, properties, and events.

❑ All new methods, properties and events added to objects that were available in previous versions of Outlook. Only the enhanced methods, properties, and events are listed in this section.

❑ The most commonly used property tags for Message, Appointment, Contact, and Task items in Outlook.

New Objects and Collections

The following table lists the new objects and collections introduced in Outlook 2007, and their associated methods, properties, and events. This table is adapted from information provided by Microsoft and is used with permission.

Object or Collection	Methods	Properties	Events
Account		AccountType	
		Application	
		Class	
		DisplayName	
		Parent	
		Session	
		SmtpAddress	
		UserName	
AccountRuleCondition		Account	
		Application	
		Class	
		ConditionType	
		Enabled	
		Parent	
		Session	
Accounts Collection	Item	Application	
		Class	
		Count	
		Parent	
		Session	
AddressRuleCondition		Address	
		Application	
		Class	

Object or Collection	Methods	Properties	Events
		ConditionType	
		Enabled	
		Parent	
		Session	
AssignToCategoryRuleAction		ActionType	
		Application	
		Categories	
		Class	
		Enabled	
		Parent	
		Session	
AttachmentSelection	Item	Application	
		Class	
		Count	
		Parent	
		Session	
AutoFormatRule		Application	
		Class	
		Enabled	
		Filter	
		Font	
		Name	
		Parent	

Continued

Object or Collection	Methods	Properties	Events
		Session	
		Standard	
AutoFormatRules Collection	Add	Application	
	Insert	Class	
	Item	Count	
	Remove	Parent	
	RemoveAll	Session	
	Save		
BusinessCardView	Apply	Application	
	Copy	CardSize	
	Delete	Class	
	GoToDate	Filter	
	Reset	HeadingsFont	
	Save	Language	
		LockUserChanges	
		Name	
		Parent	
		SaveOption	
		Session	
		SortFields	
		Standard	
		ViewType	
		XML	

Object or Collection	Methods	Properties	Events
CalendarModule		Application	
		Class	
		Name	
		NavigationGroups	
		NavigationTypeModule	
		Parent	
		Position	
		Session	
		Visible	
CalendarSharing	ForwardAsICal	Application	
	SaveAsICal	CalendarDetail	
		Class	
		EndDate	
		Folder	
		IncludeAttachments	
		IncludePrivateDetails	
		IncludeWholeCalendar	
		Parent	
		RestrictToWorkingHours	
		Session	
		StartDate	
CalendarView	Apply	Application	
	Copy	AutoFormatRules	

Continued

Object or Collection	Methods	Properties	Events
	Delete	BoldDatesWithItems	
	GoToDate	CalendarViewMode	
	Reset	Class	
	Save	DayFont	
		DaysInMultiDayMode	
		DayWeekFont	
		DayWeekTimeFont	
		DayWeekTimeScale	
		DisplayedDates	
		EndField	
		Filter	
		Language	
		LockUserChanges	
		MonthFont	
		MonthShowEndTime	
		Name	
		Parent	
		SaveOption	
		Session	
		Standard	
		StartField	
		ViewType	
		XML	

Object or Collection	Methods	Properties	Events
CardView	Apply	AllowInCellEditing	
	Copy	Application	
	Delete	AutoFormatRules	
	GoToDate	BodyFont	
	Reset	Class	
	Save	Filter	
		HeadingsFont	
		Language	
		LockUserChanges	
		MultiLineFieldHeight	
		Name	
		Parent	
		SaveOption	
		Session	
		ShowEmptyFields	
		SortFields	
		Standard	
		ViewFields	
		ViewType	
		Width	
		XML	
Categories Collection	Add	Application	
	Item	Class	

Continued

Object or Collection	Methods	Properties	Events
	Remove	Count	
		Parent	
		Session	
Category		Application	
		CategoryBorderColor	
		CategoryGradientBottomColor	
		CategoryGradientTopColor	
		CategoryID	
		Class	
		Color	
		Name	
		Parent	
		Session	
		ShortcutKey	
CategoryRuleCondition		Application	
		Categories	
		Class	
		ConditionType	
		Enabled	
		Parent	
		Session	
Column		Application	
		Class	

Object or Collection	Methods	Properties	Events
		Name	
		Parent	
		Session	
ColumnFormat		Align	
		Application	
		Class	
		FieldFormat	
		FieldType	
		Label	
		Parent	
		Session	
		Width	
Columns Collection	Add	Application	
	Item	Class	
	Remove	Count	
	RemoveAll	Parent	
		Session	
ContactsModule		Application	
		Class	
		Name	
		NavigationGroups	
		NavigationModuleType	
		Parent	

Continued

383

Object or Collection	Methods	Properties	Events
ExchangeDistributionList		Position	
		Session	
		Visible	
	Delete	Address	
	Details	AddressEntryUserType	
	GetContact	Alias	
	GetExchangeDistributionList	Application	
	GetExchangeDistributionListMembers	Class	
	GetExchangeUser	Comments	
	GetFreeBusy	DisplayType	
	GetMemberOfList	ID	
	GetOwners	Name	
	Update	Parent	
		PrimarySmtpAddress	
		PropertyAccessor	
		Session	
		Type	
ExchangeUser	Delete	Address	
	Details	AddressEntryUserType	
	GetContact	Alias	
	GetDirectReports	Application	
	GetExchangeDistributionList	AssistantName	
	GetExchangeUser	BusinessTelephoneNumber	

Object or Collection	Methods	Properties	Events
	GetExchangeUserManager	City	
	GetFreeBusy	Class	
	GetMemberOfList	Comments	
	Update	CompanyName	
		Department	
		DisplayType	
		FirstName	
		ID	
		JobTitle	
		LastName	
		MobileTelephoneNumber	
		Name	
		OfficeLocation	
		Parent	
		PostalCode	
		PrimarySmtpAddress	
		PropertyAccessor	
		Session	
		StateOrProvince	
		StreetAddress	
		Type	
		YomiCompanyName	
		YomiDepartment	

Continued

Object or Collection	Methods	Properties	Events
FormNameRuleCondition		YomiDispayName	
		YomiFirstName	
		YomiLastName	
		Application	
		Class	
		ConditionType	
		Enabled	
		FormName	
		Parent	
		Session	
FormRegion	Reflow	Application	Close
	Select	Class	Expanded
	SetControlItemProperty	Detail	
		DisplayName	
		EnableAutoLayout	
		Form	
		FormRegionMode	
		Inspector	
		InternalName	
		IsExpanded	
		Item	
		Language	
		Parent	

Object or Collection	Methods	Properties	Events
	BeforeFormRegionShow	Position	
	GetFormRegionIcon	Session	
	GetFormRegionManifest	SuppressControlReplacement	
FormRegionStartup	GetFormRegionStorage		
FromRssFeedRuleCodition		Application	
		Class	
		ConditionType	
		Enabled	
		FromRssFeed	
		Parent	
		Session	
IconView	Apply	Application	
	Copy	Class	
	Delete	Filter	
	GoToDate	IconPlacement	
	Reset	IconViewType	
	Save	Language	
		LockUserChanges	
		Name	
		Parent	

Continued

Object or Collection	Methods	Properties	Events
		SaveOption	
		Session	
		SortFields	
		Standard	
		ViewType	
		XML	
ImportanceRuleCondition		Application	
		Class	
		ConditionType	
		Enabled	
		Importance	
		Parent	
		Session	
JournalModule		Application	
		Class	
		Name	
		NavigationGroups	
		NavigationModuleType	
		Parent	
		Position	
		Session	
		Visible	
MailModule		Application	

Object or Collection	Methods	Properties	Events
		Class	
		Name	
		NavigationGroups	
		NavigationModuleType	
		Parent	
		Position	
		Session	
		Visible	
MarkAsTaskRuleAction		ActionType	
		Application	
		Class	
		Enabled	
		FlagTo	
		MarkInterval	
		Parent	
		Session	
MoveOrCopyRuleAction		ActionType	
		Application	
		Class	
		Enabled	
		Folder	
		Parent	
		Session	

Continued

Object or Collection	Methods	Properties	Events
NavigationFolder		Application	
		Class	
		DisplayName	
		Folder	
		IsRemovable	
		IsSelected	
		IsSideBySide	
		Parent	
		Position	
		Session	
NavigationFolders Collection	Add	Application	
	Item	Class	
	Remove	Count	
		Parent	
		Session	
NavigationGroup		Application	
		Class	
		GroupType	
		Name	
		NavigationFolders	
		Parent	
		Position	
		Session	

Object or Collection	Methods	Properties	Events
NavigationGroups Collection	Create	Application	NavigationFolderAdd
	Delete	Class	NavigationFolderRemove
	GetDefaultNavigationGroup	Count	SelectedChange
	Item	Parent	
		Session	
NavigationModule		Application	
		Class	
		Name	
		NavigationModuleType	
		Parent	
		Position	
		Session	
		Visible	
NavigationModules Collection	GetNavigationModule	Application	
	Item	Class	
		Count	
		Parent	
		Session	
NavigationPane		Application	ModuleSwitch
		Class	
		CurrentModule	
		DisplayedModuleCount	
		IsCollapsed	

Continued

Object or Collection	Methods	Properties	Events
		Modules	
		Parent	
		Session	
NewItemAlertRuleAction		ActionType	
		Application	
		Class	
		Enabled	
		Parent	
		Session	
		Text	
NotesModule		Application	
		Class	
		Name	
		NavigationGroups	
		NavigationModuleType	
		Parent	
		Position	
		Session	
		Visible	
OrderField		Application	
		Class	
		IsDescending	
		Parent	

Object or Collection	Methods	Properties	Events
		Session	
		ViewXMLSchemaName	
OrderFields Collection	Add	Application	
	Insert	Class	
	Item	Count	
	Remove	Parent	
	RemoveAll	Session	
PlaySoundRuleAction		ActionType	
		Application	
		Class	
		Enabled	
		FilePath	
		Parent	
		Session	
PropertyAccessor	BinaryToString	Application	
	DeleteProperties	Class	
	DeleteProperty	Parent	
	GetProperties	Session	
	GetProperty		
	LocalTimeToUTC		
	SetProperties		
	SetProperty		
	StringToBinary		

Continued

Object or Collection	Methods	Properties	Events
Row	UTCToLocalTime		
	BinaryToString	Application	
	GetValues	Class	
	Item	Parent	
	LocalTimeToUTC	Session	
	UTCToLocalTime		
Rule	Execute	Actions	
		Application	
		Class	
		Conditions	
		Enabled	
		Exceptions	
		ExecutionOrder	
		IsLocalRule	
		Name	
		Parent	
		RuleType	
		Session	
RuleAction		ActionType	
		Application	
		Class	
		Enabled	
		Parent	

Object or Collection	Methods	Properties	Events
RuleActions Collection	Item	Session	
		Application	
		AssignToCategory	
		CC	
		Class	
		ClearCategories	
		CopyToFolder	
		Count	
		Delete	
		DeletePermanently	
		DesktopAlert	
		Forward	
		ForwardAsAttachment	
		MarkAsTask	
		MoveToFolder	
		NewItemAlert	
		NotifyDelivery	
		NotifyRead	
		Parent	
		PlaySound	
		Redirect	
		Session	
		Stop	

Continued

Object or Collection	Methods	Properties	Events
RuleCondition		Application	
		Class	
		ConditionType	
		Enabled	
		Parent	
		Session	
RuleConditions Collection	Item	Account	
		AnyCategory	
		Application	
		Body	
		BodyOrSubject	
		Category	
		CC	
		Class	
		Count	
		FormName	
		From	
		FromAnyRSSFeed	
		HasAttachment	
		Importance	
		MeetingInviteOrUpdate	
		MessageHeader	
		NotTo	

Object or Collection	Methods	Properties	Events
		OnLocalMachine	
		OnlyToMe	
		OnOtherMachine	
		Parent	
		RecipientAddress	
		SenderAddress	
		SenderInAddressList	
		SentTo	
		Session	
		Subject	
		ToMe	
		ToOrCc	
Rules Collection	Create	Application	
	Item	Class	
	Remove	Count	
	Save	IsRssRulesProcessingEnabled	
		Parent	
		Session	
SelectNamesDialog	Display	AllowMultipleSelection	
	SetDefaultDisplayMode	Application	
		BccLabel	
		Caption	

Continued

Object or Collection	Methods	Properties	Events
		CcLabel	
		Class	
		ForceResolution	SendRuleAction
		InitialAddressList	
		NumberOfRecipientSelectors	
		Parent	
		Recipients	
		Session	
		ShowOnlyInitialAddressList	
		ToLabel	AddressList
SenderInAddressListRuleCondition		Application	
		Class	
		ConditionType	
		Enabled	
		Parent	
		Session	
SharingItem: Only methods and properties that are added to or differ from the base MailItem class are listed.	Allow	AllowWriteAccess	
	Deny	RemoteID	
	OpenSharedFolder	RemoteName	
		RemotePath	
		RequestedFolder	
		SharingProvider	

Object or Collection	Methods	Properties	Events
StorageItem	Delete	SharingProviderGUID	
	Save	Application	
		Attachments	
		Body	
		Class	
		CreationTime	
		Creator	
		EntryID	
		LastModificationTime	
		Parent	
		PropertyAccessor	
		Session	
		Size	
		Subject	
		UserProperties	
Store	GetRootFolder	Application	
	GetRules	Class	
	GetSearchFolders	DisplayName	
	GetSpecialFolder	ExchangeStoreType	
		FilePath	
		IsCachedExchange	
		IsDataFileStore	
		IsInstantSearchEnabled	

Continued

Object or Collection	Methods	Properties	Events
		IsOpen	BeforeStoreRemove
		Parent	StoreAdd
		PropertyAccessor	
		Session	
		StoreID	
Stores Collection	Item	Application	
		Class	
		Count	
		Parent	
		Session	
Table	FindNextRow	Application	
	FindRow	Class	
	GetArray	Columns	
	GetNextRow	EndOfTable	
	GetRowCount	Parent	
	MoveToStart	Session	
	Restrict		
	Sort		
TableView	Apply	AllowInCellEditing	
	Copy	Application	
	Delete	AutoFormatRules	
	GoToDate	AutomaticColumnSizing	

Object or Collection	Methods	Properties	Events
	Reset	AutomaticGrouping	
	Save	AutoPreview	
		AutoPreviewFont	
		Class	
		ColumnFont	
		DefaultExpandCollapseSetting	
		Filter	
		GridLineStyle	
		GroupByFields	
		HideReadingPaneHeaderInfo	
		Language	
		LockUserChanges	
		MaxLinesInMultiLineView	
		Multiline	
		MultiLineWidth	
		Name	
		Parent	
		RowFont	
		SaveOption	
		Session	
		ShowItemsInGroups	
		ShowNewItemRow	
		ShowReadingPane	

Continued

Object or Collection	Methods	Properties	Events
		ShowUnreadAndFlaggedMessages	
		SortFields	
		Standard	
		ViewFields	
		ViewType	
		XML	
TasksModule		Application	
		Class	
		Name	
		NavigationGroups	
		NavigationModuleType	
		Parent	
		Position	
		Session	
		Visible	
TextRuleCondition		Application	
		Class	
		ConditionType	
		Enabled	
		Parent	
		Session	
		Text	

Object or Collection	Methods	Properties	Events
TimelineView	Apply	Application	
	Copy	Class	
	Delete	DefaultExpandCollapseSetting	
	GoToDate	EndField	
	Reset	Filter	
	Save	GroupByFields	
		ItemFont	
		Language	
		LockUserChanges	
		LowerScaleFont	
		MaxLabelWidth	
		Name	
		Parent	
		SaveOption	
		Session	
		ShowLabelWhenViewingByMonth	
		ShowWeekNumbers	
		Standard	
		StartField	
		TimelineViewMode	
		UpperScaleFont	
		ViewType	
		XML	

Continued

Object or Collection	Methods	Properties	Events
TimeZone		Application	
		Bias	
		Class	
		DaylightBias	
		DaylightDate	
		DaylightDesignation	
		ID	
		Name	
		Parent	
		Session	
		StandardBias	
		StandardDate	
		StandardDesignation	
TimeZones Collection	ConvertTime	Application	
	Item	Class	
		Count	
		CurrentTimeZone	
		Parent	
		Session	
ToOrFromRuleCondition		Application	
		Class	
		ConditionType	
		Enabled	

Object or Collection	Methods	Properties	Events
		Parent	
		Recipients	
		Session	
UserDefinedProperties Collection	Add	Application	
	Find	Class	
	Item	Count	
	Refresh	Parent	
	Remove	Session	
UserDefinedProperty	Delete	Application	
		Class	
		DisplayFormat	
		Formula	
		Name	
		Parent	
		Session	
		Type	
ViewField		Application	
		Class	
		ColumnFormat	
		Parent	
		Session	
		ViewXMLSchemaName	

Continued

Object or Collection	Methods	Properties	Events
ViewFields Collection	Add	Application	
	Insert	Class	
	Item	Count	
	Remove	Parent	
		Session	
ViewFont		Application	
		Bold	
		Class	
		Color	
		Italic	
		Name	
		Parent	
		Session	
		Size	
		Strikethrough	
		Underline	

New Properties and Methods

The following table lists new methods, properties, and events for objects that were available in previous versions of Outlook. Only new methods, properties, and events are listed. This table is adapted from information provided by Microsoft and is used with permission.

Outlook 2007 hides a number of methods and properties that were available in the Outlook 2003 object model, such as the `Manager` property of an `AddressEntry` object. These methods and properties will still compile correctly and can be shown by right-clicking the list of methods, properties, and events in the Object Browser and selecting Show Hidden Members. It's recommended that you not use hidden methods and properties in new code, and that you use replacement methods and properties when they are provided. Methods and properties that are now hidden in the Outlook 2007 object model are not guaranteed to be available at all in the next version of Outlook.

Object	Methods	Properties	Events
AddressEntry	GetContact GetExchangeDistributionList GetExchangeUser	AddressEntryUserType PropertyAccessor	AddressEntry
AddressList	GetContactsFolder	AddressListType IsInitialAddressList PropertyAccessor ResolutionOrder	
Application	GetObjectReference	Assistance DefaultProfileName IsTrusted TimeZones	AttachmentContextMenuDisplay BeforeFolderSharingDialog ContextMenuClose FolderContextMenuDisplay ItemContextMenuDisplay ItemLoad ShortcutContextMenuDisplay StoreContextMenuDisplay ViewContextMenuDisplay
AppointmentItem: Plus the new common Item methods, properties and events.		EndInEndTimeZone EndTimeZone EndUTC ForceUpdateToAll Attendees GlobalAppointmentID StartInStartTimeZone StartTimeZone StartUTC	

Object	Methods	Properties	Events
Attachment		BlockLevel PropertyAccessor Size	
ContactItem: Plus the new common Item methods, properties and events.	AddBusinessCardLogoPicture ClearTaskFlag ForwardAsBusinessCard MarkAsTask ResetBusinessCard SaveBusinessCardImage ShowBusinessCardEditor ShowCheckPhoneDialog	BusinessCardLayoutXml BusinessCardType IsMarkedAsTask ReminderOverrideDefault ReminderPlaySound ReminderSet ReminderSoundFile ReminderTime TaskCompletedDate TaskDueDate TaskStartDate TaskSubject ToDoTaskOrdinal	
DistListItem	ClearTaskFlag MarkAsTask	IsMarkedAsTask ReminderOverrideDefault ReminderPlaySound ReminderSet ReminderSoundFile ReminderTime TaskCompletedDate	

Continued

409

Object	Methods	Properties	Events
		TaskDueDate	
		TaskStartDate	
		TaskSubject	
		ToDoTaskOrdinal	
Explorer	ClearSearch	NavigationPane	
	Search		
Folder: This is the MAPIFolder object in earlier versions of Outlook. New methods, properties and events are only added to the Folder object.	GetCalendarExporter	PropertyAccessor	BeforeFolderMove
	GetStorage	Store	BeforeItemMove
	GetTable	UserDefinedProperties	
Inspector		PropertyAccessor	PageChange
Item: Common properties and events added to all Outlook item types, such as MailItem and ContactItem.		SendUsingAccount	AttachmentRemove
			BeforeAttachmentAdd
			BeforeAttachmentPreview
			BeforeAttachmentRead
			BeforeAttachment
			WriteToTempFile
			BeforeAutoSave
			Unload

Object	Methods	Properties	Events
MailItem	AddBusinessCard	IsMarkedAsTask	
	ClearTaskFlag	TaskCompletedDate	
	MarkAsTask	TaskDueDate	
		TaskStartDate	
		TaskSubject	
		ToDoTaskOrdinal	
Namespace	CompareEntryIDs	Accounts	AutoDiscoverComplete
	CreateSharingItem	AutoDiscoverConnectionMode	
	GetAddressEntryFromID	AutoDiscoverXml	
	GetGlobalAddressList	Categories	
	GetSelectNamesDialog	CurrentProfileName	
	GetStoreFromID	DefaultStore	
	OpenSharedFolder	ExchangeMailboxServerName	
	OpenSharedItem	ExchangeMailboxServerVersion	
	SendAndReceive	Stores	
PostItem	ClearTaskFlag	IsMarkedAsTask	
	MarkAsTask	ReminderOverrideDefault	
		ReminderPlaySound	
		ReminderSet	
		ReminderSoundFile	
		ReminderTime	
		TaskCompletedDate	
		TaskDueDate	

Continued

Object	Methods	Properties	Events
		TaskStartDate	
		TaskSubject	
		ToDoTaskOrdinal	
Recipient		PropertyAccessor	
Search	GetTable		
TaskItem		ToDoTaskOrdinal	
View		Filter	

Common DASL Property Tags

The following sections list the most common property tags used for DASL syntax queries, searches, and property access for Outlook. The property tags are derived from the lists of schemas in the Exchange SDK, where only incomplete lists are available, scattered among many different files and locations.

Many of these DASL property tags were first compiled by Sue Mosher of Turtleflock, LLC and are used with her permission.

Messages

The following table lists common DASL property tags and data types for properties of Outlook Mail items.

Property	Property Tag	Data Type
Attachment	urn:schemas:httpmail:hasattachment	Boolean
Auto Forwarded	http://schemas.microsoft.com/mapi/proptag/0x0005000b	Boolean
Bcc	urn:schemas:calendar:resources	String
Billing Information	urn:schemas:contacts:billinginformation	String
Categories	urn:schemas-microsoft-com:office:office#Keywords	Multivalued String (array)
Cc	urn:schemas:httpmail:displaycc	String
Changed By	http://schemas.microsoft.com/mapi/proptag/0x3ffa001f	String
Contacts	http://schemas.microsoft.com/mapi/id/ {00062008-0000-0000-C000-000000000046}/8586001f	String
Conversation	urn:schemas:httpmail:thread-topic	String
Created	urn:schemas:calendar:created	Date
Defer Until	http://schemas.microsoft.com/exchange/ deferred-delivery-iso	Date
Do Not AutoArchive	http://schemas.microsoft.com/mapi/id/ {00062008-0000-0000-C000-000000000046}/850e000b	Boolean
Due By	urn:schemas:httpmail:reply-by	Date
e-mail Account	http://schemas.microsoft.com/mapi/id/ {00062008-0000-0000-C000-000000000046}/8580001f	String
Expires	urn:schemas:mailheader:expiry-date	Date
Flag Color	http://schemas.microsoft.com/mapi/proptag/ 0x10950003	Enumeration of 32-bit Long
Flag Status	http://schemas.microsoft.com/mapi/proptag/ 0x10900003	Enumeration of 32-bit Long

Continued

Property	Property Tag	Data Type
Follow Up Flag	urn:schemas:httpmail:messageflag	String
From	urn:schemas:httpmail:fromname	String
Have Replies Sent To	http://schemas.microsoft.com/mapi/proptag/ 0x0050001f	String
Importance	urn:schemas:httpmail:importance	Enumeration of 32-bit Long
Message	urn:schemas:httpmail:textdescription	String
Mileage	http://schemas.microsoft.com/exchange/mileage	String
Modified	DAV:getlastmodified	Date
Originator Delivery Requested	http://schemas.microsoft.com/exchange/ deliveryreportrequested	Boolean
Read	urn:schemas:httpmail:read	Boolean
Receipt Requested	http://schemas.microsoft.com/exchange/ readreceiptrequested	Boolean
Received	urn:schemas:httpmail:datereceived	Date
Relevance	http://schemas.microsoft.com/mapi/proptag/ 0x10840003	String
Retrieval Time	http://schemas.microsoft.com/mapi/id/ {00062014-0000-0000-C000-000000000046}/8f040003	Date
Sensitivity	http://schemas.microsoft.com/exchange/ sensitivity-long	Enumeration of 32-bit Long
Sent	urn:schemas:httpmail:date	Date
Signed By	http://schemas.microsoft.com/mapi/id/	String
Size	http://schemas.microsoft.com/mapi/proptag/ 0x0e080003	32-bit Long
Subject	urn:schemas:httpmail:subject	String
To	urn:schemas:httpmail:displayto	String
Tracking Status	http://schemas.microsoft.com/mapi/id/ {00062008-0000-0000-C000-000000000046}/88090003	Enumeration of 32-bit Long
Voting Response	http://schemas.microsoft.com/mapi/id/ {00062008-0000-0000-C000-000000000046}/8524001f	String

Appointments

The following table lists common DASL property tags and data types for properties of Outlook Appointment items.

Property	Property Tag	Data Type
All Day Event	urn:schemas:calendar:alldayevent	Boolean
Attachment	urn:schemas:httpmail:hasattachment	Boolean
Auto Forwarded	http://schemas.microsoft.com/mapi/proptag/0x0005000b	Boolean
Billing Information	urn:schemas:contacts:billinginformation	String
Categories	urn:schemas-microsoft-com:office:office#Keywords	Multivalued String (array)
Contacts	http://schemas.microsoft.com/mapi/id/ {00062008-0000-0000-C000-000000000046}/8586001f	String
Created	urn:schemas:calendar:created	Date
Do Not AutoArchive	http://schemas.microsoft.com/mapi/id/ {00062008-0000-0000-C000-000000000046}/850e000b	Boolean
Due By	urn:schemas:calendar:replytime	Date
Duration	http://schemas.microsoft.com/mapi/id/ {00062002-0000-0000-C000-000000000046}/82130003	Long
End	urn:schemas:calendar:dtend	Date
Importance	urn:schemas:httpmail:importance	Enumeration of 32-bit Long
Label	http://schemas.microsoft.com/mapi/id/ {00062002-0000-0000-C000-000000000046}/82140003	Enumeration of 32-bit Long
Location	urn:schemas:calendar:location	String
Meeting Status	http://schemas.microsoft.com/mapi/id/ {00062002-0000-0000-C000-000000000046}/82180003	Enumeration of 32-bit Long
Message	urn:schemas:httpmail:textdescription	String
Mileage	http://schemas.microsoft.com/exchange/mileage	String
Modified	DAV:getlastmodified	Date
Online Meeting	http://schemas.microsoft.com/mapi/id/ {00062002-0000-0000-C000-000000000046}/8240000b	Boolean
Optional Attendees	urn:schemas:httpmail:displaycc	String
Organizer	urn:schemas:httpmail:fromname	String
Private	http://schemas.microsoft.com/mapi/id/ {00062008-0000-0000-C000-000000000046}/8506000b	Boolean

Continued

Property	Property Tag	Data Type
Recurrence	http://schemas.microsoft.com/mapi/id/ {00062002-0000-0000-C000-000000000046}/82310003	Enumeration of 32-bit Long
Recurrence Range End	http://schemas.microsoft.com/mapi/id/ {00062002-0000-0000-C000-000000000046}/82360040	Date
Recurrence Range Start	http://schemas.microsoft.com/mapi/id/ {00062002-0000-0000-C000-000000000046}/82350040	Date
Recurring	http://schemas.microsoft.com/mapi/id/ {00062002-0000-0000-C000-000000000046}/8223000b	Boolean
Reminder	http://schemas.microsoft.com/mapi/id/ {00062008-0000-0000-C000-000000000046}/8503000b	Boolean
Reminder Beforehand	urn:schemas:calendar:reminderoffset	32-bit Long
Required Attendees	urn:schemas:httpmail:displayto	String
Resources	urn:schemas:calendar:resources	String
Response Requested	http://schemas.microsoft.com/mapi/ response_requested	Boolean
Sensitivity	http://schemas.microsoft.com/exchange/ sensitivity-long	Enumeration of 32-bit Long
Show Time As	http://schemas.microsoft.com/mapi/id/ {00062002-0000-0000-C000-000000000046}/82050003	Enumeration of 32-bit Long
Size	http://schemas.microsoft.com/mapi/proptag/0x0e0800003	32-bit Long
Start	urn:schemas:calendar:dtstart	Date
Subject	urn:schemas:httpmail:subject	String
Unread	urn:schemas:httpmail:read	Boolean

Contacts

The following table lists common DASL property tags and data types for properties of Outlook Contact items.

Property	Property Tag	Data Type
Account	urn:schemas:contacts:account	String
Anniversary	urn:schemas:contacts:weddinganniversary	Date
Assistant's Name	urn:schemas:contacts:secretarycn	String
Assistant's Phone	urn:schemas:contacts:secretaryphone	String
Attachment	urn:schemas:httpmail:hasattachment	Boolean

Property	Property Tag	Data Type
Billing Information	urn:schemas:contacts:billinginformation	String
Birthday	urn:schemas:contacts:bday	Date
Business Address	urn:schemas:contacts:workaddress	String
Business Address City	urn:schemas:contacts:l	String
Business Address Country	urn:schemas:contacts:co	String
Business Address PO Box	urn:schemas:contacts:postofficebox	String
Business Address Postal Code	urn:schemas:contacts:postalcode	String
Business Address State	urn:schemas:contacts:st	String
Business Address Street	urn:schemas:contacts:street	String
Business Fax	urn:schemas:contacts:facsimiletelephonenumber	String
Business Home Page	urn:schemas:contacts:businesshomepage	String
Business Phone	urn:schemas:contacts:officetelephonenumber	String
Business Phone 2	urn:schemas:contacts:office2telephonenumber	String
Callback	urn:schemas:contacts:callbackphone	String
Car Phone	urn:schemas:contacts:othermobile	String
Categories	urn:schemas-microsoft-com:office:office#Keywords	Multivalued String (array)
Children	urn:schemas:contacts:childrensnames	String
City	urn:schemas:contacts:mailingcity	String
Company	urn:schemas:contacts:o	String
Company Main Phone	urn:schemas:contacts:organizationmainphone	String
Computer Network Name	urn:schemas:contacts:computernetworkname	String
Contacts	http://schemas.microsoft.com/mapi/id/ {00062008-0000-0000-C000-000000000046}/8586001f	String
Country/Region	urn:schemas:contacts:mailingcountry	String
Created	urn:schemas:calendar:created	Date
Customer ID	urn:schemas:contacts:customerid	String

Continued

Property	Property Tag	Data Type
Department	urn:schemas:contacts:department	String
Email	http://schemas.microsoft.com/mapi/id/ {00062004-0000-0000-C000-000000000046}/8084001f	String
Email 2	http://schemas.microsoft.com/mapi/id/ {00062004-0000-0000-C000-000000000046}/8094001f	String
Email 3	http://schemas.microsoft.com/mapi/id/ {00062004-0000-0000-C000-000000000046}/80a4001f	String
Email Address Type	http://schemas.microsoft.com/mapi/id/ {00062004-0000-0000-C000-000000000046}/8082001f	String
Email Display As	http://schemas.microsoft.com/mapi/id/ {00062004-0000-0000-C000-000000000046}/8080001f	String
Email2 Address Type	http://schemas.microsoft.com/mapi/id/ {00062004-0000-0000-C000-000000000046}/8092001f	String
Email2 Display As	http://schemas.microsoft.com/mapi/id/ {00062004-0000-0000-C000-000000000046}/8090001f	String
Email3 Address Type	http://schemas.microsoft.com/mapi/id/ {00062004-0000-0000-C000-000000000046}/80a2001f	String
Email3 Display As	http://schemas.microsoft.com/mapi/id/ {00062004-0000-0000-C000-000000000046}/80a0001f	String
File As	urn:schemas:contacts:fileas	String
First Name	urn:schemas:contacts:givenName	String
Flag Color	http://schemas.microsoft.com/mapi/proptag/0x10950003	Enumeration of 32-bit Long
Flag Status	http://schemas.microsoft.com/mapi/proptag/0x10900003	Enumeration of 32-bit Long
Follow Up Flag	urn:schemas:httpmail:messageflag	String
FTP Site	urn:schemas:contacts:ftpsite	String
Full Name	urn:schemas:contacts:cn	String
Gender	urn:schemas:contacts:gender	Enumeration of 32-bit Long
Government ID Number	urn:schemas:contacts:governmentid	String
Hobbies	urn:schemas:contacts:hobbies	String
Home Address	urn:schemas:contacts:homepostaladdress	String
Home Address City	urn:schemas:contacts:homeCity	String

Property	Property Tag	Data Type
Home Address Country	urn:schemas:contacts:homeCountry	String
Home Address PO Box	urn:schemas:contacts:homepostofficebox	String
Home Address Postal Code	urn:schemas:contacts:homePostalCode	String
Home Address State	urn:schemas:contacts:homeState	String
Home Address Street	urn:schemas:contacts:homeStreet	String
Home Fax	urn:schemas:contacts:homefax	String
Home Phone	urn:schemas:contacts:homePhone	String
Home Phone 2	urn:schemas:contacts:homephone2	String
IM Address	http://schemas.microsoft.com/mapi/id/ {00062004-0000-0000-C000-000000000046}/8062001f	String
Initials	urn:schemas:contacts:initials	String
Internet Free/ Busy Address	urn:schemas:calendar:fburl	String
ISDN	urn:schemas:contacts:internationalisdnnumber	String
Job Title	urn:schemas:contacts:title	String
Journal	http://schemas.microsoft.com/mapi/id/ {0006200A-0000-0000-C000-000000000046}/8025000b	Boolean
Language	urn:schemas:contacts:language	String
Last Name	urn:schemas:contacts:sn	String
Location	urn:schemas:contacts:location	String
Mailing Address	urn:schemas:contacts:mailingpostaladdress	String
Mailing Address Indicator	http://schemas.microsoft.com/mapi/id/ {00062004-0000-0000-C000-000000000046}/8002000b	String
Manager's Name	urn:schemas:contacts:manager	String
Middle Name	urn:schemas:contacts:middlename	String
Mileage	http://schemas.microsoft.com/exchange/mileage	String
Mobile Phone	http://schemas.microsoft.com/mapi/proptag/0x3a1c001f	String
Modified	DAV:getlastmodified	Date
Nickname	urn:schemas:contacts:nickname	String
Notes	urn:schemas:httpmail:textdescription	String
Office Location	urn:schemas:contacts:roomnumber	String

Continued

Property	Property Tag	Data Type
Organizational ID Number	urn:schemas:contacts:employeenumber	String
Other Address	urn:schemas:contacts:otherpostaladdress	String
Other Address City	urn:schemas:contacts:othercity	String
Other Address Country	urn:schemas:contacts:othercountry	String
Other Address PO Box	urn:schemas:contacts:otherpostofficebox	String
Other Address Postal Code	urn:schemas:contacts:otherpostalcode	String
Other Address State	urn:schemas:contacts:otherstate	String
Other Address Street	urn:schemas:contacts:otherstreet	String
Other Fax	urn:schemas:contacts:otherfax	String
Other Phone	urn:schemas:contacts:otherTelephone	String
Pager	urn:schemas:contacts:pager	String
Personal Home Page	urn:schemas:contacts:personalHomePage	String
PO Box	urn:schemas:contacts:mailingpostofficebox	String
Primary Phone	http://schemas.microsoft.com/mapi/proptag/0x3a1a001f	String
Private	http://schemas.microsoft.com/mapi/id/ {00062008-0000-0000-C000-000000000046}/8506000b	Boolean
Profession	urn:schemas:contacts:profession	String
Radio Phone	http://schemas.microsoft.com/mapi/proptag/0x3a1d001f	String
Read	urn:schemas:httpmail:read	Boolean
Received Representing Name	http://schemas.microsoft.com/mapi/proptag/0x0044001f	String
Referred By	urn:schemas:contacts:referredby	String
Reminder	http://schemas.microsoft.com/mapi/id/ {00062008-0000-0000-C000-000000000046}/8503000b	Boolean
Reminder Time	http://schemas.microsoft.com/mapi/id/ {00062008-0000-0000-C000-000000000046}/85020040	Date
Reminder Topic	urn:schemas:httpmail:messageflag	String
Sensitivity	http://schemas.microsoft.com/exchange/ sensitivity-long	Enumeration of 32-bit Long

Property	Property Tag	Data Type
Size	http://schemas.microsoft.com/mapi/id/ {00020328-0000-0000-C000-000000000046}/8ff00003	32-bit Long
Spouse	urn:schemas:contacts:spousecn	String
State	urn:schemas:contacts:mailingstate	String
Street Address	urn:schemas:contacts:mailingstreet	String
Subject	urn:schemas:httpmail:subject	String
Suffix	urn:schemas:contacts:namesuffix	String
Telex	urn:schemas:contacts:telexnumber	String
Title	urn:schemas:contacts:personaltitle	String
TTY/TDD Phone	urn:schemas:contacts:ttytddphone	String
User Field 1	http://schemas.microsoft.com/exchange/ extensionattribute1	String
User Field 2	http://schemas.microsoft.com/exchange/ extensionattribute2	String
User Field 3	http://schemas.microsoft.com/exchange/ extensionattribute3	String
User Field 4	http://schemas.microsoft.com/exchange/ extensionattribute4	String
Web Page	urn:schemas:contacts:businesshomepage	String
ZIP/Postal Code	urn:schemas:contacts:mailingpostalcode	String

Tasks

The following table lists common DASL property tags and data types for properties of Outlook Task items.

Property	Property Tag	Data Type
% Complete	http://schemas.microsoft.com/mapi/id/ {00062003-0000-0000-C000-000000000046}/81020005	Double
Assigned	http://schemas.microsoft.com/mapi/id/ {00062003-0000-0000-C000-000000000046}/81290003	Enumeration of 32-bit Long
Actual Work	http://schemas.microsoft.com/mapi/id/ {00062003-0000-0000-C000-000000000046}/81100003	32-bit Long
Attachment	urn:schemas:httpmail:hasattachment	Boolean
Billing Information	urn:schemas:contacts:billinginformation	String

Continued

Property	Property Tag	Data Type
Categories	urn:schemas-microsoft-com:office:office#Keywords	Multivalued String (array)
Company	http://schemas.microsoft.com/mapi/id/ {00062008-0000-0000-C000-000000000046}/8539101f	String
Complete	http://schemas.microsoft.com/mapi/id/ {00062003-0000-0000-C000-000000000046}/811c000b	Boolean
Contacts	http://schemas.microsoft.com/mapi/id/ {00062008-0000-0000-C000-000000000046}/8586001f	String
Created	urn:schemas:calendar:created	Date
Date Completed	http://schemas.microsoft.com/mapi/id/ {00062003-0000-0000-C000-000000000046}/810f0040	Date
Do Not AutoArchive	http://schemas.microsoft.com/mapi/id/ {00062003-0000-0000-C000-000000000046}/850e000b	Boolean
Due Date	http://schemas.microsoft.com/mapi/id/ {00062003-0000-0000-C000-000000000046}/81050040	Date
Importance	urn:schemas:httpmail:importance	Enumeration of 32-bit Long
Mileage	http://schemas.microsoft.com/exchange/mileage	String
Modified	DAV:getlastmodified	Date
Notes	urn:schemas:httpmail:textdescription	String
Organizer	urn:schemas:httpmail:fromname	String
Owner	http://schemas.microsoft.com/mapi/id/ {00062003-0000-0000-C000-000000000046}/811f001f	String
Private	http://schemas.microsoft.com/mapi/id/ {00062008-0000-0000-C000-000000000046}/8506000b	Boolean
Recipient Name	http://schemas.microsoft.com/mapi/received_by_name	String
Recipient No Reassign	http://schemas.microsoft.com/mapi/proptag/0x002b000b	Boolean
Recipients Allowed	http://schemas.microsoft.com/mapi/proptag/0x0002000b	Boolean
Recurring	http://schemas.microsoft.com/mapi/id/ {00062003-0000-0000-C000-000000000046}/8126000b	Boolean
Reminder	http://schemas.microsoft.com/mapi/id/ {00062003-0000-0000-C000-000000000046}/8503000b	Boolean
Reminder Time	http://schemas.microsoft.com/mapi/id/ {00062003-0000-0000-C000-000000000046}/85020040	Date

Property	Property Tag	Data Type
Request Status	http://schemas.microsoft.com/mapi/id/ {00062003-0000-0000-C000-000000000046}/812a0003	Enumeration of 32-bit Long
Requested By	http://schemas.microsoft.com/mapi/id/ {00062003-0000-0000-C000-000000000046}/8121001f	String
Role	http://schemas.microsoft.com/mapi/id/ {00062003-0000-0000-C000-000000000046}/8127001f	String
Sensitivity	http://schemas.microsoft.com/exchange/ sensitivity-long	Enumeration of 32-bit Long
Size	http://schemas.microsoft.com/mapi/proptag/0x0e080003	32-bit Long
Start Date	http://schemas.microsoft.com/mapi/id/ {00062003-0000-0000-C000-000000000046}/81040040	Date
Status	http://schemas.microsoft.com/mapi/id/ {00062003-0000-0000-C000-000000000046}/81010003	Enumeration of 32-bit Long
Subject	urn:schemas:httpmail:subject	String
Team Task	http://schemas.microsoft.com/mapi/id/ {00062003-0000-0000-C000-000000000046}/8103000b	Boolean
To	urn:schemas:httpmail:displayto	String
Total Work	http://schemas.microsoft.com/mapi/id/ {00062003-0000-0000-C000-000000000046}/81110003	32-bit Long
Unread	urn:schemas:httpmail:read	Boolean

B

Troubleshooting Problems and Support

There are many online resources for getting information about Outlook development, and for Outlook 2007. Microsoft has outdone itself by providing articles, blogs, sample addins and other resource material. In addition to Microsoft resources, many Web sites have Outlook sample code and information about solving specific Outlook programming problems.

This appendix provides listings of many resources for Outlook developers, as well as information about online support forums and newsgroups that are invaluable for any Outlook developer. Also listed are resources for VSTO development and support, MAPI tools and SDKs (Software Development Kits) and useful developer tools such as virtual machines.

Microsoft often changes the URLs for its online resources, often without forwarding links being applied. The links listed here are accurate at the time this was written.

Resources

This section of the appendix contains a list of resources that are valuable for Outlook development projects. This list is by no means complete — many Web sites or articles focus on only one problem and don't have enough general information to make the list here. Searching for specific Outlook programming-related terms is a good way to find additional resources, using a search engine such as Google or MSN search.

Microsoft

The Microsoft Developer Network (MSDN) provides a wealth of information about developing with Outlook and other Microsoft technologies. The main entry point to the MSDN Library online is at `http://msdn.microsoft.com/library`. This library contains a huge amount of information, code samples and code snippets and the Microsoft KnowledgeBase collection of articles on techniques and troubleshooting.

The home page for the MSDN Developer Center, a gateway to information on all of Microsoft's technologies is located at `http://msdn2.microsoft.com/en-us/default.aspx`. Links to specific downloads, code samples, whitepapers, video presentations, blogs, and other sources of Outlook and Office information are listed in the following sections of this appendix.

Outlook and Office Developer Centers

The Office Developer Center home page for Outlook 2007 developers is located at `http://msdn2.microsoft.com/en-us/office/aa905463.aspx`; it organizes and highlights the new features in Outlook 2007.

The home page for more general Outlook developer information, not specific to Outlook 2007, is the Office Developer Center Outlook, located at `http://msdn2.microsoft.com/en-us/office/aa905455.aspx`.

The home page for general Office development information at MSDN is located at `http://msdn2.microsoft.com/en-us/office/default.aspx`.

Blogs and Video Presentations

Some of the members of the Outlook and Office teams have been blogging about Outlook and Office 2007, presenting interesting information about the decisions that went into the Outlook and Office 2007 architectures and new features. Other blogs and video presentations are presented by members of related Microsoft teams such as the VSTO team. The home page for all Microsoft hosted blogs is located at `http://blogs.msdn.com`. You will probably find many blogs listed there that you can subscribe to that provide useful information about various aspects of Outlook and Office, from both the user and programmer perspectives. The following list shows blogs and video presentations of interest:

Individuals with blogs for Outlook 2007 include:

❑   Ryan Gregg, a program manager on the Outlook team, who is part of the Programmability Group, has a blog about Outlook 2007 development issues and philosophies located at `http://blogs.msdn.com/rgregg/default.aspx`. This blog contains lots of useful information, and it's highly recommended that you review it as part of a good Outlook 2007 programming foundation.

❑   Ryan and Randy Byrne, who heads up the Outlook Programmability Team, have an MSDN video presentation that discusses the new enhanced Outlook 2007 object model and some of the design decisions that went into the enhancements made to Outlook for Outlook 2007. I recommend viewing this video as a useful learning tool for Outlook 2007. The video is available at `http://msdn.microsoft.com/msdntv/episode.aspx?xml=episodes/en/20060511OutlookRB/manifest.xml`.

Two other interesting blogs related to Outlook 2007 aren't specifically developer oriented but do provide information about the uses and philosophy behind some of the new features in Outlook 2007:

❑ Michael Affronti's blog covers his areas on the Outlook team: instant search, RSS subscriptions, and sharing with Outlook. Michael's blog is located at `http://blogs.msdn.com/michael%5Faffronti`.

❑ Melissa Macbeth , another member of the Outlook team, is in charge of the new To-Do Bar and her blog at `http://blogs.msdn.com/melissamacbeth` has lots of information about the design of and decisions behind the To-Do Bar and the new task functionality related to it.

The Office blog of most interest to developers for Outlook 2007 is Jensen Harris's blog on the new Ribbon interface for Office 2007 applications. This blog isn't a programming blog, although some of the blog posts do touch on developer issues. The primary value of this blog is Jensen's inside information on the whys and wherefores of the Ribbon design and why Microsoft went in this new direction for Office 2007, from the manager of the Ribbon development project. Jensen's blog can be found at `http://blogs.msdn.com/jensenh`.

VSTO makes Outlook COM addin development much easier by hiding all the underlying addin plumbing and providing a simple startup and shutdown interface. VSTO has many advantages for Outlook development if you are supporting versions of Outlook targeted by VSTO and planning to use the .NET languages VB.NET or C#. Deployment of VSTO addins isn't part of this story however, and deploying VSTO addins presents various security problems on the target systems that aren't addressed by the VSTO package. VSTO 2005 SE is used to develop for either Outlook 2007 or Outlook 2003; VSTO 2005 can only be used to develop for Outlook 2003.

❑ The primary source of information about deployment of VSTO 2005 SE applications is located at `http://msdn2.microsoft.com/en-us/library/bb332051.aspx` and `http://msdn2.microsoft.com/en-us/library/bb332052.aspx`.

❑ The primary source of information about deployment of VSTO 2005 applications is located at `http://msdn2.microsoft.com/en-us/library/aa537173(office.11).aspx` and `http://msdn2.microsoft.com/en-us/library/aa537179(office.11).aspx`.

❑ Additional resources for VSTO development and deployment are listed at `http://forums.microsoft.com/MSDN/ShowPost.aspx?PostID=196504&SiteID=1`, in a post in the MSDN VSTO support forum.

Blogs by members of the VSTO team provide solutions for VSTO deployment problems (more details in the list that follows), but you have to seek out these solutions yourself; you won't find them in VSTO out of the box:

❑ Mads Nissen, a VSTO team member has posted blog entries explaining the deployment problems and a solution to those problems. His blog articles for VSTO deployment are located at `http://weblogs.asp.net/mnissen/archive/2005/07/01/417148.aspx` and `http://weblogs.asp.net/mnissen/articles/427504.aspx`.

❑ Peter Jausovec, another VSTO team member, has two blog articles that also are relevant to VSTO deployment issues, "Where's My VSTO Outlook Add-in?!" parts 1 and 2. The locations for these blog articles are `http://blog.jausovec.info/blogs/petersblog/articles/ovstoaddin1.aspx` for "Where's My VSTO Outlook Add-in?! (Part I)", and `http://blog.jausovec.info/blogs/petersblog/articles/ovstoaddin2.aspx` for "Where's My VSTO Outlook Add-in?! (Part II)."

❏ Two other resources that discuss various issues and architectural decisions about VSTO and Outlook development are authored by David Hill and Andrew Whitechapel, both also members of the VSTO team. David Hill's blog is located at `//blogs.msdn.com/dphill/`. Andrew Whitechapel's MSDN video presentation about VSTO Outlook architecture is located at `http://channel9.msdn.com/ShowPost.aspx?PostID=74734`.

Downloads

There are a number of sample addins and documentation on working with the new features of Outlook 2007 at the What's New for Developers in Outlook 2007 Center at MSDN at `http://msdn2.microsoft.com/en-us/office/aa905463.aspx`. The downloads and articles most interesting to Outlook developers are presented in the following table.

Download	URL
Building an Outlook 2007 Form Region with a Managed Add-In	`http://msdn2.microsoft.com/en-us/library/ms788695.aspx`
Code Security Changes in Outlook 2007	`http://msdn2.microsoft.com/en-us/library/ms778202.aspx`
Outlook 2007 Sample Add-ins: Rules Add-in, Travel Agency Add-in, and Prepare for Meeting Add-in	`http://msdn2.microsoft.com/en-us/library/ms778811.aspx`
What's New for Developers in Microsoft Office Outlook 2007 (Part 1 of 2)	`http://msdn2.microsoft.com/en-us/library/ms772422.aspx`
What's New for Developers in Microsoft Office Outlook 2007 (Part 2 of 2)	`http://msdn2.microsoft.com/en-us/library/ms772423.aspx`
Word 2007 HTML and CSS Rendering Capabilities in Outlook 2007 (Part 1 of 2)	`http://msdn2.microsoft.com/en-us/library/aa338201.aspx`
Word 2007 HTML and CSS Rendering Capabilities in Outlook 2007 (Part 2 of 2)	`http://msdn2.microsoft.com/en-us/library/aa338200.aspx`
2007 Office System Tool: Outlook HTML and CSS Validator	`www.microsoft.com/downloads/details.aspx?familyid=0b764c08-0f86-431e-8bd5-ef0e9ce26a3a&displaylang=en`
2007 Office System: Updated Developer Content	`www.microsoft.com/downloads/details.aspx?familyid=066f9f31-9d7b-4d5e-8759-55fb4bf24d52&displaylang=en`

Download	URL
2007 Office System: XML Schema Reference	www.microsoft.com/downloads/details .aspx?familyid=15805380-f2c0-4b80-9ad1- 2cb0c300aef9&displaylang=en
Outlook 2007 Add-In: Form Region Add-In	www.microsoft.com/downloads/details .aspx?familyid=932b830f-bf8f-41fc-9962- 07a741b21586&displaylang=en
Outlook 2007 Add-Ins: RulesAddin, TravelAgencyAddin, and PrepareMeAddin	www.microsoft.com/downloads/details .aspx?familyid=f871c923-3c42-485d-83c7- 10a54a92e8a2&displaylang=en
Outlook 2007 Document: Deploying Outlook 2007 with Business Contact Manager in a Remote Database Configuration	www.microsoft.com/downloads/details .aspx?familyid=f24267ee-9ad5-4be5-b888- c9a50ae395ca&displaylang=en
Outlook 2007 White Paper: Web Service Development Guide for the Outlook 2007 Mobile Service	www.microsoft.com/downloads/details .aspx?familyid=505c17a6-5598-4fd8-a448- 820d8bae5f07&displaylang=en
Outlook 2007 Reference: Business Contact Manager for Outlook Developer Guide	www.microsoft.com/downloads/details .aspx?familyid=5b847e87-5736-4511-a7de- 9d8dc91d7ae2&displaylang=en
Outlook 2007 Sample: Ribbon Extensibility Add-In	www.microsoft.com/downloads/details .aspx?familyid=11ab93bf-48dc-4f73-8f6b- 62b4482a92bc&displaylang=en
Outlook 2007 Sample: Visual Studio 2005 Templates	www.microsoft.com/downloads/details .aspx?familyid=0cab159a-0272-4635-b158- 10553779a3df&displaylang=en
Outlook 2007 Sample: What's New Add-Ins	www.microsoft.com/downloads/details .aspx?familyid=aabf127d-d069-4549-a1b1- 667a698c3ef6&displaylang=en

The Download Center also has some Office 2007 articles important for Outlook 2007 development, as shown in the following table.

Download	URL
2007 Office System Document UI Style Guide for Solutions and Add Ins	www.microsoft.com/downloads/details .aspx?FamilyId=19E3BF38-434B-4DDD-9592- 3749F6647105&displaylang=en
2007 Office System Document Lists of Control IDs	www.microsoft.com/downloads/details .aspx?FamilyId=4329D9E9-4D11-46A5-898D- 23E4F331E9AE&displaylang=en

Three other articles useful for Outlook developers are given in the following table.

Download	URL
Known issues that may occur when you use the Outlook 2007 object model	http://support.microsoft.com/default.aspx?scid=kb;EN-US;929593
How to make the Design Form feature unavailable in Outlook	http://support.microsoft.com/default.aspx?scid=kb;EN-US;190890
Deploying Visual Studio 2005 Tools for Office Solutions Using Windows Installer Walkthroughs (Part 2)	http://msdn.microsoft.com/office/default.aspx?pull=/library/en-us/odc_vsto2005_ta/html/officevstowindowsinstallerwalkthrough.asp

Non-Microsoft Web Sites

Microsoft isn't the only source for information about programming Outlook, although the depth and quality of information provided for Outlook 2007 are better than anything Microsoft has ever provided previously for a rollout of a new version of Outlook. Third-party Web sites, blogs and other resources provide additional information, some of it about undocumented Outlook properties or features, code samples, tips and tricks, and general Outlook and Exchange information.

The Web sites in the following table provide useful Outlook code samples, information, tools, and articles.

Web site	URL	Description
Outlookcode	www.outlookcode.com	Most comprehensive third-party Web site, with code samples, forums, and articles about all things Outlook and Exchange
Slovaktech	www.slovaktech.com/code_samples.htm	Outlook code samples and addin templates
Wrox Press	www.wrox.com/WileyCDA	Wrox Web site with articles and forums on programming related topics
CDOLIve	www.cdolive.com	Definitive CDO 1.21 Web site with code samples, lists of undocumented property tags, and downloads
MicroEye	www.microeye.com/resources/index.html	Outlook KB article listings, whitepapers, and sample code
X4U	www.x4u.de	Outlook samples using C#
T.S. Bradley .NET	www.tsbradley.net	Outlook samples using VB.NET and VSTO

Web site	URL	Description
Redemption	`www.dimastr.com/redemption`	Documentation, code snippets and tricks for using the Redemption third-party library for Outlook development
RDO objects	`www.dimastr.com/redemption/rdo`	Documentation and code snippets for the RDO (Redemption Data Objects) part of the Redemption library.
MAPI33.NET	`www.mapi33.adexsolutions.com`	Information and download for the MAPI33 third-party library, another COM wrapper for Extended MAPI
MAPILab	`www.mapilab.com`	Information and downloads for the MAPILab product line of Outlook Extended MAPI extenders as well as some sample code for directly accessing MAPI properties using VB
Add-in Express	`www.add-in-express.com/outlook-extension`	Addins for making .NET programming for Outlook and Office easier and for creating the equivalent of Outlook 2007 form regions in earlier versions of Outlook
MVPs.ORG	`www.mvps.org`	Code samples, FAQs and other information about various Microsoft technologies created by Microsoft MVPs
CodeProject	`www.codeproject.com`	Code samples and articles for VB.NET, C# and VB 6 among other languages and technologies
VBAccelerator	`www.vbaccelerator.com/home/index.asp`	VB.NET, C#, and VB 6 code samples provided under a version of the Open Source license
MAPI Spying Tool	`http://mapispy.blogspot.com`	Blog with some interesting MAPI information and some simple tools

Tools

This section of the appendix contains information about Outlook developer tools such as MAPI viewers, software development kits, and providers of virtual machine software that enable you to leverage a development computer into a development test bed for different versions of application and operating system software.

MAPI Viewing Tools

The development tool I probably use most often for my Outlook development work is a MAPI viewer. This tool enables you to view, change and add various MAPI properties and to get the DASL or other property tags for various properties that aren't well documented or documented at all. Using a MAPI viewer, you can examine items, folders, stores, and other pieces of an Outlook session and also run scripts that can help in debugging Outlook programming problems.

A MAPI viewer of choice is OutlookSpy, an application from Outlook MVP Dmitry Streblechenko. This tool installs as an Outlook addin and integrates into Outlook. This has an advantage over the free, stand-alone viewers available from Microsoft, because you don't have to run a separate session for the viewer and because of the integration into Outlook. Another advantage of OutlookSpy, as shown in Figure B.1, is that it provides the property tags, GUIDs, IDs, and other information about named and standard properties on items, folders, and stores.

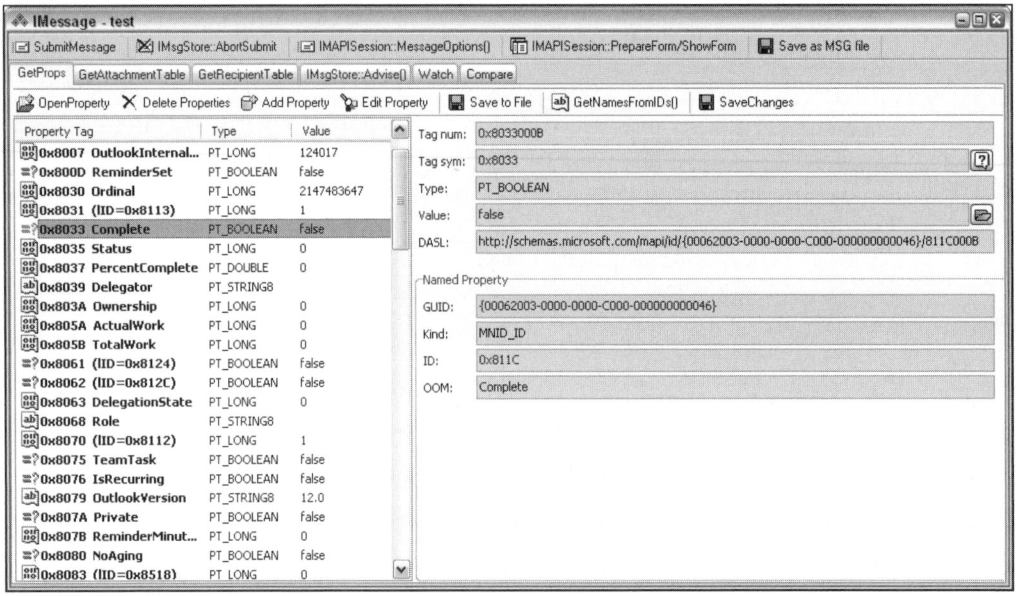

Figure B-1

Microsoft provides MAPI viewers that are more limited than OutlookSpy and run as standalone applications, but they are free. These viewers have some advantages in certain circumstances over OutlookSpy, especially when running a session not tied to a running Outlook session. The older viewer, MDBView, is a server tool that requires the Exchange server versions of the MAPI libraries, so it's not suitable for running on a computer with Outlook installed.

Microsoft's newer MAPI viewer can run on client machines with Outlook installed, and is also a free download. The earlier version of this viewer is called MFCMapi and the download includes the C++ source code for the viewer, which has valuable examples for coding Extended MAPI using C++. You can download this version at http://support.microsoft.com/default.aspx?scid=kb;EN-US;291794.

The new, enhanced version of the MAPI viewer is now named the Microsoft Exchange Server MAPI Editor, and you can download it at www.microsoft.com/downloads/details.aspx?FamilyID= 55fdffd7-1878-4637-9808-1e21abb3ae37&DisplayLang=en. Figure B-2 shows the main window of the newer version of the Microsoft Exchange Server MAPI Editor.

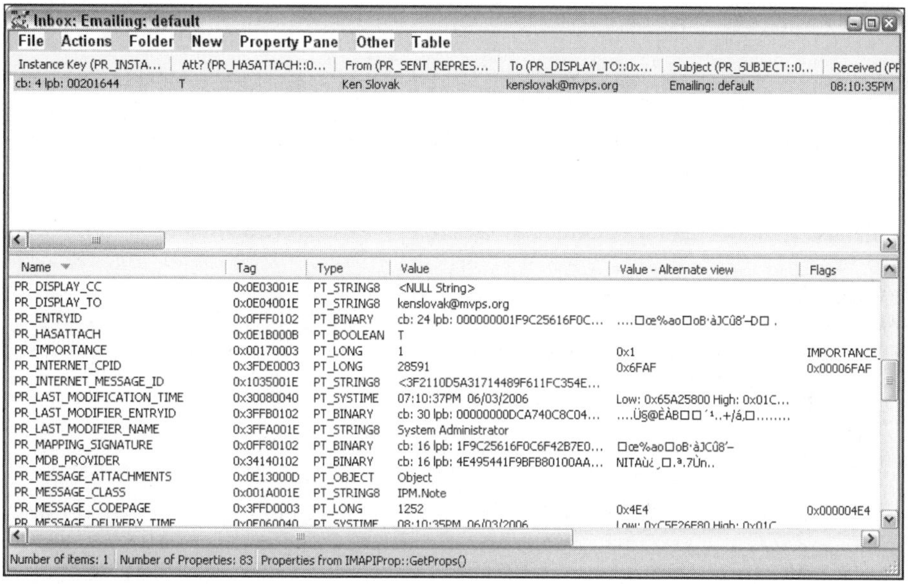

Figure B-2

Software Development Kits

Microsoft provides many software development kits (SDKs) for its servers and applications, and some of these SDKs are very useful for Outlook developers if you need to dig down into the development guts of the server or application. The two SDKs highlighted in this appendix are for Exchange server and for Windows, both of which have information and header files for Extended MAPI.

The Exchange SDK can be downloaded at www.microsoft.com/downloads/details .aspx?FamilyId=4AFE3504-C209-4A73-AC5D-FF2A4A3B48B7&displaylang=en. You can download additional Exchange server information and code samples at www.microsoft.com/downloads/ details.aspx?FamilyId=57414A35-CF6B-460A-8F99-D76DC9E4ED31&displaylang=en.

The Windows Platform SDK contains useful information and samples for Windows; you can download the Windows SDK at http://msdn.microsoft.com/library/default.asp?url=/library/ en-us/sdkintro/sdkintro/devdoc_platform_software_development_kit_start_page.asp.

Virtual Machines

Virtual machines are invaluable developer tools that enable you to set up multiple virtual computers that can run all the versions of Office and Windows that you need to support with your Outlook applications. I run virtual machines in my development lab that have Outlook versions from Outlook 2000 to 2007 installed and that run a variety of Windows versions from Windows 98 to Windows Vista. Without using virtual machines, you would need over 20 computers to maintain this type of testing base for Outlook applications. Of course, you need licensed copies of any operating system and version of Windows you plan to put on a virtual machine, the virtual machines do not supply licensed copies for you to install.

Microsoft offers a free virtual machine provider, Virtual PC that you can downloaded for free. The location for the Virtual PC download is at `www.microsoft.com/windows/virtualpc/default.mspx`.

VMWare is the other major supplier for virtual machine software. The free version of the VMWare software is called Virtual Server and can be downloaded from `www.vmware.com/products/server`. This version installs on nonserver versions of Windows, although the remote monitoring functions won't work unless the VM (virtual machine) is running on a server operating system.

VMWare Workstation is another product for setting up virtual machines, but it isn't free. It does have features that make it very useful, however, and is the virtual machine provider that the author uses. This version provides for cloning existing virtual machines for quick setup of variations of existing VMs and can take snapshots of existing VM states that can be returned to at any time. The link for information about VMWare Workstation is at `www.vmware.com`.

Support

Support for Outlook development is available in paid and free support venues. Paid support from Microsoft's product support technicians, third-party support vendors, and paid consultants are not discussed in this appendix. Free support is available from newsgroups, forums, and mailing lists online, and from many user groups at user group meetings and support forums.

User groups are geographically organized and are not covered in this appendix. To find a user group for a specific geographic area and product search using the tools at `www.microsoft.com/communities/usergroups/default.mspx`.

Newsgroups

Newsgroups offer mostly peer-to-peer support, whereby users help other users. Some managed newsgroups exist, where a response from a Microsoft support person is guaranteed within a certain time frame, but those newsgroups are only available to Microsoft partners, subscribers to Microsoft Developer Network, and participants in certain other special programs. Often, the managed newsgroups are overlaid on peer-to-peer newsgroups, and the answer comes from another user instead of from a Microsoft support person.

Many knowledgeable users answer questions in the public newsgroups, often learning themselves in the process of researching and answering a question. Some users are recognized by Microsoft for their support for specific products and technical excellence in the quality of the support they provide. Users who have been recognized by Microsoft for the support they provided in the previous year are awarded the designation of MVP (Most Valuable Professional).

Many servers for newsgroups exist, and many ISPs slurp the Microsoft news feeds into their own news servers. It's recommended that you use the Microsoft news servers instead of other servers for these newsgroups. Many other servers carry groups that are no longer active and that have few knowledgeable answers from other users. The Microsoft news servers are either `news.microsoft.com` or `msnews.microsoft.com`. You can set up Outlook Express to connect to those servers to subscribe to various newsgroups, as you can many other newsreaders or browsers capable of reading newsgroups. When you set up a newsreader, you can view a list of all groups available on that server, including all the Outlook-related newsgroups.

The following table lists the most popular Outlook newsgroups. Many of these groups also have a Web interface that you can use if you prefer that to a newsreader, or if NNTP (Net News Transfer Protocol) isn't available on your server. Any Web browser can visit the Web interface to a newsgroup. In cases where there is more than one group for an area of Outlook programming, the groups with the most traffic are listed first.

Programming Area	Newsgroup Address	Web Interface
Addins	`microsoft.public.outlook` `.program_addins`	
Addins	`microsoft.public.office` `.developer.com.add_ins`	`msdn.microsoft.com/newsgroups/` `default.aspx?dg=microsoft` `.public.office.developer.com` `.add_ins&lang=en&cr=US`
Addins	`microsoft.public.developer` `.outlook.addins`	
Forms	`microsoft.public.outlook` `.program_forms`	`msdn.microsoft.com/newsgroups/` `default.aspx?dg=microsoft` `.public.outlook.program_` `forms&lang=en&cr=US`
Forms	`microsoft.public.office` `.developer.outlook.forms`	
General Outlook Programming	`microsoft.public.outlook` `.program_vba`	
General Outlook Programming	`microsoft.public.office` `.developer.outlook.vba`	`msdn.microsoft.com/newsgroups/` `default.aspx?dg=microsoft` `.public.office.developer` `.outlook.vba&lang=en&cr=US`
VSTO		`forums.microsoft.com/msdn/` `showforum.aspx?forumid=` `16&siteid=1`
MAPI	`microsoft.public.win32.program-` `mer.messaging`	`msdn.microsoft.com/newsgroups/` `default.aspx?dg=microsoft` `.public.win32.programmer` `.messaging&lang=en&cr=US`

An index to all Microsoft Office newsgroups, many of which have Web interfaces, is located at `http://msdn.microsoft.com/newsgroups/topic.aspx?url=/MSDN-FILES/028/201/008/topic.xml`.

Forums

The two main public, nonsubscription forums for Outlook programming topics are both moderated by Sue Mosher, a prominent Outlook MVP and developer. The highest-traffic forum is the forum at `Outlookcode.com`, a Web site that's also a prominent Outlook programming resource for code samples and compilations of information and related links on most Outlook programming topics. Moderated forums are useful for avoiding spam, flame wars, and other unpleasant aspects of open forums and newsgroups.

The Outlookcode forums are divided into basic code areas, such as Outlook code essentials, basic Outlook programming, Outlook forms design, expert techniques, and .NET programming for Outlook. The home page for the Outlookcode forums is `www.outlookcode.com/forums.aspx`. Another, lower-traffic forum is hosted on Yahoo groups, and is located at `http://tech.groups.yahoo.com/group/outlook-dev`. Both of these forums have mailing lists that you can subscribe to, instead of or in addition to their Web interfaces.

MAPI Mailing List

The MAPI mailing list, MAPI-L, specializes in Extended MAPI, the foundation of all things Outlook and Exchange. The list has a searchable archive that's a treasure trove of MAPI information both documented and undocumented. The forum home for the MAPI list is located at `www.lsoft.com/scripts/wl.exe?SL1=MAPI-L&H=PEACH.EASE.LSOFT.COM`.

Support Catalogs

A list of newsgroups and mailing lists for various Outlook, Exchange, SharePoint, and related technologies is maintained at `www.cdolive.com/ngml.htm`. The list also includes groups and lists for Outlook for nonprogramming topics.

A catalog of mailing lists is maintained at `www.lsoft.com/catalist.html`. You can search this list to find other lists that look like they might be interesting. This catalog is large, and some of the mailing lists require being accepted as a member or are otherwise limited in membership.

Self-Help

There are many other resources for support located on the Internet, directed at helping you solve your support questions by yourself. These resources range from self-published articles providing fixes and workarounds for various Outlook programming problems to the enormous Microsoft KnowledgeBase. Performing a Google search can often result in many sources for solutions, and often better search results for the Microsoft KnowledgeBase than directly searching the KnowledgeBase at Microsoft's Web site.

The primary location for Outlook 2007 developer information is `http://msdn.microsoft.com/office/program/outlook`, which has links to documentation, support articles, and support forums. The links for other primary support locations are listed in the following table.

Description	Link
Microsoft Office Outlook 2003	`www.support.microsoft.com/out2003`
Microsoft Exchange Server 2003	`www.support.microsoft.com/exch2003`
Microsoft Help and Support home	`www.support.microsoft.com`

The MicroEye Web site maintains a list of many Outlook programming-related articles from Microsoft's KnowledgeBase at `www.microeye.com/resources/res_outlkb.htm`. This list is not up to date but is still useful on many occasions. There are also links to many whitepapers and other information about developing for Outlook using .NET code at `www.microeye.com/resources/res_outlookvsnet.htm`.

It's recommended that you locate some newsgroups and forums that provide the level of information you need and spend some time there seeing what questions and answers are being posted. The author spends time in the Outlook programming newsgroups, answering questions and learning things almost every day and encourages you to join the forums of your choice to learn and to participate when you know the answers to questions.

Index